# d Civilizations (BC)

| rew | Hittite | Indian | Phoenician | Roman | | Year |
|---|---|---|---|---|---|---|
| | | | | | | ...BC |
| | | | | | First use of irrigation / Growth of city states / First script – cuneiform / Invention of Bronze | 3000 BC |
| | | First civilization in the Indus valley. Harappa and Mohenjo-daro founded (c. 2500) | | | Dominance of Ur over other cities (c. 2800 – c. 2370) | 2500 BC |
| | | First Indian writing / Towns built on grid system / Drainage and central heating | | | Ur conquered by Sargon of the Semites (c. 2370) | 2400 |
| | | | | | | 2300 |
| | | | | | | 2200 |
| | | | | | | 2100 |
| es from Ur, Abraham, er to Palestine 00) | Arrival of Hittites in Asia Minor (c. 2000) / Invention of iron | | | | Last days of Sumer / Rise of **BABYLON** (c. 2000–1900) | 2000 BC |
| | | | | | | 1900 |
| ws welcomed ksos in Egypt 00) | | | | | | 1800 |
| | | | | | Reign of Hammurabi (c.1790–1750) | 1700 |
| | | | | | Hammurabi's Legal Code / First libraries | 1600 |
| | Reign of Hattusilis I (c. 1550) | Indus civilization overrun by Kassites (c. 1500) | | | | 1500 BC |
| | | | | | | 1400 |
| ws persecuted pt (c. 1550–) | Reign of Suppiluliumas (c. 1380–40) | | | | | 1300 |
| s leads Hebrews Egypt (c. 1250) | Hattusilis III makes treaty with Rameses II of Egypt (c. 1270) / Hittite civilization overrun (c. 1200) | | | | Decline of Babylon and rise of **ASSYRIA** (c. 1200) | 1200 |
| lected king 30) | | | Phoenician cities begin to rise on coast of Levant (c. 1100) | | | 1100 |
| king (c. 1010– Jerusalem built | | | Hiram, king of Tyre, builds harbour at Tyre | | | 1000 BC |
| non's reign e built | | | Development of commercial shipping (c. 950) | | | |
| w state divided rael and Judah | | | Introduction of alphabet. Spread of Phoenician civilization to coast of North Africa. Foundation of Carthage | | | 900 |
| r (853) | | | | Rome founded (753) | Reign of Sennacherib (c. 705–680) | 800 |
| n II of Ayssria omes Israel 0) | | Publication of first Vedas (c. 700–600) / Growth of caste system / First records of events (Upanishads) | | | Reign of Ashurbanipal (c. 670–625) / Library of clay tablets | 700 |
| overrun by chadrezzar of on (586) | | Introduction of coinage | | Republic created (509) | Assyria falls. Nineveh taken by **PERSIANS** (613) / Babylon falls to Persians under Cyrus (539) | 600 |
| ws returned to by Cyrus of (539) | | Career of Buddha (530–480) | | Twelve Tables of the Law (c. 450) | Reign of Darius (521–486) | 500 BC |
| ws (now d to as Jews) t to successive ion (c. 539 rds) | | Alexander the Great reaches India (326) / Chandragupta founds Mauryan kingdom / Builds capital at Patna / Creates new army | | Brennus sacks Rome (390) | The King's Highway built / Persia conquered by Alexander the Great (c. 330) | 400 |
| | | Asoka's reign (c. 275–235) / Art and building encouraged: first stone buildings / Decline of Mauryan kingdom after Asoka | Hannibal's war against Rome (221–202) | Samnite Wars (c. 340–280) | | 300 |
| | | | Hannibal crushed at Zama / Carthage destroyed by Romans (146) | Careers of the Gracchi brothers (c. 133–121) / Career of Marius (c. 110–86) | First Arsacid king (c. 160) | 200 |
| of Herod the (c. 37–5) | | | | Conquest of Gaul (58–48) / Caesar master of the Roman world (45) | Mithradates' wars with Rome (123–87) | 100 |
| | | | | | | 0 BC |

# THE
# HISTORY
## OF THE
# WORLD

## PLANTAGENET SOMERSET FRY
### Material updated by BRIAN WILLIAMS

### Foreword by Leonard Cottrell

## DEAN

First published 1972 by The Hamlyn Publishing Group Limited

This edition first published 1994 by Dean, an imprint of Reed Children's
Books, Michelin House, 81 Fulham Road, London SW3 6RB
and Auckland, Melbourne, Singapore and Toronto.

ISBN 0 603 55412 1

British Library Cataloguing-in-Publication Data
A catalogue record for this book is available from the British Library.

Printed in Slovakia
52146/2

# Contents

# Foreword

'Let Observation, with extensive view,
Survey Mankind from China to Peru'
– wrote Doctor Samuel Johnson some two hundred years ago. It is doubtful, however, if Johnson would have anticipated how literally his ebullient injunction would be carried out by the author of this book. Mr Somerset Fry has endeavoured to explain in simple language, in one volume, the whole history of mankind: not just one civilization or linked group of civilizations, not just one area of the earth's surface where Man has settled, not just one stretch of time, but the whole story from the emergence of our primitive human ancestors from their ape-like forebears some half million years ago, down to our own time when men have walked on the moon.

We travel in the steps of the earliest known civilizations, the Sumerians and the Ancient Egyptians of 3000 years B.C., on through other major cultures of the Middle East such as Babylonia and Assyria, and at the same time see what was happening in, for instance, India and China. Europe comes into the picture with Greece, Rome, and the modern civilizations which have sprung from them, and to which we in the West belong, but Mr Somerset Fry also pays due attention to the rise of other cultures in Central and South America, the Aztecs, the Mayas and the Incas.

It is a complex story and must have been a mind-stretching task, but not, as the author has presented it, something beyond the comprehension of an intelligent child of nine onwards. Moreover, it is an excellent reference book for children. One lesson among many learned is that groups of human beings, though separated by vast differences of time and distance, with no possibility of communication, but faced with similar problems – political, military, agricultural, economic – tend to go about solving them in similar ways. Altogether this is an excellent account of how we come to be what we are.

*Leonard Cottrell*

# Introduction

This book is called 'A History of the World'. Strictly speaking, it ought to be called 'A History of World Civilizations', for, apart from the first chapter it is devoted entirely to the story of the last seven thousand years of world history, which is but a fraction of the actual age of the earth.

There are many ways of looking at world history. You can regard it as the history of Man's development from primitive and inarticulate savage to modern and sophisticated technician. It can be the record of never-ending efforts by bigger and stronger people to dominate smaller and weaker ones. Someone else has already said that history is but the dismal tale of different people of different nations making the same mistakes. You can say that history is the story of groups of people in different parts of the world developing, over the centuries, characteristics of civilization, some in common with other people and some uniquely original and individual.

I prefer the last approach because I believe it to be the most satisfactory one with which to summarize the story of the world for young readers in one volume.

What is civilization? At what stage in the development of a people do we say they have shed their barbarism and become civilized? When men come together to live in an ordered society, grow their own food and rear their own livestock, erect permanent buildings, and develop their language and art, then they may be said to be civilized. But to be civilized does not mean that one is good or honest or gentle-mannered or just or even clever. These are qualities which can be enjoyed by primitive people as well, while even the most civilized people can be cruel, dishonest and unjust. This is because so far in the story of the world no civilized people has yet entirely rid itself of its savage characteristics. Three examples serve to illustrate this point. Spain, England and Germany have been at the forefront of European civilization for centuries. Yet how can one overlook the frightful cruelty and treachery of the Spaniards among the Aztec and Inca people in America in the sixteenth century, the systematic degradation and exploitation of the Irish and Welsh peasantry by the English over several centuries after the conquest of Ireland in 1171 and that of Wales in 1282, or the horrifying murder of six million Jews and more than four million non-Jews by the Germans between 1933 and 1945.

There are many other examples.

There have been twenty-two main civilizations in history, and these are plotted in terms of approximate duration on both end papers. Some have lasted much longer than others, but they are not necessarily accorded more space in this book. This is because it is the influence and not the duration of a civilization that matters. The Indian and Chinese civilizations have lasted by far the longest and they have, on the whole, been the most peaceful, but their influence has not been as widespread or as far-reaching as the Graeco-Roman and European civilizations, which have been short in duration and, in the European case, marked by exceptional violence. Therein lies the tragedy of Civilized Man; his advance has been accompanied by belligerence and cruelty, and the improvement in material benefits has been more than matched by the decline in moral standards. This is the story of the development of European civilization, known as Western civilization, and its extensions in those countries of the world which formed the 'colonial' empires. Of course Europeans brought benefits, but could not these perhaps have been accomplished without wars of annexation, or coercion of the native inhabitants? Was so much greed and arrogance necessary? There is really no single land of which it can be said that its occupation by European powers brought it more good than harm.

In many ways it must seem that Man has in fact progressed very little since his great transformation from barbarism into a civilized state six or seven thousand years ago. Despite technological achievements such as lunar landings, nuclear power, transplant surgery, and computer control, there are still such things as slavery, racial intolerance, injustice, religious persecution, and exploitation of minorities.

Compressing the story of the world's civilizations into one volume means that some things receive scant treatment or get left out altogether. I have tried to compensate for many of these omissions in the text by the extensive use of illustrations and captions. The text is intended to contain the facts, with some indication of the movements of men's minds on great issues. The morals to be drawn from the story of the world are confined to this Introduction.

# The Beginnings of Man

The earth is believed to be about 4,500,000,000 years old (four and a half thousand million years old). In this vast unimaginable time span, Man and our evolutionary ancestors have existed for less than 4 million years. And of that time human beings have been civilized for little more than 10,000 years. This is a tiny fraction of the earth's age. To put it another way, suppose you stretched out a roll of paper for 45 kilometres or so, and made this represent the age of the earth. Then Civilized Man's history would occupy only about 10 centimetres of the roll, that is, about the diameter of an orange or the length of the words in the heading of this chapter.

In this time, Man has progressed from being a simple herdsman, who invented the wheel, who knew how to make pottery, and who began to need a society governed by laws, to a highly sophisticated creature

Pithecanthropus man was a hunter and scavenger of small game

able to pilot himself away from the earth and land on the moon.

Man lived for hundreds of thousands of years as little more than an animal, a member of the primate order of mammals (which includes apes and monkeys). His development was extremely slow. Much of the time the earth was engulfed in thick sheets, or layers, of ice, and all over the globe there were huge glaciers. This period is called the Ice Age, though it would be more correct to regard it as a series of ice ages because there were also intervals of warmer weather. For near-Man life was one long struggle with nature, cold winds, storms and floods, now and again relieved by the respite of better weather, which we believe enabled him to adapt himself to changing conditions.

We have said that Man and his evolutionary ancestors have existed for less than 4 million years. By this we mean that the view of many biologists today is that Man is a descendant of *Homo habilis*, a

species of human being (or hominid) who evolved about that time. *Homo habilis*, however, had an ancestor of about 12,000,000 years ago, called *Ramapithecus*, who is generally regarded as the 'founder' of the hominid family tree. *Ramapithecus*, a small ape-like creature, appeared in Europe, Asia and Africa. He evolved gradually into two distinct branches. One was *Australopithecus*, who appeared between 6 and 3 million years ago, in two types: *Australopithecus africanus* and *Australopithecus boisei*. Both gradually became extinct. The other was *Homo habilis*, who appeared at the later end of the 6 to 3 million year time span and who shared some characteristics with the Australopithecines. But he was essentially a different being and he did not disappear.

*Homo habilis* was discovered in the form of fossilized remains in the Olduvai Gorge in Tanzania, in 1961 by Louis Leakey, the famous British anthropologist. *Homo habilis* appeared to have been capable of using tools, hence his name which means Skilful Man. In 1972, Leakey's son,

Richard, discovered a fossilized skull and other remains at Lake Turkana in Kenya. It was clear to him that these belonged to the same family as the Olduvai Man. His find is generally called '1470' Man because that is the number given by the Kenya National Museum in its catalogue to the remains which were placed there. Near the fossils Leakey also found pebbles, from which it seems '1470' Man probably made simple tools. This means that in a sense, one can date the beginning of the Stone Age to about this time, that is, about 2,500,000 B.C.

The next major stage in the evolution of hominids was about 500,000 to 1,000,000 years ago when *Homo erectus* appeared in many parts of the world, notably Java, China, Europe and Africa. *Homo erectus* was a fully upright man. His head rested straight on his spine, without the hunched appearance of his ancestors. He was discovered as long ago as 1891 in Java (then part of the Dutch East Indies, now Indonesia). A second set of remains of *Homo erectus* was dug up near Peking in

China, in 1927. *Homo erectus* is often called Peking Man, although he has been found in many other places, including France, where a footprint about 500,000 years old was seen by one of the investigators.

*Homo erectus* had shorter teeth than his ancestors, more like ours, and his brain was larger. He was probably the first hominid to use fire. Peking Man made simple tools of stone, and hand-axes have been discovered.

The next species of developing Man appeared in about 80,000 B.C. We call him Neanderthal Man because relics of him were first found in the Neander Valley in West Germany in 1856. His brain was much larger than that of *Homo erectus* and somewhat larger than modern man's. His intelligence was of a high order, and yet, by about 35,000 B.C. he seems to have died out altogether. He was not an ancestor of ours, because though he descended from Homo erectus, as we do, he appears to have been the result of a 'branching out' of Man's family tree.

The descendant of *Homo erectus* who was our direct ancestor was *Homo sapiens* (Latin: wise man). He had appeared at about the same time as Neanderthal Man, and there are some who believe that he evolved from Neanderthal Man. This cannot yet be proved. It is possible that there were several types of *Homo sapiens*, but the one from whom we descend was Cro-Magnon Man, so-called because a skeleton of *Homo sapiens* was found in a cave at Cro-Magnon in south-west France, in 1868. The skeleton was about 30,000 years old and it resembled modern man's skeleton very closely. Cro-Magnon Man is thought to have ventured into Europe from Africa.

*Homo sapiens* proved to be remarkably adaptable to his surroundings. His skull was more highly developed than those of his predecessors, and his rate of progress was to be much quicker. He built crude tents or huts under which to sleep and to store the food he had gathered, for food gathering was his main occupation. He also lived in caves, where he could find them, and was generally clever enough to choose those whose entrances faced southwards, away from the winds and the cold of the north and east. In these caves or tents he made his own comforts, and learned to make weapons and tools and to create fire with flint stone.

As time went on, New Man, as we shall call him until he becomes civilized and learns to cultivate his own food, found better ways to gather food, and extended the range of his diet. The men hunted wild animals and fished in the rivers; they collected oysters and other shell-fish. The women and children gathered berries, fruits and root vegetables. They learned to store food for periods of bad weather, and they experimented with cooking. New Man improved the quality, the range, and the ingenuity of his tools and instruments, which were made from bone, flint, stone and wood. You can see fine examples of these developments in most museums. Archaeological evidence makes it clear that these improvements spread widely over the world. By the end of the Upper Palaeolithic (Early Stone) Age, between about 15,000 and 10,000 B.C., Man had arrows, axe-heads and daggers for war, tools with handles, awls and simple saw blades for crafts and industry, harpoons for fishing, and needles for making clothes from wool, flax and leather. Jewellery began to be made, as Man came upon precious stones, shells and ivory; and we have evidence from bone fragments and from cave paintings that some men had their arms tattooed with designs.

These advances show the marked superiority that New Man had over his ancestors. And he began to take an interest in things around him, that went beyond whether he could eat them or use them for shelter. New Man felt the need for self-expression, and perhaps wanted to experiment with communicating ideas. We find the beginnings of art: crude portrayals of those parts of his environment which he considered important or dramatic. Carvings of animals have been found in the Sahara, an area which was once habitable. Caves in Spain and France have revealed fascinating pictures drawn by New Man – Cro-Magnon Man in this case. At Altamira, near Santander, in Spain, there is a life-like drawing of a bison, probably 15,000 years old. In the caves at Lascaux in south-west France, the horses, deer, oxen and cattle painted on the walls have become the most famous examples of early art in the world. These paintings were done in colours such as red, black and yellow, so early Man must have understood how to make some dyes and pigments.

By the end of the Upper Palaeolithic Age New Man had spread widely over the earth. He had organized small communities in many districts where he had settled, whether in the Near East, or Britain or Central Africa.

The next period of Man's development was the Middle Stone Age (Mesolithic Age). This was much shorter in time, depending upon the area of the world where it flourished, and it was distinguished by a rapid advance in the accuracy and use of stone implements. In the Fertile Crescent, a stretch of land extending from the foothills of north-western Iraq to the Persian Gulf (later, to become the 'cradle of civilization'), the Mesolithic Period began in about 12,000–10,000 B.C. and lasted for about three to four thousand years. It used to be thought that the Mesolithic Period in Europe began much, much later, and that the advanced technology of Mesolithic Man was introduced into Europe by

THE EVOLUTION OF MAN

Ramapithecus

Homo habilis

Homo erectus

Australopithecus boisei

Australopithecus africanus

Homo sapiens

Cro-Magnon man, a hunter-gatherer, produced the first forms of art

Near Eastern people. This view is now questioned, and our European forebears were probably advancing at an almost equal rate with their Near Eastern neighbours.

By about 8000 B.C. New Man had become settled in the Fertile Crescent in isolated 'village' communities. He had observed that the effects of water on earth encouraged vegetables and corn to grow. He had begun to see that the sun hardened chunks of mud and made them firm. And he had started to make small, shed-like houses from mud-blocks. He stood in fact upon the threshold of a great jump forward in his progress, on the border between prehistory and civilization. He was now about to grow his own food, and rear his own livestock. And this was to be one of the most significant steps in Mankind's development.

This new age, called the Neolithic (or New Stone) Age, because stone implements were developed to a high degree of usefulness, witnessed the birth of what we call agriculture: the organized growing of plants for food and the domestication of animals for use as beasts of burden and for slaughter for food. The Neolithic Age occurred spontaneously in different places, just as the Mesolithic Age had. In China and east India, Man began to grow rice and millet; in the Americas (Peru and Mexico in particular) he grew beans and potatoes; and in the Fertile Crescent he grew wheat and barley. The technique of growing one's own food spread, and we see the emergence of the first skilled profession, farming.

When farming got under way, New Man also began to think of organizing his life in many other ways. He started to domesticate animals to avoid the need to hunt them. Goats, sheep and cattle were tamed. He also began to trade with his neighbours, exchanging one crop for

another, or one animal for another. This idea, known as barter, spread, and it brought New Man more into contact with other New Men, and in time communities became aware of each other. They began to navigate rivers and lakes in crude boats and ships, in order to get from one place to another, and they began to explore natural tracks and paths across the land, in the hills and down in the plains.

By about 8000 B.C. the first (known) buildings of mud-brick were being erected, in and around Jericho, in what later became known as Palestine. This settlement was eventually surrounded by a high stone wall, probably of about 7000 B.C., which is thought to have risen above four metres or so and had round towers placed along its length. The occupants of Jericho knew how to farm, and it is likely that they at least had the beginnings of some form of government. To that extent we could say that they had become civilized. But they do not appear to have proliferated their

towns, nor spread their way of life in Palestine in such a way as to earn for themselves the credit for founding the first civilization in world history. That distinction more properly belongs to the Sumerians who settled in the Fertile Crescent in about 5000 B.C., or perhaps even earlier.

Cave painting in Lascaux, France (c. 12000 B.C.) of a wounded bison attacking a man

# The Story of Sumer

If you look at a map of the Middle East you will see two large rivers, the Euphrates and the Tigris. They both rise in Turkey and run roughly together in a south-easterly direction through Iraq. At Kurna they meet and form what is now called the Shatt-al-Arab River. This is about one hundred miles long and runs into the Persian Gulf.

The plains between the lower ends of the two rivers are known as Mesopotamia (from the Greek meaning 'between the rivers'), and the area is very fertile. Here a dark-skinned race from north-west India settled. They called themselves the 'black-headed people', or the people of Sumer, and we call them the Sumerians. They were the first people in the world to become civilized who left some form of written records.

The Sumerians probably began to move into the Mesopotamian plains before 5000 B.C. These people understood the working of metal and could make many useful tools. They were already skilful farmers, and in the rich soil of Mesopotamia they found the opportunity to develop their agricultural skills to a high degree. It was not long before they were growing far more than they needed for themselves, and so they began to trade with their less skilful neighbours.

The Sumerians were builders as well as farmers. There was no natural stone for building in Mesopotamia, nor was there much timber. So they made bricks by moulding the thick clay of the river banks into blocks and leaving them in the scorching sun to bake. At first they built small houses of two or three rooms. Then, as their prosperity grew, they constructed larger houses. Some had two storeys, and some had rooms built round a paved courtyard. Soon they discovered that settlements farther away had natural stone, and they traded their surplus farm goods for the stone. Many of the bigger Sumerian buildings were made of brick and stone.

Meanwhile, they developed the potter's wheel and with it were able to fashion a great variety of useful vessels, such as bowls, plates, cups, vases and storage jars. They decorated their pottery with beautiful designs and shapes. They also knew how to make sculpture and how to work copper, bronze and gold and precious stones.

The Sumerians built small boats of plaited reeds which they covered with animal skins and pitch. This building of boats was a milestone in their development, since they could sail from one bank of the Tigris to the other, or up and down the Euphrates, and thus keep in much closer touch with neighbouring settlements than when they first came to the plains. In other words, the Sumerians had found a means of communication, which is vital to a developing civilization. This communication between the early small settlements led in time to the creation of great cities, and the main part of the story of Sumer revolves around city-states.

The flat summit of this ziggurat in Ur was used for astrological observations, and the building contained a temple as well as storehouses for grain

This period began in about 3500 B.C., and it lasted for around fifteen hundred years.

In the last hundred years, archaeologists have excavated in Mesopotamia and have made many exciting discoveries. One of the most important was the remains of a Sumerian city called Ur. Since it is thought that other cities, such as Erech, Kish, Eridu and Lagash were similar, an outline of Sumerian history can be sketched by telling briefly the story of Ur.

Ur was built on the eastern bank of the Euphrates River. Excavation has shown that the city was encircled by a high brick wall and a wide canal which was used for defence as well as for transport. On the river's edge was a harbour for the trading boats which brought goods to and from the other settlements along the Euphrates.

The city itself was threaded with narrow streets which were paved with sun-baked earth. Along the streets were houses, shops and public buildings. In many respects the Sumerian house was like ours, but it had no windows. Glass had not been discovered, and the inhabitants of Ur considered that they had enough air and light if there were doorways in the walls, sometimes curtained with reeds.

Somewhere near the middle of Ur there

was a large temple in the shape of a tower, called a ziggurat. The Sumerian gods governed natural forces such as the earth (Enlil), the sky (Anu), water (Ea), the sun (Shamash) and the moon (Nannar). Each city of Sumer had its own special god, but also worshipped other gods. The chief god for Ur was Nannar, and for the city of Eridu it was Ea. Nannar's temple was the large one at Ur, and was the chief place for worshipping him. The Sumerians believed, like most ancient people, that the gods were human in form and so they had to have houses, or temples, food, clothing and household furniture. The Sumerians must have devoted much time to ensuring that the temples were properly equipped and served. Furniture and clothing were made, and acres of land outside the city walls were allotted for corn and barley for use in the temples.

Inside the temple at Ur there was a large sculptured image of Nannar. It rested upon the top of three brick platforms, and was reached by a staircase. We know the temple was built by Ur-Nannu, an early Sumerian king, because some of the bricks which have been found bear his name.

The temple was enclosed by a high wall. Inside this enclosure there was a palace for the reigning king. His house was like the others in the city except that it was much larger, for it had to accommodate his advisers and servants as well as his family. The priests of the gods also lived in the enclosure.

Nannar was also worshipped in many smaller temples throughout the city, and there were several small temples for his wife, Ningal.

As in every civilization that followed, the family in Sumer was the most important unit of society, and the father was its head. To keep the family together he usually had land which could be handed on to his wife or son.

There were three main classes of people in Sumer. The highest contained the priests, the government officials and the army officers. The middle class included the traders, farmers and craftsmen, and last were the slaves. The most important people were the priests, for they were the servants of the gods. Since the Sumerians believed that the gods were responsible for the people's safety, good health and prosperity, the gods had to be kept happy.

Map of the Fertile Crescent

It fell to the priests to supervise the many jobs that this entailed. They tended the temple lands outside the city; they managed the storehouses; and they conducted trade, exchanging surplus food for stone, timber and precious metals with which they adorned the temples and chapels.

The priests were also looked upon as the wise men of the city. They held lessons in the temple enclosure, prescribed medicines for the sick, sat in judgment over disputes between one person and another and managed the calendar. The Sumerian year was calculated on the behaviour of the moon and had twelve months divided into hours and days. The months, however, were only thirty days long which equalled a year of 360 days. Therefore, in order to make the seasons coincide properly with the calendar, every so often the priests announced that another month would be added to the current year.

We have already mentioned the Sumerian kings. In the earliest days of Sumer, however, there were no kings, and the cities were ruled by chief priests. But as the cities grew and the business of government proved too much for one chief priest, a worthy man was picked from the ranks of the priesthood to handle some of the city's affairs, and from this stemmed the principle of kingship. The king managed the business of state that was not connected with the temple. He ensured that law and order were enforced among the people. He maintained the canals and kept the streets in good repair. If there was a war with a neighbouring city or tribe, he led the army into battle.

The king was helped and advised by priests and other officials. Some of them assisted him in dispensing justice for, as the populations of the cities expanded, business in the law courts became too heavy a burden for the king alone.

Traders and farmers kept the city well stocked with food and other necessities, and with many luxuries as well. They increased the prosperity of the whole community by successful trading with other cities and with less civilized races further away. The craftsmen turned their skills to making the city beautiful. Sculptors carved exquisite statues, carpenters fashioned splendid gates, doors and furniture, and smiths made jewellery out of silver, gold and precious stones. Armourers wrought copper for weapons of all kinds, for the Sumerians were a warlike people and needed arms on many occasions.

Among the most skilled craftsmen in Sumer were the seal-cutters. The kings, the court officials, the high priests and the merchants all needed seals for their letters, orders, legal documents and accounts. The seals were made of clay or stone,

The Standard of Ur, found in a royal tomb, dates from c. 2500 B.C. It is made of shells, red limestone and lapis lazuli stuck on to a bitumen base.

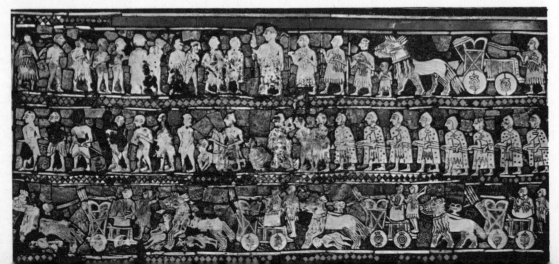

A Sumerian pictogram on a fragment of clay tablet. This is an example of cuneiform script, more than 4,500 years old

alabaster or ivory, and were carved with images of gods, animals or human beings. Many seals that have been found are exceedingly beautiful.

The slaves were the servants of the rich in the households or on the land. They were often enemy soldiers who had been defeated and captured in the field of battle. Slaves also cleaned the streets, emptied the rubbish, and carried water to people's homes. Some were able to buy their freedom and purchase their own land.

The Sumerians have communicated a great deal about themselves through their unusual form of writing, called cuneiform. As far back as 3500 B.C., they drew pictograms, or outlines of objects incised on clay tablets with reed pens. These tablets were then baked and became almost indestructible. The huge number of clay tablets unearthed at the site of Ur has given us a vivid picture of the lives of the Sumerians. The pictograms developed into a mixture of pictures and symbols which represented pronunciations of word syllables. Eventually, they had a kind of script which included some 600 symbols.

One surviving Sumerian inscription reads: 'For Nannar, his king Ur-Nannu, the mighty man, king of Ur, king of Sumer and Akkad, has dug the great canal, his beloved canal.'

As the number of cities on the Euphrates and the Tigris grew, some of the richer and more powerful ones tried to bring their neighbours under their control. Thus arose the succession of dynasties (or royal families) which held supreme power in Sumer.

It is not possible to draw up a complete family tree of the Sumerian dynasties. But we do know of some of the rulers. From about 2700 to about 2280 B.C., Ur was the leading city. The tomb of Shub-Ad who lived there has been uncovered, and from its magnificence and wealth we can be fairly sure that she was the wife of a powerful king. Among the possessions buried with her was a harp, adorned with a bull's head and inlaid with lapis-lazuli and shells.

Probably in about 2370 Sumer was conquered by a strong neighbouring Semitic chief, Sargon I. He defeated the kings of Ur, Lagash and other cities, and for about one hundred and twenty years his family dominated the Sumerians and their Amorite and Akkadian neighbours.

Sargon's grandson Naramsin called himself King of the Four Quarters of the World, but he was eventually defeated in battle by a Sumerian army from Ur. Once more Ur led the cities of Sumer, under a new dynasty, but by 2000 B.C. neighbouring peoples were again pressing on the cities of Sumer. Sumerian greatness was coming to an end.

Sumerian civilization did not die out, however, but was absorbed by Babylon, which adopted and developed its best characteristics. The Sumerians had reached a high standard of legal and social organization, at a time when Europe was inhabited by Neolithic men who were not yet civilized.

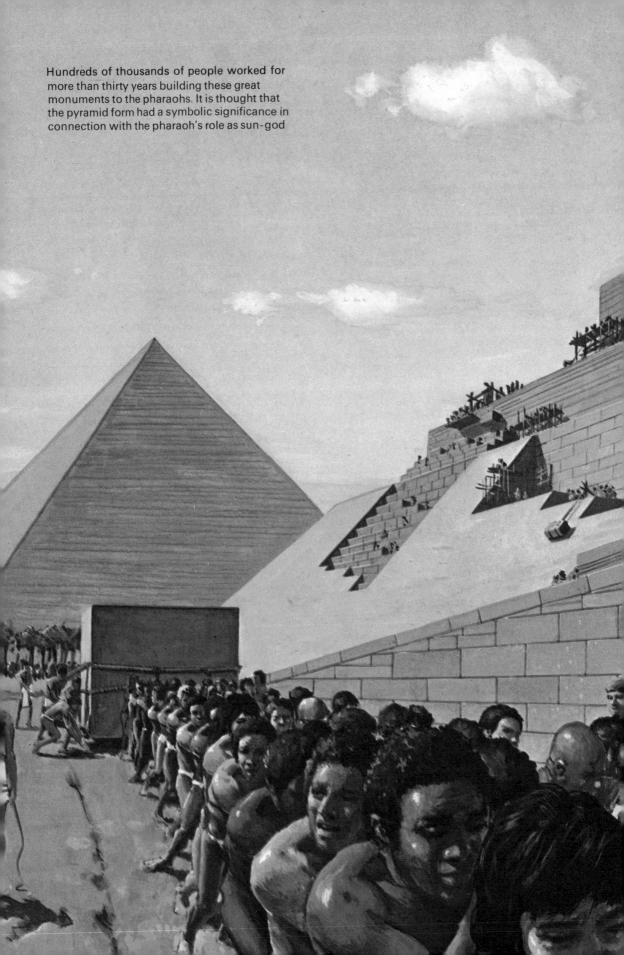

Hundreds of thousands of people worked for more than thirty years building these great monuments to the pharaohs. It is thought that the pyramid form had a symbolic significance in connection with the pharaoh's role as sun-god

# The Land of the Pharaohs

Once the Sumerians settled in the plains of Mesopotamia, they soon became prosperous farming the fertile soil there. A similar growth of early civilization occurred in Egypt. There, in the valley of the River Nile a number of races gathered along the fertile river banks, probably as early as 5000 B.C., and settled down to live together. These races included Libyans, who were descendants of early European Man, Semites from Asia, and Nubians from the warmer parts of Africa.

This mixed population settled in two separate areas, the valley below Assiat which became known as Upper Egypt and the Fayum district, Lower Egypt. For a long time the peoples remained completely separate, until in about 3100 B.C. (according to legend) the king of Upper Egypt, Menes, invaded and conquered the Northern (Lower) Kingdom. From then onwards, Egypt existed as a joint kingdom under one ruler.

In about 3500 B.C., a wave of Semitic people from around the Persian Gulf came to Upper Egypt. They soon mingled peacefully with the Egyptians. This proved to be of great benefit to Egypt because the Semites were intelligent and more advanced culturally. They had traded for some years with the Sumerians; they had learned the use of bronze; and they could make pottery. They were also familiar with Sumerian cuneiform script.

This settlement enabled the Upper Egyptians to advance more quickly than the people of Lower Egypt, but later more Semites migrated into the Northern Kingdom. By the time that Menes had conquered the whole country, Egyptians and Semites had intermingled and had

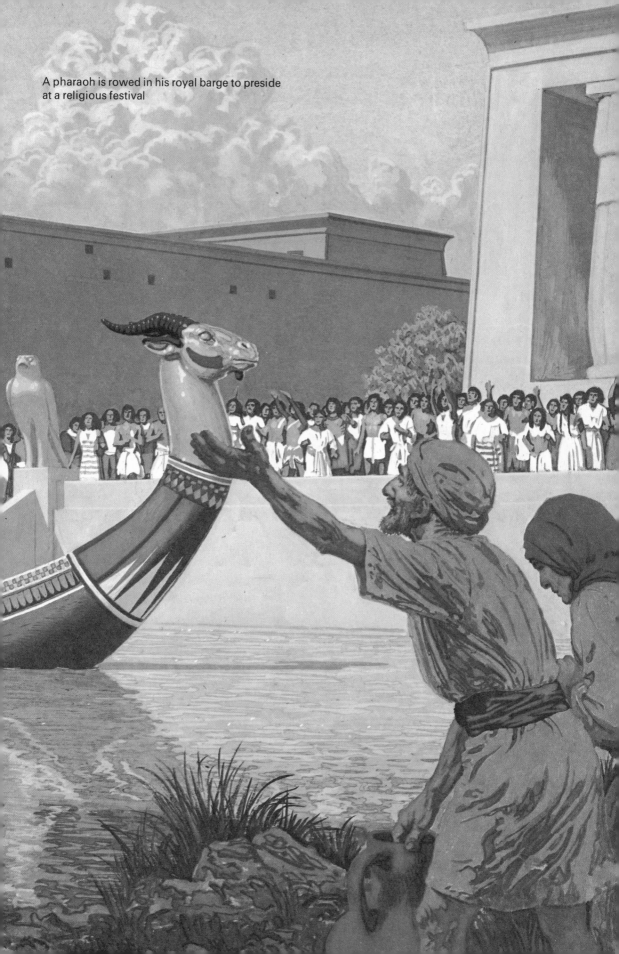

A pharaoh is rowed in his royal barge to preside at a religious festival

begun to develop one language. They were still a nation of farmers, but since farming was relatively simple, the people had time for some of the refinements of civilization such as handicrafts and the pursuit of recreation.

Unlike the Sumerians, the Egyptians did not at first build large cities. Villages grew up along with a few larger market towns where trading activities could be carried on. The only town of any large size was the king's capital, and its location changed according to the whims of the reigning dynasty.

Menes was the first king of all Egypt. He and his successors formed what is called the First dynasty, or the first ruling family. The descendants of Menes ruled for many years after his death. And although quite a lot is known about Menes and something about his descendant Zoser, (who lived about 500 years later), the period between the two rulers is almost a complete blank. These periods about which we know very little occur throughout the story of Egypt – as indeed they do in the stories of all early civilizations.

From our knowledge of early Egypt, we can judge that Menes was an active and very intelligent pharaoh, as the Egyptians called their ruler. One of his most important contributions was to bring order to Egyptian farming methods. He introduced the nilometer, an instrument which recorded the level of the River Nile at different points along the bank. At these points, observers were stationed to watch the level of the river and warn farmers in the locality of the coming of the flood. This enabled the farmers to take advantage of the flooding of the Nile to water their lands.

(Left) Menes officiating at a dyke-cutting ceremony. A shaduf, a means of raising water with a bucket, can be seen in the background

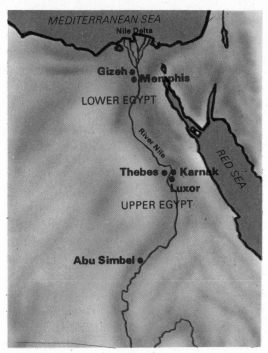

Map of Ancient Egypt

The Nile Valley was – and still is – flooded every year from the middle of August for about two months. This was very helpful to farmers, for it meant that they could plan their sowing and harvesting. The waters would rise soon after the harvest, irrigate the hard, sun-dried earth, and cover it with a layer of silt. The flood would recede in October and then it would be time to start sowing. The newly-enriched earth would produce fine crops.

It is easy to see that under such conditions even the smallest farmer could grow far more than he or his family needed, and so he could sell off the surplus. But in time, the number of people to be fed grew so large that the flood-irrigated earth could no longer provide enough crops. New fields farther from the river's edge had to be sown, but they also had to be watered – in a land that has very little rain.

The Egyptians invented a method of watering land which was beyond the reach of the Nile flood. A canal was cut from the river bank across the fields. The flood water would pour through the gap in the bank and run down the canal. When there was enough water to irrigate the land, the gap would be closed, and another canal would be opened further downstream. Practically the whole Nile Valley was irrigated on this principle, and the farming communities prospered.

Menes introduced the ceremony of 'dyke-cutting' which was continued by his successors. Dykes would be cut on farms before the actual ceremony and a small amount of earth left to separate the channels from the river. As the waters reached their peak, the king shovelled off a few spadefuls of earth from one channel, and the water would begin to trickle over the earth into the dyke. Before long, the earth would be washed away and the water would cascade into the channel. The king would then go down river and carry out the ceremony on another farm.

Menes built a large city near Memphis and made it the capital of Egypt. There he set up his government. Officials were appointed to undertake various duties. For example, a list of all landowners and their lands, a land-registry, was established. This was very important because after the Nile's flooding, boundaries between neighbouring farms were often erased by the new silt deposits, and fierce quarrelling would break out between landowners.

Menes's people worshipped him as a god. Probably both he and his descendants fostered this worship and by the time of Zoser (c.2650 B.C.) Egyptians believed that their pharaohs were gods who had descended from the heavens to rule over them. A structure of religious government – a 'hierarchy' of priests – was organized in Menes's time to ensure that the pharaoh was properly worshipped. The priests were the cleverest and most learned men in the pharaoh's service. They could, by skilful use of words and writings, make sure that ordinary people regarded the pharaoh as superhuman. They invented legends and stories about him and his ancestors, and ensured that religious rituals were carried out. In the process, the priests no doubt acquired a worshipful attitude towards the pharaoh, too.

Two very important gods evolved by the priests, perhaps from earlier, more primitive deities, were Isis and Osiris. There were many other Egyptian gods and goddesses, but of all of them the gods Ra and Isis and Osiris were worshipped the most devoutly by the Egyptians.

The legend of the origin of the gods said that Ra, the sun god, was the first being in the universe. He had four children, Geb, Shu, Tefnut, and Nut. Shu and Tefnut stood on Geb when he was a young boy, and raised Nut, a young girl, to the sky. Thus Geb became the earth god and Nut became the sky goddess. Geb and Nut had four children, Osiris and Seth, who were boys, and Isis

Statues of three Egyptian gods: (left to right) Horus, god of the sky, Isis mother of all things, and the supreme god, Osiris

and Nepthys, who were girls. Osiris succeeded to the throne of Geb and ruled the world wisely, aided by his sister, Isis, whom he later married. Seth, however, was very jealous of Osiris and he murdered him, cutting his body into pieces which he buried in several places in Egypt. The head was buried at Abydos.

Isis was broken-hearted, and collected the parts of her husband. With the aid of the jackal god, Anubis, she brought Osiris back to life, but he was not allowed to return to earth. Instead he went to the underworld where he became the god of the dead. Eventually, his son, Horus, pursued Seth and defeated him in a great battle. Ra then banished Seth to the desert, and Horus reigned in his father's stead.

Ra, the sun god, was the prime Egyptian deity – the giver of light and life, but Osiris, too, was worshipped for many centuries, and his shrine at Abydos became a place of pilgrimage. Isis, too, was a very important deity, and from the Middle Kingdom onwards, her cult which later became joined with that of the cat goddess, Pasht, was widespread.

The Egyptians believed in a future life after death and so they believed that when

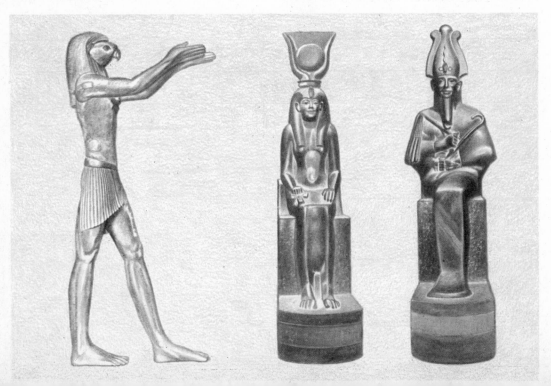

Head of Nefertiti, a renowned beauty and the wife of Pharaoh Akhenaton

2100 B.C.). The largest – and the most famous – was the Great Pyramid at Giza, built for the Pharaoh Khufu (Cheops) in about 2550 B.C. This huge building was more than 480 feet high and nearly 760 feet along each side of its square base. Despite centuries of natural decay, the measurements today are not much less. Khufu's pyramid was made of more than two-and-a-quarter million cut stone blocks, each with an average weight of two-and-a-half tons. Some of the bigger blocks over the inside burial chamber weigh as much as fifty tons. Napoleon Bonaparte, who was very much interested in the history of ancient Egypt and is said to have started the science of Egyptology, calculated that there was enough stone in the pyramid to construct a wall around the whole of France ten feet high and one foot thick.

Pharaohs entombed in the pyramids had many of their possessions buried with them, treasure chests of priceless jewels and metals, fine pottery and elaborate clothing. Not long after the end of the Tenth dynasty, gangs of robbers, who evidently had knowledge of the construction of pyramids, broke into some of them and robbed them of their valuable contents, leaving the mummified pharaohs lying in their tombs, stripped of any jewellery.

The pyramids were not the only great Egyptian achievement which had a connection with the people's religious beliefs. Because religion played a great part in Egyptian daily lives, many early Egyptian manuscripts were devoted to religious matters and religious legends and stories.

The early Egyptians developed a form of writing in pictorial symbols called hieroglyphics. This written language used pictures of things drawn not to represent the things themselves but rather the sounds of names of things. The symbols

a pharaoh died his soul went back to the heavens where he took his place among the other gods. But how could this happen if his body was allowed to rot in the ground? The Egyptians found the answer. The pharaohs must be embalmed as soon as they were dead and entombed in some vast and solid mass, to protect them. These tombs must be constructed so as to be ready for them when they died. This was why the great Egyptian pyramids were built.

Zoser was the first pharaoh to have one built, on the banks of the Nile at Sakkara, and it is called the Step Pyramid. Zoser employed an architect called Imhotep, whose skill was so famous that he was worshipped by later generations of Egyptians as a sort of god. Imhotep's pyramid (which is 200 feet high) is still standing, after nearly 5000 years.

There are several other pyramids in Egypt that were built after Zoser's and before those of the pharaohs of the Tenth dynasty (who ruled between c. 2200–c.

were very complicated and took a long time to carve or write. So, before long, the Egyptians developed a more rapid, somewhat shorter and simplified hieroglyphic script for everyday purposes.

Hieroglyphic inscriptions were first carved on pottery, tablets and tombs. Later they were inscribed on papyrus rolls. The development of writing was greatly helped by the invention of papyrus – from which we get the word paper. Papyrus was made from papyrus reeds which grow abundantly in the Nile Valley. Strips of the stem of the plant were laid out side by side in lengths. More strips were positioned across them at right angles. This double layer was dried and pressed together, and eventually a serviceable sheet of papyrus was ready to be written on with a reed stylus and ink. Papyrus could be produced in any length, and rolls of more than twenty or thirty

feet constituted what we would regard as books. Some manuscripts longer than one hundred feet have been found.

Although Egypt remained an agricultural nation, its civilization continued to develop throughout the centuries, reaching greater and greater heights in architecture, the arts and science. Early Egyptian mathematicians, for example, devised a calendar which has lasted, with modifications, until the present day. It did not take the Egyptians long to observe that the regular flooding of the Nile was related to the climate, nor did it escape them that there was a full moon every twenty-eight days. So they drew up a calendar based upon these natural occurrences which proved to be of great benefit to farmers of the Nile Valley and to everyone else.

Towards the end of the Twelfth dynasty (c. 2000–1790 B.C.) the Pharaoh

Amenemhet III led an invasion into Syria and succeeded in overrunning the country from Gaza, in the south, to Ugarit. He established himself as overlord in Syria, but this was to have disastrous results for Egypt. The invasion brought Egypt into conflict, for almost the first time, with other Middle Eastern empires.

Amenemhet's triumph was short-lived. About 1700 B.C., a fierce wave of Semites, whom the Egyptians called Hyksos (meaning foreigners), drove the Egyptians out of Syria and Palestine. The Hyksos overran the Nile Delta and captured splendid towns and buildings there. They even set up their own capital at Avaris, and built a strong wall around it for protection.

Two things gave the Hyksos superiority over the Egyptians. One was their horse-drawn chariots: the Egyptians had not

Hyksos forces attack the Egyptians, using horse-drawn chariots to great effect

seen horses or chariots before. The other was the Hyksos's skilful use of bronze (a mixture of copper and tin) for war weapons. The Hyksos may even have had iron weapons.

Before long the Hyksos had moved up the Nile Valley and overrun the whole kingdom, which they dominated for about two centuries. The pharaohs were allowed to remain on the Egyptian throne, but their powers were curtailed. This conquest was not altogether bad for Egypt. The Hyksos taught the Egyptians many things; perhaps the most important was a new approach to warfare. They introduced the idea of a regular army with an officer corps, and they instructed the Egyptians in the use of war chariots.

In about 1567 B.C., Ahmose I (c. 1575–c. 1550 B.C.), founder of the Eighteenth dynasty, carefully built up an army of men eager to restore the old power of the pharaohs. The Egyptians attacked the Hyksos in the Nile Delta and drove them out. Ironically it was the horse-drawn chariot which proved decisive in this struggle; the Egyptians had learned well from their masters how to manipulate this engine of war. Ahmose pursued the Hyksos into Palestine, and his successors extended the conquest into Syria.

Ahmose's victories over the Hyksos gave him great popular support, which in turn enabled him to foster the ideas that Egypt's territory should be expanded and that the Egyptian way of life should be spread far and wide beyond the country's boundaries.

The pharaohs of the early Eighteenth dynasty pursued a policy of conquest. In a short time thay had built up a large empire that was to last many years and that produced the most splendid period in Egyptian history. At its greatest extent, this empire stretched from what is now the Sudan in the south, including the

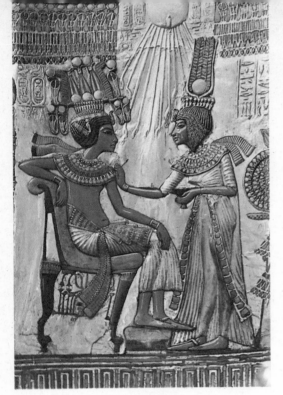

A panel from the back of Tutankhamun's throne, showing the king and queen together

western coast of the Red Sea, to the Euphrates River, including all Palestine and Syria.

Thutmose I (c. 1530–c. 1500 B.C.) defeated the Assyrians and Babylonians in Mesopotamia. His reign appears to have been a glorious one, for carved upon the wall of his great temple to Osiris at Abydos was the inscription:

'I have increased the achievements of others, those kings who ruled before me. The gods have been well worshipped and their temples adorned. I extended the boundaries of Egypt as far as the sun and I have made Egypt greater than any other land . . .'

Thutmose I was succeeded by Thutmose II who married his half-sister Hatshepsut. She was Thutmose I's daughter by his second wife. Thutmose II consolidated his father's gains and organized fresh conquests, but at his death in about 1490 B.C. there was a change in Egyptian policy when his queen assumed control of the empire.

Hatshepsut was a remarkable queen. When Thutmose II died, she immediately began to devote her energies to improvements at home rather than to empire building. The hordes of prisoners captured and enslaved by her predecessors were put to work on great engineering schemes – the construction of palaces, temples, roads and houses. The enormous riches taken in the course of the conquests were used to beautify the cities of Egypt and to provide money for the great trading fleets. Merchants, craftsmen, artisans, shopkeepers and farmers all benefited from the increased flow of money and goods, and the standard of living in Egypt was very high.

Of the many buildings that survive from this time, the tombs Hatshepsut had carved out of the cliffs of the Valley of the Kings near Thebes, as a memorial to her father and a burial place for herself, are magnificent. Her chief architect, Senenmut, one of the greatest of all Egyptian designers, spared neither time nor expense adorning these tombs. They were approached by a wonderful set of stepped terraces, with colonnades branching off at right angles.

Some of Hatshepsut's successors also had tombs built in this part of the Nile Valley with secret entrances, in the hope that grave-robbers would not find the pharaohs' resting places.

Hatshepsut's policy of maintaining peace with her neighbours had severely weakened the empire, and when Thutmose III became pharaoh he reverted to the former policy of expansion. Thutmose, who ruled from c. 1480 to c. 1450 B.C., seems to have been a strong and aggressive ruler and was probably the greatest pharaoh of the Eighteenth dynasty. He led many expeditions into

Palestine and Syria – and beyond – and succeeded in establishing Egyptian power on a more lasting basis by setting up permanent military garrisons in the conquered cities. He also set up local government institutions and put trusted officers of Egyptian birth in the senior positions. Thutmose's rule in these areas was continued by his successors and the stability which followed brought great prosperity to the whole Egyptian empire.

The next pharaoh whose reign is of special interest was Amenhotep IV (or Akhenaton). He succeeded in about 1375 B.C. to a splendidly rich and powerful kingdom and an empire which had hardly been disturbed for eighty years. Amenhotep had little interest in anything other than religious and social reform, and as a result the empire declined. Syria and Palestine, which were semi-independent states governed by Egyptian-born officers, became easy prey to the Hittites who had

for some time been expanding their territory north of the Fertile Crescent, and it was not long before the two areas were overrun and absorbed by the Hittites.

Amenhotep resented the power that the officials and priests had over the pharaohs. The most powerful priests were those of the god Amen, a fierce god. So Amenhotep adopted the worship of another god, Aton, a gentle, even-tempered, shepherding deity, and he surrounded Aton with a new ritual. Aton became the 'one god' and his symbol was the sun. To protect the new religion from the priests of Amen he moved his court from the royal capital of Thebes to Amarna and there set up a temple to Aton. The pharaoh also decreed that the people should worship no other god but Aton. He even changed his own name to Akhenaton which means, roughly, 'he who makes Aton happy'. Then Akhenaton chose a new council of advisers and excluded priests from membership.

Akhenaton is credited with introducing the first real civil service in Egypt. He

The figures are graded in size of importance in this scene of 'fowling' in the marshes from a tomb in Thebes

The ante-chamber of Tutankhamun's tomb as it was found in 1922

appointed governors in the various districts of Egypt and ordered that the proceedings of council meetings should be recorded by scribes.

Akhenaton was married to a beautiful queen, Nefertiti, who has become famous because of the beautiful portrait bust of her which survives. Art under Akhenaton broke away from the usual stylistic Egyptian conventions, and people were portrayed naturally for the first time.

When Akhenaton died in about 1360 B.C. he was succeeded by his son-in-law, Tutankhamun, who was only a boy. At once the priests of the older religion of Amun reasserted their power, and from the boy-pharaoh's name it is clear that they managed to restore the worship of Amun to its former prominence. Even Akhenaton's capital of Amarna was abandoned.

Tutankhamun reigned for only a few years and was still in his teens when he died. His tomb, which has become the most famous of all Egyptian archaeological discoveries, was opened in 1922 by Howard Carter. Inside were the most amazing riches, all jumbled up carelessly in an ante-chamber just outside the burial chamber itself. One item was one of the oldest chairs in the world. Tutankhamun's corpse was found inside the tomb, mummified and in a state of excellent preservation.

After Tutankhamun Egypt was governed by a military chief, Haremhat, who tried to restore Egyptian power in

Syria and Palestine. He made little headway, however, and his successor, Rameses I, one of his officers, was no more fortunate.

Rameses was followed by his son, Seti I, who was pharaoh from about 1310 B.C. to about 1290 B.C. Seti proved to be a forceful ruler, and a fine army commander. He replaced corrupt local government officials; he tried to bring some order into the country's programmes; and he sought to ensure that a fairer standard of justice prevailed in the courts. Then he turned to the business of re-establishing Egyptian dominion in Palestine. He led three armies into the country and defeated every force which the Hittites sent against him.

Seti had a vast temple-palace built for himself in the Nile Valley, near Hatshepsut's tombs.

Seti was succeeded by his son, Rameses II, who was pharaoh from about 1290 B.C. to about 1225 B.C. He is often referred to as Rameses the Great. His fame, in fact, rests largely on a long epic poem about his reign in which he is praised in very exaggerated terms.

Not long after Rameses came to power he marched with an army into Palestine, and there met the Hittites in a great battle at Kadesh. The armies fought fiercely all day, and by sunset both sides had lost enormous numbers of men. The Hittites withdrew and so Rameses regarded the day as a great victory for himself. He returned to Egypt in great pomp and celebrated a triumph.

The Egyptians may have saluted their pharaoh with joy and congratulations, but it was not long before it became quite clear who had really won the war. The Hittites, having withdrawn to regroup their forces, moved southwards again, and in a short time had overrun Palestine as far down as Jerusalem, about two hundred miles south of Kadesh. What is more, they held these newly conquered lands and compelled Rameses to recognize them by treaty.

Rameses's troubles were not confined to Palestine. At home his subjects were on the verge of revolt. Tax collecting, local government, and the administration of justice, all left much to be desired as far as fairness to the people was concerned. The pharaoh devoted an inordinate amount of time and labour to erecting vast monuments to himself. At Abu Simbel, for example, he ordered the construction of a huge temple in the cliffs of the Nile Valley, and on the cliff face he had four statues of himself carved, each over sixty feet in height. These were recently cut out of the cliff and raised to a position two hundred feet higher, so that the great Aswan Dam project might be completed in modern Egypt.

Another of Rameses's monuments is in the hall of the temple at Karnak. This huge building, which is considered an architectural masterpiece, was built in stages by many pharaohs. Its principal feature is a great hall over three hundred feet long, whose roof is over seventy feet high.

While these feats of engineering were being undertaken by Rameses the Great, the pressing internal problems of Egypt were not being dealt with, and the decline of Egypt as a great civilization began during this long reign.

By the end of the twelfth century B.C., Egypt had been overrun by Libyans and by Indo-Europeans, people who were also forcing the decline of Hittite, Mycenaean and early Indian civilizations. As a great and powerful empire Egypt had come to the end of its influence, but in later chapters we shall see how Egyptian culture affected subsequent civilizations, in particular the Assyrians and the Greeks.

# The Babylonians

The Sumerians and the Egyptians were surrounded by other races which were not as civilized or as highly developed politically and militarily. But because they had to trade with these less civilized neighbouring peoples – Sumer needed metal and stone and Egypt required wood – it was not long before the secrets of their civilizations and their benefits became known, exciting envy as well as wonder.

In the years between 3000 and 2000 B.C. both the Sumerians and the Egyptians were subjected to invasions by several races, although generally the rulers had been able to overcome them. Either the invaders were absorbed and became useful members of the Sumerian or Egyptian communities, or they were driven back to their own territories. These invasions, however, became much worse after about 2000 B.C.

In about 1950 B.C. Semitic Amorites from the western Arabian Desert and Semitic Elamites from the east began to move into the richer plains of Mesopotamia. There they captured the cities and thus destroyed the supremacy of Ur and other Sumerian city-states. In time, Ur itself fell to the Elamites and its last king, Ibi-sin, was captured and taken to Elam.

The Amorites, meanwhile, had been overrunning the more northerly Sumerian settlements. One of the villages on the Euphrates River which was captured was to grow into the great city called Babylon, the chief city of Babylonia. Sometime before 1800 B.C. the Amorites set up a king called Sumnabum. He was the first Amorite king of Babylon. Once his rule was established, he began to have dreams of building an empire. For the next hundred years, he and his successors struggled to dominate the plains of Mesopotamia.

But Babylon did not succeed in dominating Mesopotamia until the time of its sixth king, Hammurabi, who was one of the greatest rulers of ancient history. Hammurabi, who was descended from Sumnabum, ruled Babylon for over forty years c.1790–c.1750. Although a great part of his reign was taken up with fighting, he also accomplished considerable social reforms.

By the time Hammurabi came to the throne the Babylonians had reached a high standard of civilization. Although they developed their own language – and the Sumerian language sank into a position where it was only used by priests, in much the same way that Latin today is used by the Church of Rome – the best elements of Sumerian culture were absorbed and improved upon by them. Their knowledge of mathematics had been increased by contact with the Egyptians, and probably by 1700 B.C. the Babylonians were using multiplication tables, square roots and even some algebra. They understood geometry, especially the principles which were later stated as a basic theorem by Pythagoras. Babylonians also used a system of numbers from which we derive the 60 minutes of an hour and the 360° in a circle.

The first library in the world was established in Babylon. The books it contained

Babylon, one of the most famous cities of antiquity, was built overlooking the Hilla, a tributary of the Euphrates

were not volumes as we know them, nor indeed were they made of papyrus rolls like Egyptian books. Stories, poems and even letters were written on stones or clay tablets of varying shapes. Some were prisms, others cylinders, and others flat slates. This early library was important. Apart from providing a place for storing records and historical and religious writings, it encouraged both reading and writing, in particular poetry. The Babylonians were great readers of poetry; one of their favourite epics was the legend of Gilgamesh. This was the story of a mythical Sumerian hero-king which was absorbed into Babylonian folklore. The legend has survived in varied forms to the present day.

Babylon had a regular standing army, probably the first in the world. The existence of a permanent fighting force made it easier for the kings to hold sway over neighbouring states; it also meant that in Babylonian society there was a new class of people—the warrior class—made up of officers and soldiers. Because these men enabled the ruler to maintain his power, they naturally had special privileges. One of these was the right to own land, which as a rule in ancient times was held by the king who only granted it to his people for farming. The king, of course, could withdraw the right to farm his lands, but he ran the risk of inciting a rebellion if he tried to remove the farming rights on a wide scale.

The first thirty years or so of Hammurabi's rule were devoted to wars with his neighbours. After that he succeeded in overrunning the Assyrians in the north of Mesopotamia and the Elamites in the east, thus bringing a large part of Mesopotamia under the rule of Babylon.

After the success of these conquests, Hammurabi turned his attention to the governing of Babylon, and he was equally successful in times of peace. He is most famous for the Code of Laws that he assembled. Hammurabi's Code is, in fact, the oldest surviving code of law in the

history of the world, and it was the model for many states which followed Babylon. Some of the laws mentioned in the *Book of Exodus* in the Old Testament, for example, are derived from Hammurabi's Laws. The Code was inscribed on a huge pillar of black basalt rock. The original is in the Louvre in Paris and a copy is in the British Museum in London.

The Code reveals Hammurabi to have been a most thorough and painstaking ruler. The laws show the depth of his interest in government and in the welfare of his people. The Code in itself is also a wonderful record of his splendid services to the state. Here is part of Hammurabi's own view of what he achieved in Babylon:

> 'I rooted out the enemy above and
> below.
> I made an end of war.
> I promised the welfare of the land.
> I made the peoples rest in friendly
> habitation.
> I have governed them in peace.
> I have sheltered them in my
> strength.'

There were some two hundred and eighty parts of the Code, which provided rules and regulations for the three main classes of Babylonian society, the *amelu* (nobles, warriors and officials), the *mush-kinu* (commoners, merchants, craftsmen,

The great Babylonian ruler and law-giver, Hammurabi. Above him is part of his Code engraved upon a pillar of black basalt rock, which is now in the Louvre in Paris

farmers) and the *wardu* (slaves). The laws and penalties varied according to the classes:

> 'If a noble has broken another noble's
> bone, they shall break his bone.
> 'If he has destroyed the eye of a
> commoner or has broken the bone
> of a commoner, he shall pay one
> mina of silver.'

According to the Code, theft from a noble had to be repaid thirty times, but theft from a commoner only ten times. If a house collapsed and killed the owner, the builder was put to death; if the house killed the owner's son, the builder's son had to die.

This was, of course, a stern code, but we should remember that the times were both hard and harsh. The Code was also fair, for, above all, Hammurabi was determined that the mighty should not be allowed to oppress the weak.

Hammurabi was concerned about the treatment of women, particularly widows. He enacted laws which allowed women to inherit their husband's house, land and possessions, which was not the case in other civilizations. This splendid ruler also insisted on legal formalities in business transactions. No one could sell property, or transfer it, without a written contract, duly signed and witnessed. There are many surviving tablets illustrating this strict attention to contract law. Hammurabi is even credited with regulating wages, and setting down maximum rates for work in various trades.

Hammurabi, of course, did not invent all these laws; he assembled existing laws, revised them and added new ones of his own in order to bring the whole system of laws up to date. The Code was inscribed on a huge pillar so that all his people would know what their legal rights were.

Hammurabi not only recast the law; he supervised its carrying out. He wrote many letters telling people to do this or that. One letter which survived was very rude. It was written to an official who was taking a long time cleaning out a canal. Hammurabi's letter gave the man three days to finish the work.

Hammurabi was also a builder. He improved Babylon and constructed a fine wall around the city. He extended the canal system, and built temples at Nippur and Eridu, two other Mesopotamian cities.

When Hammurabi died Babylon fell on hard times. He left no successor capable of maintaining the power he had wielded or of enforcing the laws he had drawn up. So it was not long before Babylonia became a prey to invasion, first by the Hittites and then by the Kassites, another Indo-European race who lived in the mountainous regions of what is now Persia. The Kassites were deeply impressed by Babylonian civilization and decided to remain in Babylon. They maintained the city's dominant position for many years, until in the end Babylon was overcome by the powerful Assyrians.

The Assyrians came from a kingdom in north-eastern Mesopotamia. When Sumerian greatness ended and Babylon became the ruling city in Mesopotamia, the Assyrians continued to develop their own separate civilization in the northern district around the Tigris River. They prospered because they managed to control the trade routes between Asia Minor and the Persian Gulf, but they remained under the dominion of Babylon, although for centuries they fought to break free. Eventually, however, the Assyrians built a splendid empire with territories stretching from Egypt to India.

The Babylonians thoroughly understood the principles of mathematics and geometry

# The Rise and Fall
# of the Minoan Civilization

South of Greece, in the Mediterranean Sea, lies the narrow island of Crete. This small isle, about one hundred and twenty miles long and no more than thirty miles wide at its broadest point, was for some 1500 years the centre of one of the greatest ancient civilizations. It is usually referred to as the Minoan civilization because the chief priest and ruler was called the Minos.

Because Crete is an island and naval warfare on a large scale was unknown at the time, the Minoans did not continually have to ward off invasions by jealous

The famous palace of the Minos at Knossos, in Crete, about 3500 years ago. Sir Arthur Evans's excavations in 1900 revealed a complex system of apartments, bathrooms and storehouses, many of them decorated with elaborate and colourful friezes

neighbours, as did Sumer and Babylon. These peaceful times greatly encouraged the development of civilization and culture in Crete.

The Minoans depended entirely on ships for trading, and their merchants visited many places up and down the coasts of the Aegean Sea and the Mediterranean. This brought them into contact with the civilizations in the Near East, especially Egypt, and enabled them to take advantage of the culture, knowledge and innovations of other peoples which helped in the development of their own civilization.

Minoan civilization began in about 3000 B.C., but it did not reach its greatest period, which lasted for about two hundred years, until around fifteen hundred years later. A great deal about the story of Crete was revealed by the remarkable excavations of Sir Arthur Evans, at the beginning of the present century. Since then, other archaeologists have been able to add more details to – and in some ways to correct – Evans's original interpretations.

We now have some good ideas of how this peace-loving people lived and went about their business. Although Minoans learned the art of writing from contact with their neighbours across the seas, they do not appear to have kept records of the special achievements of their leaders like those of Hammurabi of Babylon; so an historical picture of the Minoans cannot be presented in the same way as for other civilizations.

In the first period of Minoan civilization, which we call the Early Age (*c.* 3000–*c.* 2000 B.C.), Indo-Europeans came to Crete via the mainland of Greece. Finding the climate agreeable and the soil fertile they stayed and quickly developed an organized way of life. Their agriculture proved so successful that before long they were able to export grain and wine to Greece, to Asia Minor and even to Lower Egypt.

These early Minoans lived in villages of small square houses, and were particularly skilled in stone-work. They knew how to work bronze and make knives, axes, pincers, and ornaments with a great degree of skill and beauty. They also fabricated jewellery out of gold and silver. They were very skilful and imaginative potters, and manufactured a whole range

Map of the Aegean world in south-eastern Europe showing the mountainous Greek peninsula and island of Crete

One of the favourite sports was bull dancing. Skilled youths and girls somersaulted over the horns of bulls, risking serious injury

A bronze dagger blade, decorated with silver and niello inlay on copper (16th century B.C.) and an earthenware jar (18th century B.C.) found at Phaestos

of utensils and ornaments decorated with geometric and animal designs.

By about 2000 B.C., the Minoans seem to have taken a great leap forward in civilization, for a period of marked development has been dated as beginning at about this time. This is called the Middle Age (c.2000–c.1700 B.C.). During these centuries, the Minoans built large cities with vast palaces and public buildings. They devised a written script, and they organized a central government. Their arts and crafts flourished and became perhaps the most skilful and beautiful in the Near East.

The main city built by the Minoans was Knossos, which lay on the northern side of Crete on the side of a hill not far from the sea. On the hilltop was a huge palace, the residence of the ruler, the Minos. The palace was really a group of buildings around a paved courtyard. The principal building contained the ruler's rooms. These were approached by a wide staircase leading from the court-

yard. The rooms had windows which overlooked the sea and the valley.

Indoors, the rooms were brightly decorated. Walls were painted, and decorated with colourful frescoes–paintings done on wet plaster – which depicted scenes of everyday Cretan life. Remains of these frescoes show what Minoan citizens looked like. The walls of the palace of Knossos also depicted bulls – animals which played an important part in Cretan games and festivals – and young men and women engaged in bull dancing. The legendary Minotaur, a creature half-animal and half-human, was supposed to have inhabited a labyrinth, possibly part of the palace of Knossos, and demanded human sacrifice. It is likely that the Minoans had some sort of religious cult centering around bull worship which may have been connected with the Minotaur legend.

The bathrooms and kitchens of the palace were connected to an elaborate drainage system, said to be the best in the Near East. Water was supplied by means of clay piping from wells outside, and the waste was carried away through other pipes to a vast drain situated in the cellar. This emptied into an outside gutter.

In addition to the ruler's apartments there were residential quarters for the host of craftsmen who worked for the Minos. The workshops of carpenters, stonemasons, goldsmiths, potters and metal founders were part of the palace, too. Accommodation and offices were also provided for government officials.

Since Crete probably did not, for a long time, suffer from foreign invasion, the palaces were not fortified. The pillars, stone walls and parapets were very strong, however, and could withstand considerable damage. When the palace of Knossos was destroyed in about 1550 B.C., archaeologists believe it was not due to the arms of an invader, but to an earthquake.

Below the palace was the city of Knossos. There people lived in two- or three-storey houses. The foundations and ground floors were made of stone and the upper storeys of brick interlaced with timber. The houses were also equipped with drainage systems and were gaily decorated and furnished.

What kind of people were the Minoans and what did they do? The men, if they were not in the service of the ruler, worked on the land, fished off the coasts, or built ships and sailed them for merchants, or worked as skilled craftsmen. The Minoans were extremely enterprising. For example, merchant-sailors not only transported merchandise to and from the mainland, but they also set up the first transport agencies in history, carrying, among other things, linen from Egyptian manufacturers to Hittite importers in Asia Minor.

Minoan women dressed gaily, usually in woollen clothes. They wore ankle-length skirts, open bodices, and wide, tight girdles around their waists. Their hair was worn very long. Young girls and boys who were bull dancers wore very short, thigh-length skirts and waist girdles.

Minoan art in this period reached an extraordinarily high standard. Their paintings, for example, are regarded as more beautifully executed than any of those of their contemporaries. They mastered the craft of making very thin pottery, an art that is still difficult today. Jars and vases were moulded on wheels, operated by treadles, into the finest shapes and then decorated with beautiful patterns of seaweed, oyster shells, squids, or flowers like lilies and irises.

Minoan writing, on clay tablets, was developed from both Egyptian and Sumerian models. They began with a

The legendary bull-headed monster, the Minotaur, was slain by Theseus who was brave enough to confront the beast

completely pictorial script and then added a syllabic system. Some of it is still indecipherable and archaeologists are examining what are called Linear A and Linear B scripts to try to find out more about Crete.

Knossos was not the only important city on Crete. Another large one was Phaestos, in the south-west, and it is thought that at some time the island was divided into two rival kingdoms. There was a third, smaller city at Hagia.

Sometime about 1500 B.C., all of Crete was devastated by a series of earthquakes, which are not uncommon in the Aegean Sea area. Knossos was very severely damaged, and archaeologists have shown that the palace of the Minos had to be rebuilt.

The third and last period of Minoan civilization, the Late Age, began soon after these earthquakes and for a little more than a century it was Crete's greatest age. The main difference between Cretan civilization in the Middle and Late Ages was that the latter was a more luxurious version of the Middle Age. The reconstructed palace of Knossos was more beautiful, the Minoan sailing fleet was larger, and the country was richer. Trade with Egypt and the Levant (the eastern Mediterranean coastline) was more vigorous and extensive. Even the art is regarded as more exquisite. Finally, the language evolved into something like the earliest form of Greek, which is a sort of link between modern Western civilizations and the Minoans of thousands of years ago.

Not long after, about 1400 B.C., Minoan civilization began to decline very rapidly. Crete had for some years been subjected to raids by more backward people from Greece, whom we call Mycenaeans because of their principal city, Mycenae. Knossos itself was captured and burnt, as it had no proper defences. The Minoans never recovered from the destruction of their capital. They drifted into semi-slavery, and their former greatness became only a memory.

The Mycenaeans were less civilized descendants than the Minoans or Indo-Europeans from the Greek mainland. The Mycenaeans took Minoan culture to the

The great city of Knossos was badly damaged by an earthquake in about 1500 B.C.

mainland and for two hundred years or so they enjoyed an age of civilization which was based upon the Cretan model.

They built great palaces at Mycenae and Tiryns, at Pylos, on the Acropolis at Athens, and in northern Greece (Thessaly). These were decorated rather like the Minoan ones, and adorned with magnificent rows of columns. They buried their chiefs in vast rock or stone tombs. The Mycenaeans also adapted Minoan writing, and reduced it to a workable alphabet of some ninety characters.

But the Mycenaeans never reached the heights of civilization of the Minoans – or for that matter of the Hittites. They did not build great cities. They devoted a lot of their time to warfare, invasion and conquest. They were cruel to their prisoners. Troops or sailors captured on their expeditions were brought back to Greece and forced into slavery to work on the land.

The Mycenaeans raided the Syrian coast; they landed in Cyprus; and they made continued descents on the vast coast of Asia Minor. One of these raids was on Troy. By about the beginning of the twelfth century B.C., the Greek peoples were loosely united under the Mycenaean kings, and the king, Agamemnon, led the expedition against Troy from which grew one of the best known stories of all time, the legend of the Trojan War.

Mycenaean civilization came to an abrupt end. Towards the end of the twelfth century B.C., Mycenae was attacked by Dorian invaders from the area that is now Bulgaria and Yugoslavia and burned down. Pylos and Tiryns were also destroyed. Indeed, all the buildings of the Mycenaeans suffered, except the Acropolis in Athens.

The new invaders were semi-barbarous. They had little use for art, and did not care much for constructing beautiful buildings, and they were not interested in trading. Their sole purpose in life seemed to be in conquest and destruction.

So Mycenae sank into lethargy. Many of the peoples scattered throughout Greece, and all traces of the Minoan-Aegean culture and civilization disappeared for a long time. But from this obscurity was to rise the Greek civilization in all its splendour and greatness.

Greek soldiers, concealed in this wooden horse, emerged at night to overpower the city of Troy whose unsuspecting citizens had accepted it as a gift.

# The Hittites in Asia Minor

In the story of early Babylon we saw that Sumer and Egypt either beat off invading armies or they absorbed the incoming population. Then, after about 2000 B.C., the raids of the invaders became more dangerous and their effects more lasting. And in the second millenium (2000–1000 B.C.), there were two main streams of migration and invasion into the Near East – Semitic and Indo-European.

The Semites, a grouping of tribes from the more southerly areas, mingled with kinsmen from the north-east, moved westwards and northwards and settled in the area of Syria, Palestine and Assyria.

The second stream of invaders consisted of Aryan, or Indo-European peoples. Aryan, or Indo-European, loosely describes a large group of peoples who came down into the fertile plains of the Near East from the area that is now Russia. These people spoke different languages of a related group called Indo-European languages, from which Sanskrit, Greek, Latin, Russian and Welsh, among others, were to develop.

Babylon was overrun by the Kassites as was ancient India. The Kassites were Indo-Europeans. Another important Indo-European group of races was the Hittites.

The Indo-Europeans, who invaded the civilized parts of the Near East, were themselves very backward. Their raids were prompted by jealousy of Egyptian, Sumerian and Indian civilizations and of the other nearby regions that had acquired a veneer of civilization. In about 2000 B.C. the Hittites came from Armenia over the Caucasus mountains and settled in Asia Minor, south of the Black Sea. They were as barbarous as any of the other Indo-Europeans; but they had one advantage not shared by Sumer, Egypt, India or Babylon: they had mastered the use of iron, which is harder than bronze and melts at a much higher temperature. The Hittites discovered and held the secret of producing this high temperature for centuries. When their greatness came to an end in about 1200 B.C., the Assyrians became masters of iron founding and this helped them to build the most powerful empire in the Near East.

The Hittites settled in the valley of the winding River Halys and established themselves as farmers of the rich plains. They were the first of the Indo-European peoples to become civilized. Contact with Mesopotamia and Egypt enabled them to develop scripts for their own language. They used two scripts, one a cuneiform variety rather like that used in Babylon, and the other a form of hieroglyphic picture-writing.

The Hittites were a group of allied races, and when they settled in Asia Minor they divided up into separate 'states'. But those that lived on the River Halys asserted a sort of leadership which was not seriously contested. They began by electing kings, who were advised by a council of nobles. With the passage of time, however, the power of the king grew and that of the nobles declined until they became more or less administrators of the king's decrees.

The first Hittite king to make his mark

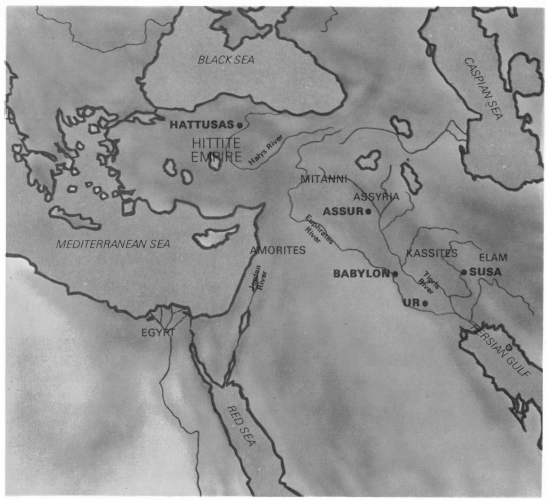

Map of the Hittite and other kingdoms in about 2000 B.C.

in history was Hattusilis, who ruled in the middle of the sixteenth century B.C. He built a large city about seventy-five miles north of the southern-most bend in the River Halys. This city had grand walls, large temples, a spacious palace, and rows of fine houses for the nobles and officials. The city was later named Hattusas after him, and today the modern Turkish town of Boghazkoy marks the original site.

Hattusilis was the first king to extend Hittite power outside Anatolia, the area which today forms the main part of Turkey. He invaded Syria at a time when the part of the Near East known as the Levant was in turmoil. There the Hittite secret of using iron for weapons of war proved decisive.

Hattusilis's successor, Mursilis I (who died about 1550 B.C.), went further on through Assyria and reached the great city of Babylon which he plundered, slaying the last of Hammurabi's successors. Mursilis then withdrew his forces and returned to Hattusas.

Mursilis was said to have been assassinated, and on his death the Hittite kingdom appears to have lapsed into a state of anarchy for many years. Not until about 1450 B.C. did an ordered kingdom emerge,

49

by which time the principle of hereditary succession of kings appears to have been established. The organization of a more central form of government also seems to have taken several steps forward. Once more, the Hittites embarked upon a series of expeditions into Syria, Mitanni and Assyria. This brought them into contact with Egypt which had interests in Palestine and Syria.

The incursions were to some extent successful, and by the time of King Suppiluliumas (*c.* 1380–*c.* 1345 B.C.) the Hittites were well established in northern Syria. Mitanni, which acted as a buffer state between the Hittites and the Egyptian interests in Palestine, soon dissolved into anarchy, and the Hittites took control of the kingdom.

Suppiluliumas was probably the greatest of the Hittite kings. He enlarged Hattusas and adorned it with grand buildings of stone. He strengthened the power of the monarchy over the smaller Hittite states, and he added to the dominions of the Hittites outside Asia Minor. Indeed,

by the end of his reign, the Hittite empire stretched from the western coast of Anatolia on the shores of the Aegean Sea to Assyria and down the Levantine coast to Jerusalem. In his time, Suppiluliumas was looked on as the arbiter of disputes in the Near East, and the widow of the young pharaoh, Tutankhamen, is said to have begged him to arrange for her to marry one of his sons, so that she could have a husband to rule Egypt. The death of the son on reaching Egypt led to a Hittite campaign against Egypt.

What was Hittite society like? The Hittites were a confederation of tribes which were centrally controlled by the reigning king at Hattusas. Under the king were three classes of people throughout the Hittite states. The upper class was the *mariannu,* whose ranks were hereditary, and who pledged their allegiance to the ruler at Hattusas. They were usually the most important people in the states, and owned large tracts of land. Next came the *haniahu,* who were tradesmen, farmers, gardeners, royal husbandmen, grooms

Perhaps the Hittites' main contribution to Western civilization was the discovery of iron

and officials. The most numerous class was the *hupsu*, semi-free labourers who paid taxes and had to go into military service when called upon by the *mariannus* to whom they owed loyalty. Beneath these three classes there were slaves, mainly of foreign origin.

In Hittite law there were rules for freemen and rules for slaves. Both codes were, by comparison with those of Assyria, Babylon and Egypt, humane. The death penalty, for example, was limited to a few serious offences and was enforced only if an offence had been committed by a freeman. Even then, the sentence had to come from the king's own court.

Another characteristic of the Hittites, once they had developed their written scripts, was their interest in history and in keeping records. A great many documents in the form of tablets have survived. These include reports, speeches of kings, and texts of treaties and ordinances. Treaties were often preceded by brief historical summaries of the events leading up to them.

The Kassites destroyed much of Babylon and looted valuable objects

One of Suppiluliumas's successors, Mu-watallis, fought the Egyptians, led by Pharaoh Rameses II, at Kadesh in 1285. Both sides claimed victory – and Rameses actually celebrated a triumph for it at home. But it was the Hittites who really derived the benefit from the war, for they proceeded to advance across Syria to Damascus, and the war went on.

Some years later (*c.* 1269 B.C.), Muwa-tallis's successor, Hattusilis III, made a peace treaty with Rameses, which was recorded by both the Hittites and the Egyptians. The terms in it recognized existing frontiers, and set up schemes for mutual trade and financial aid. It was confirmed later on by the marriage of Rameses II to one of Hattusilis's daughters. The Hittite king went to Egypt for the wedding celebrations.

Not long after the death of Hattusilis III the Hittite kingdom was invaded by barbarians from the north – Phrygians from the Balkans as well as various other nomadic tribes. As the Hittites had not really evolved an independent culture of their own, but had adopted and developed aspects of older cultures, they did not have strong enough roots to survive these invasions.

By 1200 B.C. Hittite power had come to an end and Asia Minor remained in a semi-barbarous state for many years. The Hittites were never heard of again. But they had influenced the history of the Near East in many ways: they had introduced the use of iron, they had stopped the expansion of the Egyptian empire, and they had kept eastern nomadic invaders away which helped the civilizations of the Near East to develop.

The marriage of Pharaoh Rameses II to the daughter of the powerful Hittite king, Hattusilis III, his former enemy, confirmed the peace treaty made several years before. It was celebrated in the most magnificent style, festivities continuing for days

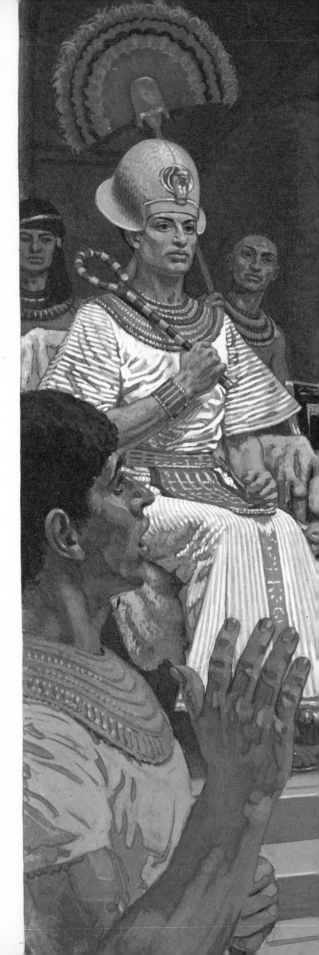

# Early Civilization in the Indus Valley

In the western part of the Indian sub-continent, in what is now Pakistan, flows the great River Indus. The Indus River has given its name to India and to the country's people. The valley of the Indus is a huge plain, some one thousand miles long and more than five hundred miles wide in places. This valley was once extremely fertile, and there, 4,500 years ago, the Indus civilization began.

Where did the people of this civilization come from? It is not known for certain, but one or two guesses have been made. Some historians think they came from the Mediterranean area through Turkey, across Assyria and into north-west India. Others believe that when the 'black-headed' people set out from north-west India and founded the Sumerian civilization, some stayed behind in India. Then, many years later, when travellers from Sumer visited them and displayed the benefits of a more civilized way of life, they moved south from the hills into the fertile plains of the Indus Valley.

This might explain why the Indus civilization appeared to rise almost overnight, for the people would only have had to imitate the Sumerians to achieve a fairly high degree of culture, and so would not have needed long years of unassisted development.

However it developed, the Indus civilization was an intensely individual one, with many characteristics not shared with any other civilizations.

Excavations carried out over forty years ago in the Indus Valley revealed that there were two large cities, three hundred and fifty miles apart in the plain of the

Indus seals featured a wide range of animals, and are thought to have represented personal names. The bronze dancing girl (right) is one of the most outstanding Indus figurines

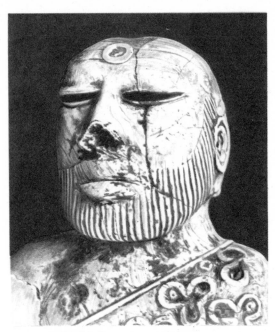

An example of Indus stone sculpture representing a 'priest-king' or deity

which had obviously been submerged under water.

The building and operation of canals would have required some kind of central organization and control, which could not have been exercised merely by village communities. It is believed that the cities and towns of the Indus Valley were run on similar lines to the city-states of Sumer.

That there was contact between the Indus people and the Sumerians is clear from the large number of seals and letters in Indian script that have been excavated in Mesopotamia. The ties between Sumer and India seem to have been closest in the time of Sargon I, the Assyrian ruler of the Sumerian city-states.

The story of Harappa and Mohenjo-daro is a strange one. In about 2500 B.C. the Indus civilization became mature rapidly. Then, over the next thousand years it did not really develop but remained more or less as it was. Buildings were destroyed from time to time by floods, and new ones were put up on the old foundations, but the quality of building declined rather than improved. The styles of construction did not vary, but the skill with which the buildings were erected became more and more haphazard. The

Indus. Both cities were over a square mile in area; they were called Harappa and Mohenjo-daro. The discovery of these cities gave archaeologists and historians evidence, for the first time, of the earliest civilization of the Indian people.

Besides these cities there were several smaller towns in the plain, built in a similar manner, which suggests that the two big cities governed the whole area between them. Harappa, which was the largest of the cities, seems to have left its influence on the other towns. Possibly, therefore, at some time one of the city's rulers attempted to bring the whole area under Harappa's control.

The Indus Valley, like the Nile Valley, is flooded every year—in this case from May to August. The Indians, therefore, had the same problems of irrigation as the Egyptians, and they built canals. Possibly the floods were less regular than those of the Nile, or the canals less effective, for there are signs both in Harappa and in Mohenjo-daro of rebuilding on old sites

Map of the Indus River Valley

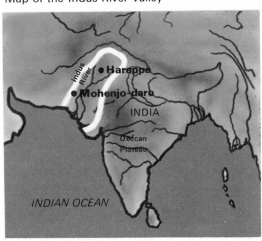

A view of Mohenjo-daro showing the immense and complex granaries, baths and two-storeyed houses which existed in about 2000 B.C.

builders subdivided large rooms to provide extra accommodation rather than building extensions or erecting new buildings close by.

The Indus Valley towns, especially the large ones, were exceptional. They were laid out on a rectangular grid system, with wide main streets running parallel to each other, cut at right angles by smaller streets. The streets were lined with large blocks of houses, many of them two-storeyed, all of them with flat roofs.

The Indians were the first people to use bitumen on walls, floors and roofs, to keep out the damp.

The houses were built of baked bricks. Access to the upstairs rooms was by a narrow stone staircase at the back of the house. This staircase sometimes continued upwards on to the roof. The houses had bathrooms and water closets (which were sometimes upstairs), rubbish shoots and excellent drainage systems. The drains were incorporated in the walls and led outside into covered sewers which ran down the side of the streets. The kitchens had serving hatches into the dining rooms.

The Indus Valley people had an assortment of furniture. Pieces most usually found in houses were wooden storage chests with bronze or copper fasteners, beds, and benches. Carved chair legs dating back to about 2000 B.C. have been found in the ruins.

Indian houses usually had their own wells, for in that part of the world a lot of water was used. Bathing was an important part of the day's activities. There were public bath-houses, and these were used frequently; a public bath-house was a good place to meet one's friends.

We are not yet certain about the kind of social structure the early Indians had. Some of the houses in Mohenjo-daro and Harappa are much bigger than others,

A terracotta figurine of a 'mother goddess' wearing what we might call a 'mini-skirt', and laden with jewellery and an elaborate head-dress

and this must indicate that there was a rich class which was superior to ordinary people. The Indians were great traders. Examples of their pottery, jewellery, and metal work have been found in many places in the Middle East and so perhaps it was the merchants who owned the larger houses.

The Indians used copper and bronze in great quantity. They learned to exploit the mineral resources of Rajputana, and with these metals they made fish hooks, copper-headed arrows, razors and bronze mirrors.

Clothing which early Indian women wore was very gay. They wore short, scanty petticoats rather like mini-skirts. Their clothes were made of cotton, linen or wool. They wore bright, sparkling jewellery made of gold, silver, or shell, inlaid with stones like jade and lapis-lazuli. In general, men wore a sort of cloak, rather like a Roman toga, which went over one shoulder and under the other.

The early Indians were great craftsmen. They knew how to make fine pottery on the wheel. Some of their works were remarkably like ours today.

Potters usually engraved or painted their pottery. Their favourite designs were geometric, but they used also the figures of animals as decoration. The designs were often painted in black ink, probably a liquid similar to the thick, indelible India ink used today.

The Indians kept pets, such as song-birds and dogs. They also raised cattle, sheep, pigs and poultry for food, and used cattle for drawing vehicles. The Indians are believed to have invented the ox-cart. Animals played a special part in Indian life, for evidence from excavations seems to indicate that they were worshipped along with other gods, a similarity to the Egyptian animal-god worship.

The early Indians were just as accomplished artists as they were craftsmen. Some of their sculpture is very beautiful, particularly when it depicts movement, as do some pieces showing dancers which were found at Mohenjo-daro.

Despite their considerable abilities and their artistic genius, the Indians did not advance very far in the period from 2500 to 1500 B.C. They made finer pottery without ensuring that it was also more useful. They built no palaces or temples,

and their rulers do not seem to have had splendid tombs constructed. They imitated the things that their fathers did, and so remained a stagnant society. They were an easy prey to foreign invasion.

In about 1500 B.C., the Kassites, kinsmen of the tribes who overran Babylon, moved into the Indus Valley, overthrew the cities and established their own society. They were simple, barbarous people, who neither adopted nor improved the existing Indian culture. Harappa and Mohenjo-daro, and the smaller cities, were left to decay.

For the next thousand years Indian history is almost unknown. When once again the Indians moved in a civilized and ordered society there was little, if any, trace to be found of their earliest age of development. Until 1921 there was not a building in India which had originated earlier than 500 B.C. Perhaps archaeology will ultimately reveal something of the interim period in the Indus Valley civilization between 1500 and 500 B.C.

A reconstruction of a public bathing house in Mohenjo-daro. The bath, which measured 39 × 23 feet, was lined with asphalt to make it waterproof. A large well provided the source for the bath

# The Beginnings of Chinese Civilization

The civilization of Sumer, Egypt, Babylon and India all had one thing in common: they all grew up in valleys along the banks of great rivers. So it was with the Chinese civilization, which began along the shores of the Hwang-Ho (Yellow) River in north China, some 320 kilometres south of modern Peking.

The country's ancient legends say that Chinese civilization began as far back as about 3000 B.C., but there is no real historical or archaeological evidence to support so early a start. In those times, there were certainly advanced Neolithic peoples enjoying a progressive Stone Age,

as in many other parts of the world. And we must not forget that a specimen of *Homo erectus* was found near Peking in 1927. These Neolithic people settled in the Hwang-Ho valley and in time began to develop an agricultural way of life in its fertile, yellow soil.

The Hwang-Ho often broke its banks and flooded vast areas. Indeed, the torrents were sometimes so great that the whole river changed its course. Many of the earlier settlements built up over years would be destroyed and field of crops would be washed away. The whole story of China has to some extent been domi-

nated by battles against these floods, and it contains many tales of leaders who rose up to organize people to cope with them.

Before very long, draining the fertile plains had become common practice among the settlers. Deep ditches were cut running from the river banks far away into the fields. These ditches also provided valuable irrigation for crops and eventually the valley farmers prospered. The drainage system, however, needed some planning, so that the ditches were not too unevenly spaced or too shallow. It also required much labour and so teams of workers had to be organized. Thus, village and town communities – an essential element in the beginning of any civilization – were developed from groups of people who joined forces to fight the floods.

Early Chinese written historical records mention a dynasty of rulers called the Hsia Dynasty. The Hsia dynasty is said to have begun in about 2000 B.C., and some rulers are named, like Fu Hsi, Shen Nung, and Yu the Great (possibly the first ruler)

who is reported to have saved the world from a catastrophic flood. There is a Chinese saying, "We would have been fish but for Yu." Probably he was no more than a first-rate engineer who successfully stemmed one of the more violent floods of the Hwang-Ho River, but because of this he was remembered as a man with superhuman powers. There is no archaeological support for the dynasty, however, though that is not to say that some artefacts of the Hsias may not one day be discovered.

The earliest archaeologically supported dynasty of rulers of China is called the Shang Dynasty, whose first king, or emperor, reigned sometime in the 16th century B.C. (between 1600 and 1500 B.C.). His name is said to have been T'ang. He ruled from a capital at Cheng-Chou on

A Shang warrior in traditional costume

the Hwang-Ho. He was a powerful monarch, for he appears to have built a new order in China. He organized society on feudal lines (similar to those organized in north-west Europe in and after the time of Charlemagne, see pages 252–4). T'ang assumed ownership of all land in the country, and then leased it out to his followers who had to render him various services in return. These included providing armed men when he went to war. The system was extended to the neighbouring lands conquered during his reign. T'ang established the idea of hereditary succession of the Shang emperors and when he died he was followed by his son.

During the early Shang period, Chinese civilization advanced steadily. The Chinese developed a written language which was quite different from other early scripts. It was made up of characters, each of which was a picture representing a complete (idea) word. This script was unique in that it has hardly changed over thousands of years, and the Chinese people to-day can read the ancient characters without difficulty, whereas the British, for example, would find it almost impossible to read and understand the original text of the Domesday Book, unless they had a knowledge of the language in which Norman clerics wrote in the 1080s.

The Chinese also developed a form of movable type which was the forerunner of printing. Unfortunately, this Chinese invention never spread to the other great ancient civilizations – Egypt, Greece or Rome – and their literature, laws and records were only preserved in handwritten form. Therefore, much ancient literature and many legal records have been lost to us forever. Printing did not begin until the middle of the 15th century A.D. in the Western World.

Under the Shang emperors the Chinese mastered the use of bronze and other metals, and in time progressed to the use of iron. Local supplies of metal ores were limited, so the Chinese had to rely upon imported ore from further west, especially from the area south of the Caspian Sea. Egypt, Mesopotamia and India also traded in the same area and the Chinese came into contact with these other civilizations. To a limited extent, early Chinese metalwork shows some influence of them. But the Chinese developed their own particular styles, too, and to a very high standard. Some marvellous early examples of their work can be seen in England's Victoria & Albert Museum, in London. Some of the designs produced are now considered superior to anything created by contemporary civilizations.

The Chinese had already invented the wheel – independently of other civilizations in the Near East – and from that they developed carts and war-chariots which had wheels and axles. They also invented ploughs and were among the first people to use horses to pull them. Another Shang invention was the Chinese calendar, which enabled farmers to plan the time for sowing and harvesting in the fields, which had usually to be completed by July when the floods began to come down the rivers.

The Chinese were the first to discover the secret of spinning silk from silk-worm cocoons. They kept the discovery a secret for many hundreds of years. When people from other civilizations first saw their exquisite silk products they wanted to know how to make them. But the traders were never told, and so they had to be content to buy rolls of ready-made silk and take them back to their own lands. The Chinese did not develop a wool industry to the same extent as other peoples, probably because they did not look upon sheep-rearing as very economical, so they had to buy woollen goods in turn from the Near East. The trade routes established for this trans-Asian traffic were very long and hazardous, for China was a very long way away from the rest of the "known" world.

Sometime about 1400 B.C. the capital of the Shangs was moved up the Hwang-Ho valley, and established at Yin (An-yang). There have been many excavations in this district. One revealed a whole regiment of soldiers, together with charioteers and their vehicles and horses, all buried together. It is thought these men were

Map of the cradle of Chinese civilization in the Hwang-ho River Valley

The Chinese invented movable type many centuries before it came into use anywhere else

sacrificed. Curiously, in the same tomb was found a fine collection of metal and jade objects. One of the early emperors was P'an Keng, said by some to have been responsible for the move to An-yang.

Under the Shangs, towns were built in many places, and Chinese society was gradually converted from a rural to an urban basis. A stratified social structure emerged: the nobles of the upper class consisted of military officers; under them were the officials who served the emperor and the army commanders; and then followed the merchants, the craftsmen and the farmers. The Chinese, in common with other ancient civilizations, had slaves, who were usually foreign prisoners taken 'in war. They were referred to as *ch'iang*.

How did the upper class live in ancient China? They appear to have led an elegant and probably easy life, hunting, feasting and sporting, when they were not engaged in warfare. They lived in houses built of wooden pillars which had plaster partitions inside, mounted on foundations of packed earth. The roofs were gabled, and the walls were often decorated with beautiful silks of many colours, bearing very attractive landscape paintings.

The lower classes' houses were not so grand at all, and some poorer people lived in holes in the ground covered only with reed mats.

The Shangs maintained their power for centuries, largely through their skill as metal founders, horsemen and charioteers. This combination proved too strong for the barbarous tribes from the north and west which from time to time descended from the mountains to threaten the peaceful civilization in the river valleys. Shang soldiers were almost invincible. Accoutred

A nobleman's house and walled garden provide a distinct contrast to the simple shacks of the farmers and slaves working on the estate

with bronze helmets, greaves and breast-plates, armed with sharp-bladed axes or bow and bronze-tipped arrows, and pulled in chariots drawn by two or four horses, they must have presented a terrifying spectacle.

The Shangs do not seem to have been bent upon military conquest for its own sake, but they were anxious to spread their superior culture among their neighbours.

One group of peoples especially claimed the attention of the Shangs. This was the Chou who came from the western uplands of China. They moved into the central plain between the Hwang-Ho and the Yangtze Rivers and absorbed much of the Shang culture. Eventually, the Chou over-threw the Shangs in about 1030–1020 B.C. The last Shang emperor probably died, or was deposed, in 1027.

# The Eastern Mediterranean Peoples

The earliest civilizations of Mankind all developed into empires of one kind or another. In the Near East, the rise of Egypt and the later development of Hittite power meant that these two empires shared control of the Levantine coastal area of the Mediterranean (roughly, Syria, Israel, and the Lebanon today). Over the course of several hundred years the amount of influence the Egyptians and the Hittites wielded varied according to the success of their armies. In about 1200 B.C. the Hittite empire was destroyed by the Indo-European invasions, and Egypt, thought not similarly crushed, lapsed into the status of a minor power.

The Levantine coastal area was part of the Fertile Crescent and so was attractive to Semitic peoples migrating from Arabia, to barbarian tribes from the north-east looking for arable land, and also to traders from Egypt, and from Mesopotamia. Syria, the northern part of the Levant, was well placed for trading with the great empires of the time. Even by the time Egypt and the Hittites began to vie with one another for dominance of the Levant, cities of considerable size and splendour had sprung up and were prospering in Syria. Ugarit became prosperous and Damascus, located inland, became a Syrian cross-roads for traders throughout

Carthage

the eastern Mediterranean region. Sidon, Byblos and Tyre became important seaports and trading centres in Phoenicia, the narrow strip of land on the northern coast. Jericho and Jerusalem and Gaza flourished, too, further south in Palestine.

The peoples of all these cities were influenced by the civilizations of the large empires of the time. Ugarit, for example, which was destroyed by the invasions in 1200 B.C., has been excavated and many relics of Egyptian, Sumerian, Hittite, and Babylonian origin have been found. Ugarit was a cosmopolitan and coastal city at the northern-most tip of Phoenicia, bordering on Assyrian territory. It exported a variety of wooden utensils and ornaments, cosmetics, and textiles that were coloured with the famous purple Tyrian dye extracted from a shellfish which was plentiful off the coast. It also had a large measure of self-government under the alternating dominion of

Egypt and the Hittites, and like some of the other Levantine cities it had its own dynasty of kings.

Ugarit and its neighbouring cities were constantly under the power of the great empires. They had more self-government than would normally be tolerated by Imperial masters, but they were prevented from forming any kind of confederation which would constitute a danger to their overlords. Phoenician and Syrian art and culture did not develop distinct and individual characteristics. Architecture, jewellery and pottery from the Levantine cities were good copies of other peoples' arts and crafts, rather than fine original works.

When the Indo-European invaders came, it was not only the peoples of the Levantine cities that suffered conquest. Both the Hittites and the Mycenaeans were crushed and the Near East became a jumble of warring tribes.

Who were these invaders? They were half-civilized Indo-European tribes from the north. Some of them drifted as far west as Italy and western Europe. Others pushed down towards the Persian Gulf and some even went as far as the borders

Eastern Mediterranean civilizations about 1200 B.C.

of the Shang empire in China. Many of the invaders did not settle, for they had only come to plunder.

Despite the destruction of Ugarit and other cities, the years which followed the invasions were ones of opportunity for the peoples of the Levantine coast. Surviving towns, no longer the subject of rivalry between bigger powers, had a chance to develop individually. The main developments occurred in three areas of the Levant: Palestine, Phoenicia, and Syria.

The Hebrews, descended from Abraham's people, who for a while lived in Ur during early Sumerian times, established a state in Palestine, and built the city of Jerusalem.

Phoenicia was a strip of land about two hundred miles long and twenty miles wide lying between the Lebanon mountains and the Mediterranean Sea, stretching from just north of Mount Carmel up

Solomon, king of the Hebrews

A Phoenician princess, assisted by her maid, dresses herself in elaborate jewellery. She wears purple material which the Phoenicians specialised in dyeing

alongside the River Orontes. All along the coast maritime towns grew up, which were governed by local ruling dynasties. These towns had well laid out streets of houses which were generally three- or four-storeyed.

The principal towns were Byblos (where the papyrus was made on which the Old Testament chapters were first written), Avadus, Sidon and Tyre. Tyre was perhaps the greatest city of Phoenicia.

One ruler of Tyre, Hiram (c. 970–c. 940 B.C.), was very friendly with the Hebrew king, Solomon, the son of David, and the two rulers had a joint merchant fleet. Hiram developed the harbours of Tyre, for the Phoenicians were great sailors and needed good ports for their growing fleets of merchant and fighting ships.

At Tyre, the Phoenicians built most of their ships. They had to import much of the materials – fir-trees for deck planks,

Tyre, one of the busiest harbours on the Phoenician coast, was built originally on an island, a convenient site for shipping and one which was easily defended against attack

cedar for the masts, and oak for the oars. The sails were made from linen bought from Egypt. In return they sold precious stones, embroidered cloths, spices, wine, and also the valuable commodity, iron. The Minoans had handled most of the cartage of goods between the seaports of the various empires in the Near East, but the Phoenicians took over this important and lucrative role, and by about 800 B.C. they had expanded their interests to include new ports and colonies along the Mediterranean seaboard as far north as Africa and Spain. They also traded with Cyprus, and Sardinia and at these establishments they erected new harbours and warehouses, some of which have been excavated and found to contain a variety of riches. Before long the Phoenicians dominated the entire Mediterranean basin.

The Phoenicians were skilled craftsmen. Their utensils, ornaments and weapons were made in great quantity and became popular throughout the Near

Expansion of Phoenician colonies between 700–400 B.C.

East. They were exceptionally gifted in the use of ivory, bronze and wood. They made a lot of money from their rich purple dye.

The Phoenicians were a cosmopolitan Semitic people and they spoke many languages. One of the most widespread was a Semitic tongue which had about thirty signs representing consonants and a few vowels which made up a complete alphabet. The Phoenician traders spread their alphabet to the Persians and later to the Greeks from whom we derive our present alphabet. All Western alphabets are based upon variants of the original

The camel is able to carry a load of 500 lb. 25 miles a day for three days without drinking. It quickly proved to be an invaluable means of transport

A slab inscribed in Phoenician script. Although in no sense a literary people, the Phoenicians developed an alphabet which formed the basis of Greek, and of all European, writing

Phoenician alphabet which they had adapted probably from Egyptian hiero-glyphics.

One colony set up by the Phoenicians in North Africa was destined to play an important part in the history of the world. This was Carthage, which was situated near the site of modern Bizerta. The struggle between Carthage and Rome for domination of the western Mediterranean area greatly influenced the course of the Roman empire.

During these times of Phoenician development the land of Syria was no less busy. There, in many small city-states – some originally had been founded by the powerful Hittites – new ideas of industry, transport and iron-foundry were being explored.

The use of iron, first brought to the Near East by the Hittites, became widespread. Iron ore was obtainable in many parts of Asia and Europe and this meant that more tools of iron could be made and sold. It also meant that the stronger iron weapons superseded bronze ones, and the side in battle that wielded more iron swords or spears, axes or daggers, had a better chance of winning than the side still clinging to bronze weapons.

The Syrians became the chief traders of early times. Their bazaars were famous throughout the then civilized world. Goods from India, from Egypt, from Mesopotamia, and from far-flung foreign ports could be purchased in the Syrian cities.

By about 800 B.C. Assyria was starting to grow into the mightiest empire the world had yet seen. Within a century or so the whole Levantine coast came under the influence of Assyria and the cities lost much of their independence. The Phoenicians and Syrians, however, were still the most skilled merchants and sailors in the Near East, and the Assyrians and the Egyptians used the services of the Levantine towns and their peoples on many occasions. As late as about 600 B.C. Necho, an Egyptian pharaoh, commissioned a sea voyage beyond the Straits of Gibraltar for the first time, and the Greek historian Herodotus wrote that the Phoenician ships and crews took two years and sailed round Africa.

The people of the Levantine towns continued to contribute much to the development of civilization in the Near East by spreading their culture far and wide—to Greece and later on to Rome. These trading and sea-faring people were in many ways a link in the story of world history for they formed a bridge between Eastern and Western civilizations and between ancient and mediaeval times.

In building Jerusalem between the desert and the sea, and off the main trade routes, it meant that her influence would always be military, political and religious rather than commercial

# The Hebrews

In the lower part of the Levant another civilization was taking root, one which was quite different from all the others. This was the Hebrew civilization and it was important not only for its early and unique characteristics, but also because it eventually gave birth to Christianity.

A great deal of what we know about the early Hebrews comes from their own writings in the Old Testament of the Bible, and excavations over the past century or so have amply substantiated the background of many stories in the Bible.

The Hebrew people were descended from wandering tribes of Semites in the Near East. They were not at first one people, although their languages were very similar, and they did not all arrive in what was to become their land at the same time. The first tribe had been living in Mesopotamia at the end of the third millennium B.C. In about 1900 B.C. they seem to have tired of life under the Sumerians

Moses presents the Ten Commandments to the Hebrews

and Babylonians and, led by Abraham, an experienced farmer, they emigrated westwards in search of new land where they might set up their own political organization.

After much wandering they settled near Hebron in lower Canaan. Before long other Semitic tribes joined them, or set up separate communities nearby. There these Semites, later called the Hebrews, continued their life of sheep farming and, when the climate was favourable, crop growing.

There is not much rain in Palestine and so the crops were generally poor. The sheep, too, suffered, and from time to time the descendants of Abraham and his tribesmen endured terrible famines. Some of the more enterprising Hebrews left the country and sought a new and more secure living in the fertile Nile Delta where, more often than not, the pharaohs accepted them and made use of their abilities and special skills.

In about 1750 B.C. Egypt was invaded by the Hyksos (*See* page 31). These Semitic warriors were kinsmen of the Hebrews, and when they overran the Nile Delta they were welcomed by the Hebrews who, under the Hyksos, enjoyed some prosperity. One person who was rich was Joseph, one of Jacob's children.

But when Pharaoh Ahmose I (*c.* 1570– *c.* 1550 B.C.) finally expelled the Hyksos from Egypt, the Hebrews had to pay the price of their kinship. They were enslaved and had to spend their lives working on the enormous monuments and tombs that the pharaohs had erected for themselves. This bondage lasted some three hundred or more years. Meanwhile, the Hebrews who remained in Canaan continued to endure hardship and famine,

Abraham led the Hebrews westwards from Sumeria to Canaan in about 1900 B.C.

Moses, the leader of the Hebrews, was given permission by the pharaoh to lead his people out of bondage in Egypt. After forty years of wandering in the desert, they reached Canaan. The event is known as the Exodus

not only because of the climate but also because of the incessant warfare between the tribes.

One thing kept the Hebrews going – their unique faith. They were the only people in the world at the time who believed in one God.

In about 1250 B.C. there arose among the Hebrews in Egypt a new religious leader, Moses. This great man, of high intelligence and strong moral principles, determined to win a better life for his people. He organized a resistance campaign against their Egyptian masters and so undermined the stability of the Egyptian state that the pharaoh, Rameses II, allowed Moses to lead his people out of the country altogether. This movement back towards Canaan is called the Exodus and it was an event of vital significance in Hebrew history, for it gave them the feeling of national unity for the first time.

Moses turned to the formulation of laws and the establishment of religious principles. The Biblical story of the Laws of Moses is a simple one; the great leader presented the Ten Commandments dictated to him by God to the people in the Sinai desert. But there is more to the story than that. Over the centuries the Hebrews had developed – and after Moses they continued to develop – a whole moral and practical code of living which they called the Torah. The basis of this is found in the first five books of the Old Testament (that is, Genesis, Exodus, Leviticus, Numbers and Deuteronomy). The Torah has similarities with the Code of Hammurabi, from which some of it is derived. What Moses did was to organize the compilation of these laws and principles as he found them and provide a background for his successors to improve upon.

As a result, for the next few centuries

at all events, few Hebrew leaders of war or government were not also religious leaders. Many of them were prophets, as well, whose careers and sayings are preserved in the books of the Old Testament.

Moses, meanwhile, died before the Hebrews actually reached Canaan. When they did get there they split up into tribal communities, each retaining a sort of independence under the accepted laws. But it was not long before the Hebrew

settlers ran into trouble with the other peoples who had already been living in Canaan for a long time. Among these were the warlike cousins of the Phoenicians, the Philistines, who occupied a series of small towns along the coast below Mount Carmel. These warriors had iron weapons and tools, and they were continually raiding in the interior of Canaan. Gradually, with the plunder they acquired, they built up a chain of strong and beautiful cities, joined loosely by a sort of federation. Some of these cities, Joppa and Gaza, for example, are mentioned in the Old Testament.

The Philistines regarded the Hebrews

(Top) Solomon built a huge temple to the Hebrew God in Jerusalem. It was destroyed by Nebuchadrezzar in 586 B.C., rebuilt with the help of the Persians about sixty years later, and destroyed again by the Roman emperor Vespasian's son, Titus, in 70 A.D. (Left) Moses erected a tabernacle, or portable sanctuary, in the wilderness as a place of worship for the Hebrew tribes

77

as a dangerous threat to their security and the two peoples often went to war. More often than not the Philistines were victorious. Indeed, not until the time of Samson did the Hebrews score their first major success against the Philistines.

After Samson's death the Hebrews set up their first royal dynasty by electing an able statesman Saul, as king, in about 1030 B.C., giving him full military authority. Saul was not a good general, however, but he did set in motion the beginnings of a workable political organization which was continued by his son-in-law, David.

David was elected king of the Hebrews in about 1010 B.C. He was an excellent example of the type of Hebrew leader mentioned earlier, a soldier, statesman, prophet and law-giver. He is best remembered from the Bible for his exploit in slaying the Philistine giant, Goliath, with a stone hurled from a sling, an allegory for what must have been the real achievement of a defeat of the Philistines by a Hebrew army of much smaller size.

David reigned for nearly forty years. In that time he enlarged Hebrew territory, and took the small town of Jerusalem and made it into the capital city of his kingdom. He scored a number of successes against neighbouring states, and made alliances with others. He also organized a central government which devolved some powers to regional governors in the provinces.

David died in about 970 B.C., and was succeeded by his son Solomon, who has earned the reputation not only for being extremely rich but also for being very wise.

Solomon ruled for as long as his father and he was in most ways as able and as successful, although he did not have David's military skill. He devoted considerable efforts, however, to building up alliances with neighbours, not least with the Phoenicians whose artists and craftsmen he encouraged to come and work in Jerusalem and elsewhere. This particular alliance led to a greatly increased volume of trade between the two peoples, and the resulting riches were reflected in Solomon's vast building programme. One project was a huge temple to the Hebrew God. This took fourteen years to construct and it was decorated with all manner of ornaments, many of them the work of Phoenician craftsmen.

Solomon organized the Hebrew civil service and he introduced a system of taxation on a clear-cut regional basis; that is, richer regions were assessed more highly than the less prosperous ones.

Despite the Hebrews' feeling of national identity, their political unity collapsed almost as soon as Solomon died in 930 B.C. The kingdom was divided into two unequal and independent states, Israel, the larger, in the north, with its capital in Samaria, and Judah, the smaller, in the south, retaining Jerusalem. The split had been to some extent engineered by the Egyptians who had long feared the growing strength of David and Solomon.

Israel lay next to Phoenicia, and its leaders continued where possible to cooperate with their more powerful neighbour. In the ninth century B.C. a Hebrew noble, Omri, seized power and ruled. He married his soldier son Ahab to a Phoenician princess, Jezebel, and this was to prove a useful alliance.

In about 853 B.C. Ahab demonstrated splendid military gifts when he led a combined army of Phoenicians, Israelites and other Levantine peoples against the all-powerful Assyrians and defeated them in a great battle at Qarqar. But the success was short-lived and soon the Assyrians were again in the ascendant.

The kingdom of Israel began to decline

as the old habit of tribal quarrelling continued. In 721 B.C., Sargon II, king of Assyria, invaded Israel, captured Samaria, and deported the Israelite's leaders and most of the people to Mesopotamia, from which they did not return. In their place the Assyrians settled their own people, and everything was done to obliterate the traces of the Hebrews.

The smaller kingdom of Judah, meanwhile, did not suffer the severe Assyrian domination. But in 586 B.C. the Babylonian-king, Nebuchadrezzar II, invaded the country and captured Jerusalem. He destroyed much of Solomon's great temple and many other public buildings. The leaders and part of the population were transported to Babylon.

When Cyrus the Great of Persia (*See* page 86) conquered Babylon in 539 B.C., he granted the remaining Judeans and their families, known as the Jews, leave to return to Jerusalem. Although he incorporated Judah into the Persian empire, Cyrus gave the Jews a large measure of self-government. The governor was usually chosen from the ranks of the Jews, the faith was not interfered with, and the new priests were granted the same sort of

powers as their predecessors had once held. Allowing peoples whom they conquered to rule themselves was a characteristic of the Persian rulers.

The Jews rebuilt Solomon's temple and reconstructed the decaying city of Jerusalem. For five hundred years or so they existed in comparatively peaceful self-government, although Jerusalem was severely damaged by Antiochus of Syria in 167 B.C. Then in 70 A.D., when the Jews resisted some Roman edicts, the Emperor Vespasian's son, Titus, took Jerusalem after a struggle in which the Jews displayed a heroism which astonished the ancient world. Thereafter, the Jewish people were dispersed, and left to make a living as best they could in different countries throughout the world.

Not until after the Second World War did they have a national home again, when the modern state of Israel was founded in 1948. But in those eighteen and a half centuries the Jews, no matter where they were in the world, maintained their religion and their unique way of life, and they have demonstrated their exceptional talents in every nation on earth. Their influence on Christianity is traced in Chapter Twenty-Six.

The Hebrew king, Ahab, helped defeat the Assyrian army at the battle of Qarqar in about 853 B.C

# The Assyrian Empire

Assyria was one of the few kingdoms in the Near East to survive the Indo-European invasions of 1200 B.C., but its strength was greatly reduced and its territory confined to northern Mesopotamia. Assyria had absorbed old Babylon earlier and throughout the second millennium B.C., it developed slowly but surely, until at the time of the invasions it was beginning to expand by attacking surrounding wealthy cities and deporting the population for slave labour. One Assyrian king, Tukulti-Ninurta, made a few conquests,

and a successor, Tiglath-Pileser I (*c.* 1115–1075 B.C.), conquered Hittite lands and advanced as far as the Mediterranean Sea in Asia Minor.

About the beginning of the tenth century B.C., Assyria began on its path towards becoming the greatest empire in the world up to that time. Its people, a sturdy and warlike collection of tribes, who were excellent farmers and traders and who thoroughly exploited the richness of the Fertile Crescent, had been toughened by fighting off a series of

The Hanging Gardens of Babylon, one of the Seven Wonders of the ancient world.

invaders and had acquired a feeling of national pride. This was the first step towards empire building, and within three hundred years the Assyrians dominated almost the whole of the Near East, including Egypt, Syria, Palestine, Asia Minor, Mesopotamia and Arabia.

The Assyrians were blessed with a number of extremely able and diligent rulers, though naturally they did not always follow in succession. Adadnirari II (*c*. 910–*c*. 890) created the first civil service and encouraged the development of local government. His grandson Ashurnasirpal II (*c*. 885–*c*. 860) constructed a

beautiful city at Calah and made it the capital of the empire. He reorganized the army and led it successfully into battle against many of his neighbours. Prisoners captured in his victories were transported back to Assyria and put to work building a great palace.

When Ashurnasirpal died his place was taken by Shalmaneser III (*c*. 860–*c*. 825 B.C.). In a few years a combined army of Phoenicians, Hebrews and Syrians, led by the Israelite general Ahab, fought the Assyrians under Shalmaneser at Qarqar, in 853 B.C.

In about 750 B.C. there came to the throne a very powerful king, Tiglath-Pileser III (who is mentioned in the Old Testament). He actually seized the throne from his predecessor and at once made it known that he was going to rebuild the power of Assyria. He trained and equipped a new army which defeated all enemies which came against it. He crushed a rebellion in Babylon and invaded Syria, capturing its capital, Damascus.

This new Assyrian army was more successful because it was disciplined, organized and better equipped. Its troops were picked from Assyrian nobles and yeomen farmers. Then, when large numbers were needed, the king hired mercenaries who were well paid for their services. Above all, the army had iron weapons and swift

Map of the Assyrian empire

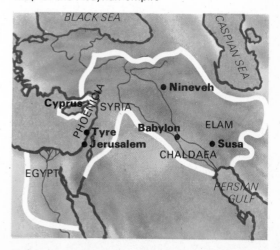

chariots. The chariots were used in squadrons as shock forces, and the drivers were armed with bows and arrows. Behind them marched the solid ranks of the infantry, helmeted, and armed with sharp spears and tough shields.

This army was all but invincible, and it is believed that Tiglath-Pileser never lost a battle. It was the same kind of well-equipped, highly disciplined and fearless army that Sargon II later led against the Hebrews of Israel when that state was destroyed and its leaders and people were deported.

Sargon's successor was Sennacherib, who ruled from *c.* 705 to *c.* 680. He conquered and burned Babylon because the inhabitants had rebelled against the law. Then he made Nineveh the new capital of the Assyrian empire. The rebuilding of Nineveh was a remarkable feat of engineering for the time. Nineveh's streets were relaid, large open parks were built and the city was enclosed by a double wall and a string of moats, over eight miles long. To supply it with water an aqueduct some three hundred yards long was built across a river valley thirty miles away. More than half a million tons of stone went into the building of the aqueduct, which channelled water into a canal that went right to the heart of the city.

Sennacherib was succeeded by his son, Esarhaddon, who rebuilt part of Babylon, possibly in the hope that the Babylonian people might refrain from constant rebellion against Assyrian rule. He also conquered much of Egypt and Cyprus. Under his rule, the mighty Assyrian empire stretched from the Mediterranean Sea to the Persian Gulf and from Ararat to Thebes.

Esarhaddon's son was Ashurbanipal (*c.* 670–*c.* 625) who was a great leader and renowned as 'the King of the World'. Hearing reports that Egypt was in revolt,

A stone relief of King Ashurnasirpal on a lion hunt, c.860 B.C. Hunting episodes such as this have a double significance, as the king personified the good vanquishing the evil powers

he assembled an army and marched into the country along the banks of the Nile. At Thebes he crushed the rebel force and then sacked the city.

When he was not fighting to preserve the unity and strength of the empire, Ashurbanipal turned his attention to more intellectual matters. He organized educational schemes for the children of his courtiers, soldiers and servants. He assembled a huge library of thousands of clay tablets, many inscribed in foreign languages. He also reformed the civil service and extended the already large network of roads which enabled his officials to travel more quickly to and from the various cities of his empire. He encouraged trade and commerce, favoured merchants, and allowed local authorities to have considerable powers over nearly all civic matters.

The Assyrian empire reached its zenith in the time of Ashurbanipal. But succeeding kings had an unending struggle to keep the empire's subject races under control, and the chief trouble spot—Babylon, was very close at hand. The wide local government powers which the Assyrians gave to provinces they had conquered encouraged rich nobles and landowners to set up little kingdoms of their own. Power assumed by these men was not easily taken away, since the king and his officials were hampered by the very vastness of the area they had to govern.

When Ashurbanipal died, the kingdom was in disorder and many provinces broke away from Assyrian control. Babylon was not the only danger to Assyria. South of Mesopotamia lay Persia, which was growing steadily in strength and biding its time. In 612 B.C. a combined force of Persians, Medes and Chaldeans (who had first taken over Babylonia) invaded Assyria, when the country was ruled by a weak king and government. Nineveh was captured with ease. Because this beautiful city represented the hated might and majesty of Assyria it was razed to the

Gilgamesh, a famous hero and the winged deity, Enlil

The Ishtar Gate in Babylon, named in honour of the chief goddess, was faced with glazed bricks in rich colours

ground. When Nineveh fell, the Assyrian empire fell too. Within about fourteen years the greatest empire the world had seen had vanished, and its territories were divided among the conquerors.

The Chaldean tribes who had helped sack Nineveh founded a dynasty of Kings of Babylonia, conquered most of Mesopotamia and there they tried to create a new empire similar to the Assyrian empire. One Babylonian king, Nebuchadrezzar (*c.* 605–*c.* 560), rebuilt Babylon and surrounded it with a double wall ten miles long. Inside the walls he erected the famous hanging gardens, a roof garden on top of a series of huge brick arches, which was considered one of the Seven Wonders of the ancient world.

Nebuchadrezzar's palace was decorated with the finest friezes, statues, ornaments and tiles that he could find or commission, and the library was well stocked. Employment was given to a huge number of workmen, skilled and unskilled, who were required to run and maintain the powerful Eastern king's establishment.

He was also a conqueror, and in 586 B.C. he invaded Judah, captured Jerusalem, carried away thousands of Jews into captivity, and put an end to the last bastion of Jewish independence.

But Babylon's new glory was not to last. In 539 B.C., Cyrus the Great, king of Persia, invaded the country and stormed the capital. Babylon, weakened by attacks from surrounding nations who were rising to power, surrendered peacefully. Cyrus treated his defeated enemies with typical clemency, for, as a great trading city, Babylon was a source of wealth for her Persian conquerors. It was Cyrus's aim to recreate the empire that Assyria had once controlled, and in a relatively short reign he went a long way to achieving that goal. Persia was indeed the real successor of Assyria and Babylon.

# Persian Greatness

The Persians were a race of Indo-Europeans who occupied lands just north and east of the Persian Gulf, in roughly the same area as the country of Iran today. They had settled there as far back as about 1200 B.C. when the Near East was overrun by the Indo-European invaders.

When the Assyrian empire was at its height in the seventh century B.C., the Persians had attained a state of development not far behind that of their neighbours. Assyria disintegrated very quickly after the fall of Nineveh and the Near East broke into several independent states.

In about 560 B.C. there came to the throne of Persia a remarkable young man, Kyrash of Anshan (whom we know as Cyrus), who was destined to become the greatest of the Persian kings. No sooner had he succeeded to power than Cyrus determined to take over the mantle of supreme power in the Near East. To do this, he realized that Persia needed to be well organized internally and equipped with a tough army. So he set to work.

He began by courting the support of the Persian people, especially the landowners who wielded a great deal of local power. Then he arranged for the army to be trained and equipped, outfitting the men with fine new weapons of iron. By 550 B.C. he felt ready to make his first expedition and he attacked Media, a neighbouring kingdom. He overran it in a matter of weeks. The Medes and Persians joined forces under Cyrus, and he then set out on a long march right through Asia Minor, and on the western coast he conquered the kingdom of Lydia, whose king was the fabulously wealthy Croesus. The booty captured was enormous and much of it was used to improve the Persian capital, Pasargadae, and to finance important social reforms.

Cyrus then overthrew Babylon in 539 B.C., and when the city itself was captured he allowed the Palestinian exiles he found there to return home and rebuild their temple to Yahweh.

These conquests, together with the annexing of Syria and the subjection of the Greek cities of Asia Minor, made Persia the biggest empire in the world, an empire that was to last for two hundred years and that was to bring many benefits to its subject races. It was indeed a great tragedy for Persia when Cyrus was killed in 530 B.C. in a skirmish with some barbarian tribes near Afghanistan, on the empire's eastern border.

Cyrus was succeeded by his son, Cambyses, a strange, morose young man who was highly skilled as a general but given to

(Left) Darius I, who extended the Persian empire to stretch from Europe to the boundaries of India (*See* map).
Map of the Persian empire in about 500 B.C.

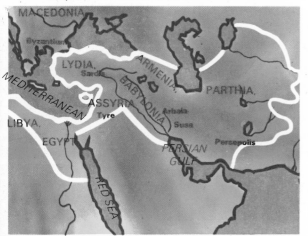

fits of depression during which he would inflict harsh injustices on people around him. He was given the full support of the people of Persia, however, who had grown to love his father, and carried on the task of expanding the empire.

In 525 B.C. Cambyses led an army into Egypt and in a short campaign conquered it, and was recognized as pharaoh. He continued the conquest into Ethiopia but was forced to return home when supplies ran short and rebellion in Iran broke out. Then, three years later, in one of his black moods, he committed suicide. This, too, was a great tragedy for he left no direct heir and civil war broke out. The very heart of the new empire was seriously weakened.

A brother-in-law of Cambyses, Prince Darius, crushed the rebels, and in 521 B.C. was made king. Darius was as great a ruler as Cyrus, and he devoted his energies to expanding the territories of Persia and to beautifying the empire's cities. By the time of his death in 486 B.C. the Persian empire stretched from northern Greece and the area of modern Turkey in Europe to the banks of the River Indus in India where, two thousand years before, the Indus civilization had arisen.

To control these vast tracts of land Darius realized that the government of the empire had to be extremely efficient. Moreover, his own authority had to inspire fear and reverence. So he surrounded himself and his court with trappings more generally accorded to gods. His beard was worn long and cut square. His clothes were unique and distinctive. His robe was purple and on his legs he wore white silk trousers. To keep the sun off his head he carried a parasol. He also arranged that whenever he appeared anywhere in public – even before his court – his feet would be supported several inches off the ground –

gods must not deign to soil their feet with the earth. Servants stood behind him with fly whisks to swat the insects that buzzed around in the intense heat of the oriental sun.

An inscription on a cliff described Darius as 'King of Kings, King of land peopled by all races, for long King of this great Earth'.

Darius and his predecessors selected their councils of state from the Persian nobles who advised the ruler in matters of peace and war. Each of the empire's twenty subject-provinces was governed by Persian-appointed governors, or *satraps,* as they were called. They were usually people of local origin. Satraps were responsible for law and order and had to organize the raising of taxes, the bulk of which were remitted to Persia. Taxes were paid not only in money but also in horses, or ships for the navy, or even troops for the army. In return, the Persian government undertook to keep rebellion down, to maintain law and order, and to encourage and organize commerce and trade.

The king and his officials kept control of the satraps and their local councils through a service of secretaries, military liaison officers and travelling inspectors, who were popularly known as the king's 'ears and eyes'. Their work was made easier by the splendid network of roads which the Persians developed from the earlier Assyrian framework. These roads radiated from the capital and went to the heart of every subject kingdom. The most important and the biggest was the King's Highway, which stretched 1,600 miles from Susa to Ephesus on the western coast of Asia Minor. Riders on horseback could cover the distance in just under a week, but trade caravans and passenger coaches could spend anything up to three months on the same trip.

In many respects the Persians were the most highly-developed civilization up to the time of Darius. They took over the ideas of the Assyrians and improved on them. They ruled their subjects with far less severity; and although they had a good many revolts with which to deal, they probably endured less consistent rebellion than previous empires. Local customs and religious beliefs were as a rule tolerated.

The Persians strove to maintain peace throughout their lands. They bent their energies to the maintenance of an improvement of trade, and long periods of peace kept the gold and silver coinage at a stable value.

The Persians tried to unite all the different traditions, arts and cultures of the empire. They left very little literature

Persepolis, where Persian kings celebrated elaborate rites to win favour from the gods

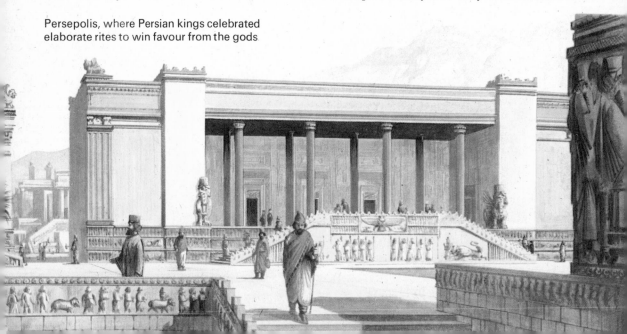

of their own but made it possible for much to come from regions under their rule. Babylon, Egypt and Phoenicia excelled in the fields of science and inventions, and scientists were accorded every encouragement by the Persians. Persian art seems to have been copied from earlier Egyptian or Mesopotamian models.

They were builders on a grand scale. Their architecture contrived to combine the best and most impressive elements of earlier ages. At Persepolis, for example, a new city was built by Darius with a vast fortress on a site over 5,000 feet high. He built a huge terrace there and began to decorate it with stairways and colonnades. The whole area of construction was more than twice the size of the Acropolis in Athens. This construction at Persepolis is magnificent evidence of how great the Persian empire was at its height.

Down to the time of Alexander the Great, Persia dominated the Near East, but there had always been the danger of the growing civilization of Greece in the Mediterranean. When Cyrus defeated Croesus in Lydia he also captured several Greek outposts in Asia Minor. His successors pushed further into Europe itself, and Darius conquered Macedonia. In 512 B.C. Darius advanced into what is now Bulgaria and Rumania and crossed the River Danube in pursuit of the savage

An Eastern merchant leads transport camels along the famous King's Highway which extended from Ephesus to Susa and took nearly three months to cover

Scythian tribes who came from the wastelands of Russia.

The Greek tribes on the eastern coast of the Aegean Sea, though unable for a long time to agree among themselves, disliked the power of Persia and separately, or in coalitions, rebelled against it with the help of Greeks from Europe. In 490 B.C., Darius decided to punish the Athenian Greeks but was severely defeated by them at the battle of Marathon. Darius died in 486 B.C. and left the task of avenging the defeat to his son, Xerxes.

The defeat at Marathon was followed by others at Salamis and Plataea during Xerxes's campaign against the Greeks, and before long the Persians gave up their ambitions to expand their empire in Europe and concentrated on stabilizing the territories already controlled in Asia. They retained dominion in the Near East for about another one hundred and fifty years, until Alexander the Great, king of Macedonia, defeated them.

Ancient Persia never rose again to such heights, but it left its legacy to the world. One of Rome's most deadly enemies for several centuries was Parthia, a nation descended from the Persians.

# The Aryans in India

A sandstone statue of Buddha

Chapter Seven dealt with the very early civilization that arose in the valley of the River Indus, centred on two cities, Mohenjo-daro and Harappa. Advanced though this civilization became, it reached a stage of stagnation and so became easy prey to the Aryan invaders in about 1500 B.C. These Aryans were tribes of semi-civilized people who spoke various dialects of the Aryan tongue, the Indo-European language that developed into Sanskrit. The Indus civilization collapsed under the might of the Aryans and what occurred during the next nine hundred or so years of Indian history is almost unknown.

Life in the northern part of India was essentially agricultural. People lived in small communities and no cities – certainly none the size of Harappa – existed. The sub-tropical climate tended to reduce human energy, and the Aryans, who came from colder areas, were content to eke out a quiet existence on the land. What traces we do have of Aryan life seem to bear no resemblance at all to the earlier Indus way of life. The art of writing, the culture and the ideas of government from the Indus peoples did not survive at all.

The south of India, which had a more tropical climate, was unaffected by the Aryan migrations, as it had been untouched by the development of the Indus civilization.

Whatever we do know of these mysterious nine hundred years we get from ancient Aryan hymns and religious rituals, folklore spells and charms, which are collected in four books known as *Vedas* (for 'Knowledge'). The most comprehensive *Veda*, called the *Rig-Veda*, or *Royal Veda*, because it was associated with the religious rituals surrounding the Aryan kings, was a compendium of more than a thousand hymns, prayers and sacrifices to Aryan gods, such as Varuna, god of the sky, and Indra, god of thunder and battle. The *Vedas* were handed down by word of mouth for many centuries, and the collection provides a vague picture of life in Aryan India in the years about 700–600

Gradually, the whole community was divided into four main classes, or *varnas*, of people – and they were the forerunners of the strict caste system that was the basis of Indian society for more than two thousand years to come.

The highest caste was the Brahman, the educated priests and the scholars. Their role was to dictate the religious life of the community, to prepare the hymns and prayers, and to arrange sacrifices to the gods. They also supplied the men to govern, whether locally or in central government.

The next caste was the Kshatriya class which included kings and warriors. They provided the troops for the kings or local chiefs. They were the most important people next to the Brahmans.

The third class were the Vaisyas, who were merchants, farmers, tenders of cattle or tillers of the soil. Since they provided the food for everyone they were vital to society, but all the same their station in life was somewhat lowly.

The humblest class were the Sudras, or labourers, whom we would equate with serfs in the feudal system of the Middle Ages. More often than not, as in other civilizations, they were slaves – soldiers captured from invading armies or pre-Aryan Indians still living in isolated communities.

Under these four main classes were the Pariahs, men without caste, the 'untouchables'. The caste system expanded until every Indian community had its own special class system. Soon there were literally thousands of castes throughout India, all with their own rules and their own conceptions of the place they occupied in society. With this developed a multiplicity of languages or dialects of languages, and many of these have survived to this day.

Some time towards the end of 600 B.C. the Aryan religions were modified and became known as the Hindu faith, one all-embracing religion combining the different beliefs, adapted to suit all the people and the different castes.

Brahmans pondered on the real meaning of life, why mankind was placed on the earth. Their thinking guided the progress of religion and provided the backbone of the law. The central theme of their thought was the search for Brahma, the name they gave to the spirit of the world, the reason for existence.

The Brahmans wrote down their thoughts and their teachings, either as *Vedas* or in the form of *Upanishads*, which were records of discussions between seekers after the truth, and comments on ritual and on laws, which were to have a great influence on people's lives.

Brahmans taught that when men died they reappeared on the earth in some different form, perhaps as animals or even as plants. This is called reincarnation, and the goal of the Indian was to be re-incarnated as something at least as good as before, if not better. But because existence was considered to be evil itself, the best future was to arrive at *nirvana,* which was a state in which the soul was free from earthly wants and desires, and was at peace.

By about 500 B.C., when Darius of Persia was making inroads into Europe and Rome had thrown off its dynasty of kings, India had reached a high standard of civilization. Iron was in general use for weapons, tools, farming implements and household utensils. Metal coinage existed. Trade routes with the Near East – and with China – had been opened up and a brisk interchange of goods was being systematically organized. A new form of writing, based on Levantine alphabets, was in use.

By this time, too, the Indians had started to build cities again. Local government was developed and this brought the curse of inter-city rivalry.

The new society in India spread throughout the sub-continent and soon the south, up to then more primitive than the north, began to enjoy the benefits of civilization. But with this growth there also developed a discontent with the extravagant orthodox rituals of Hinduism. There was a ferment of religious ideas.

The most influential of the new religious ideas stemmed from the teachings of Gautama Siddhartha, who lived from about 560 to about 485 B.C. His followers called him the Buddha, which means 'The Enlightened One', and he was the founder of the Buddhist faith.

Buddha was born in what is now Nepal,

Buddha leaves home to seek enlightenment.

the son of a king. He came from the military (Kshatriya) caste but had led a quiet life, protected by his family from the hardships of the world. He had lived for little more than pleasure. Then, when he was twenty-nine, he decided to seek an answer to the meaning of life by meditation.

For the rest of his life he devoted his time to thinking and preaching. His message, in essence, was: 'There are two paths to follow throughout life: pursue the desires of the heart and give in to earthly temptations, or live without feelings and without enjoyment of any kind. Neither way is right. There is a third way: enjoy desires in moderation, be kind to all other people, do not harm living creatures of any kind, help people less fortunate than yourself.'

Buddha's teachings were really quite practical and before long he had obtained a large following. His disciples, like those of Jesus, spread the word throughout the

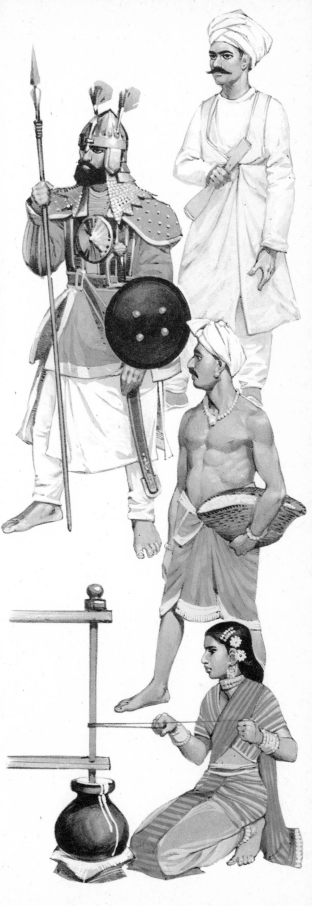

Four classes of Aryan society: Brahmin, Kshatriya, Vaisya and a Sudra woman making butter

land and went some way towards establishing Buddhism as the principal faith of the Indians. Hinduism, however, and the caste system, were traditionally too strong in India and by the beginning of the third century B.C. Buddhism declined in India although the religion spread throughout other eastern countries.

India in time came into direct contact with the Near East, first through peaceful trade, and then through war. Persian expansion threatened to be a serious danger to India, and when that had passed, it was the turn of Alexander the Great, who dreamed of a vast dominion stretching as far as the River Ganges, and who came surprisingly close to achieving it. After Alexander reached the borders of India in about 326 B.C., Indian civilization faded more or less into obscurity, dominated as it was by a superior power. It did not become really important again for about a hundred years, until the time of the Mauryan monarch, Asoka, in 273 B.C.

# China Under the Chous

China is a long way from Europe and even from the Near East. It is separated from India by the massive range of the Himalaya mountains, which include the highest peaks in the world. By sea the only way to reach the country was to sail round the difficult coast of Malaya. And to the north and west of the country are vast tracts of desert.

Cut off from other civilizations by natural barriers, Chinese civilization had a chance to mature almost unaffected by outside influences. In about 1027 B.C. the Chous displaced the Shang dynasty and promptly absorbed all that was best in Shang culture, art, government and industry.

China did, in fact, become one united civilization in the first millennium B.C. and its influence spread throughout the whole of the Far East. But the path to this state of power was not an easy or uneventful one.

The Chous, who came from the southwest, extended the Shang dominions to include the rich land along the banks of the Yangtze River. By the tenth century

B.C., they controlled a large empire, but they did not keep it for long. Defeated in battle on several occasions by envious barbarians from the west, they moved eastwards and built a new capital city, Loyang, 160 kilometres or so west of Cheng-Chou. There the Chou civilization was centred for several hundreds of years.

During these centuries the Chous were continually harassed by barbarians who attacked their borders. This did not affect the development of the Chous for, as has happened so often in Chinese history, when invaders gained a foothold in the country they were absorbed by the native population.

The Chou empire grew so large that it had to be divided into regions for governing. Before long the regions were quarrelling among each other. The principal offenders were the Ch'u in the south and the Ch'in in the western hill region. The Ch'in were eventually to dominate the whole country for a time, and it is from them that China gets its name.

This pattern of strife between regions was repeated between the classes of people

Map of the Chou empire in 800 B.C.

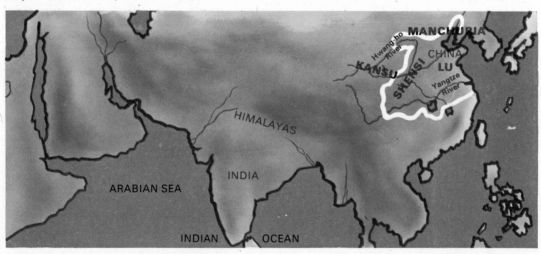

Confucius discusses a philosophical point
with a pupil

in each of the regions. The land was held by powerful lords who granted it to small farmers to work. The whole system was based upon the fact that labourers owed loyalty and their very livelihoods to the feudal lords. Landlords were greedy and ill-treated the peasants, to such an extent that the latter formed gangs to kill the worst offenders. Officials over-loaded the people with taxes and made their lives a misery with many petty regulations. People with ambition sought high office, but they paid dearly if they failed at their jobs. One official is recorded as saying, 'If you are successful at your work, you get promotion: if not, you are boiled alive.' The times were extremely hard for nearly everybody. And worst of all, the government at Chengchow was powerless to control the landlords, so great were the distances and so limited the means of communication and transport.

In spite of everything, Chinese civilization advanced enormously during this period. Irrigation of fields was properly planned and carried out on an extensive scale, so that the two main food products – millet in the northern part and rice in the warmer southern part – were produced in abundance. Trade flourished, markets opened up all over the land, and a vigorous export drive was set in motion. This gave the Chous greater contact with other civilizations; for example, Persia ordered large quantities of silk, the manufacturing process of which China kept secret for centuries.

The buffalo was tamed and trained to pull the plough, which was, of course, an enormous saving in time and labour for the peasant farmers. Metal coins were minted, and the casting of iron was introduced, becoming one of the most widespread industries.

In the field of the arts, China set an example for the rest of the world. The early Shang bronze-work, which itself was very fine indeed, was improved upon and new forms were created. Histories were written and the folklore and legends of old China were set down. The Chinese script, already more than a thousand years old, was modified to include word forms to express new ideas and developments.

These interesting advances would not have been possible but for the work of a new class of people, the scholars. They were, for the most part, the innovators, the teachers, and the record-keepers. Their influence was powerful and they were regarded as the most important people in the land (unlike, for example, the scholars in Imperial Rome who were largely slaves from conquered and occupied countries). So it is not surprising that in China scholars could be found at the head of the government or in charge of the civil service.

The scholars none the less found time to reflect upon the purpose of life. They considered the troubled times in which they lived. The main problem was the preservation of the order which they had helped to create, and they pondered on ways to regulate everyday existence so as to bring the greatest benefit to the greatest number of people.

Some scholars travelled far and wide throughout China discussing these problems with any men who wished to learn from them. Open meetings were held in

all sorts of places, and in an age when death by the sword was still the final punishment or the ultimate solution in a quarrel, the scholars appear to have had remarkable freedom of expression even though they often suggested radical changes in the structure of Chinese society.

The greatest of these scholars was Kung Fu-Tze, who lived from about 550 to about 480 B.C. He is better known as Confucius. Many legends surround the life story of this man. Early Chinese writings describe him as more than six feet tall with large flapping ears, a squashed nose and buck teeth; in fact, the ugliest

Bronze ornamental plaque depicting a tiger attacking a gazelle. It was made in about the third century B.C.

man in China. He was supposed to have
been extraordinarily clever as a child.

Confucius had been a magistrate for
much of his life and was interested in the
betterment of living conditions around
him. He believed this might be achieved
by a more reasonable attitude to life and
to its purpose. In his sixties, he gathered
round him a school of disciples who were
to spread his ideas throughout the land.
Before they could go out to teach the
people, however, he subjected them to
extensive sessions of mental discipline.
Long periods of meditation were followed
by serious discussions on everyday topics,
especially the problems of order and of

Emperor Huang-Ti ordered the destruction of the
records and written laws of China. This came to
be known as the 'Burning of the Books'. The
emperor wished to unite all China and believed
that this was one way to ensure that the people
accepted union

government which needed urgent attention.

Confucius himself put few of his ideas
to paper, except in the form of poetry.
The sayings and words of wisdom
ascribed to him have come from the writings of his disciples or were recorded long
after his death from hearsay. These sayings were published in a volume called
*The Analects* (Conversations) *of Confucius,*
which became perhaps the best-known

book in Chinese literary history. *The Analects* reveal the full character of the man—dignified and conscientious, but with a strong sense of humour. As one of his pupils wrote: 'He took nothing for granted; he was never arrogant or cocksure; and he was never stubborn.' His message was a simple one: live a good, ordered life within the bounds of the requirements of state, of family, and of reason.

Confucius's ideas and political philosophy were considered at length by succeeding generations of scholars. Mencius (*c.* 370–285 B.C.) believed that the welfare of the people should be the highest aim of the state. Hsun Tzu (*c.* 300–235 B.C.) said that man was essentially wicked and that good could only be achieved by a system of laws enforced by wise rulers.

By the third century B.C., China was in a state of continual warring, the ideas of the great philosophers were not heeded, and each region was independent of its neighbours. All this, however, was changed by one ruler.

In about 220 B.C. a powerful and intelligent emperor, Ch'in Shih Huang-Ti, came to power. Within ten years he had united the regions of China into one state. To stave off the continuing barbarian incursions which contributed to the general disorders in the regions he began the construction of the Great Wall of China (*c.* 218–204 B.C.), a fabulous piece of engineering much of which still exists. It was over fourteen hundred miles long, and had turrets at regular intervals which served as outposts for border guards.

He built roads and canals, and so ensured that communication between the states was improved. Huang-Ti was also a severe man. To force the regions to accept the idea of union he ordered the destruction of their records and their written laws and statutes in 212 B.C. This is known as the 'Burning of the Books'; into the flames of the bonfires organized by his agents went volumes of sayings of Confucius and Mencius. This was a tragedy for the Chinese people. The people came to hate Huang-Ti for his severity; he put more than four hundred scholars to death, and he also forced many of the peasants to work on the Great Wall.

The emperor, Huang-Ti, organized the building of the Great Wall of China, between 218 and 204 B.C. When completed, it was more than 1400 miles long

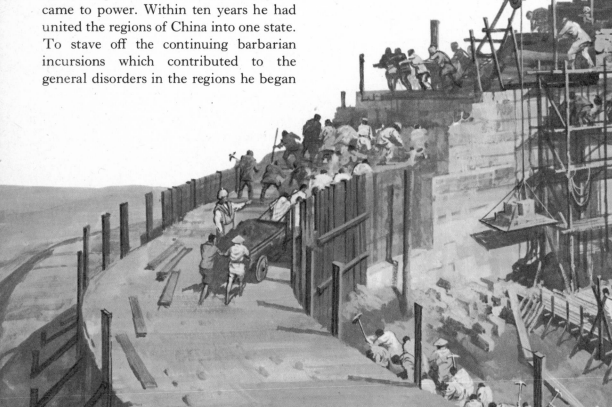

Despite this, Huang-Ti gave China a good, if severe, central government and his work introduced a new age of greatness for the country. He ushered in emperor-worship and travelled throughout the land in disguise so that people were never sure where he was and grew to feel he was all-seeing, all-knowing, and all-powerful.

Huang-Ti's successor was merely a puppet in the hands of Imperial advisers, and so four years after the first Ch'in emperor's death, the kings of the Han dynasty succeeded to power. The great contribution of Huang-Ti – a united nation with a strong central government – survived under the splendid Han emperors.

# Greece—The First European Civilization

In Chapter Five on the Minoans and Mycenaeans we saw that Mycenae was eventually overrun by hordes of semi-barbarous people from central Europe. These people, whom the Greek poet Homer called Achaeans, sacked the fine cities of Mycenae, slew the men or put them to servitude on the rich farms, and seized their wives. When they had settled in Mycenae they began a series of wars against their neighbours, especially the cities on the west coast of Asia Minor, for they were a warlike race who believed that the highest activity of man was fighting.

One of the Asian cities which the Achaeans attacked in about 1200 B.C. was Ilium (or as we know it, Troy), and the siege of the city has become, through the poetry of Homer and later of Virgil, one of the greatest stories of history. Homer's account is partly based on fact, but is largely legend. The facts were that the Achaeans attacked the city and besieged its high towering walls for several years. Finally, they succeeded in breaking down its defences and then sacked the interior.

The Achaeans continued on their path of aggression in the eastern Mediterranean for many years. Then their own territory was invaded in about 1000 B.C. by races of northern people. Chief among these were the Dorians, and these powerful warriors drove the more cultivated Achaeans into the remote corners of the Greek mainland. Many Achaeans found refuge in Attica.

The Dorians established cities at Sparta, Corinth, Megara, and Argos and they introduced new ideas of government.

The Achaeans attacked the Mycenaeans and besieged their cities, taking many by storm. The city of Mycenae fell after a long struggle when the Lion Gate was captured

Usually they made slaves of the Achaeans who remained there, but in some places the Dorians mixed more freely with the conquered people and became merged with them. The Dorians also established colonies elsewhere in the Mediterranean, in particular in Sicily and southern Italy. Later on, the Romans, in their struggle for mastery of Italy, fought desperately with these Greek colonies. (The name 'Greek' was in fact given to the Achaeans by the Italians who settled in the western Mediterranean.)

The Achaean farmers had been small-holders and many of them had barely scratched out a living on their tiny farms. They had laboriously turned the soil with wooden ploughs which broke easily on sharp stones or wore out after only a little use. They did not use bronze and they did not know how to make iron.

But the Dorian invaders brought with them considerable skill in iron-founding

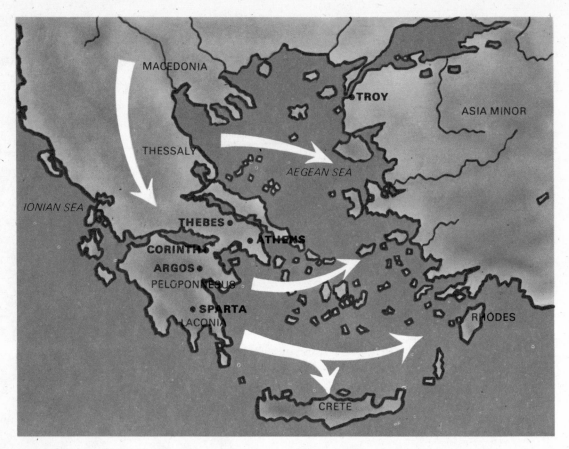

Map showing Greek city-states and paths of aggression of the Achaeans, Dorians and Ionians

and a wide range of iron tools. One was an iron plough and with this they expanded farming into a thriving industry from large and prosperous holdings.

This expansion of farming brought about a change in the Greek way of life. The Greeks began to live in cities, some of them new ones and others villages which they restored. They continued to run their farms outside, but gradually their wealth grew so that they could employ slaves to do the work, while they turned to the task of developing the cities which became centres of trade. These cities became city-states, each with their own government.

When they first came to the country the Greeks had arrived in tribes, led by kings or chiefs. Over the years kingship had disappeared and government passed into the hands of the richest farmers and traders, for these people quite naturally regarded themselves as the most important and the best fitted to rule in the cities. The poorer classes were allowed to meet to discuss the cities' affairs, but in the end they had to conform to the decisions of the ruling farmers. This form of government was called 'aristocracy', from two Greek words – *aristos*=best and *kratos*=rule. Unfortunately, in Greek history the aristocrats were not always the people most fitted to govern.

By about 800 B.C. all the Greek city-states were governed in this way and they remained so for a long time. Next in importance and social standing to the aristocrats came traders and merchants, artists and craftsmen, who had a few privileges, and beneath them were the peasants and slaves who had no rights.

As the city-states grew, the Greeks came into contact with other civilized peoples, especially the Persians and the Phoenicians. Quite often this contact resulted in war, for the Persians regarded Greek control of the mainland of south-eastern Europe as a threat to their subjects in Asia Minor, and the Phoenicians did not like the rapid expansion of Greek naval power in the Mediterranean and the Black Sea, spheres where they claimed predominance.

When the space within the walls of a Greek city became too crowded for comfortable living, and the surrounding lands were farmed to the maximum productiveness, groups of people were sent out to form colonies in other Mediterranean lands. Many of these people were not happy in the cities living under the aristocrats and they hoped to build a new life in a new place. Citizens from Megara, a Dorian city, founded Byzantium which, a thousand years later, became the capital of the eastern Roman empire. Corinthians from Corinth founded Syracuse in Sicily, and were soon followed by others so that the heel and toe of Italy eventually became dotted with Greek colonies.

Each colony the Greeks founded was modelled on the city from which its colonists had originated; it had the same sort of government, worshipped the same gods, and was generally built on the same plan. To begin with, the mother-city had to provide food and other essential supplies to the colonists, but it was not long before the colonists set up their own industries and developed their own markets, to become, in some cases, great trading centres.

The third race of Greek people was the Ionians. These people, of ancient Mycenaean origin, came to Asia Minor and mingled with the Indo-Europeans there. The Ionians founded city-states along the western coast and among the Aegean islands and they became prosperous. They developed a particularly high standard of civilization and in later years provided Greece with many of its mathematicians, philosophers and engineers, and not a few of its artists. The Ionians' city-states also founded colonies. One, Miletus, established several on the shores of the Black Sea and in the Dardanelles.

By the eighth century B.C. the Greeks had constructed an alphabet from the Phoenician script and before long a grammar emerged which, with minor local variations, became the ancestor of most western European languages.

Something else the Greek city-states had in common was their religion. Each had its own local gods, but there was also one family of gods which dwelt on Mount Olympus in which all Greeks believed. The king of the gods was Zeus, lord of thunder and lightning, and his wife was Hera, goddess of the home. The most important of Zeus's children were Athene, goddess of wisdom, Artemis, goddess of hunting, Apollo, god of youth and music, Hermes, messenger of the gods, and Aphrodite, goddess of love. Zeus also had two brothers, Poseidon, king of the sea, and Hades, god of the underworld.

Around these gods and their associates and enemies was woven the most wonderful collection of myths and legends ever conceived, and these have been the subject of plays, poems and books throughout the world ever since.

The development of the city-states brought many problems for the ordinary people. For the most part they were very poor and they had no say at all in the running of the city or in the framing of

Pheidippides runs the 25 miles to Athens to announce the Greek victory over the Persians at the battle of Marathon, and falls dead with exhaustion after gasping out the good news

A street scene in sixth century Athens

the laws. They endured this for a long time, but it was a situation that could not last forever. It was in Athens that changes first took place.

Athens was built round the base of a huge rocky mound, which the Athenians called the Acropolis. On the top of the Acropolis they constructed a temple to the goddess Athene, after whom the city was named. Around the outskirts of the city was some very rich and fertile land which the farmers put to good use as cornfields and vineyards. Nearby were groves of olive trees, the source of olive oil, a commodity the Athenians began to export in great quantities.

On the slopes of the hills not far away farmers pastured goats and sheep and nurtured extensive ranges of beehives for the production of honey, another valuable export.

With these geographical advantages it might seem that Athens had all the ingredients necessary for a peaceful and prosperous existence. But that was not so. By the seventh century B.C. there was very serious discontent in the city. Farm owners had become enormously rich, while those who worked the land had reached the depths of poverty. Many were so burdened with debt that to discharge it they sold themselves as slaves to their landlords. There was no written code of laws such as had existed in Babylon in the time of Hammurabi, a thousand years earlier, and what the aristocrats decreed was law. Worse, they changed the law whenever it suited them. These conditions often breed revolt, and eventually the people in Athens rebelled.

In about 590 B.C. one of the Athenian lords called Solon, disgusted with conditions as they were and filled with compassion for the poor, decided the time had come to put matters right. He solicited the co-operation of friends and introduced into the government a radical programme of reform.

He devised a just code of laws for all Athenians and had the laws engraved on granite pillars. These were set up in the main market place, or 'agora'. Everyone had to obey the code. Then he cancelled all mortgages, freed those who were imprisoned for debt, and redeemed with state money those who had sold themselves into slavery. He also fixed limits on the amount of land that any citizen could own.

Having relieved the distress of the poor, Solon encouraged trade to bring them better work. He also changed the whole structure of the government. No longer were the city's affairs to be run solely by rich farmers and exporters. Instead, a new governing council of four hundred members was to oversee the administration of the city's affairs. Membership was drawn from all classes, except slaves who had not been freed. Courts were established in which the juries, too, were selected from all classes. This was the first occasion in history when the jury system was used to try cases. Now it is the accepted system in many – but not all – civilized countries of the world.

The overall aim of Solon's wise and just reforms was to make Athens a good place to live in. But at his retirement some of the new schemes were dropped by the inconvenienced nobles who seized power from his colleagues. The poorer classes, however, having had a taste of better times, were not going to allow this for long. They overthrew the nobles in a rebellion and elected their own leader, Pisistratus, in about 560 B.C. and gave him the powers of tyrant. Tyrant, in Greek, meant a ruler who had complete power. It did not mean a harsh and oppressive dictator, as we understand it today.

Solon was an Athenian noble who, in about 590 B.C., introduced a code of laws which ensured a better life for the poor

Pisistratus governed Athens for the best part of twenty years and he proved an able and just leader. He continued Solon's reform schemes and introduced some of his own. He expanded trade and opened up new export markets by encouraging and financing merchants to take their wares much further afield. One new trading area was the Black Sea coast. Pisistratus also put up a number of public buildings and temples. He succeeded, too, in getting the Greek gold and silver mines working properly, partly by commissioning goldsmiths and silversmiths to decorate the buildings he erected.

Soon Athens became first among the Greek cities, and the other city-states, except for Sparta, looked to her for leadership, especially in times of trouble.

Pisistratus died in about 527 B.C. and was succeeded by two sons. As so often happens when a great leader dies, the heirs proved unworthy of their father. One was murdered, and the other, Hippias, who began to let affairs return to what they had been before Solon, was driven out. Then the people elected a new leader, Cleisthenes.

Cleisthenes was a political reformer who attempted to implement Solon's ideas and expand them. He is credited with being the first leader to introduce democratic government. Democracy (demos=people) in those days, however, was not entirely the same thing as it is today. Then, democracy meant that power was in the hands of all free citizens to elect and, if dissatisfied, to dismiss leaders; but not everyone had these rights – foreigners living in the city, or slaves, were excluded. Nowadays democracy means that a government, at regular intervals, must submit itself to the test of free election by the whole adult community, and that the judiciary, that is, the administrators of the law, must be independent of the existing government.

Cleisthenes introduced the principles by which every free Greek citizen could attend an assembly of the people and discuss the affairs of the city. A new Council of Five Hundred was set up. Its members were elected by the people. As it was so large, it was divided into groups, or committees, of fifty, each of which managed affairs for one-tenth of the year. The archons, officials appointed to execute the orders of the Council, were elected from among the people by lot, and the people also elected ten generals to form a board to manage the army and lead it into battle when required. Thus the people had a voice in everything to do with the city's welfare, and Athens became the best example of a truly democratic community for hundreds and hundreds of years.

Another city-state whose development was very different from Athens was Sparta. To begin with the city had been ruled by two kings, reigning jointly. Then power passed to elected magistrates, called ephors. The city people kept for themselves the right to elect these ephors and would not allow either the country peasants or the slaves to vote. In the seventh century the slaves, called helots, rebelled several times against the city people but without much success. Finally, the Spartan city people reorganized their state on military lines so that such risings could not occur again. This meant that democracy, such as the Athenians knew it, could not function.

Spartan boys from the city were taken from their homes at the age of seven and put into state military schools for training. This continued until they were old enough to fight. Farming trades were left to slaves. Thus the Spartan army became

The Council of 500 meets in Athens

Spartan boys were usually taken from home at the age of seven and brought up in military schools. They led severely disciplined lives without any luxury, and spent much of their time learning the arts of war. They took great pride in their well kept hair which they grew long

the best in Greece, but it did not always bring its great strength into battle on the side of other Greek states against common enemies. Instead, Sparta vied with Athens for the position of dominant city-state of Greece.

The Greeks first ran into trouble with the Persians when Darius was king of Persia. He had conquered large areas of south-eastern Europe, including Macedonia, while his predecessors, Cyrus the Great and Cambyses, had won many cities on the western coast of Asia Minor. These places were granted a large measure of self-government, which was the keystone of Persian policy towards its dependent people.

At the beginning of the fifth century B.C. some of the Ionian cities tried to throw off the Persian overlordship altogether. They asked the Greek city-states of the mainland to help. Sparta declined, but Athens lent some ships and the crews to man them.

The Persians put down the revolt with sternness. Then Darius decided that Athens should be taught a lesson for aiding the rebels. An army was prepared with a view to besieging the city.

In 490 B.C. commissioners were sent by the Athenian Council to Sparta and other city-states to ask for help against the impending Persian invasion. Again Sparta refused to help her fellow Greeks, and other states declined on the ground that they needed all their resources in case the Persians should attack them. There was one exception, the little city-state of Plataea, which volunteered a regiment of one thousand men.

Meanwhile, the Persian monarch assembled his army, some 40,000 strong, and embarked in a vast fleet to sail across the Ionian Sea to the mainland near the small town of Marathon. There, on the plains outside, Darius found the Greek army drawn up, waiting for him.

Dawn rose, and the Athenian general in command, Miltiades, gave the signal to begin battle. The Greek army, drawn up in a solid, strong body, all gripping their shields, charged across the plain right into the heart of the Persian force. For some hours the two sides fought fiercely, with neither giving ground, until gradually the Greeks began to weaken. Then, Miltiades sent two squadrons of cavalry to attack the Persian flanks. This threw the invaders into confusion and before evening they were retreating towards their ships.

Marathon was an outstanding victory for the Greeks. The Persians had outnumbered the Greeks many times, but

Five of the gods of ancient Greece: Hermes, messenger of the gods, Aphrodite, goddess of love, Poseidon, god of the sea, Zeus, king of the gods, and Artemis, goddess of hunting

they left thousands of dead on the field. The Greek losses were heavy, too, and there were hardly any reserves left for further fighting.

As soon as the Persians began to retreat, Miltiades despatched the athlete Pheidippides to Athens to announce the victory. He ran all the way, some twenty-six miles. This famous run is nowadays commemorated by the comparable distance covered by runners in what are called Marathon races, especially at the Olympic Games.

Athens had saved herself and her neighbours for a while - and with no help but that of the gallant band of Plataeans, few of whom returned to their homes. But no one in Greece really believed that this was the last they would see of the mighty Persian king. All the same, the Persians were made painfully aware that they were not invincible, and in future years they preferred to extend their dominion eastwards rather than westwards.

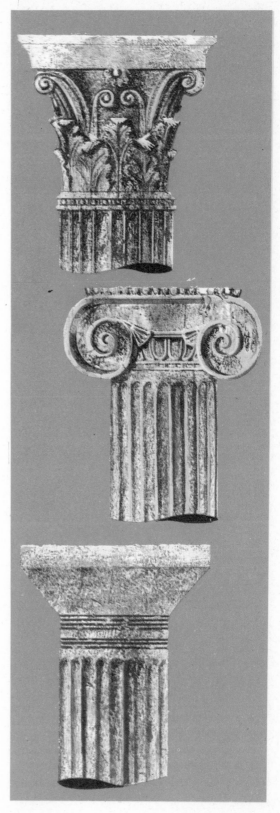

The three classic orders of Greek architecture: (bottom) Doric, (middle) Ionic, (top) Corinthian

# The Seven Kings of Rome

Of all the civilizations of world history that of the Romans is the most famous. It had the greatest influence on history, and yet there was very little about it that was original. The Romans produced few native artists or thinkers; most of them came from Greece or Asia Minor, Egypt, or some other colony. The alphabet, the language and the grammar were adapted from Greek, as was much of the architecture. Even the system of law, although more highly developed than that of any civilization up till then, was derived from Babylon, Persia and Greece.

Why then do we owe so much to Rome? Primarily, because the Romans were such practical people. They developed, in fact, an uncanny skill of seizing upon an idea,

improving it and bringing the benefits to an enormous number of people. The Romans would have been the first to admit that they lived largely on borrowed ideas. Their buildings were of course grand, and in some cases beautiful, but they were also functional. Their engineering works were constructed on an unparalleled scale for the time.

The Romans also had an amazing amount of courage, and their powers of endurance enabled them to lose battle after battle and still triumph in the end. It is doubtful whether any other civilization could have withstood the losses which the Romans suffered in the war against the great Carthaginian, Hannibal, and still have emerged the victor. On many other

Aeneas, son of the Trojan king, and founder of the Latin race, was blown ashore at the mouth of the Tiber in Italy after escaping from the Greeks

occasions the Roman empire was in danger of breaking up, but it survived again and again over the centuries.

How did these remarkable people manage to build an empire larger than anything the world had seen, starting as they did from one small town on the banks of the River Tiber in Italy?

The Romans believed that they were descended from a group of people who had accompanied Aeneas, one of the sons of Priam, king of Troy, on his escape from the burning city, when the Achaeans sacked it. Aeneas sailed across the Mediterranean and was blown ashore at the mouth of the Tiber where he founded a city called Lavinium.

What in fact happened was that when the Indo-European peoples overran most of Asia in about 1200 B.C., uprooting many civilizations and empires, some of the Indo-Europeans moved westwards and settled in Italy. As the Trojans were also Indo-Europeans of about the same period, there was some substance to the

Roman belief, though they probably did not realize it.

The iron-using Indo-Europeans who settled in Italy broke up into various tribes, Umbrians, Latins, Samnites, and Etruscans, all of whom were warlike and spent much of their time fighting. The Etruscans and the Latins occupied the land between the River Tiber and the western coast of Italy. This land was very fertile indeed, excellent for growing corn, grapes or olives. There was also fine fields for pasturage. The Samnite land, further south, was quite productive as well.

At the bottom of the Italian peninsula, and in Sicily, the Greeks and the Phoenicians had founded colonies whose principal means of living were trade and shipping, for the land there was dry and dusty and hard to work.

Roman legends date the founding of Rome as 753 B.C. The city was located on a hilly site twenty or so miles inland along the banks of the Tiber. Rome's founding father, a Latin chief called Romulus, believed the site to be a better place for a city than Lavinium, for it was away from the sea and out of reach of Greek and Phoenician raiders. The first buildings were erected on one of the hills on the site, later called the Palatine Hill where, in Imperial days, the emperors raised their huge palaces and furnished and decorated them with every conceivable luxury.

Romulus made himself king of Rome and ruled until 716 B.C., during which time he fought a number of battles with his neighbours.

He was succeeded by a young friend of his, Numa Pompilius, who came from a different tribe, the Sabines. He is believed to have introduced the first religious institutions to Rome, and these followed the pattern of Greek religion. The Romans even had many of the same gods, though they gave them different names. Zeus became Jupiter, Hera became Juno, Hermes became Mercury, and Athene, Minerva. The Roman god of the sea was Neptune and the king of the underworld was Pluto.

Numa (716–673 B.C.) was a wise and gentle ruler, and under his guidance the new city grew rapidly. Numa annexed some farmlands around the city so that the citizens could be assured of regular food supplies. He arranged the construction of temples to the gods. One temple dedicated to Janus, the two-faced god who looked both ways, to peace and to war, had its doors closed only if Rome was not at war. After Numa, in fact, the doors of the temple of Janus were very seldom closed until the time of Augustus, the first emperor (27 B.C.–14 A.D.).

Tullus Hostilius (673–641 B.C.) was the next king and he, too, was a wise ruler, although a much more warlike one. He conquered the neighbouring state of Alba Longa, destroyed its villages and brought its people into Rome. He also continued with the building of the city.

Tullus was followed by Ancus Marcius (641 616 B.C.) who spent much of his reign expanding the city. He built the first bridge across the Tiber and on the south bank he erected buildings to accommodate the Latin peoples whom he had defeated in various battles. So the city began to grow on both sides of the river. Ancus also constructed a port and harbour facilities at Ostia, at the mouth of the Tiber,

Romans believe that Romulus, the founder of Rome, and his twin brother Remus, were orphaned as babies and saved by a she-wolf

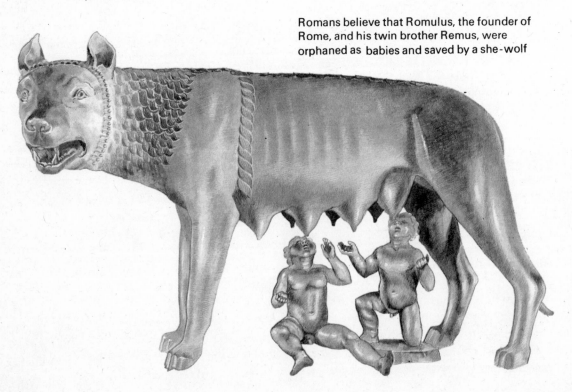

Bronze statue of an Etruscan warrior

in the talks which followed, their leader, Tarquin, said he would like to bring some of his people to live in Rome. The Roman commissioners agreed and at the same time elected Tarquin king. He ruled for thirty-eight years and in that time did much good work for the city and its people.

He constructed Rome's principal drainage system, the Cloaca Maxima, which made the city healthier. Parts of the Cloaca Maxima still exist in Rome today. He devised works to carry off the excess water in the valleys when the Tiber overflowed. This system saved the rich fields from being swamped and the crops from being ruined, and also helped to irrigate dry areas.

On the Capitoline Hill Tarquin built a temple to the king of the gods, Jupiter, which became a very sacred place. Down beyond the Palatine Hill he laid out the Circus Maximus. This was a huge ovalshaped race course for chariot racing and for individual running. Festival games were held every year in the Circus, too, for like the Spartans the Romans believed in keeping the body fit and supple.

so that Rome could be supplied easily with imported goods. Ostia was really a miniature Rome. Eventually it had its own meeting place, its own public baths and its own theatre, all on a small scale.

Rome was quite a large city by the time of Ancus's death. It sprawled over the seven hills in the northern part. These hills were very famous, and they were called the Palatine, the Capitoline, the Esquiline, the Aventine, the Caelian, the Quirinal and the Viminal. Rome was often known as the 'City of the Seven Hills'.

Like the Spartan people, the early Romans were tough, stern, disciplined, and devoted to warfare. The height of ambition for a man was to be a general in war. The Romans had to be strong and warlike because their rapid expansion excited the envy of their neighbours who continually harassed them. The worst enemies of Rome were the Etruscans, a similarly tough and ruthless people who were quite civilized and who had perfected the use of iron.

When Ancus died there was no capable leader to follow him. Then some Etruscans led a raid on Rome. They defeated a Roman force sent out from the city, but

Map of Italy showing the tribes round Rome

- Etruscan
- Roman territory
- Other Italic
- Samnite
- Apulli, Messapii
- Greek States
- Carthage

Servius Tullius, sixth king of Rome, built an extensive wall round the city, parts of which can still be seen today

When Tarquin died in 578 B.C. he was succeeded by one of his closest advisers, Servius Tullius, a peaceful man. In Servius's time Rome was acknowledged head of the Latin League, a loose association of Latin cities which tried to combine forces, like the Greek city-states, to ward off invasions from aggressive neighbouring nations.

Most of Servius's achievements were of a domestic nature. To start with he organized the construction of a large, strong wall around the whole city which embraced the seven hills. Part of this wall still stands.

Servius regularized the Roman class systems. The patrician class consisted of Romans who were freemen and who had a right to attend the assembly of high-born people who advised the king. Over the years this assembly grew into one in which the qualification for attendance was the ownership of property. These patricians became as powerful as the Greek aristocrats. On many occasions there were serious disturbances in Rome over the injustices which people suffered under the patricians. They held all the seats in the government for a long time and they did not always act for the best interests of the Roman people.

The plebeian class were freed slaves, strangers who had just come to stay in the city, or immigrants and their descendants. The third class of Roman people were the slaves who, despite their servitude, had some rights in Roman law.

Servius reorganized the army. Both patricians and plebeians could serve, provided they owned property. They had to supply their own uniform, weapons and provisions, but they were also allowed to share in any booty captured in a successful campaign. Many soldiers in fact made a lot of money over a period of years and were able to retire in comparative luxury.

When he died Tarquin had left a son too young to rule, and that is why Servius was elected king. But not long after he reached manhood, this child, also called Tarquin, began to resent the fact that he was not king. Most of all, as he was an arrogant and cruel man, he hated Servius's kindly nature and good works. Despite the fact that he had married Servius's daughter, Tarquin still harboured a grudge. He prevailed upon Servia, his wife, to help him get rid of her father and in 534 B.C. they murdered Servius.

The people of Rome were appalled at this deed, but because Tarquin had bribed the palace guards to protect him, no one dared to do anything about it.

Tarquin, to whom the Romans gave the name Superbus which means arrogant or proud, ruled very badly. He involved the city in a number of expensive wars, had people imprisoned or murdered, without trial, and generally subjected Rome to a reign of terror. He surrounded himself with a powerful bodyguard, as he grew afraid of the crowds and could not even trust his own counsellors.

Eventually, in 510 B.C., two leading Roman patricians, L. Junius Brutus and L. Collatinus, organized a revolt. They were supported by nearly the whole of the upper classes – and by the plebeians as well. Tarquin and his wife were ordered to leave the city, together with all the members of their family, and were refused the right to return under any circumstances.

To make the expulsion of Tarquin effective it was decided that Rome should have no more kings at all. Instead, the state would be run jointly by two officials called consuls. They were to be elected every year for a one-year term of office by the assembly. Their duties were to administer the government, lead the army in time of war, and generally supervise the smooth operation of the law.

The Romans always referred to the deposing of the last Etruscan king as the Expulsion of the Kings, and even five hundred years later the Tarquins, as the the Etruscan kings were known, were remembered with such hatred that the name of king could not be used by a Roman sovereign.

The first two consuls under the new system were Brutus and Collatinus, who were elected in 509 B.C. They can be said to have been the founders of the Roman republic.

The Temple of Jupiter Capitolinus

# The Decline of Persian Power

The defeat of the Persian army at Marathon in 490 B.C. showed Darius, the Persian king, that the Greeks were tougher adversaries than he had expected. So he decided to organize a new and much larger army with which to avenge the disaster. But his plans were interrupted by reports that serious rebellion had broken out in Egypt. In 485 Darius prepared to march across Syria to the Nile to put the rebellion down, but he died on the way. His throne passed to his son, Xerxes, a tough and stern man who had spent many years on active service in different parts of the Persian empire.

Xerxes led the Persian army to Egypt and there he dealt swiftly with the rebels. He then returned to Asia Minor and continued with his father's preparations for a new expedition against Greece. In 481 he marched a huge army along the King's Highway, picked up extra divisions of men at Sardis and turned northwards to go to the Hellespont. Xerxes bridged this thin strip of water by having two rows of ships tied together, over which he led hundreds of thousands of troops. After crossing the Hellespont the army was to march along the coast down to Greece, while ships of the Persian navy sailed close to the coast line so that supplies could easily be landed for the troops.

The Greeks, meanwhile, had had nearly ten years to prepare themselves for the Persian invasion, but because of disagreements between the city-states their armies were in an unprepared state when news of Xerxes's crossing of the Hellespont was announced. Fortunately, Themistocles had persuaded the Athenians to construct an entirely new fleet of about two hundred ships which assembled at Piraeus harbour. The Spartan army was the natural leader of the Greeks, as its men had been trained for years, and the other city-states agreed at last to accept Sparta as the head of the coalition of Greeks which would be required to meet the Persians in battle.

The Greeks managed to assemble an army of some twenty thousand men, so in the spring of 480 B.C., when the Persians reached the pass of Thermopylae which was the main route to central Greece, they found Leonidas, the Spartan king, waiting with a body of hand-picked men. For two days the armies fought. Then a Greek betrayed to the Persians a secret route through the pass. The Greeks had to retreat before the weight of the enemy troops, but their withdrawal was helped by the brave action of the Spartan Leonidas, who with a troop of only three hundred defended the pass to the last man.

Soon all northern and part of central Greece was in Persian hands and Athens had to be evacuated. The Persians entered the city and set fire to the buildings on the Acropolis.

Meanwhile, the Greeks retired to the Isthmus of Corinth where the Athenian fleet lay in wait in the Bay of Salamis for the Persian troops transport ships and supply vessels. Led by Themistocles the Greek fleet fell upon the Persians as soon as they reached the narrow waters and

300 Spartans defend the narrow pass of Thermopylae against the Persians

Xerxes, king of the Persians, took a huge army across the Hellespont by building a bridge of ships in an attempt to conquer the Greeks

A stone-relief sculpture of Xerxes, the last great king of the Persians. After his death the empire gradually fell into decay

Xerxes in 465 B.C. a series of ineffective and weak kings ruled in turn. As a result, subject peoples on the borders of the empire were encouraged to break away. They were helped to do so by the Greeks.

In about 400 B.C. there came to the Persian throne Artaxerxes II. He ruled for more than forty years, but the reign was marked by one disaster after another. His brother Cyrus, appointed viceroy in Asia Minor, made a bid for the throne, and offered self-government to some of his subjects if they would help him. He was defeated at Cunaxa and killed, but the damage had been done. Indeed, the whole Persian empire was in serious danger of falling to pieces.

Egypt won her independence after a swift and well-timed revolt. Several satraps in Asia Minor apportioned themselves more self-government than even the tolerant government at Susa had been accustomed to allow. Finally, Artaxerxes had to face great personal tragedy. Three of his sons met violent deaths in a short space of time. This broke the king's heart and hastened his death.

Artaxerxes was succeeded in 359 B.C. by a fourth son, Artaxerxes III, who ruled for twenty years. He succeeded in re-uniting the satrapies in Asia Minor and curbing their powers. Then he conducted a lightning campaign to restore Persian power in Egypt. He was murdered by one of his chief ministers, with the result that once again Asia Minor and Egypt revolted.

The next king of note was Darius III – no relation to King Darius who lost the Battle of Marathon. He was king when Alexander the Great invaded Persia in 334 B.C. (*See* page 133). At Arbela, in what was Assyria, the great Macedonian general defeated Darius III and drove the Persians off the field. Darius's own officers then murdered him, and Alexander took

destroyed them. Xerxes's army could not continue without supplies, so he withdrew to Thessaly. This gave the Greeks another breathing space.

In the following year the Persians attacked the Greeks at Plataea, but were severely defeated. Here, the Persians' bows and arrows proved no match for the Greek spears. This Greek victory was followed by a naval battle at Mycale near Samos in which the Greek navy also emerged the victors. The Persians were forced to retreat.

For the next thirty years Persia and Greece continued to wage warfare against one another, though not on the same large scale. Finally, in 450 B.C. they came to terms. Persia agreed not to send fleets into Greek waters, and the Greeks undertook to call off their raids on Persian outposts, harbours, and cities.

The wars with Greece had severely weakened the Persian empire. Although it was still very rich in men, materials and money, the vast extent of its territory became increasingly difficult for a king to govern. Following the assassination of the title of king of the Persians for himself. As Arbela was on the King's Highway, Alexander was able to march on to Babylon, Susa and Persepolis without difficulty.

As an independent empire, Persia soon ceased to exist since the remaining areas subject to Persian rule fell to Alexander's invincible army. After the death of Alexander at Babylon, much of the Persian empire fell to one of his principal generals, Seleucus. He was the first ruler of the Seleucid dynasty, and he tried to rule the empire in the same way as the old monarchs. His reign was troubled by wars with his former brother-generals and their successors. Eventually, he was assassinated in 280 B.C. and was succeeded by Antiochus I (c. 280–260), known as the 'saviour' because he restored law and order in the empire. He and his son, Antiochus II (260–247), established a powerful monarchy and fought hard to maintain their territories, with varying degrees of success. When the second Antiochus died, however, the empire fell apart once more. The Egyptian part of the Persian empire was ruled by Ptolemaic kings who were descended from Ptolemy, one of Alexander the Great's generals. But for several decades it was not clear who controlled the various parts of the old empire.

By 220 B.C., however, a descendant of Antiochus the Saviour had become king. He was Antiochus III, later known as Antiochus the Great. He recaptured nearly all the Seleucid provinces, including Media, Parthia, Bactria (Afghanistan), Syria and Palestine. The old Persian empire seemed to exist again. But the Persians themselves were a different people. They had been heavily influenced by Greece and Macedonia, and they appeared to have forgotten how to live together in harmony.

Antiochus died in 187 B.C., and once more Persia dissolved into anarchy and thus was left an easy prey to other empires, especially Parthia, a state that had broken away from Persia many years earlier under a tough and ruthless leader, Arsaces. His descendants, who are called the Arsacids, continued their aggressions against neighbours to the east and west. Under Mithradates I (171–138 B.C.), the Parthians overran Media and Persia and set up a new capital at Seleucia on the Tigris, only a few miles from old Babylon.

Mithradates was succeeded by his son, Mithradates II, who ruled from 123 to 87 B.C. He was to prove severely troublesome to the Romans.

Routes taken by the Persian army and navy against the Greek city-states

# Pericles and
# Alexander the Great

Although their defeat by the Greeks at Marathon, Salamis and Plataea had compelled the Persians to give up their ambitions of conquering Greece, they still remained a danger to all the Greek city-states. This meant that the states had to consider the advantages of uniting under one leader. Which should that leader be – Sparta, whose armies were the strongest, or Athens, whose naval fleet had become very powerful? A combination would seem to have been the best insurance against attack, but the Greek city-states had a long history of not being able to co-operate, even for defence purposes, a situation that continued until they destroyed each other and then fell an easy prey to Philip of Macedonia and his son, Alexander the Great.

The difficulty was solved for the time being when the Spartans decided that it was more important for them to maintain their position as head of the cities of the Peloponnesus, the peninsula which stretches into the Ionian Sea below the Greek mainland. The Spartans did not wish to be bothered by defence preparations against possible Persian attacks. So the Athenians stepped into the leadership and, despite their own troubles – Athens had been all but destroyed by Xerxes – they formed a league of states that included the Ionian cities (*See* map) which had thrown off Persian dominion.

This league was called the Delian League because the original plans were discussed on the island of Delos. The money paid by member states was sent to Delos for safekeeping. The Delian League was to have a fleet with which to guard the Aegean Sea and the Greek coasts from Persian attack, and the members of the league were to contribute either gold or ships. Athens provided the first commander-in-chief of the fleet, Cimon, son of Miltiades, the victor of Marathon.

As it turned out, most of the cities sent money, and only Athens, together with the small islands of Samos, Chios and Lesbos, supplied ships. While there was

no real shortage of ships or materials, this meant that Athens had to provide nearly all the crews. At the same time she had only one vote at the Delos meetings, the same as the other members who were only providing money. It was a situation that could not last, and eventually it was agreed that Athens should have more votes.

Cimon took the fleet into action on one or two occasions and he defeated a Persian fleet outside the mouth of the river Eurymedon. As a result every Greek city on the shores of the Aegean Sea was free from Persian power. The aim of the Delian League had been achieved.

But Cimon then displeased the Athenians when he was discovered making approaches to Sparta to invite her into the

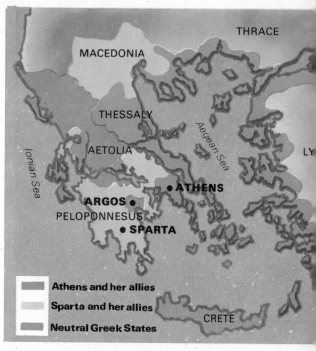

Greece at the beginning of the Peloponnesian War, 431 B.C. Red—Athens and her allies, Yellow—Sparta and her allies, Green—Neutral Greek states

Delian League. He felt, quite rightly, that the League would be more effective if all the Greek city-states belonged to it. Sparta rebuffed the approach to the further indignation of the Athenians who had not forgiven the Spartans for leaving them on their own at Marathon. Cimon was accordingly sent into exile. Eventually, the Greeks and the Persians came to terms in 450 B.C., and the Greek right to Aegean waters and the coast of Asia Minor was established. This truce was not broken for many years.

When Cimon was exiled a new leader began to make his name in Athens. He was Pericles, destined to be one of the greatest men in the history of ancient Greece. A descendant of Cleisthenes,

Pericles (right) approves the finished front of the Parthenon in Athens, the temple of the goddess Athene. The architect, Ictinus, holds a scroll of plans

Athenians climb the Acropolis in a ceremonial procession, bearing gifts and leading sacrificial animals to present to the ivory and gold statue of Athene

Pericles, was elected to the Board of Commanders, and was so popular that he was re-elected every year for the next fifteen years. Thus he became virtual head of the Athenian state.

Pericles was of noble birth, but none the less imbued with the spirit of true democracy. It is said that even those who opposed him also admired him. He was incorruptible, that is, he would take no bribes, a rare characteristic in Athenian politicians of those days. He was a fine and colourful orator, and a clear thinker. He believed that men were good at heart and that they only required gentle guidance to keep on the right path.

The leadership of Pericles brought Athens a period of calm and order in internal affairs that enabled her to rebuild her strength and become the dominating power among the Greek cities. Pericles believed that the Athenians were the people most fitted to lead the states and he also thought that external affairs should be handled for all the states by one city, Athens. This was the germ of a projected Athenian empire, a dream that Pericles turned into reality during his period in power.

By moving the headquarters and treasury of the Delian League from Delos to Athens he made it clear that Athens was head of the League. Athens began to take command of the other cities and sent fleets of ships against them if they did not obey. So the League gradually changed into an empire. One by one the cities lost their independence and the ship money they paid to Athens became a sort of tribute instead; Athens' allies became her subjects.

The Greek city-states resented Athens' rule, for the empire conflicted with the Greek idea that every city should be a free, self-governing state. But being part of the Athenian empire was beneficial to the other cities in many ways. Athens kept peace in the Aegean area. Piracy was controlled and made unprofitable. Trade was encouraged and the Athenians subsidized

certain industries which they knew would eventually become prosperous. Each state was urged to set up democratic government on the Athenian model and to run its law courts fairly and efficiently. Delegations were invited to the Panathenaic festival and games, a meeting held at Athens every so often to show that all the states were part of a united and contented empire.

Meanwhile, Pericles and his colleagues had been making Athenian democracy work better. Officials who were chosen by lot were investigated by the Council of Five Hundred to ensure that they possessed the necessary qualifications for their jobs. Every official who had anything to do with public money was carefully supervised. No financial officer could embezzle funds and expect to get away with it. Jobs were switched round at short notice so that no one could tell in advance who might be on a jury and so be open to bribes. Service on the juries was open to any citizen. The juries, the magistrates, and the members of the Council

were paid by the state – one of the characteristics of Athenian democracy. Above all, democracy in Athens was government by the man in the street. Most citizens of Athens were small farmers, craftsmen or traders, and they were chosen by lot to sit on juries or in the Council. Athenians sought to get rid of a 'governing class' of men by paying state wages so the average citizen could afford the time to participate in government. Only the ten generals – men such as Cimon and Pericles, of wealthy, noble families – achieved office by direct vote.

In the time of Pericles people actually felt they were taking part in government for any man could propose a motion in the Assembly of the people and, if he and his proposal were popular, he could expect it to be carried. This participation helped the Athenian system to work.

A year before he died Pericles delivered a speech which has come down to us through the Greek historian Thucydides, who lived at the same time. Thucydides mentions the justice meted out equally to everyone and admits that favours were given to those people in public service who deserved it, regardless of class. Citizens were stopped from breaking the law because they had a healthy regard for authority.

But despite the comparatively happy times enjoyed by the Athenians, the subject states were growing restive. Some could not afford to pay the tribute; others did not like the new idea of government. Sparta was also jealous of Athens. And when Athens went to war with Sparta in what was called the Peloponnesian War (431–421 B.C.), some of the states did not support her.

In 429 a fearful plague ravaged Athens and tens of thousands died. To the great grief of the survivors one of the victims was Pericles. He had run the state for more than thirty years (461–429 B.C.).

Before turning to the history of Greece after Pericles's death, we should look at what kind of life the average Athenian led, and the kind of art and culture he enjoyed.

After its destruction by Xerxes, Athens was rebuilt in a much more magnificent way. The city and harbour were surrounded by thick stone walls, some of

which were originated by Pericles himself. A new temple to the goddess Athene, called the Parthenon, was erected on the Acropolis – its ruins can be seen there today, massive, splendid and dominating. On one slope of the Acropolis a huge open theatre dedicated to the god Dionysus was built. This had circular rows of seats surrounding a stage and a forestage for the orchestra. Much of this theatre still remains today.

Ordinary houses in Athens were built of brick and plaster. The size of the house usually indicated the amount of money the owner had, but all houses were constructed in the same simple style. Athenians all used the same kind of furniture which, because they were Greeks and loved beautiful things, was designed with graceful lines. The richest people generally lived on large country estates a few miles outside Athens.

Athenian citizens spent a lot of time in the public buildings and streets discussing politics and business, even if they had one of the sumptuous mansions outside the city. On one day a citizen might sit on the council and on another he might be a member of a jury, which often consisted

The Acropolis, crowned by the Parthenon, is a mass of rock 260 feet above Athens

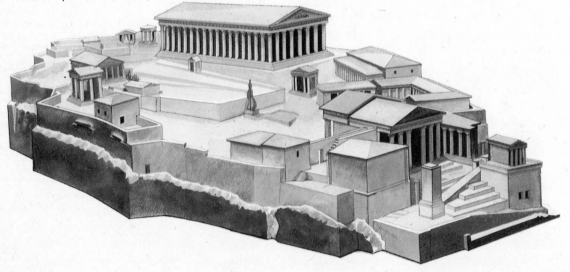

A play in progress at the open-air theatre of Epidaurus which was built 2,300 years ago and seated 14,000 people.

of as many as two hundred men. Jury service could last all day and carry on for longer. Otherwise, an Athenian might spend an afternoon with his friends at the baths or in public meeting houses arguing about the topics of the day or listening to speakers in the Agora, the open market square in Athens.

Athenians were very keen on keeping fit so they would only eat a light lunch of bread and cheese, perhaps washing that down with fine wine. Then they might go to an athletic field or a gymnasium for an hour or two, where they might throw the discus or javelin, or run several laps round a track, perhaps in competition with one of the track keepers.

The baths and gymnasia, athletic fields and public buildings were open to everyone, so there was plenty of opportunity for Athenian citizens to mix with each other freely, regardless of wealth or social status.

Their main meal would be in the evening and if a citizen were rich this might be a banquet. This was not an excuse to overeat or get drunk – rather the Greeks would enjoy the chance to discuss politics, or business or art with their friends or with strangers.

Above all, the Athenian citizens were, as Pericles said, 'lovers of beauty, yet simple in our tastes, and lovers of wisdom, yet strong of heart.' He appreciated the extraordinary grace and beauty of the sculpture and architecture in Greece in those times. Pheidias was probably the greatest of the Greek sculptors, though Praxiteles, in a later age, was hardly inferior. Pheidias had a school in the time of Pericles. He and his pupils carved the exquisite figures on the friezes which adorned the Parthenon. Some of these were taken to Britain by Lord Elgin in the nineteenth century and can be seen today in the British Museum. Pheidias also made the famous statue of Olympian Zeus.

There were many other fine artists in Athens. Myron sculpted the Discobolus

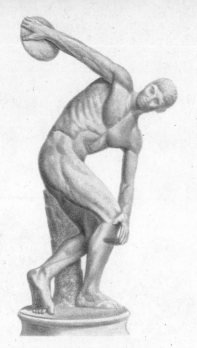

The famous statue of the Discus Thrower (the Discobolos), sculpted by the fifth century B.C. artist, Myron

and Polyclitus carved a figure of a young man so life-like that other sculptors and artists used it as a model.

Greek buildings were marvels of design and beauty. The Parthenon, for example, was a perfect piece of architecture. Each section of the temple was exactly proportional to the next section, so the whole structure was harmonious. Architecture is a science that is based on proportions in size and shape, and also in weight.

Greek artistry was taken indoors into the home. The pottery was finely carved or decorated, and statuettes and ornaments were made with the greatest skill. The artistic skills of earlier civilizations were highly developed, but in Greece art seems to have reached a state nearing perfection.

The Greeks enjoyed good plays and the theatre of Dionysus was usually packed at every performance. A number of playwrights were producing fine plays at this time; plays which are still produced today both in the original Greek and in translation. Three Athenian playwrights stand out above their contemporaries, Sophocles, Aeschylus and Euripides. The plots of their plays were mainly taken from Greek legends, and quite often there would be a moral to the story which was understood by the audience. Most of the work was serious and tragic, but the Athenians also had their comedy writers. The best known was Aristophanes who wrote his most brilliant plays after Pericles's death. One of his plays, *Lysistrata,* is about the women of Athens who, sick of war, tell their husbands that they cannot come home until they give up fighting altogether. The dialogue is extremely funny and the play is often produced today.

· The Greeks also had their own schools of thinkers just as China produced the philosopher Confucius (*See* page 96) and India Gautama Buddha (*See* page 92). One of the best known philosophers, as we call them, was Socrates. He lived in Pericles's time, and he believed that good conduct was the result of reasoning out how one should behave and not the result merely of following convention. He gathered round him a school of pupils

and discussed at length his ideas, which embraced the whole purpose of life and the theory of proper government. Pericles would often speak with Socrates and never minded if he was outspoken against the state. But when the great leader died, Socrates incurred the wrath of other people in the government. They put him on trial for being subversive, found him guilty and sentenced him to die by drinking hemlock.

Socrates's most famous pupil was Plato (*c.* 427–*c.* 347 B.C.), the author of the *Republic,* a book that described Plato's ideas on correct government, ideal human society and ordinary behaviour. Plato in turn had a brilliant pupil, Aristotle (384–322 B.C.), who became the greatest thinker of his time and the tutor of young Alexander, son of Philip of Macedonia.

Pericles's splendid period of rule, then, represented the height of Greek achievement in government, art, philosophy and science. This magnificent era ended when Pericles died. The Second Peloponnesian War, with Sparta, had begun and the fighting continued over the next century, with only short intervals of peace. Most

states stood behind Sparta, who had the strongest army, but Athens still had her great navy. To begin with, Sparta usually triumphed on land and Athens at sea. But by 421 B.C. both sides had had enough and a truce was arranged.

As early as 415 B.C. the war had begun again, and in 405 B.C. the Athenians defeated the Spartans at Arginusae. Less than a year later, however, they were crushed by Sparta at Aegospotami and their fleet was forced to surrender to the Spartan general, Lysander. This defeat marked the end of Athenian domination of Greece.

The Spartans ruled their new empire with much more severity than the Athenians had done, and before long those states which had so gladly switched sides began to regret it. Meanwhile, the Persians, never willing to give up the chance of regaining power in Greece, made alliances with some states and played them off against each other. Even Athens, Persia's oldest enemy, was in league with

Socrates is handed a fatal dose of hemlock in a cup. It was his punishment for 'corrupting youth' with his advanced ideas

them against the Spartans, and an Athenian admiral commanded the Persian fleet.

Athens no longer presented any threat to Sparta; instead it was Thebes which dared to vie with the Spartans for supremacy in Greece. The Theban general, Epaminondas, began a successful campaign against the Spartans and defeated them at Leuctra and again at Mantinea where, unfortunately for Thebes, he was killed.

While all this inter-state fighting and rivalry in Greece was going on, a kingdom further up the mainland was watching events with some interest, waiting to see when to move and in which direction, hoping to exploit the troubles. This was Macedonia, under the courageous and artful king, Philip. At the right moment he invaded Greece and defeated a combined army at Chaeronea in 338 B.C. All Greece came into his dominion.

Macedonia was, by Greek standards, a semi-barbarous state; it had borrowed some Greek ideas, but it was autocratic. Philip who was king from 359 to 336 B.C. had spent part of his youth at Thebes and had acquired a love of Greek culture. So, though he wanted to conquer the states, he did not want to destroy their culture. He passed on this love of Greek things to his son, Alexander the Great, who, once he had overcome all his enemies, tried to infuse his empire with the Greek spirit.

Soon after Chaeronea, Philip planned an invasion of Persia through Asia Minor, but before he could set out he was murdered by one of his nobles who, it is said, was in the pay of the Persian king. Philip was immediately succeeded by his son, Alexander.

Alexander was one of the most remarkable men in the history of the world. Coming to the throne of Macedonia before he was twenty-one, in thirteen

A mosaic portrait of Alexander the Great (356–323 B.C.), king of Macedon, and conqueror of most of the known world west of India by his death at 33

years he conquered a large part of the known world. When he died at the age of thirty-three he had built up the largest empire yet seen. Julius Caesar, who was himself to become the greatest man of the ancient world, was once seen weeping in a temple in Spain, when he was thirty-four. He was asked why. 'At this age,' he replied, 'Alexander was master of the world, and I, I have achieved nothing.'

Alexander had commanded one of the wings of the Macedonian army at Chaeronea, and had more than proved his courage and skill as a leader of men. He was extremely good-looking, tough, and energetic. Like Caesar he shared all the hardships which he asked his troops to endure, and so earned their love as well as their obedience. He was also ruthless, cruel if he had to be, bad-tempered, and impetuous.

He inherited a full treasury of gold from

his father, and took over a strong army which had been trained in revolutionary new battle tactics. With these two assets, he set out to dominate the world and in the thirteen years that followed he succeeded, to all intents and practical purposes.

Alexander's path of conquest was as follows (*See* map): Asia Minor, Syria, Phoenicia, and Egypt, where he founded the city of Alexandria. Then he went back to Tyre, and crossed over to Mesopotamia. At Arbela, on the King's Highway, he crushed Darius III of Persia. He took over the Persian throne and put his own officers into the highest state positions in Persia.

From Susa, Alexander marched to Persepolis and then back; then he turned northwards to Ectabana where he defeated the Parthians. He crossed the mountainous borders of western India and marched down into the Indus valley. He planned to go on to the Ganges River, and possibly then to the borders of China itself, but disturbances in Persia compelled him to return to Babylon.

To please the Persians he married one of their princesses, Roxana, thus uniting Greece, Macedonia and Persia. But both at court and in the army the Greek and Persian officers did not get on at all. The Greeks made insulting jokes about barbarians to the Persians. The Persians criticized the Greeks for being effeminate and overfond of the arts.

While at Babylon, Alexander contracted a severe infection and died there, in 323 B.C. He was nearly thirty-three years old and the master of a huge empire – which broke up almost immediately after his death.

As he had no suitable heir, Alexander's dominions were divided between three Macedonian generals. Ptolemy took Egypt and at once asserted his independence from the rest of the empire. Seleucus took the Asian territories except those west of the Indus River, which Chandragupta, the first Mauryan emperor in India had obtained by destroying Macedonian troops. Cassander occupied the European districts of Macedonia, Greece and the colonies.

The history of Greece after the death of Alexander is a sad one of divisions, rivalries, and conquest by other nations. This sorry state of affairs lasted until the Greek states passed into the dominion of the Romans.

Alexander's empire and the route he followed

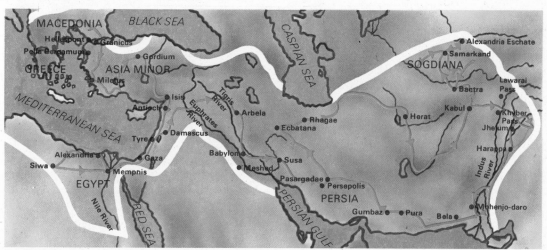

# The Roman Republic

In 509 B.C. the Romans had expelled Tarquin the Proud (Tarquinius Superbus) and all his family, and put an end to the monarchy. In its place they set up a republic which was controlled by two consuls elected for one-year terms of office. Later, other officials beneath the consuls were also elected in pairs for one year at a time. The praetors were administrative chiefs and legal officers. The quaestors were financial officers and responsible for assessing and collecting taxes. The aediles looked after the policing of the republic. All acted as magistrates in the courts to a greater or lesser degree. It was usual, though not invariable, that a man wishing to be consul should go through all other offices first.

What did the first consuls do for Rome? They shared out among the Roman poor the immense riches accumulated by the Tarquins. Their lands near the city were converted into a huge public park for military exercises, and it came to be called the Campus Martius. And it was as well that they did this, for before long Tarquin persuaded one of the Etruscan chiefs, Lars Porsena, to march on Rome and reinstate him as king.

A huge Etruscan army marched down the plains from Clusium and outside the city of Rome a fierce battle was fought. Although the Romans had been well trained and armed, they were defeated. Rather than surrender, they retired behind the walls of the city and held out against a prolonged siege. Finally, they

Four officials of the Republic: (from left to right) a praetor, a lictor (a magistrate's attendant who carried the *fasces*), an aedile, and a consul

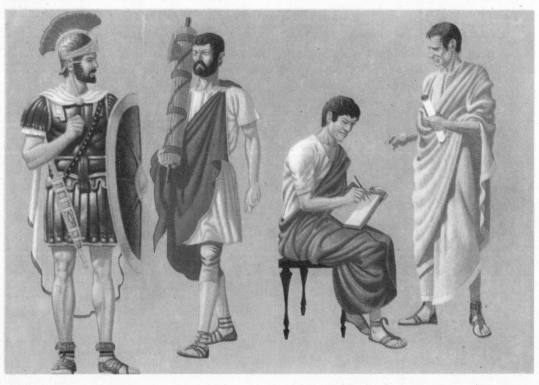

had to yield, and peace was made. The Etruscan terms were not harsh. Lands north of the Tiber River were given up, but Rome did not have to accept Tarquin as king again.

In 496 B.C., Tarquin, having been – as he thought – let down by the Etruscans, persuaded the Sabines (*See* map) to lead an army against Rome. On the way they invited other Latin peoples to join them, and some did.

Tarquin and the Sabines met the Romans in a great battle at Lake Regillus, and after a bitter struggle lasting all day, the Romans triumphed. That put an end to the revenge of the Tarquins.

Meanwhile, the state of affairs in Rome was not at all happy. The patricians, or aristocrats – like the nobles and landlords of early Greece before the wise Solon – were running the country with no thought for the poor. They had managed to ensure that the qualification for getting a seat in the Senate was the possession of a certain minimum amount of land, which was beyond the reach of many men.

So the plebeians, or common people, decided to leave the city in a great mass, and start a new life in the central plains of Italy. This secession was planned at the precise moment when Rome was threatened by another Latin tribe. The patricians were alarmed. Who would labour on the farms that made them rich? Who would put up the buildings which made them comfortable? And who would serve in the army and protect Rome from the enemy?

They begged them to return, offering all kinds of reform in government and the law. Reluctantly, the plebeians came home and helped the patricians against the invaders. Then they waited to see what reforms the patricians would introduce.

To protect the plebeians in the courts

Map of Italy in about 496 B.C.

in future, special officers called Tribunes of the People were appointed, to whom any plebeian could turn for help in matters of injustice. The tribunes were regarded as sacrosanct – that is, it was the gravest possible crime to attack or harm them during their term of office.

The next thing the plebeians obtained was a proper written legal code. In 454 B.C., experts were sent to examine the legal codes of Greece which was at that time ruled by the great Pericles. Three years later, after they had reported to the Senate, the laws of Rome were written down and published on twelve bronze tablets in the Forum, the Roman main square, similar to the Greek Agora. These Twelve Tablets of the Law, as they came to be called, were the foundation of Roman Law and, subsequently, of the legal systems of many European nations and New World countries today. All Roman schoolchildren were expected to know the laws by heart.

The third thing that the plebeians won, after many bitter riots and at least one other threatened mass exodus from the city, was the right to stand for all the city magistracies, and for the offices of praetor,

Cincinnatus is begged by Roman officials to assume the dictatorship of Rome and to lead an army against the Aequi

quaestor, aedile and even consul. That way they could get seats in the Senate since these officials automatically had a seat. Marriage between plebeians and patricians was made legal.

For more than a hundred years after the expulsion of Tarquin, Rome fought continually with her neighbours. Either they were jealous of her growing strength and of her rapidly developing civilization and the benefits it brought, or they were themselves greedy to add more lands to their own small territories. One war produced the first really famous general in Roman history – Cincinnatus.

Map of area surrounding Rome

In 458 B.C. the Aequi (*See* map) surprised a Roman army and all but trapped it within a huge circle of trenches and ramparts. But a few Roman cavalrymen slipped out in the dark and rode to Rome to warn the Senate and get help. Delegates were chosen from the Senate to call upon an elderly farmer who was an experienced general. His name was Lucius Quinctius Cincinnatus.

At first Cincinnatus could not be bothered with the delegations; there was some ploughing to be done before lunchtime. But when the delegates pleaded with him, he gave way. Taking up an old toga from the wall in his small house he gird it round him and set out for the city. There the Senate invested him with extraordinary powers. He was appointed dictator and given the power to raise an army.

The position of dictator was equal to that of king – with one important difference: the dictator held office for only a fixed period. As dictators were only appointed in times of national emergency when the city was threatened with destruction their terms of office lasted only until the danger passed. One exception was Julius Caesar who was appointed dictator for life, but this was an honour in recognition of his supreme services to the state.

Cincinnatus, then, marshalled an army and set out for the plains where the Romans were trapped. As the evening approached he ordered his men to spread out and encircle the Aequi positions. In the morning the attack was sounded and the Aequi found themselves surrounded. So they surrendered, were spared, disarmed and then sent home.

The Romans also fought for many years with the people of Veii, a city on the Tiber occupied by a tribe of Etruscans. Their struggles were long and bitter and, though from time to time there were intervals of peace, it was clear that there was not room for two powerful and growing cities on the river. One had to go.

In 396 B.C. another of Rome's earliest heroes made his name, in the war against Veii. He was Marcus Furius Camillus. The city of Veii had been under siege by

the Romans for several years, but had not surrendered. Camillus, given dictatorial powers for the campaign, thought of a new idea. Tunnels were dug by the Romans starting several hundred yards outside the walls of Veii and ending right inside the city. When the Veientines were absorbed in dealing with the Roman army attacking the walls, Romans suddenly began to appear in the city through holes in the ground and started to attack the defenders from the rear. It was not long before the city fell. To put an end to the rivalry the Romans destroyed the city and made slaves of the inhabitants. Camillus was publicly thanked by the Senate and the people, and he in turn offered to sacrifice some of the spoils of war to the gods.

In the years that followed the fall of Veii, Camillus conquered other Etruscan towns and lands. But in 390 B.C. the Senate quarrelled with the great Camillus, and he left the city and retired to his country estates.

Then down from central Europe poured thousands and thousands of Gauls, Celtic tribes who were in turn

By crawling through tunnels from outside, Roman soldiers capture the city of Veii

being pressed by savage Huns to make way for more living space. Under their leader Brennus, the Gauls surged across the Apennine mountains in search of spoils and new farmlands.

In great alarm the Romans sent messengers to Camillus asking him to return and save the city, but he would not. So the Gauls reached the city of Rome and plundered it. Those who were not slaughtered managed to escape to the Capitoline Hill, the fortified citadel of Rome, where they held out for several months.

Meanwhile, Camillus relented and agreed to help. Accepting office as dictator again, he assembled an army of Romans and Latins and marched towards the burning and desolated city. On the outskirts he found Brennus waiting for him. In a short battle, Camillus completely out-generalled his enemy and drove the Gauls across the Tiber away to the north. The Romans, however, had not seen the last of the Gauls.

Camillus entered Rome and relieved the garrison on the Capitoline Hill. Then he set out to reconstruct the city. Temples, baths, meeting houses, blocks of flats, were all lying in heaps of rubble or with only the walls still standing. It was a great opportunity to rebuild, and Camillus seized it. Many of his new buildings lasted until the dreadful fire in Rome in 64 A.D. (*See* page 185).

Camillus also organized the keeping of records and documents about the city's history; the earlier records had been destroyed by the Gauls and a fresh start had to be made. It is from these times that the true history of Rome may be said to have begun, for much of the earlier material was based on legend and memory.

Camillus had much to do in his reconstruction programme. He also had to deal with the Latin states which had broken away from the League when they heard of the sack of Rome. In 367 B.C. news reached Rome of another mass of Gauls moving down towards the Tiber. Now a very old man, Camillus was once more made dictator to save the state. He sallied into battle in the plains not far north of Rome and there defeated the Gauls. Then he went into retirement, loaded with honour and praise, having earned the gratitude of every Roman.

The threat of the Gauls was removed, but it was replaced by a series of dangerous wars with the Samnites (*See* map), a tough and aggressive group of tribes who were bent on mastering all Italy. In 343 B.C., war broke out between the Romans and the Samnites, and with a few short intervals, lasted for nearly sixty years. This was a very severe struggle for the Romans. When the Samnites were pressing in one direction, the Etruscans or discontented Latins would attack in another. Time and again the Romans beat off attacks. Sometimes they were defeated.

But they never gave up because they believed that Rome should be mistress of all Italy. When the Samnites were eventually overcome they agreed to become part of the Republic, for they had much to gain. The Romans built them a wonderful new road from the city down towards the south, called the Appian Way (after Appius Claudius, the man who planned it). They were also given a large measure of self government, but they were not to engage in war without Roman consent. They also had to administer justice in the Roman manner.

These terms were the same as those offered to many states that Rome conquered. In Italy all the people were encouraged to look upon themselves as part of Rome. Some even were accorded the special privilege of being Roman citizens, which meant that they could stay in their

The first few miles of the Appian Way, which led from Rome to the Campania, were lined with tombs

own territory but still vote at meetings of the Assembly in Rome.

Before long the Romans came into conflict with the Greek cities in the south of Italy. Rome wanted to absorb all the cities, but some did not wish to lose their city-state independence. One of them, Tarentum, not only resisted, but also sent for help to Pyrrhus, king of the state of Epirus in northern Greece. Pyrrhus, a ruler of considerable courage and ambition but not much judgment, dreamed of turning his small kingdom into an empire as big as Alexander the Great's. So he jumped at the chance to get a foothold in Italy, especially as Tarentum obligingly offered to pay his expenses. He sailed for the toe of Italy with a huge fleet of transport ships conveying not only twenty-five thousand troops but also a herd of elephants.

At Heraclea, in 280 B.C., Pyrrhus drew up his army in an advantageous position not far from the town. In the distance the formidable ranks of the Romans were marshalled. The signal was given and the two armies clashed. At first the Romans, who had not seen elephants before, seemed to ignore their potential destructive power, and fought fiercely with the Epireans. Then, Pyrrhus ordered the huge beasts to be driven against the Roman flanks. Roaring and screaming, the animals lumbered across the plain into the thick of the Romans. Almost at once the Romans panicked and began to flee from the field.

But it was no great victory for Pyrrhus. He lost more men than did the Romans, whose fighting power so impressed him that he said: 'With troops like these I could have conquered the world.' Today the word 'Pyrrhic' is used to describe any victory that is dearly bought.

Pyrrhus stayed on in Italy but was eventually defeated at Beneventum. He returned to Greece with the shattered remnants of his forces. Tarentum, meanwhile, had been compelled to become part of Rome.

The success against Pyrrhus, together with other swift and successful campaigns, served to make Rome mistress of Italy. She soon put fear into the heart of the great Phoenician colony, Carthage, which had over the years built itself into a powerful independent state in North Africa, and was virtually the mistress of the Mediterranean Sea.

Carthage had numerous colonies which stretched all along the coast of North Africa and Spain. It possessed Sicily and Sardinia. In Spain it had exclusive use of the rich silver mines near Gades (Cadiz). It was also the leading trading power in the Mediterranean; and to keep this power the Carthaginians had a huge fleet of ships, special quinquiremes (so-called because it took five men to pull each oar). It also had a large army composed mainly of mercenaries, foreigners who were paid

well to fight. These mercenaries included swift cavalry from Numidia, stone slingers from Majorca, and archers from Gaul.

For many years Roman and Carthaginian interests had hardly clashed at all, since Rome was fully occupied building up her dominion in Italy. Once this was achieved, Rome began to look elsewhere and started by interfering with Carthaginian trading fleets. This provoked reprisals and by the middle of the third century B.C. war was inescapable. In 264 the First Carthaginian or Punic War (264–241 B.C.) began, and it was confined largely to the sea. Rome soon showed that she had good shipbuilders and sailors as well as soldiers, and despite a number of reverses she emerged at the end of the war in a stronger position than the enemy. Carthage had to give up Sardinia and Sicily, and also to pay a huge sum of money in tribute.

Then, in 219, by which time Rome had pushed the Gauls out of northern Italy and extended her dominion right up to the Alps, the Carthaginians threatened Rome again. They were led by Hannibal, a brilliant young man destined to become one of the greatest generals in history.

Hannibal had been brought up by his father, also a general, to hate Rome, and he had sworn that he would devote his whole life to crushing the new and dangerous state in Italy. In 219 B.C. he put together an army in Spain and began to march northwards towards Italy. He had about one hundred thousand foot-soldiers, thirteen hundred cavalry, and forty elephants, brought all the way from Africa. He planned to bring this force across the Pyrenees, through the south of France and over the Alps down into the Italian plains.

It was a very ambitious plan, but it was

Pyrrhus defeated the Romans at Heraclea

typical of this slim, agile and energetic young man. Despite severe hardships especially in crossing the cold, snow-packed Alps – where he lost all the elephants – the plan was successful. By the end of 218 he was in Italy. Though depleted in numbers, Hannibal's army was in high spirits and full of enthusiasm about conquering the land that could boast such rich plains stretching for miles.

Meanwhile, at Rome, the Senate was concerned at the reports it received of Hannibal's progress. At first the Romans had been inclined to dismiss him as a youthful and unimportant adventurer, but when he was actually sighted in Italy itself their scorn turned to alarm. At once two armies were despatched to meet him and drive him out, and this was the start of the Second Punic War (218–202 B.C.). By skilful manoeuvres, in which he managed to separate one from the other,

Hannibal defeated each army in turn, on the Ticinus and on the Trebia, respectively. The Roman losses were enormous.

The following year Rome managed to raise fresh forces. One army was sent under Gaius Flaminius, a popular general who had been responsible for the construction of the Flaminian Way, a straight road running through the Apennine mountains from coast to coast. Hannibal watched the approach of this army as it came towards the pass leading into Lake Trasimene. His troops were positioned on the hillsides.

When the Romans came into the lake bowl, Hannibal sent detachments to seal off the entrance and exit, thus cutting off any means of retreat. At the same time he ordered the rest of his forces to charge down the hillsides. There, terrible slaughter was inflicted. Flaminius was

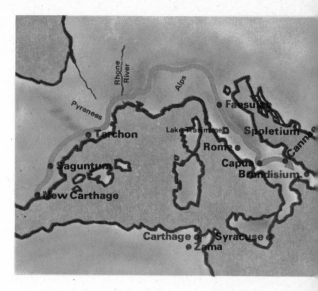

Hannibal's march to Rome across the Alps

Hannibal's army, which included elephants, endured terrible hardships crossing the Alps into Italy

slain and nearly the whole Roman army cut to pieces.

It was a black day for Rome. The remainder of her forces were under the command of Quintus Fabius Maximus, an elderly general (nicknamed 'the Delayer') whose bravery was matched by his caution. Three major armies had been destroyed in open battle. Clearly, then, Hannibal had to be defeated by other means. Fabius decided to march his troops towards Hannibal as if to engage in battle, and then at the last moment retire. These delaying tactics did not of course defeat Hannibal, but they did aggravate him and exhaust his men. Thus vital months were obtained for Rome to recruit fresh forces.

By 216, many Romans were becoming tired of Fabius's wise strategy and wanted a show-down with the Carthaginians. A group of senators, led by P. Terentius Varro, clamoured for open battle. An army was raised amounting to nearly eighty thousand infantry and six thousand cavalry. According to custom, two generals were appointed to command the army, each on alternative days: one was the brave but cautious L. Aemilius Paullus; the other was the hot-headed Varro.

Hannibal was only too willing to fight,

Map-plan of the battle of Cannae in 216 B.C. where Hannibal inflicted a disastrous defeat on the Romans

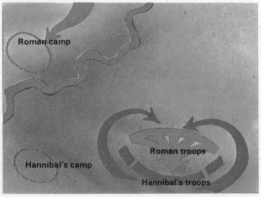

and on the plain of Cannae he waited for the Romans. Paullus believed that the position was too good for the Romans to dislodge the Carthaginians, but Varro insisted on risking all on a frontal attack – and it was his day of command. The Romans surged forwards right into the Carthaginian centre, which had been drilled to let the enemy through with little resistance. Then the Carthaginians closed in upon the Romans and cut them down in their hundreds. On the flanks the Roman cavalry were outmatched by swift Numidian horsemen and driven off the field.

Before the day was over the entire Roman force was destroyed. It is said that nearly eighty thousand lay dead. At least one member in every family of the republic perished; among the dead was Paullus. It was the worst defeat in Roman history.

Miraculously, few of the allies rose against Rome in her hour of defeat. What they had heard of the Carthaginians – who believed in human sacrifices and other barbarous practices – did not encourage them. Worse still for Hannibal, he was finding it difficult to get supplies from Carthage. His own government did not seem to want to support him, possibly through envy of his success, so he could not take advantage of his great victory and march on Rome. A sustained assault was out of the question, and the city was thus saved.

Although Hannibal could not take Rome, fresh Roman armies also failed to defeat him. One under T. Claudius Nero, utterly vanquished Hannibal's brother Hasdrubal, who was bringing reinforcements from Spain, at a great battle on the River Metaurus in 207 B.C. But Hannibal stayed in Italy until 203 B.C. Then, when he heard that the Romans were planning to attack Carthage itself in North Africa, he left to go to the city's rescue.

After a number of skirmishes with the Romans in North Africa, Hannibal was ready for a final battle. At Zama he assembled his tired troops and waited for the Romans to attack. Under P. Cornelius Scipio, a dashing, brilliant, good-looking young patrician, whose father had been in command at the Ticinus, the Romans charged once more, this time in the blazing sun of Africa. All day they fought, but by sunset the Carthaginians were on the run. Roman endurance and Roman courage – to say nothing of Roman skill at arms – had triumphed, with the help of Numidian horsemen who were on Rome's side in this battle, even against the brilliance of the greatest general of the day.

Hannibal knew when to accept defeat, and he persuaded the Carthaginian government not to argue with the peace terms which Rome might dictate. As it was the terms were very generous, considering the frightful losses the Carthaginians had inflicted on Rome over the years. Carthage was allowed to retain its own government but it had to give up its colonies. It had to pay a huge war debt spread out over the years. It was not to

Rome destroyed Carthage in 146 B.C.

make war or treaties with anyone without obtaining the permission of Rome.

This Second Carthaginian War cost Rome dear, but the ultimate success left her very powerful indeed. She now controlled most of Spain, all Sicily, and parts of France, and she dominated the western Mediterranean Sea, with its rich and important trading routes and ports. It was as well that Rome won, for her civilization was a progressive and humanitarian one, whereas Carthage was in many ways barbarous and unwilling to develop along more civilized lines. Carthage itself was finally destroyed in 146 B.C. as a result of Cato's persistence in calling for the city's destruction.

But directly after the defeat of Carthage in 202 B.C. Scipio became the hero of the day. He was given the name Africanus, and was accorded a tremendous welcome when he returned to Rome in triumph.

If we now pass over the next century of Roman history more quickly, it is because the struggle with Carthage was a decisive period of Rome's story, whereas what followed was not attended by the same degree of risks, sacrifices, losses or glory which had been the substance of the Roman struggle with Hannibal.

# Roman Expansion
# in the Mediterranean

Hardly had the war with Carthage been brought to an end than the Romans had to intervene in troubles in Greece. There, since the death of Alexander, the old greatness of Greece had steadily declined as the city-states continued to quarrel among themselves, taking different sides in the struggles between the three parts of Alexander's empire: Egypt, Seleucia and Macedon.

Rome's new position as mistress of the entire western Mediterranean naturally extended her interest much further than before, and warfare anywhere near her borders was a matter of concern. Moreover, the Roman people had begun to learn something of the ways of Greek civilization, and wished to learn more and to benefit from it. This could best be done by protecting the Greeks from aggressors and also from themselves in their ceaseless quarrels.

The Macedonian king, Philip, was trying to subject all the Greeks to his rule. He had also made a pact with Antiochus the Great of Seleucia to invade and divide that rich kingdom between them. These intentions threatened Roman interests

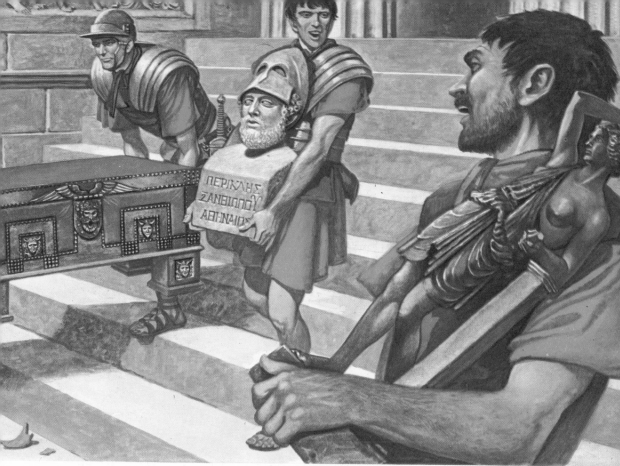

Greek treasures taken to Rome greatly influenced Roman art of all kinds

and so the Senate sent an army to Greece under T. Quinctius Flamininus who, in 198 and 197 B.C. won two shattering victories against the Macedonians at Antigonea and at Cynoscephalae.

These victories guaranteed the Greeks their freedom. When Flamininus announced to a huge assembly of Greeks at games held in Corinth that Rome would protect them but would not interfere with their liberties, the great roars of approval could be heard as far away as the sea.

In 192 B.C., however, Antiochus invaded Greece, but he was defeated by M. Acilius Glabrio, and again at Magnesia in 190 by L. Cornelius Scipio, brother of Africanus. This Scipio was given the name Asiaticus because the victory of Magnesia gave the Romans a firm foothold in Asia Minor – where they were to develop and extend their power until, in time, they possessed or protected territories up to the borders of Parthia (*See* page 153).

Peace between Greece and Asia Minor was not an easy thing to maintain, and throughout the second century B.C. Roman armies had to be sent to restore order and to fight off invaders from other Asian states.

It is one thing to win a series of wars and thus acquire an empire. It is quite another to hold that empire together and to rule it wisely. This the Romans had to learn to do and in the process they made many mistakes.

When they gave Greece its freedom they also tried to move Greek culture wholesale from the land of its origin to Italy. Famous sculptures were lifted from their pedestals and taken to adorn the private houses and gardens of the rich in

Rome. Greek teachers and scholars were enslaved and brought to the city to teach the children of the upper classes. Some of the Greek gods were worshipped by Romans who had grown bored or dissatisfied with their own. Of course in bringing Greek civilization to Rome – and then spreading their adaptations and improvements upon it throughout the empire – the Romans saved Greek culture for later generations. At the time it was a most hazardous experiment. The introduction of Greek ideas into Italy, coupled with the material wealth acquired through Rome's new position in the world, brought about a great change in the character of the Roman people. Up to the time of Hannibal they had led hard lives, and most of the people were poor as well. The Romans were not used to the luxuries that began to arrive in great quantities from the East

Roman audiences, including women, enjoyed the spectacle of gladiators fighting to the death

– new foods, richer clothes, more exciting entertainments such as wild beast shows and gladiatorial contests, new building materials, pottery, glass, furnishings, and wines. Nor had they ever conceived of living an idle life, leaving the chores entirely to slaves. But the latter became possible with the arrival of vast numbers of enslaved peoples of foreign birth, captured for the most part in wars.

Much of this new wealth could well have been put to good use at home or in the new colonies or states. But men became greedy and spent it on themselves, their families and their properties. They bought land and then bought slaves to work on it, throwing thousands of free men out of work. The riches also bought Romans important positions in the state for they used their money to bribe voters at elections. Many a praetor or quaestor – even some consuls – were elected by spending vast sums entertaining the public.

As the rich got wealthier the poor became more and more debt-ridden and distressed; those out of work had nothing to do all day, except listen to agitators making political use of their misery.

Two people of noble birth who tried to put matters right were Tiberius Sempronius Gracchus and his brother Gaius, known as the Gracchi. In 133 B.C. Tiberius had himself elected Tribune of the People promising to restore land to farmers so

Two brothers, Tiberius and Gaius Gracchus,
tried separately to put right political injustices

that free men could work again. He
brought in a law which enabled the state
to regulate the amount of land held by one
person. He also had some of the land
belonging to greedy owners divided into
allotments for the poor to work.

Ten years later Gaius was elected tribune and he introduced further reform
measures to help the poor: one was a
regular supply of corn to be made available very cheaply to anyone who applied
for it in person; another was to extend the
vote to Rome's Latin allies who served in
the Roman army but had not previously
been allowed to vote at elections.

Both Gracchi brothers died as a result
of mob violence after their terms of office.
They had done some good but most of the
social evils remained. Thousands of idlers
hung about in taverns drinking and gam-
bling, and often arguing to the point of
fighting. Gangs of terrorists were formed
among younger people to rob rich merchants or senators, sometimes in broad
daylight. The Senate seemed powerless to
prevent this and had to resort to the use of
troops to keep order.

The discontent was not limited to Rome
itself. The new provinces were often
badly governed by greedy Roman administrators. The spirit of lawlessness spread
to the seas where fleets of pirates raided
seaports, attacked trading fleets and
generally made travelling by ship a dangerous experience. In Italy – and in other
parts of the empire – more gangs were at
work making a good living out of highway
robbery.

Worse was to come. All Italy was
threatened by vast hordes of German
barbarians who descended upon the
northern territories south of the Alps.
Several Roman armies sent to deal with
them were wiped out, and one, in 105 B.C.,
under Q. Servilius Caepio, was destroyed
at Arausio (*See* map) and seventy thousand men were killed or captured. When
Caepio returned to Rome he was dis-
graced and his property was confiscated.

In 104, however, one of Rome's greatest
men was elected consul. He was Gaius
Marius, the son of a farm labourer who
had risen from the ranks of the army to
become a general, and who had defeated
a dangerous enemy, Jugurtha, a North
African king who had made trouble for
Rome. Marius promised to defeat the
German barbarians. Before setting out he

Map showing where the battles of Arausio,
Aquae Sextiae and Vercellae were fought

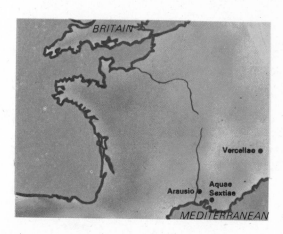

raised an army of tough soldiers and put them on a regular pay basis; this was the first professional army in the history of Rome. Previously soldiers only received rewards if they were victorious in battle. This army took three years to prepare and Marius had to get himself elected consul every year to see the programme through. He managed to do this with the support of the popular party, for he had no money with which to bribe electors. Of plebeian stock himself, he was hated by the patricians because he had insulted them for their idle way of life.

In 102 Marius marched northwards, and at Aquae Sextiae he met the German hordes in battle and utterly defeated them. A year later he routed another force of Germans at Vercellae, and thus brought the barbarian danger to an end. When he returned to Rome, where he was elected consul for the sixth time, in 100 B.C., Marius received the most splendid welcome accorded any general since Scipio Africanus. He immediately allied himself with the popular party against the Senate in an effort to redress the wrongs that still abounded in Rome. But as a politician he was a failure, and even his marvellous record as a general was not enough to enable him to stop the endless quarrelling between plebeians and patricians (street fighting and violence had now become part of the Roman scene) and between Rome and her allies who felt they should have Roman citizenship and the privileges it brought. Moreover, Marius himself was constantly quarrelling with the patrician general, L. Cornelius Sulla, who had served with him in Africa.

Marius bitterly resented it when the Senate appointed Sulla as commander-in-chief of the Roman army to be sent to the East to deal with Mithradates of Pontus, a ruler who had invaded Asia Minor and started to overrun Greece. Civil war broke out and Sulla marched on Rome with his legions. It was the first time a Roman army had ever marched against Rome. The Senate welcomed Sulla and gave him powers to restore order. A warrant was issued for the arrest of Marius but he had escaped to North Africa. Sulla then left for Greece.

In five years, 87–83 B.C., Sulla crushed Mithradates in a brilliant campaign. In the process he acquired enormous wealth. Before returning to Rome he reorganized the governments of the provinces and collected taxes which had not been paid for several years. Leaving trusted lieutenants in charge in the East, he set sail for Italy in 83 and landed at Brundisium. Marius, meanwhile, had returned to Rome in 86 and got himself elected consul for the seventh time, but he died a few days after taking office. His party, led by his son,

Gaius Marius (centre), who was elected consul seven times by the popular party, receives leading plebeians after an election to express his gratitude for support

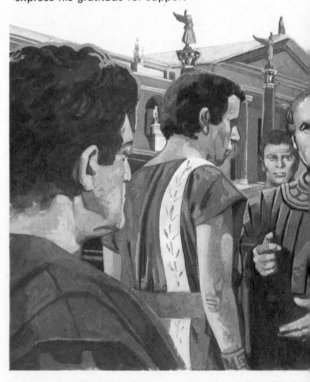

was no match for the disciplined and hardened veterans of Sulla's campaigns, and Sulla's march to Rome was an easy one. He celebrated his success by publishing a list of people who were to be put to death for having supported Marius or his son. These lists, called proscriptions, were the first of their kind in Roman history, but they were not the last. More than five thousand senators, knights (a class of business men which had grown up with Rome's conquests), merchants and commoners had their property and wealth confiscated, and subsequently died on this occasion.

Sulla then reconstructed the government in Rome. Having had himself appointed dictator, he strengthened the Senate and cut down the rights of the people. Even the powers of the sacred tribunes were curtailed. Only by these means did Sulla see any hope of maintaining order in the empire. Then, satisfied with his reforms, he retired from

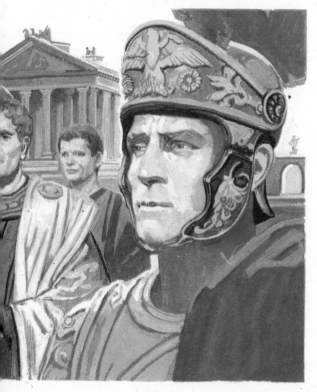

office to enjoy his riches and died in 78 B.C. He was accorded a splendid funeral.

Unfortunately, his reforms were short-lived. The Senate proved incapable of wielding its new powers either at home or in the empire. Corruption in high places continued unchecked. For a while no leaders arose who could command popular support. L. Licinius Lucullus was an able general but was hated by his troops. When the Senate sent him to the East because Mithradates had declared war again, he started by driving the Pontine king back into Asia, but after a great victory at Tigranocerta in 72 B.C., his troops mutinied. He was recalled and another general, a younger man whom Sulla had favoured, Gnaeus Pompeius (Pompey), was sent out in Lucullus's place. Pompey easily defeated Mithradates and, at the same time, added four new provinces to the empire. When he returned to Rome he received a splendid welcome.

Always popular with his troops, Pompey now aimed at winning the favour of the people of Rome. He wanted to settle lands in the colonies on his victorious troops, but the Senate was unwilling to ratify his requests. Instead, the senators became alarmed at his power and feared he would become a threat to their power as Marius had been.

The senators need not have feared Pompey. He did not understand politics; he lacked strength of purpose, and his vanity clouded his judgment. On his own he was unlikely to be any danger.

There was, however, someone else at the time of whom the Senate should have been afraid – someone who was soon not only to alter its powers, but also to change the very constitution of Rome. That man was Gaius Julius Caesar (100–44 B.C.). It has been said that the history of the world could be divided into two parts, the times before Caesar and the times after him.

# Parthia

In Chapter Seventeen we traced the decline of the great Persian empire, how it was transformed after the conquests of Alexander the Great, and how, during the second century B.C. the Arsacid kings of Parthia occupied large tracts of land belonging to their former masters. Mithradates I of Parthia invaded Mesopotamia and set up a capital on the River Tigris at Seleucia. Two other cities expanded into thriving commercial centres, Ctesiphon and Ectabana, and by the time of his death his empire stretched from Bactria to Syria, and from the Caspian Sea to the Indian Ocean.

The skill with which the Parthian archers fired arrows backwards while they charged on horseback enabled them to defeat almost every army set against them

Powerful though the Parthians were, they lacked many qualities generally associated with civilized peoples, despite their long contact with more civilized lands. They do not appear, for example, to have recorded details of their history and most of what we know about them comes from outside sources. Even today archaeology has revealed little about them. The Parthians seem to have suffered from the early growth of a class of greedy landlords who held down a much larger but poorer peasant class in conditions amounting to slavery. This is a disadvantage from which other early civilizations also suffered.

After he had secured Mesopotamia, Mithradates was wise enough not to extend his dominions any further and concentrated on consolidating the territory he held. This policy was continued by his able successor Mithradates II who ruled from 123 to 87 B.C. For the next three centuries Parthia more or less succeeded in keeping its frontiers secure

against all challengers, including Rome, although the Emperor Trajan made perhaps the biggest inroads.

In 91 B.C. Mithradates II first came into contact with Rome when L. Cornelius Sulla was governor of Cilicia, a Roman province in Asia Minor. An embassy of Parthian delegates called on Sulla and exchanged courtesies, offering assurances of peaceful relations. But the Romans were not anxious to allow the power of a neighbouring nation to remain unchecked in Asia, and for the next seventy years there was intermittent warfare between Rome and Parthia. In 54 B.C., M. Licinius Crassus, one of the members of the First Triumvirate (*See* page 163) set out from Rome with a large army and landed in Syria. Bent on defeating the Parthians in battle, he entered into a great engagement at Carrhae, in northern Mesopotamia.

The Parthians were successful at Carrhae, and Crassus's army was defeated and he was killed. The Parthians had the most skilful archers in the world. They were usually mounted on horses and they could shoot backwards with deadly accuracy while riding at high speed. Gripping the flanks of their horses with their knees, they galloped off the fields of battle in pretence of flight so that their enemies would pursue them. They then presented

An example of Parthian craftsmanship, this clasp is decorated with a symbolic eagle and deer, and is made of gold with turquoise inlays

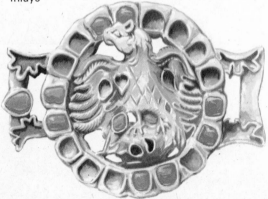

a terrifying spectacle when they turned and drew back their bow strings. It is said that at the banquet held to celebrate the victory, the Parthian king ordered Crassus's head to be displayed to the guests and then filled with molten gold, in mockery of the Roman general's avid interest in money.

Twenty years later, Marcus Antonius, a member of the Second Triumvirate, failed to avenge the death of Crassus and was lucky to escape with his life, when an army he commanded was defeated by the Parthians. Finally, in 20 B.C. the Roman emperor, Augustus, came to terms with Parthia and peace was maintained for nearly eighty years. The only Roman general ever to defeat the Parthians in war was the Emperor Trajan who actually succeeded in capturing their great town of Ctesiphon on the Tigris. Even so, his successor, Hadrian, withdrew Roman forces from this area in order to remain on more peaceful terms.

The great trade routes to the East went through Parthia. The famous Silk Route from China to Asia Minor passed through Parthian territory for nearly a thousand miles (*See* map) and the Parthians guarded it well. The silk was moved along the trail in caravans and much of it was purchased en route by Parthian merchants for the upper classes, who enjoyed decking themselves with silk costumes and their homes with silk furnishings. They also traded in pearls, spices and jewels brought from India, either across the southern part of the country or by sea up the Persian Gulf to Seleucia and Ctesiphon. According to Chinese historians, the Parthians maintained excellent relations with China.

The Parthians have left little evidence of any artistic achievement. Their buildings were built, like those of old Persia, on a grand scale, clearly copied from

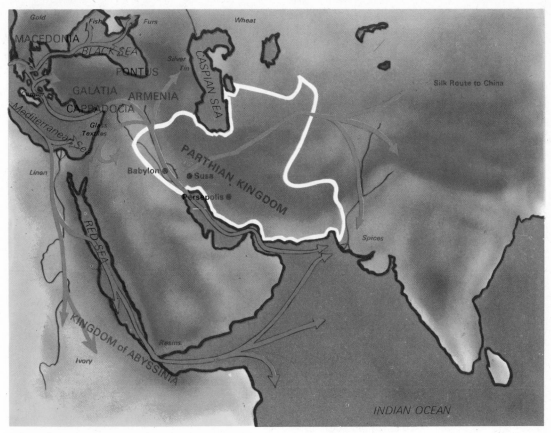

Map of the Parthian kingdom at the height of its expansion (14 A.D.)

Assyrian or Babylonian models in their monumental design. Their sculpture and pottery depicted, for the most part, warlike scenes or statuary. There are many relics of Parthian art showing, to full effect, the terrifying appearance of their archers on horseback.

The subject nations of the Parthian empire did not develop anywhere near as swiftly as most of the peoples under the rule of Rome. The Parthian kings, for the most part, failed to provide any kind of central leadership for their subject states. A considerable amount of self-government was accorded to these people, which meant that power was in the hands of the local landlords instead of the kings. The empire would have profited more from a stronger central government.

Unlimited power in the hands of a few powerful land owners usually means that little progress is made towards a more just and tolerable way of life for all. The land-owners resist change to the utmost, especially if change threatens either their power or their control of land. So it was in Parthia, until the Arsacid kings were removed from power by a new dynasty, the Sassanids, who were of Persian origin.

When the Sassanid dynasty came to power the Near East began to surge forward as a developing civilization well able to hold its own against the enormous power of Rome or the hordes of barbarians who continually pressed down upon their northern borders. In Chapter Thirty-two we shall see how this revival of power under the Sassanids took shape and paved the way for yet another great empire, the empire of Islam.

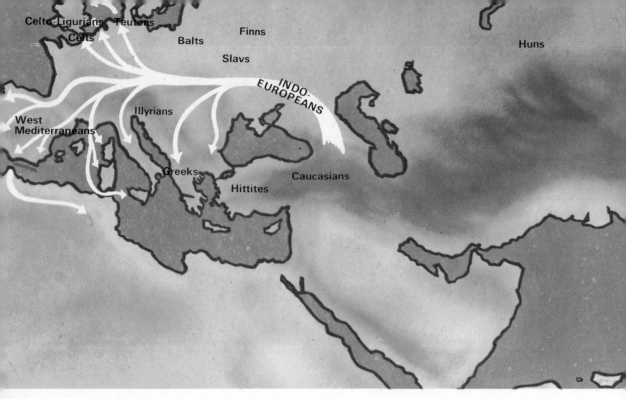

Map showing the routes of the Indo-Europeans who emigrated into Europe

# The Celtic Peoples

The story of Celtic civilization is of special relevance to Britain and to those nations of the world which began with British emigrant families, like the United States, Australia, and New Zealand. Celtic civilization survives in Wales, Scotland, Ireland, the Isle of Man, and Brittany and is mingled with Anglo-Saxon and Norman cultures in England. The Celtic languages are still spoken in Wales (Welsh), Ireland (Erse), Scotland (Gaelic) and Brittany (Breton), despite centuries of effort by England and France to stamp them out.

Who were the Celts? They were Indo-European people who, while still in the Stone and Bronze Ages of development, lived in large areas of Europe ranging between eastern France and Czechoslovakia. On the northern and eastern borders of Europe they were gradually pressed by other prehistoric peoples to give up some of their space. So they moved westwards and southwards, to western France, northern Spain, across the Alps into northern Italy and over the sea to Britain. In Italy they clashed with the Romans, and in 390 B.C., under their leader Brennus, they sacked Rome. By this time they were in many respects as advanced as the Romans, certainly in iron technology. But they had not mastered the idea of central government or of military organization, in which the Romans were supreme.

The Romans succeeded in containing the Celts after the sack of Rome, and by the time of Julius Caesar they had been confined to Gaul and Britain. Caesar conquered Gaul and invaded Britain, and when the Romans occupied Britain as far as Hadrian's Wall, the Celts only retained their independence in Scotland, the Isle of Man, and Ireland.

Wherever they went the Celts took their culture with them, and in many respects it was quite unlike any other in history. Their contact with Rome and Greece, for example, introduced them to the arts of designing and making pottery and fashioning bronze vessels. The Greek designs usually depicted battle scenes, scenes of nature, pictures of home life or representations of nobles' life, but the Celts did not copy these designs. Rather, they painted beautiful abstract forms and geometrical shapes. Bronze brooches or shields, for example, might be adorned with coloured enamel, a Celtic speciality. If there were scenes from life, the figures were usually grotesque and unrealistic.

The Celts were extremely warlike. Their most beautiful carvings were invariably on shields, helmets or other accoutrements of war. Unfortunately their predisposition for fighting was not confined to skirmishing with their enemies, for they have one of the worst records in history of fighting among themselves, a tradition that was observed – and exploited–by Caesar and which persisted into the Middle Ages. Thus it was comparatively easy for the English, later on, to conquer both Ireland and Wales, as the Celts would not co-operate with each other in resisting their common enemy.

This Celtic habit – for it is the only word we can use–of continuous fighting, made any form of practical central government impossible. The tribes, ruled by elected chiefs or kings, would as soon throw off their leaders and pick new ones as change their garments after it rained. If a chief built up any sort of dominion, as did Cunobelinus in Britain in the time of the Roman emperor, Tiberius (14–37 A.D.) it would not last. No chief could depend upon the word of an ally in times of emergency. The story of King Arthur, which stems from Celtic legend mingled with some fact, abounds in examples of brother kings breaking their word or betraying their own relatives.

This extraordinary civilization developed entirely along its own lines, almost uninfluenced by any other. Naturally the Celtic merchants traded with Rome and Greece, but this did not encourage them to adopt Mediterranean ideas. Consequently, when Caesar invaded Gaul – he later wrote a most interesting account of the campaign – he was fascinated by the strange customs of these people.

They believed in human sacrifices to their gods, until the Romans succeeded in discouraging this practice. They were not particularly interested in the idea of a proper legal system. Justice was dispensed in the main by their priests (the Druids)

A Celtic bronze flagon with coral stone inlay, of about the 4th century B.C.

The Gauls fought well against the Romans, but they were usually defeated by the superior discipline of the Roman legionaries

or by their chiefs, and it was usually rough and inexorable. At the same time they were gifted poets and songsters; their bronze work was considered among the best in Europe; and they knew how to build the most complicated fortifications. These strongholds abounded in Britain. The ramparts were constructed of packed earth or of stone blocks, and many were so well built that when the Romans came they merely took them over and improved on them.

The Celts seem in some ways to have earned the description 'barbarians' given them by the Romans, but it is not really the correct word to describe them or their culture. And it should not be overlooked

that it took Julius Caesar, perhaps the most successful general in history, nearly ten years to subdue them completely. Caesar always gave the Celts credit for their skill in war. He comments upon the craft and cunning of some of their chiefs, and highlights their most civilized characteristics wherever he can.

In 59 B.C., Caesar was allotted Gaul for his proconsular province. There were then about seven million Celts in the country. They were a race of farming tribes, preferring to raise livestock (cattle, sheep, pigs) rather than to grow crops, especially in Britain. They lived in small village communities, some large enough to constitute a town, and they knew how

to build roads and bridges. These were to prove of great help to Caesar in his campaigns.

On the seacoasts of France and Belgium the Celts were skilled shipbuilders and sailors. They made skiffs of leather and wood, with wooden oars, for short distances, and they also made much larger vessels of oak, with flat bottoms, high bows and sterns, which were capable of riding the great rolling waves of the Atlantic Ocean. These ships had anchors of iron on iron chains, and their sails were made of leather. The Atlantic winds were too strong for the type of sailcloth used in the Mediterranean. In these craft they frequently visited their kinsfolk in Britain and traded with them. The British Celts, too, were keen shipbuilders.

The leather sails of the Celtic navies were one day to prove a disastrous liability. One of the seacoast tribes, the Veneti, who lived in the area around the mouth of the Loire River, fought the Romans at Quiberon Bay in 56 B.C. The Romans had secretly studied Celtic ship construction and had devised long-handled sharp sickles with which to lean over the sides of their ships and cut the halyards of the Celtic sails. Down came the heavy water-laden sails on to the crews below, rendering the vessels unsteerable. Thus the Romans destroyed the Venetian fleet.

When Caesar met the Gauls in battle he was astonished at their fighting clothes. They wore helmets of metal, heavily adorned with huge animal horns. They wore bronze breastplates, decorated with peculiar abstract designs. They also wore trousers, chiefly to keep out the cold but also to afford some protection to their legs. Their weapons were conventional long swords, bows and arrows, and spears. In battle they were fanatically brave, but they simply did not understand how to fight in an ordered line or in a formation in response to the leadership of a general. When the Celts went into battle each man fought for himself. If some fled from the field because they had had enough, the chances were that the rest would follow. Thus in many cases Caesar's victories were complete routs.

The Celts that Caesar found in Britain when he invaded the island in 55 B.C. were very interesting. They had many substantial buildings. They grazed cattle on a wide scale. They had a sort of coinage, either in the form of copper discs or iron rings. There was a lot of natural tin and iron ore which they knew how to mine and work. And they had animals like geese, hares and chickens as pets, which were prohibited as food by their religion.

As fighters they were extraordinarily brave but, like their Gallic cousins, hopelessly unable to unite. Caesar landed in Kent and defeated the Britons in several

Sodden wet leather sails hampered the Veneti in their sea battles with the Romans

skirmishes. Then he left for Gaul when he heard of a revolt that seemed to require his personal attention. In the spring of 54 B.C. he returned in a larger fleet, led his army on a victorious path across the Weald of Kent to the Surrey plains south of the Thames, near Chertsey and Staines. Near Sunbury he crossed the Thames and marched into the interior in the direction of Hertfordshire. At Wheathampstead, not far from St Albans, he met the southern British chief, Cassivelaunus, and defeated him in a quick engagement. Peace terms were agreed by which the British undertook to send hostages and goods to Gaul every year, but no sooner had Caesar returned to the mainland than the British conveniently forgot to fulfil the terms.

Back in Gaul, Caesar dealt swiftly with a number of risings, but in 52 B.C. a serious rebellion broke out. Led by a

Base-plate from the interior of the Celtic Gundestrup cauldron showing a warrior – or deity – about to plunge his sword into the neck of a bull

brave and resourceful young chief, Vercingetorix, it was no less than a cunningly planned general revolt of all Gaul. The first move was a sudden attack on the Roman garrison at Cenabum (Orleans), which was overrun. Immediately the success was communicated throughout Gaul by means of signals of flags and smoke displayed on hill tops and high tree tops. The men of Gaul flocked to join Vercingetorix to rid the country of the hated Romans.

Vercingetorix won a small victory over Caesar at Gergovia, the only recorded reverse ever sustained by the general. The Gallic chief then led his army to Alesia and entrenched himself, waiting for reinforcements from other parts of Gaul.

Caesar surrounded Vercingetorix with an enormous series of ditches, earthworks and ramparts, preventing anyone escaping from Alesia. The Gauls thought they could sandwich the Romans between their two forces, but when the Gallic reinforcements arrived they were quickly overcome by the outer ring of Roman troops. Then Caesar turned on Alesia. Vercingetorix surrendered and the major part of the revolt was over.

The Gauls saw that further resistance was useless and they abandoned the struggle. They settled down under Roman dominion, and Caesar treated the Gauls so justly and sensibly, allowing them to retain their own customs, that they soon came to admire him and like the Roman way of life. They appreciated, perhaps more swiftly than any other province, that the benefits of Roman civilization and Roman protection outweighed the disadvantages, even the loss of freedom. Thereafter the Gauls proved the staunchest of Rome's supporters for several centuries, especially when later the whole of western Europe was threatened by the Vandals, the Goths, and the Huns.

Boundary of the Roman Empire
at its greatest extent 167 A.D.

Roman Territory in 133 B.C.

Acquired up to the death of
Caesar 44 B.C.

Acquired after 44 B.C.

# Julius Caesar

The Roman republic was beginning to break down in the years after Marius's victories over the German barbarians. A saviour of the country (Marius) was driven into exile, a consul (Sulla) led an army into Rome itself to restore order, and a successful general's (Lucullus) own troops mutinied against him at the height of his campaigns in foreign fields. Law and order could not be maintained without the help of the army. Corruption ran riot throughout Rome in high places, and governors of foreign provinces seemed anxious only to line their own pockets with wealth.

Clearly, this state of affairs could not continue if the Roman empire, which was already enormous, was to grow or even to survive. Kingship had been tried and discarded. An aristocratic republic had not worked, nor had a democratic one. Dictatorship seemed the only answer. In Julius Caesar Rome found a ruler more than equal to the task.

Gaius Julius Caesar, who was born in about 100 B.C., was tall, with a fair complexion and dark eyes. From quite an early age he began to lose the hair on his head and, in later life, he combed it forward to cover the baldness. He was a remarkable horseman, and was said to have been able to ride bareback at great speed with his hands tied behind his back. He had extraordinary powers of endurance, would sleep in the open and share the worst dangers and bitterest weathers with

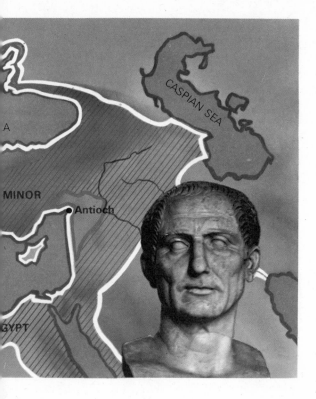

In about 70 B.C. Caesar had begun to make his name in Rome. Born of a patrician family, one side of which claimed direct descent from the gods themselves, he was also the nephew of Marius, the popular plebeian general. All his life Caesar's sympathies rested with the plebeians rather than with his own class, which he despised for its weakness. Until the time of his dictatorship he was one of the leaders of the democratic party.

In 68 B.C. he won special affection from the mob when at the funeral of his aunt Julia, widow of Marius, he displayed busts and relics of the great man. Despite his failure as a politician, Marius had always been loved by the people for his splendid martial career. A few years later Caesar was elected aedile and in that office, on the road to the consulship, he spent huge sums of money (most of which he borrowed from rich men who believed in his destiny) on entertainments for the public. Once he gave a banquet for ten thousand people.

Caesar joined forces with Pompey, the popular general who had defeated Mithradates of Pontus, and with Crassus, one of the richest men in Rome – who would have given most of his wealth to have enjoyed some real affection from the populace. Caesar realized that if all three worked together they could achieve their individual aims: Pompey would get his veterans settled in the lands he had promised them (*See* page 151); Crassus would get elected consul and so win popularity as well as be given an army with which to attack Parthia; Caesar would get the consulship, and finally a province in which to prove his worth as a general.

Caesar, Pompey and Crassus were very powerful, and their combined rule of the state was called the First Triumvirate, that is, rule by three men. In 60 B.C. Caesar was elected consul whereupon he

the hardiest of his troops; he was braver than any man in his armies, and his troops adored him for it and would follow him anywhere.

This unique man, whom Shakespeare called 'the noblest man that ever lived in the tide of times', excelled in everything that he did. He was gifted with the most varied talents of any human being. 'He was at one and the same time a general, a statesman, a lawgiver, a jurist, an orator, a poet, an historian, a mathematician, and an architect . . . . He would have surpassed all other men in any subject to which he devoted the energies of his extraordinary mind.' He was also kind and munificent, and more generous to defeated enemies and to wrong-doers than any ruler of ancient history.

The career of Caesar amply testifies to this seemingly exaggerated combination of virtues and characteristics.

Gnaeus Pompeius Magnus, known to history as Pompey

immediately introduced legislation to ratify Pompey's requests of land for his veterans. He also arranged for himself to be allotted Gaul as his province for military conquest. This provided him with an army which would later stand him in good stead for use in enforcing his aims which were directed towards two ends: the establishment of permanent order in Rome and the empire, and the reconciliation of the classes.

Caesar spent nine years in Gaul and Britain where he proved himself the equal of any general in history. On many occasions he demonstrated his personal bravery. Sometimes if the front line seemed ready to break before a Gallic charge, he would go up to the front, seize one of the standards, and crying out 'Follow me', rush into the thick of the fray. This rallied the men and brought about their eventual triumph. At the same time he found enough hours in the busy days to write the story of the war, and the eight volumes of the *Gallic War* are among the most famous books of ancient history.

When at last, in 49 B.C. Caesar was ready to return to Rome to receive the honours and thanks that his generalship had merited, and to get the rewards for his troops ratified by the Senate, he found that the Senate wanted to brand him as a public enemy and to put him on trial. What had happened?

In his absence, his friend Pompey, who had married his daughter Julia – she had died in 54 B.C. – had been gradually turned against him by the conservative members of the Senate. They feared that Caesar was aiming to bring the republic, ineffectual as it was, to an end. Against his better judgment, Pompey, no longer tied by his marriage to Caesar's daughter, threw in his lot with the conservatives. It was to cost him his life.

The Senate ordered Caesar to disband his victorious army and return to Rome alone, otherwise he would be declared a public enemy.

This was a crucial moment of decision for Caesar. He stood on the cross-roads of

Caesar decides to cross the Rubicon into Italy, 49 B.C.

his career. Should he obey the Senate and so end his distinguished career? Or should he, like Sulla, march on Rome and exert his will, which he did not wish to do? Standing on the northern bank of the River Rubicon, which separated Italy from Gaul, he hesitated for a moment, and then, exclaiming 'The die is cast', ordered his advance troops to cross.

When they heard that Caesar was marching against Rome, Pompey and the conservative senators hastily fled from the city for Brundisium where they took ship to Greece. There, other Roman armies were stationed and Pompey assumed command of them.

Caesar reached Rome and entered it in peace. There were no proscriptions. No one was punished, no one's possessions were confiscated. Even those conservative senators who had not managed to get away in time were given leave to pack up and go, if they wanted to, and Caesar guaranteed their safe conduct. Such was the clemency of the man.

Caesar followed Pompey to Greece and after many adventures he and his erstwhile friend and former son-in-law met in battle at Pharsalus. Pompey was defeated and fled to Egypt where he was treacherously murdered by one of the king's officers. It was a crime for which Caesar later made Egypt pay, for he had loved Pompey.

Pompey's supporters continued the struggle and it took all of Caesar's resources, skill and leadership, to defeat them in battles in Egypt, North Africa and Spain. When finally he arrived in Rome in 45 B.C. he was master of the entire Roman world, which stretched from the British Isles to the borders of Parthia, and from Gibraltar to Palestine.

He was appointed dictator for life by those members of the Senate who had not fled with Pompey. It was the end of the republic. Now Caesar set out to introduce his programme of reform. He planned to maintain order, improve trade, reduce warfare with neighbours, and bring the benefits of Roman civilization to the widest possible number of people. He founded colonies in Italy and elsewhere for the majority of the unemployed citizens of Rome who still hung about the streets looking for free food and stirring

When building their famous roads, the Romans laid down a hard core of small stones and rubble. Paving stones were placed on top

up disorder. He regulated the supply of free corn so that only the really needy received it. To supervise his revisions of the law in the provinces, and in Rome itself, he enlarged the Senate by making distinguished non-Romans members. Roman citizenship was extended to all inhabitants of Italy. He also established local authorities in all parts of the empire and thus may be said to have been the founder of municipal government.

Caesar also revised the calendar, and it lasted in western Europe, at all events, right into the eighteenth century. He started the construction of many grand buildings in Rome, among them the Julian Forum (named after his family), remains of which are standing today. He planned to drain the Pontine marshes and thus liberate much-needed arable land near the city. He arranged road building programmes in the provinces.

He discussed the possibility of cutting through the Isthmus of Corinth and he even contemplated building a new city in Greece that would vie with Rome in size, splendour and importance.

Once these plans were under way Caesar gave some thought as to how the government should continue after him. Elected representatives had failed to govern Rome or the empire satisfactorily for a long time, but the people would not tolerate the idea of kingship. What the empire needed, he felt, was one ruler with absolute power, including the right to hand that power on to a worthy successor from the same family.

There was one young member of his family to whom Caesar felt such power could be passed, provided the boy was properly trained and given the opportunity to obtain the necessary experience. That was his great-nephew, Octavianus

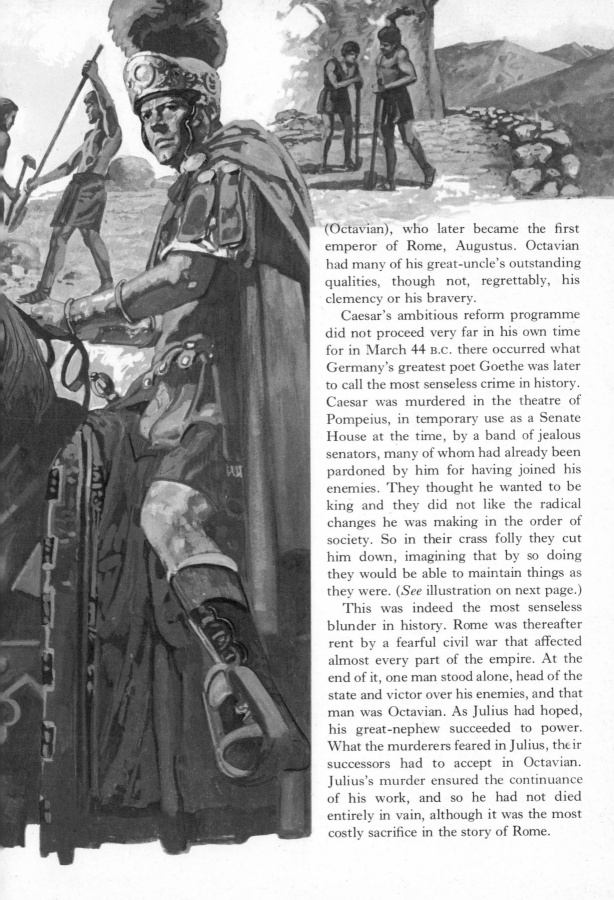

(Octavian), who later became the first emperor of Rome, Augustus. Octavian had many of his great-uncle's outstanding qualities, though not, regrettably, his clemency or his bravery.

Caesar's ambitious reform programme did not proceed very far in his own time for in March 44 B.C. there occurred what Germany's greatest poet Goethe was later to call the most senseless crime in history. Caesar was murdered in the theatre of Pompeius, in temporary use as a Senate House at the time, by a band of jealous senators, many of whom had already been pardoned by him for having joined his enemies. They thought he wanted to be king and they did not like the radical changes he was making in the order of society. So in their crass folly they cut him down, imagining that by so doing they would be able to maintain things as they were. (*See* illustration on next page.)

This was indeed the most senseless blunder in history. Rome was thereafter rent by a fearful civil war that affected almost every part of the empire. At the end of it, one man stood alone, head of the state and victor over his enemies, and that man was Octavian. As Julius had hoped, his great-nephew succeeded to power. What the murderers feared in Julius, their successors had to accept in Octavian. Julius's murder ensured the continuance of his work, and so he had not died entirely in vain, although it was the most costly sacrifice in the story of Rome.

# The Mauryan Kingdom in India

Alexander the Great marched his army into India along the banks of the Indus River. On the journey he covered the famous route from Kandahar to Kabul. He founded colonies in India and left governors in the various territories. When he died, however, the dominions in India did not long survive. Seven years afterwards, Chandragupta, a northern Indian prince, founded the Mauryan kingdom, which stretched from the Indus to the Ganges and included what is now Afghanistan.

Chandragupta devised a new system of government which was based on a combination of Egyptian, Greek and Indian ideas. He also changed the order of society for he did not really like the class system that had grown up under the Aryans.

Setting up his capital at Patna, he created a firm central authority. This was ruthlessly maintained by the use of a new professional army, one of his innovations. The army consisted of four parts. There were the elephants and their skilful riders; the chariots, fast-moving, two-wheeled

vehicles which his warriors learned to handle with deftness and speed; a cavalry arm, with sleek horses ridden by well-trained riders; and, finally, the infantry, men who could shoot fast and straight with bow and arrow or wield an axe, or sword, with undaunted courage.

The army was paid for by special taxation levied on all other people in the kingdom. Naturally, the army became a privileged class, but it had a difficult task, trying to keep safe the territory of a new kingdom which was likely to attract the envious eyes of more westerly empires. After Alexander's death it was feared that some other military genius might arise, take his place, and so prove a danger to India.

Chandragupta then regulated irrigation of the land and controlled the distribution of water in dry areas. Inspectors were sent to all farming districts to see that his rules

Chandragupta reviews his army. At right are the elephants and their riders who acted as shock forces in battle

were obeyed, thus ensuring that there would be enough food for all Indians to eat and some crops left over for export purposes. The king also took charge of all the copper and iron mines in Bihar and charged heavy royalties to anyone who wanted to extract the ores for metal-work. This money was not squandered on idle pursuits, but was spent on improving the general standard of building, of transport and of communications throughout the Mauryan kingdom.

This great prince died in 297 B.C. and was succeeded by his able and diligent son, Bindusara. He reigned for over twenty years and continued the good works of his father, improving roads, building comfortable barrack houses for the army and strengthening the borders of the kingdom.

Bindusara died in 275 B.C. and the throne passed to his son, Asoka, said to have been the greatest ruler in all Indian history. He was king for about forty years.

Asoka was a remarkable man. He started his career as a conqueror, and then, suddenly disgusted by the slaughter

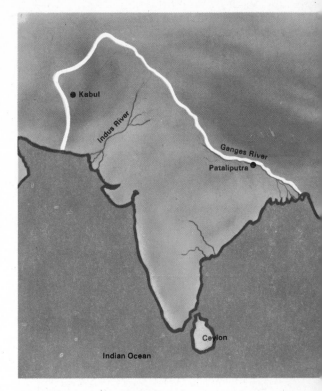

Map of the Mauryan kingdom

and misery of war, turned his back on campaigning and devoted his life to religion.

At the start of his reign he took the great Mauryan army on an expedition to Orissa in the south-west and swiftly beat the enemy forces, adding their lands to his kingdom. But in this, his only war, he became horrified at the slaughter and suffering, not only of troops on both sides, but more especially of the innocent people who were not in the army but who nevertheless lost life or limb because they happened to be in the path of the army.

Asoka returned to Patna, the magnificent capital built by his grandfather, and there sought comfort in the religious teaching of the Buddha. He accepted the faith and spent the remainder of his reign spreading its doctrines. It has been said that at the beginning of his time Buddhism was little more than a sect of

Hinduism, and that by the end it was the state religion.

Asoka's devotion to Buddhism is evident in many places in India today. Edicts carved on pillars throughout India proclaim his beliefs and his hopes that people will follow his new way of life. He urged kindness to the old, the poor, the slave, and the cripple. He preached peace and gentleness, as did Jesus later. He also sent missionaries to spread the faith to such places as Ceylon, Syria and even Egypt. So keen was he to get his message across that he used several languages. One rock recently found in Kandahar is engraved in both Greek and Aramaic.

Despite his devotion to Buddhism, Asoka was a realist and he did not overlook his more practical duties as king. He organized a vigorous export drive and granted special tax concessions to exporters. He maintained the huge Indian army in a high state of readiness though he never had to give it orders to march. And he opened the royal treasury to help the new upsurge of artistic genius in India that occurred during his reign.

Asoka, regarded as the greatest of all Indian kings

Hitherto, many important buildings had been constructed mainly of wood, with stone pillars here and there. Under Asoka's rule stone was used for whole buildings, and craftsmen excelled in carving embellishments on gates, parapets and columns. Many of the sculptures were connected in some way with Buddha or his teachings, or with animal life, and they all seemed to convey something of the new spirit of happiness and kindness that Asoka had instilled throughout the kingdom.

Asoka was not averse to outside influences, however, provided that they were not warlike. His encouragement of trade

Asoka was an enthusiastic builder. He introduced the use of stone as the principal material for buildings, especially for temples for Buddhist worship. The temple here is a substantial edifice, bearing distinct Persian architectural features

naturally increased the contacts made with other civilizations, and their influence was reflected in some buildings of Asoka's time. A vast council chamber built at Patna, for example, is distinctly Persian in style.

Asoka's rule is still commemorated by Indians today, many of whom regard him as the greatest king in all their long history. He was the first king to rule an empire on principles of non-violence – a unique achievement in an age when violence was more or less the order of the day, especially in India which had a long history of it.

Those Indians who think of Asoka with pride also regret with deep sorrow that no sooner had he died in 232 B.C. than the Mauryan empire disintegrated. India reverted to its traditional state of continuous warfare between smaller kingdoms. The history of the sub-continent for the next several hundred years is obscure, and no clear picture can be seen until about A.D. 300 when a new empire, the Gupta empire, emerged.

# The Great Han Dynasty
# of China

In Chapter Fourteen brief mention has already been made of the last Ch'in emperor, Shih Huang-Ti (*See* page 98), who began the construction of the fabulous Great Wall of China. While in many ways he was severe and autocratic, Huang-Ti helped to bring about a change in the order of Chinese society that was to flourish under the Han dynasty.

Huang-Ti united the squabbling regions of China, and then created a number of administrative districts and appointed trusted and efficient officers to manage them. This was the foundation of what later developed into the great Chinese civil service, a bureaucratic machine which preceded its Roman counterpart by two centuries and its western European imitators by about seventeen to eighteen hundred years.

Huang-Ti realized that to provide effective central government for China he would have to break the power of the landlords. So he compulsorily purchased large areas of land belonging to rich owners and distributed it among the poorer class. Then he took measures to strengthen the executive powers of his officers who managed the districts. He and his chief minister Li Szu ordered the standardization of the Chinese language which had altered very little in basic

The silk trade route

Huang-Ti brought the country rapidly along the path of civilization, and his ordering the destruction of many local books on law, religion and political theory, can be understood, even if not forgiven, for he saw that these locally traditional adjuncts of civilization were potentially dangerous to strong central authority.

It was a considerable tragedy for China when Huang-Ti died in 210 B.C., for almost immediately there was a widespread revolt against his reforms. The new laws and the land distribution were the things that had caused the greatest annoyance to the landlord class and they began to reverse the situation.

In the general turmoil which followed – for Huang-Ti left no worthwhile successor—a peasant adventurer of ability and courage, Liu Pang (206–195 B.C.) seized power. Instead, however, of undoing all the good organizational work of the Ch'in emperors, he retained it. He was the first ruler of the great Han dynasty, which was to hold power in China for nearly four centuries.

The Han dynasty proved as decisively influential in the Eastern world as the Roman empire was in the West. The economic and social reforms of the Hans helped to keep the unity of China which had been forged by Huang-Ti. And in their time many of the remarkable developments associated with China that have never ceased to amaze Western historians began. Irrigation and transportation by water, by means of canals and river diversions, were developed to an almost modern degree. The population grew very quickly. There was a steady increase in trade, markets opened up everywhere and the use of money became popular as a means of buying goods in preference to the barter or exchange of goods.

structure over the years but had developed a variety of local dialects. This improved communications within China, and meant that everyone could understand the instructions, advice and exhortations issued by the central government.

It followed that Huang-Ti would also standardize the laws, and that is just what he did. One set of laws was to be applied to the whole country.

The growth of prosperity had other results. Scholarship became more widespread, and education was extended to a wider section of people. Historians began to compile serious and factual accounts of the story of China, of the Shangs, the Chous, the Ch'in and, of course, of the Han dynasty.

It was an age, too, of order and peace. This allowed agriculture to develop and farming techniques to improve. New crops such as grapes and oranges were grown, and it was during the Han dynasty that the Chinese discovered that pouring hot water on finely chopped tea leaves produced a satisfying drink. So tea planting came into its own as a separate industry.

The Chinese under the Han emperors began also to extend their territory, embracing South-East Asia as well as infiltrating into central Asia. They dominated more or less the same amount of territory as did the Romans at the fullest extent of their power.

At home great strides were also made in other industries, especially in the manufacturing of pottery and porcelain. The beginnings of this major industry stem from Han times, and the pictures show some examples of the kind of utensils that were made, how delicately turned they were, and with what exquisite artistry the various designs were executed. Towards the end of the dynasty, when tea-drinking became a national habit, a variety of vessels were used for holding the liquid. Today most people use cups with handles, but the Chinese preferred small bowls.

The Han dynasty kept a strong grip on China, which was to the country's advantage. They monopolized the mining of most of the raw materials found inland, such as iron ore, clay, silver and tin. They regulated the coinage, and introduced and kept under control a new taxation system.

A Chinese noble entertains guests to tea. The tea table has cabriole legs, a design invented by Chinese furniture makers

They developed the civil service. The senior posts were kept usually for people of high birth. Three principal officers controlled the civil service, the chancellor, the minister for war and the secretary of state for land.

Other things that made China such a source of wonder to other peoples were the invention of paper in about A.D. 100 and the introduction and widespread

practice of writing with brush pens and ink. At this time scholars produced dictionaries and grammars. The Chinese discovered gunpowder but only used it for spectacles of fireworks.

The dynasty itself has been divided by historians into two parts: the early Han (*c.* 200 B.C.–*c.* 10 A.D.) and the later Han. The early Han overcame the landlord class and united the people into thirteen provinces which have survived to the present day. Although they managed to preserve order and peace internally, many

of the emperors were constantly involved in wars with the barbarian Huns from the Russian steppes. One great emperor, Han Wu Ti (140–87 B.C.), spent most of his long reign engaged in these and other external wars. He conquered Manchuria and Korea, southern China and Indo-China (now Vietnam, North Vietnam, Cambodia and Laos), and added them to the empire. From that time onwards Chinese civilization dominated those parts of the East, and so it is not difficult to see why today, for example, the Vietnamese

Transportation of people and goods by river was developed in China by the Han emperors as a practical alternative to road travel. A variety of craft was devised for these purposes

have so much in common with the Chinese.

Han Wu Ti also reinstated the books destroyed by Huang-Ti, and encouraged the spread of Confucian doctrines (*See* page 97). He was followed by Tchao Ti (86–74 B.C.) and Sivan Ti (73–49 B.C.), two worthy successors who continued his good work. Sivan enlarged the empire to an extent not known before him and this included the vast area of Mongolia. He also dealt the Huns a series of pulverizing blows which kept them from attacking Chinese territory for many years.

The emperors of the later Han dynasty were no less able or successful than those of the early Han period. In 9 A.D. Wang Mang usurped the throne. His predecessor was a relative who had been a weak ruler, and Wang succeeded in persuading the people that a new reign would usher in a new era in China. And so it did, for Wang nationalized all land in the country and redistributed it among the peasants. He also made loans of money to farmers to help them get their farms going. He stopped the use of gold in coinage and replaced it with bronze. He fixed prices at reasonable levels, and he took over production and distribution of various raw materials, salt and iron among them.

China, in fact, enjoyed a period of socialism more than nineteen hundred years before the nation had Communism under Mao Tse tung. But unfortunately China was not then ready for a Communist experiment. Wang's ideas were unpopular, not only, as may be expected, with the upper class, but also with the peasants. So he decided to undo all his reforms, but it was too late. In a rebellion in 23 A.D. he was killed and one of his officers, Kwang Wu Ti, succeeded him.

Kwang and his successors made extensive conquests in eastern and central

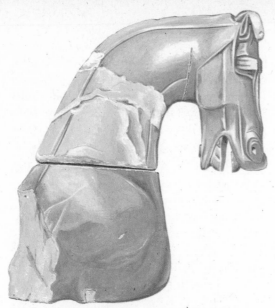

A fine ornamental horse's head of the Han dynasty, carved in light green jade. Jade is a silicate of lime and magnesia, usually in green, blue or white, and it was a favourite material for Chinese ornamental sculpture

Asia and gave the areas firm rule. One of the emperor's generals, Tchao, who was head of the army from 72 to 96 A.D. was responsible for introducing a properly organized police guard for the Silk Trade Route with the Roman empire.

But the days of Han rule were coming to an end. The emperors had been relying increasingly on their generals and ministers to govern the empire and keep order, and had gradually detached themselves from affairs of state, devoting their lives to refining court life and collecting beautiful objects of art. The landlord class, though severely checked for centuries, had never given up hope of restoring the old order of things under the Chous, and they now saw their chance. The peasants, who had enjoyed a wide measure of freedom under the Han emperors, were gradually forced into serfdom as the landlords reasserted themselves. The situation was not helped by internal rivalry among court and government officials for power.

At the very end of the second century, Tsao, a courageous and ruthless general, seized control of the government and put an end to the Han dynasty.

The Han dynasty played a part in Far Eastern history that was no less vital than the part played by Rome in Europe and the Near East. During the period of the Han emperors a structure of Chinese civilization was established that has lasted up to the present day, despite many attempts to disrupt it. The Han dynasty brought Chinese power and culture to a position of equality with Roman civilization, and in some respects of superiority.

A bronze goblet-shaped incense burner of the Han dynasty

# The Rome of Augustus and his Family

The assassination of Julius Caesar achieved exactly the opposite of what the conspirators had hoped. A long and terrible civil war was followed by pro-scriptions on the same scale as in 82 B.C. during Sulla's time (*See* page 150), and at the end of it all in 31 B.C. Gaius Julius Caesar Octavianus, Caesar's great-nephew and adopted son, was master of the Roman world. All opposition was crushed, all jealousies were silenced and war was at an end. The doors of the temple of Janus (the god of war) were closed, signifying peace, for the first time since the First Punic War.

What did Octavian, who had reached the pinnacle of power in Rome, do with this power? He knew that the Romans hated the idea of kings and emperors, even though they had been willing to accept dictators. So he declined to accept the honours and titles the Senate offered him except 'princeps', that is, chief citizen, and Augustus, which meant 'to be revered'. Henceforth he was known as Augustus and his successors carried the name Caesar, after the great Julius.

When Augustus came to power he faced many problems at home and in the provinces. The far-reaching reforms his great-uncle Julius started had been put aside during the civil war. Now they had to be taken up again and seen through. The incessant wars and civil strife of the past century had taken its toll of the sena-torial class and Augustus was hard put to find new men to undertake the responsi-bility for the reforms. So he began to look to the middle class, as Julius had done, for public servants. Two men, who were already distinguished in their own field, came to be Augustus's principal advisers. They were M. Vipsanius Agrippa, a suc-cessful general and admiral, who had defeated M. Antonius at Actium in 31 B.C. thus leaving Augustus as sole ruler of Rome, and Maecenas, a skilled statesman and diplomatist who was also a generous patron of the arts.

Under these three men the affairs of Rome and her empire took a turn for the better. At home the restoration of order stabilized the currency and stimulated the revival of trade. Soon the people were enjoying that rare combination, peace and prosperity. The provinces were well governed by new types of governors, honest, hard-working and loyal men who cared more for the welfare of those under their control than for their own gain. Both the assessment and collecting of taxes was fairer, and in the provinces, the people had a hand in the government, for they were allowed to elect their own magistrates.

Augustus, meanwhile, embarked on a big building programme throughout the empire. In Rome he completed the pro-jects begun by Julius and added a great number himself. He also encouraged his richer advisers, like Agrippa and Mae-cenas, to spend money on beautifying the

city. Towards the end of his long life, he said 'I found Rome a city of brick and am leaving it a city of marble.'

In the military sphere, Augustus was not at all like his great-uncle, and his success against his enemies after Julius's death was provided by the skill of his associates like Agrippa. So it is not surprising that Augustus preferred to consolidate the new large territories recently added to the empire by giving them just government. Most of the military activity of his long rule was in fighting the Germans on the northern borders of the empire. The new province there won by his stepson Drusus Nero Germanicus, in 9 B.C., was lost eighteen years later when P. Quintilius Varus, the governor, was overcome and three Roman legions were destroyed.

In 14 A.D., when he was seventy-six Augustus died, to the great grief of all the empire. He had been a wise ruler who cared for the welfare of his people. Behind him he left an empire at peace, its borders well guarded by garrisons of troops, its provinces content with living as the Romans lived in Italy. His life's work was to last more than two hundred

Augustus

Tiberius

Caligula's handsome good-looks hid a personality of great cruelty and corruption

years, despite the bloodthirsty careers of some of his immediate successors.

Augustus left no sons and so the Senate accepted his stepson Tiberius Claudius Nero as heir to the empire. In many ways he was worthy of the great honour. He had held command of the legions in Germany and had beaten off a number of serious attacks. At home he had assisted Augustus in the administration of the government in the latter's last years. But he was a moody and suspicious man, who became capable of extreme cruelty and injustice towards the end of his reign.

Tiberius, who was over fifty when he succeeded, ruled for twenty-three years. In that time his nephew Germanicus, son of his brother Drusus Nero Germanicus, avenged the defeat of Varus (*See* page 181) and recaptured the eagles of the lost legions. Germanicus was one of the most popular generals ever to command a Roman army. When the troops on the Rhine mutinied for more pay, it was Germanicus who quelled it. But Tiberius was envious of his nephew's popularity and arranged for him to be posted to the Near East, where shortly afterwards he was poisoned. It is generally believed that Tiberius was responsible.

Although Tiberius ruled well and the provinces remained quiet and orderly, the Roman people did not love the emperor. His suspicious nature led him to imagine that people were always plotting against him. During this period there arose a type of man called a delator, who made a living out of denouncing people to the government for complicity in 'plots' against the emperor or the state, whether or not they were really involved and whether or not there were indeed any plots. Tiberius encouraged these people by handsome payments, often taken from the heirs of the men denounced and subsequently executed. It was a dangerous time to live in for any man of wealth or position.

Then Tiberius decided suddenly to give up ruling. He retired to the island of Capri, off Naples, and left the government in the hands of unworthy, avaricious and cruel favourites such as Sejanus, the prefect or head of the praetorian guard (the emperor's bodyguard), and after his death to Macro his successor. The denunciations by delators went on and so did the murders of well-known people.

In 37 A.D. Tiberius died, hated by the entire empire, which nevertheless had remained in peaceful and prosperous order. Amid great rejoicing and celebrating he was succeeded by his great-nephew Gaius (Caligula), son of the younger Germanicus. It was not long before the Romans bitterly regretted their rejoicing, for Caligula proved to be a monster of iniquity, with all of Tiberius's vices and none of his virtues. As a boy Caligula had acquired a sense of pleasure in torturing animals, such as pulling spiders' legs out of their bodies and singeing cats' tails. As an adult his cruelty extended to his fellow human beings. High-ranking senators or

The Emperor Claudius died of poisoning, believed to have been administered by his fourth wife, Agrippina, sister of Caligula and mother of Nero.

officials were humiliated before the court or in public, and then tortured to death.

In a short time Caligula spent the bulk of the huge fortune left by Tiberius and began to extort money from the rich on a number of unjust pretexts. His heavy taxation of the provinces endangered the order there and to prevent any further deterioration, the praetorian guards murdered him in 41 A.D.

Caligula was succeeded by his uncle, Tiberius Claudius Drusus Nero Germanicus, known as Claudius, brother of the younger Germanicus. Claudius was partly crippled and had a severe stutter. For years he had been the butt of Tiberius's and then Caligula's jokes at court but had kept out of trouble by pretending to be a lunatic. He was no such thing, but was instead a great scholar and historian.

Claudius's reign of thirteen years was especially notable for his repression of the delators, his construction works and the conquest of Britain, which began under Aulus Plautius in 43 A.D. The government was given into the hands of highly educated sons of Greek slaves or freed-men. Narcissus and Pallas were two outstanding examples. The haughty Romans disliked this intensely, but these intelligent men did a great deal to found a structure of government supported by a civil service that was to last until the barbarian invasions of the fifth century, and thenceforth to be adopted by the hierarchy of the Christian Church.

Claudius was married four times. After his marriages to Urgalanilla, Aelia and Messalina he took the unprecedented step of marrying his niece Agrippina, the sister of Caligula. From the very start she dominated him and carried out many unjust acts in his name. He died in 54 A.D. from mushroom poisoning, and it was believed that Agrippina had been responsible. All her affection and ambition was centred on her son by her first

Nero was at a banquet when news was brought that Rome was on fire. Contrary to general belief, he did not play the fiddle, but rather did everything he could to help

husband, L. Domitius Ahenobarbus. The son's name was Nero, and he became one of the most disgraceful men ever to sit on any throne in any age.

Nero was seventeen when he became emperor. Despite years of careful instruction by his tutor, Seneca, and of advice from the wise and genial commander of the guard, Burrus, Nero absorbed little that was of use to him in ruling the great Roman empire. All he cared about was acting and singing and playing musical instruments. The business of government he left in the hands of his mother, Agrippina, until, tired of her strictness, he had her murdered. He then asked Burrus and Seneca to take over, which they did with considerable success.

Nero refused to take Imperial dignity seriously. He wandered about the streets of Rome at night, in disguise, with a gang of young men, attacking prominent senators and holding them to ransom. One member of the gang, Salvius Otho, had a beautiful but wicked wife, Poppaea, with whom Nero fell in love. Otho was compelled to divorce Poppaea, so that the emperor could marry her.

When Burrus died, Nero selected a ruthless and vicious new prefect of the guard Ofonius Tigellinus, who encouraged the young emperor in both cruelty and vice. Soon it was clear that the Roman people were to endure times even worse than those under the maniac Caligula.

Rich men and officers were murdered without reason or trial, and their estates confiscated. Nero put his first wife

Octavia to death for no better reason than that Poppaea asked him to. Vast sums of money were spent on useless, vulgar entertainments and banqueting; the coffers of the treasury, carefully nurtured by Claudius, were emptied, and brutal taxation was enforced to replenish them. Worst of all, the emperor himself began to play and sing before the public at entertainments, which disgusted the Romans who considered that acting should only be done by slaves.

Then in the month of July 64 A.D. a terrible fire broke out in Rome. It raged for a week, day and night, and when it was over, more than half the city had been reduced to rubble and smoke. Many famous old buildings were destroyed or severely damaged; priceless treasures, relics of ancient days, were ruined. For once Nero seemed to be shocked out of his irresponsibility. He did not start the fire, as legend has suggested; rather he organized fire brigades, opened the

Imperial gardens to the homeless and set up a relief fund for the distressed. Afterwards he began to rebuild Rome on a grander and, in many ways, more beautiful scale.

To keep the people contented he put to death hundreds of Christians, on the grounds that they had caused the fire. Who were these Christians?

During the reign of Tiberius, the Roman world first heard of Jesus of Nazareth, a Hebrew carpenter's son, who was to become the founder of a new religious faith, Christianity. This was so called after the name his followers gave him, the Christ, or Messiah, meaning the anointed one. Jesus had been born in or about 4 B.C. near Jerusalem, and had probably been trained as a carpenter in his youth. He worked for a number of years, and then, suddenly, when he was about thirty, he changed his whole way of life. Believing that he had been born on this earth in order to accomplish great things, he is said to have set out into the Palestinian desert to fast and pray in the scorching sun. He spent forty days in conditions of severe discomfort, and at the end of it he had decided what it was ordained for him to do.

He was to teach the Jewish people in Palestine about the kingdom of God (or Heaven) and to show them the need for a new kind of relationship between God and man and between men, based on love. The sermon on the Mount best expresses the basic principles of his teaching. He succeeded in gathering about him a number of devoted friends, called disciples, to whom he entrusted the task of spreading the teachings. His ability to perform miracles, especially of healing, certainly gave force to his message that he

To avert suggestions that he had caused the fire of Rome, Nero put the blame on the new and illegal sect of Christians. Many were thrown to the lions in the gladiatorial arena

The chief priests of the Jews brought Jesus Christ before the Roman governor of Judea, Pontius Pilate, on charges of blasphemy, because he claimed to be the Messiah. Pilate wanted to let Jesus go free, but he gave into the Jews' demand to put him to death

was the Messiah sent to prepare the way for God. But his teachings and actions aroused the bitter hostility of strict Jewish believers, especially the priests and elders of the Jewish faith, and they determined to suppress him. It seems he was convinced that his new ideas could only survive if he were to lay down his life for them, and during the last months he set out for Jerusalem to fulfil that purpose.

He was handed to the Jewish authorities who put him on trial before the Roman governor, Pontius Pilate, for blasphemy. Pilate was inclined to spare him for, as he said, he could find no fault in him, but sensing that the Jews were bent on Jesus's destruction, he allowed him to be crucified as a common felon.

Two days after his crucifixion Jesus is believed by Christians to have risen from the tomb wherein he had been placed after his death, and then to have ascended into Heaven. Certainly his disciples accepted this, for they swore it had happened. They believed that he was the Son of God and they were ready to die for their belief.

The belief spread rapidly. One early convert was Saul, a Jewish official, who was suddenly convinced of the genuineness of Jesus and of his disciples' claims. He changed his name to Paul, and immediately became the first Christian missionary and organizer. Paul travelled widely up and down the Mediterranean coastline but eventually he ran into trouble with the authorities in Rome who regarded the new faith as dangerous to the

Jesus Christ was crucified, along with two felons, on a hill outside Jerusalem, in about 33 A.D.

preservation of order in the empire. For one thing, Christians did not accept the condition of slavery on which the empire depended for most of its work force. For another, Romans worshipped several gods, while Christians accepted only one. Thirdly, Christians continued to hold meetings and to try to win converts despite the prohibitions of the administration.

Paul was eventually arrested, as was Peter (the most loved of Jesus's twelve disciples) and thrown into prison. Nevertheless the faith continued to grow, despite very considerable unpopularity among pleasure-loving Romans who were quite incapable of appreciating the point of selling all they had to give to the poor.

So when Nero blamed the Christians for the great fire and put hundreds of them to death, the people of Rome, perhaps for the only time, applauded the emperor for a particularly cruel action. Among those who suffered were, it is believed, both Peter and Paul, who were to become the two principal saints in the Christian faith.

Meanwhile, the rebuilding of the city proceeded, but before very long Nero relapsed into his former pattern of behaviour. Delators were again encouraged to uncover 'plots' against the emperor, with the usual results for accused men: arrest, execution and confiscation of property.

Governors and army commanders in the provinces grew more and more disgusted with the conduct of government at Rome. A number of risings took place in the year 68 A.D., and Nero was driven to suicide. Because Nero had had all possible heirs murdered, there was a struggle for power after his death. In the space of twelve months four people were declared emperor: Galba, governor of Spain, who was shortly slain by Otho, who in turn was forced to commit suicide by Vitellius, commander of the Roman forces in Gaul.

Meanwhile, in the east, the Roman general T. Flavius Vespasianus (Vespasian), was declared emperor by his troops and before long the rest of the empire acknowledged him as well. Vitellius fought to save his position, but at Cremona he was utterly defeated. Retiring to Rome he was killed by an advance party of Vespasian's troops. Rome once again fell to the power of a victorious general.

# Four Centuries of the Roman Empire

Vespasian, a rugged, thickset and ungainly man, had great strength of character and will. It was just as well, for when he assumed power the Roman empire was in considerable disorder. The treasury was empty. The provinces were restive. The Jews were in revolt in Judea. Rome itself had been damaged by the advance troops of his army. The machinery of government created by Augustus seemed about to disintegrate.

Vespasian attacked the problems with the vigour and intelligence which characterized his splendid military career. He raised enough taxation, without fear or favour, to put the treasury in funds, and employed a large number of poor people on his vast new construction schemes. One of the biggest and most famous buildings in the world, the Colosseum at Rome, was begun during Vespasian's reign. When it was finished (80 A.D.), a

Trajan, one of the greatest men to rule the Roman empire (98–117 A.D.)

year after his death, the amphitheatre had seats for 90,000 spectators; today a considerable amount of the building is still standing despite several sackings of Rome.

One day, in 79, when his doctors told him he could not live for more than a few hours, he ordered his servants to lift him out of bed and put on his robes. An emperor should die standing on his feet, he exclaimed, and promptly expired.

Vespasian had two sons, Titus and Domitianus (Domitian). Titus was a fine soldier and very popular with his troops, like Germanicus. Titus was made emperor in 79 A.D., but as a young man he had contracted a fatal illness, and within two years he died. He was succeeded by Domitian in 81 A.D.

Domitian was as strong-willed as his father and in many ways more astute, but he was also arrogant, jealous and suspicious. He ignored the advice of the Senate and went his own way. If his generals were successful in the field of battle, like Agricola who conquered the north of Britain as far as the Clyde and the Firth of Forth in 85 A.D., Domitian recalled them from the front because he envied their achievements.

Meanwhile, to keep the people amused and to maintain the loyalty of the army, the emperor dug deeply into the treasury. The most lavish spectacles were staged in the Colosseum's arena, and other constructions were commissioned. Soon Domitian had to resort to forced loans from the rich, and once more the ugly days of the delators of Tiberius, Caligula and Nero returned. In 96 A.D. Domitian was murdered by a group of senators and officers who decided that Rome had had enough tyranny. In his place the Senate elected M. Cocceius Nerva, an ageing and harmless statesman, who immediately selected an heir not from his own family but from the army. This was M. Ulpius Traianus (Trajan), who had already had a brilliant career in the field. Trajan was born in Spain, although he was of Italian descent. As a young man he could never have imagined that he would one day be selected as heir to the empire, for up to then all emperors had either been Roman or Italian by birth.

Trajan reigned for nineteen years (98–117 A.D.) and in that time proved himself one of the greatest men ever to govern the Roman empire. He had two ambitions: stability along the empire's borders which, if necessary, should be extended to ensure it, and order and prosperity at home and in the provinces. His talent as a general ensured the former and his gifts as a statesman guaranteed the latter.

In his military adventures Trajan was successful almost everywhere. During a campaign of seven years (99–106 A.D.) he conquered the powerful but semi-barbarous state of Dacia, on the northern side of the Danube (*See* map) and added

it to the empire. In the Near East, when the Parthian king Chosroes invaded Armenia, a kingdom dependent upon Rome, Trajan marched against him and defeated him in a series of battles (114–116 A.D.). The emperor then conquered Parthia itself, and captured its capital Ctesiphon. The eastern boundary of Rome was for the first time pushed from the Euphrates to the Tigris, and the Roman empire reached its widest extent.

At home, Trajan governed wisely and justly. He allowed no delators to terrorize the rich and he forbade persecutions of any kind. He was fair to the Christians, who had in earlier reigns been persecuted with appalling cruelty. Christianity was becoming accepted on an increasingly wide scale in the empire, although it was officially prohibited by law. One of Trajan's letters to the scholar and administrator Gaius Plinius (Pliny) reads: 'You are right, my dear Pliny, to distinguish between the cases of persons brought to you as Christians. They should not be

A mock naval battle held in the Colosseum in Rome, the principal place of spectacles and entertainment in the city, built by Vespasian and Domitian

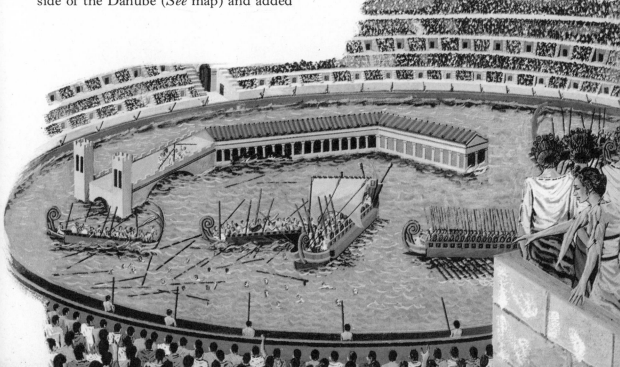

Map of the Roman empire under Trajan (98–117 A.D.)

sought out, but if they are reported and proved guilty (of worshipping God) you should punish them provided that anyone who states he is not a Christian and proves this by worshipping our gods, shall be pardoned.'

Trajan restored to the Senate a number of its functions, especially that of acting as advisory body to the emperor. He looked after the empire's finances and set a good example to others by running the Imperial court on very economical lines. Of course, great wealth was acquired from his Dacian and Parthian campaigns and now and again splendid entertainments were staged. When he died in 117 A.D., on the way back from Parthia, he left the empire peaceful, contented and rich.

It was indeed a blessing for the empire that Trajan's successor, in most ways an entirely different sort of man, proved to be as good a ruler as he. His cousin Aelius Hadrianus (Hadrian) was proclaimed emperor as soon as Trajan's death was reported in Rome.

Although Hadrian had considerable experience as a general he did not seek military glory. But events forced him to wage a few campaigns. He dealt with a rising of the Jews and an invasion of the north of Britain by hordes of blue-painted Celts. To keep the Celtic marauders out he constructed his famous wall, from the banks of the Tyne near Newcastle to the Solway Firth. Much of the wall is still standing.

Hadrian was above all a realist, and knowing that the reserves of Parthian power were very great, he decided to return Armenia and Mesopotamia, in the eastern part of the empire, to their former owners. In this way he could ensure a stable empire, provided he gave it strong, purposeful direction.

Hadrian himself was intensely curious about all the different provinces and states that made up the empire. He determined to visit them all, though the undertaking might take several years. So he reformed the governmental civil service so that it could manage the administration of the empire during the long absences which his visits would entail.

He was a cultivated person, devoted to the arts and to architecture, and forever anxious to ease the lot of the humblest of the empire's subjects. In his last months he adopted as his heir one of his close friends, Titus Antoninus, a man of great piety and wisdom.

The Emperor Hadrian visits one of the turrets along the wall he erected between the mouth of the Tyne and the Solway Firth, in Britain

Antoninus, given the name Pius which means 'gentle', took over a well-ordered and peaceful empire in 138 A.D., and he determined to maintain it in that condition. His rule of some twenty-three years was marked by few major military adventures, but during this time a wall was constructed in Scotland from the Forth to the Clyde. Today, this line marks the division between the Lowlands and the Highlands.

When he died in 161 A.D., he was mourned by the whole empire. Romans had not known such a tranquil time for many centuries – and they were never to know them again. Antoninus was succeeded by his nephew, Marcus Aurelius, who became famous for his philosophical sayings. He was a man of great piety and goodness, and in his own life he set an example of how a simple man should live. He published a volume of his thoughts, called *Meditations*, which have influenced many people since his time.

Marcus Aurelius's reign was filled with wars of one kind or another in the Near East against the Parthians, on the Danube,

The Emperor Marcus Aurelius (161–180 A.D.) dictates his *Meditations* to a secretary

and in Britain and Germany. And wars cost money, especially if they are prolonged. Worse, when he had won a victory against Parthia near the River Tigris, his troops contracted a dreadful fever and brought it back to Europe where it infected or killed thousands.

While actually in command at the front in the campaign against the Marcomanni tribe in central Europe, Marcus Aurelius died (180 A.D.), and was succeeded by his cruel, avaricious and worthless son, Commodus. The Roman empire's era of greatness, begun by Vespasian, started to decline, and by the time Commodus was assassinated by angry guards in 192 A.D., a new era of misery and strife had begun.

The army rebelled and forced the Senate to accept that in future only the soldiers should choose the emperors. For a while after Commodus's death there was some confusion, but in 193 A.D. the army elected one of their best and most beloved generals, Pertinax. Had he lived long enough he might have been as great an emperor as Trajan or Vespasian, but to the intense sorrow of many people, he was assassinated not four months after his accession.

Thereafter, for nearly ninety years, the empire was ruled by a succession of emperors, some of them able soldiers, several of them of provincial birth. Many were cruel and greedy, extravagant and unjust. Some were weak and quite unqualified to rule. Perhaps only Septimius Severus resembled the best of his predecessors.

L. Septimius Severus (193–211 A.D.) was an African, born in Morocco. As it turned out he proved an excellent, if occasionally severe, ruler. He was a cultivated man and encouraged the arts and architecture. His own triumphal arch which still stands in Rome is one of the most impressive in the world. But his time

Lucius Septimius Severus, emperor (193–211)

was largely taken up with fighting. In the east he defeated the Parthians and annexed Mesopotamia. In Britain he defeated the Picts at a great battle and kept them out of the country for a long time. He died in York in 211 and was succeeded by his two sons Caracalla and Geta. Geta was promptly murdered by Caracalla, who ruled alone.

Caracalla was a cruel and tyrannical emperor whose only achievements were the construction of some huge and very beautiful public baths in Rome and the *Constitutio Antoniniana* – laws which extended Roman citizenship to every free-born subject throughout the empire in 212 A.D.

After Caracalla the empire really began to decline. Some times there were two rival emperors, one elected by the army, the other put up by the praetorian guards. This, of course, led to civil strife which only ended when one man was killed. The provinces suffered because the quality of governors and officials deteriorated. Learning declined, taxation increased, and trade slumped to a low, precarious level. Both plague and famine flourished.

Meanwhile, barbarian Germans, Slavs, Huns, Turks and Mongolians from northern Europe and Asia increased their pressure on the empire's boundaries.

In 284 a new emperor was elected. He was G. Aurelius Valerius Diocletianus, known to us as Diocletian. This remarkable man, the son of a freed slave from Illyria (the area which is now Yugoslavia), brought some degree of law and order to the empire. Almost from the beginning he realized that the empire was really too large to be managed by one man, so he divided it into two parts in 285. The eastern part, which he chose to rule himself, consisted of the Near East, Egypt, Anatolia, Greece and part of North Africa. The western part, which he gave to his friend Maximian, consisted of Italy, Gaul, Spain, the rest of North Africa, and Britain. Diocletian remained the more powerful of the two emperors. Each of the emperors appointed a Caesar as heir, Galerius in the east and Constantius in the west. The 'Board of Emperors' ruled well for some years. Diocletian was mainly interested in civil administration and left the military side of the empire's affairs to his colleagues. Galerius defeated the Persians in 297 and Constantius suppressed a dangerous revolt of Picts and Scots in Britain in 305.

Diocletian did not reside at Rome. Indeed he rarely visited the city, and preferred to set up his court and head-quarters in Nicomedia in Asia Minor. There the court soon took on the appearance of an Eastern monarch's entourage and it dictated the style in which Roman – and later Byzantine – emperors were to live in the future. Maximian held court at Milan and Constantius at Trier on the Rhine.

Diocletian reconstructed the government and civil service so that it could cope with the demands of a huge empire. The

Caracalla, son of Septimius Severus, and emperor from 211 to 217, erected some splendid public baths in Rome. A large part of the walls and some of the vaulted roofing still survive, and these remains are among the most popular attractions to tourists in Rome

emperor was advised by a privy council. Beneath this the civil service was decentralized and divided into two sections, military and civic. The empire was sectioned into twelve dioceses (or areas of regional government), and each of these was subdivided again. Finances were reorganized and a new taxation structure introduced. Diocletian also tried to regulate the cost of living by the edict of maximum prices in 301.

In 305 Diocletian decided to retire from office, and he compelled his colleague Maximian to do likewise. Galerius and Constantius thereupon stepped into the Imperial shoes, as Augusti, and two new Caesars were appointed. One person who was passed over was young Flavius Valerius Constantinus (Constantine), son of Constantius. But when his father died Constantine seized control of his army, stationed in York, and compelled the Augustus Galerius to declare him Caesar in 306. After Galerius died, Constantine fought and defeated each of his rivals.

From the year 324 Constantine was sole

emperor of Rome and in that capacity he continued the reorganization started by Diocletian. Two major policies were pursued. First, he built a new city, which came to be called Constantinople, on the site of old Byzantium. The city lay in an excellent position commanding the crossroads from Europe into Asia. He transferred the capital from Rome, and the empire was thereafter administered from the new city. There Roman civilization, mixed with Greek and Asian elements, survived for more than a thousand years, long after the Roman culture in the western half of the empire had disintegrated under the onslaught of barbarian Goths, Visigoths and Vandals.

Secondly, Constantine decided to accept Christianity and make it the official religion of the empire. The first doctrines of the Church were formulated at the Council of Nicaea, in 325, at his instigation. These doctrines were to be hotly debated and contested in future years, but a great number of them have survived to the present day and are part of the Roman Catholic dogma.

Constantine, called 'The Great', died in 337 and the empire was divided again between his heirs. Thereafter there was less and less co-operation between east and west. And now the barbarians began to increase their raids all over the western empire. Goths and Vandals swarmed over Gaul, Spain and North Africa. Angles, Jutes and Saxons raided Britain; and behind these, in eastern Europe, pressed the Asiatic Huns and Mongols.

Towards the end of the fourth century the emperor of the west began the policy of employing one lot of barbarians to help them defeat the others. This had one result – the barbarians ceased to be their servants, and eventually became their masters.

In 410 Alaric the Goth actually took Rome and sacked it. It was the worst calamity to befall the city since the fire of 64 A.D. and the sack by the Gauls of 390 B.C. Forty years later the Huns, led by Attila, ravaged Gaul and northern Italy, but were defeated by the brilliant patrician general Aëtius at Châlons. But in 455 the Vandal chief Genseric besieged Rome. This might not have happened if Aëtius had not been put to death by the Emperor Valentinian III the year before. Twenty years after that the German chief, Odoacer, marched into the city and deposed the emperor, Romulus Augustulus (476). That was the end of Rome as an Imperial city; it was also the end of the Roman empire in the west.

But Roman civilization did not die. Here and there the barbarians took to the Christian faith and allowed the bishops and priests to help them keep the order established by the Roman magistracy. But western Europe lacked one vital thing, now that the invaders had had their own way for a century or more – and that was unity. A new Europe had to grow, made up of individual states and nations.

Map of the Barbarian migrations from the 2nd to 5th centuries A.D.

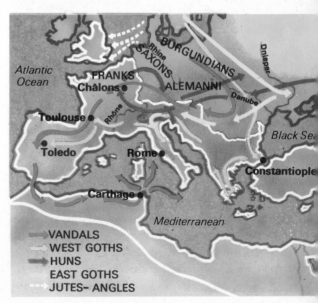

# The Byzantine Empire

When Constantine died in 337 and left the empire to his heirs, three sons and two nephews, it was not surprising that a struggle for supremacy followed. Sixteen years later Constantius II triumphed over all his rivals and became sole emperor. Constantius appointed his cousin Julianus (Julian) as Caesar in the west. Julian, who up to then had been a quiet and unobtrusive scholar, suddenly displayed great gifts as a leader of men. In 355 he defeated the Germans in battle at Strasburg. His troops, who grew to love him, elected him Augustus, although Constantius was still alive. So the two emperors prepared for war, but Constantius died before battle was joined.

Julian became emperor in 361. He was not a Christian – indeed he regarded the religion as a dangerous one, which threatened the very structure of Graeco-Roman society. He introduced measures to prohibit Christianity in the empire and encouraged men to return to the worship of the ancient gods, and some oriental ones as well. But his attentions were diverted by a war with Persia. In this campaign he was not very successful and on the return journey he was killed.

Julian was succeeded by two of his generals, first Jovian, and then Valentinian I, who at once divided the empire. He took the west and gave the east to his brother Valens. In 378 Valens marched against an army of Visigoths whom he had allowed to reside within the empire's boundaries but who had risen against him, and at Adrianople he was defeated and lost his life. He was succeeded by one of his brother's generals, Theodosius, who for a few months in the last year of his reign (395) united the east and the west.

The eastern empire, which thereafter became known as the Byzantine empire because its capital Constantinople was

Constantinople was founded on the site of Byzantium by Constantine the Great. It remained the capital of the Roman empire in the east for more than eleven centuries

built on the site of old Byzantium, was relatively safe from immediate danger from the barbarians. Not only was there the difficult Balkan countryside between them, but Constantinople itself had been built as an impregnable fortress, and it was more than a thousand years before it was conquered. The eastern emperors, by means of very skilful negotiation, bribery and occasional gestures of naval strength in the Mediterranean, succeeded in maintaining their security for a long time. Trade increased, learning advanced, and Christianity spread to a greater number of people.

In 427 Emperor Theodosius II, a man of learning and devotion to justice, ordered a new code of Roman Law to be drawn up. It was based upon the body of law that had been developing in Rome ever since the days of the Twelve Tables, but the new code also took into account the considerable changes that had taken place in society and in the provinces. At one time there had been a law exclusive to Roman citizens (that was one of the privileges of being a Roman) and another for the subjects of the empire. Both laws had been fair, but now that every citizen of the empire was also a Roman citizen, only one law was needed. Theodosius also founded a university at Constantinople, where the best elements of Roman and Greek learning were preserved and taught.

Succeeding emperors consolidated Theodosius's work and, where convenient, negotiated fresh treaties with barbarian neighbours and also with the rulers in the west. Anastasius I (491–518) reinforced the already powerful fortifications around Constantinople and built a long wall further out from the city which cut off fifty miles of the peninsula.

In 527 there came to the Imperial throne a man who is referred to as 'the last of the Romans'. He was so-called because he devoted his life to keeping western influences in Byzantium against the inevitable tide of oriental culture. Justinian was a curious mixture of characteristics. Devoted to learning, forceful, impressive to look at, he was also quick-tempered, and capable of great cruelty. Moreover, for a long time he was under the thumb of his strong-willed wife Theodora, who had favourites among the courtiers and for whom a number of injustices were committed.

Justinian wanted to revive the old empire and bring east and west together. To some extent he succeeded, aided by the very able general, Belisarius. Their first great victory was over the Sassanid Persian king, Chosroes. Then Belisarius was sent to North Africa where, in a short campaign, he defeated the Vandals and captured Carthage. Finally, Justinian planned a two-pronged invasion of Italy itself, via Dalmatia and by sea into Naples harbour. In 536 Belisarius entered Rome in triumph.

The triumph was short-lived. Belisarius was recalled to deal with a Persian invasion of the province of Armenia, and the Ostrogoths took advantage of his absence to win back much of Italy.

On his accession Justinian had found the legal system of the empire in a considerable tangle. So he set up a commission of legal experts to investigate and rearrange the laws. In the 530s they produced the Corpus Juris Civilis, a series of books. This included a code of Imperial statutes passed since the early days of the Roman empire, a digest of legal decisions that go back far into republican times, the Institutes, a kind of text book for students, and the Novels, that is, statutes made by Justinian himself.

The first books were written in Latin but the Novels, which came later, were in Greek. The main theme of Justinian's law was humanity, common sense and public usefulness. His codes lasted right down to the fall of Constantinople in 1453, and have profoundly influenced the legal systems of nearly every country in Europe up to today.

The death of Justinian was followed by a decline in the military and political fortunes of Byzantium. For nearly seventy years the empire sustained defeat after defeat at the hands of the Sassanids or the barbarians, until in about 610 a brilliant new general arrived on the scene. He was Heraclius, who had been born in Asia but who had become devoted to the Byzantine cause. Heraclius had great presence,

tremendous personal courage and considerable military skill. He won back many of the empire's lost territories, recaptured Jerusalem, pushed the Persians back to their own land and captured Ctesiphon, in 629, where he retrieved the cross on which Jesus Christ was said to have been crucified. This relic had been taken by Chosroes II from Jerusalem about fourteen years before.

The Persians were glad to come to terms with the empire. And a few years afterwards (641–3), they were to collapse before the onrush of the Arabs who had been moulded into an invincible force by Caliph Abu-Bekr (*See* page 207). The Moslems, fired with religious zeal, carried all before them in the years 635 to 643, though Byzantium did not fall.

The Arabs overran Armenia, Cyprus, Rhodes, and many other territories in the Byzantine empire, but in 678 when an Arab naval squadron attacked the capital

itself, it was severely repulsed. Thereafter, for a quarter of a century, the capital was subjected to assault, but without success. One of the main weapons of defence used by the Byzantines was their new fire power. This was a sort of charge of burning material made up of naphtha, which was shot in lumps among the Arab ships, causing terrific havoc. In the end the Arabs abandoned these naval enterprises.

For many years the Byzantines managed to beat off attacks by sea on Constantinople and elsewhere by using their great weapon, Greek fire. This was a liquid, made from naphtha, which had considerable explosive power

Byzantine cross of the 12th century. Made of silver gilt, it is adorned with enamels. Circular medallions decorate the extremities of the arms

art and learning. It is in these times that the Byzantines built magnificent cathedrals, usually with domes which they copied from the Persian model, although the greatest of them all, Saint Sophia, had been built 250 years earlier by Justinian. Beautiful manuscripts were produced by monks in the monasteries and in the universities. There was, however, continual rivalry for the Imperial crown.

In the ninth century Byzantium suffered at the hands of the Viking invaders. Waves of Nordic warriors surged down through Russia from Finland and Sweden, crossed the Black Sea in their high-prowed ships and headed straight for the capital. They failed to take the city, but the empire's armies were soon exhausted by the task of warding off these terrifying marauders who were interested only in loot and destruction, and who had already begun to scourge all western Europe and Britain. At the same time Byzantium was attacked by fleets of Arab pirates known as Musulmans, from North Africa.

Once more Byzantium was to recover and turn the tables on its adversaries. Under such generals as Bardas and the emperors Nicephorus II (963–9) and John Tzimisces (969–976), Byzantium's armies won back huge areas. The Moslems were driven out of Asia Minor altogether, out of Crete (961) and out of Cyprus. Byzantine armies also recaptured Syria which had been in Arab hands for three hundred years.

The Byzantine leaders looked upon their campaigns as religious crusades and they formed their armies on the lines of Roman legions. Their troops were fired with the same kind of religious zeal and enthusiasm as the Arab followers of Mahomet had been in the earlier days of Moslem advance. By the end of the tenth century Byzantium was once more

Byzantium, however, was not at all happily situated. Its territories all over the Mediterranean were constantly being attacked and overrun, not only by Moslems but also by savage tribes from Bulgaria who several times attempted to besiege Constantinople. The Bulgarian danger was only ended when the emperor persuaded the Bulgars to accept Christianity.

The Byzantines were forced to contract the size of the empire and to strengthen what territories were left. They gave up their interests in Italy, except in the extreme south, and by about 800 A.D. the revised boundaries limited their lands to Greece and Asia Minor. Peace treaties were made with the Caliphate of Baghdad (*See* page 208) and with the Bulgarians. The interval of tranquillity resulted in greatly increased trade and in a revival of in possession of territories nearly as extensive as those held by Justinian.

No sooner, however, had they reached this pinnacle of power than once more danger threatened them from the east. Semi-civilized Turks, called Seljuks, began to invade Armenia and places along the west coast of the Black Sea from about 1030. These invasions were to prove a major movement in history for while the Arabs had been content to allow Christians to follow their own religion in occupied countries – and even permitted pilgrimages to Palestine – the Seljuks were not as tolerant; indeed, they were very cruel. Pilgrims were ill-treated, tortured and sometimes murdered. So a deep-rooted cause of strife between Byzantium and the Turks was born, and by the end of the eleventh century almost all western Europe was dragged into the quarrel. This was the age of the crusades, about which you can read in Chapter Thirty-eight.

The Emperor Justinian accompanied by ecclesiastical dignitaries, officials and guards. Mosaic from San Vitale, Ravenna c. 540 A.D.

# The Rise of Islam

In about 600 the borders of the Byzantine and Persian empires had begun to be subjected to raids by Arab horsemen and warriors mounted on camels. These Arabs, who were semi-civilized Semitic people from the desert wastes of Arabia below Mesopotamia were, by virtue of their hard, wandering existence, extremely tough. For years they had been chased by patrols of Persian or Byzantine frontier guards and they had learned how to withstand all manner of privations – lack of shelter, shortage of food and water, and the general frustration felt by people who have nowhere congenial to settle.

These wandering Arabs were of a contemplative and religious nature. But what they knew of Christianity, Buddhism and the Persian religion did not appeal to them. They were closer to the faith of the Hebrews, who were also Semitic in origin, although they had an assortment of gods, whose images they carved and worshipped.

Then, in the seventh century, a middle-aged Arab merchant provided them with a new faith. He was Mahomet.

Mahomet was born in the small town of Mecca, on the coast of the Red Sea of Arabia, in about 570. He was the son of a merchant, and when he grew up he went into the family business. In Mecca there was a lot of money to be made out of pilgrims who came from all over the east to see the Kaabah stone, said to have been brought to the town by Abraham.

When he was about forty, Mahomet decided to give up business and lead a life of prayer and meditation, preaching and helping the poor. Mahomet soon acquired a following of disciples, just as Jesus had done in Judea at the beginning of the first century A.D. Mahomet began to preach rules of good and kind behaviour, claiming that he had been inspired by God, or in his language, Allah, and curiously he said his informant had been the same archangel, Gabriel, who had visited Mary, the mother of Jesus.

Mahomet condemned the Arabs for worshipping a host of gods, and told his audiences that Allah was the one and only true God, which was just what Moses had said of Yahweh in the first of the Ten Commandments, centuries earlier.

The contents of the Koran are extremely varied. The Almightiness of God is emphasized, idolatry condemned, and moral and legal advice provided

The victory of Islam meant that Mecca was no longer merely a commercial centre and an important holy place, but the object of pilgrimages to the Kaabah stone

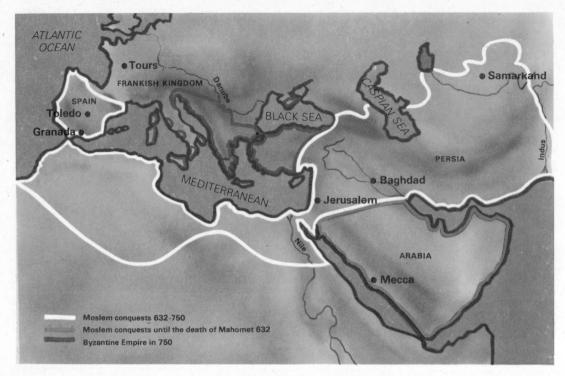

Map showing the expansion of the Arabs from 632–750 A.D.

At first Mahomet's teachings irritated the Arabs; he was driven out of Mecca in 622, and was lucky to escape with his life. He fled north to Medina and there found a more favourable climate for his ideas. Within ten years he had acquired considerable support. This included a small but devoted army of followers willing to fight to the death to spread his ideas.

Mahomet's faith became known as the Islamic faith and his followers were called Moslems. In time Islam acquired believers all over the world from North Africa to the East Indies. Today, there are perhaps more than four hundred million Moslems, and the principles of their faith have altered very little.

Islam spread when Mahomet's teachings were set down in a book called the Koran, which was as sacred to the Moslems as the Bible was to the Christians. Even the Moslem calendar was arranged so that all events were dated before or after the Hegira, the year of Mahomet's

flight to Medina. One of the main points of faith was that everyone should be given a chance to accept the doctrines; those that did not were classed as infidels. It was considered the duty of Moslems everywhere to fight infidels, but in their history they have been remarkably tolerant of other faiths. Their persecutions of non-believers were never as violent or as widespread as those of the early Christians.

By the time Mahomet died in 632, all of Arabia had been converted. At his death, there were several very able men anxious to continue Mahomet's crusade of converting the world to his faith. One was his disciple, Abu Bekr, who at once assumed the title of caliph, which means successor, and began to mobilize the Arabs into a fine fighting army. Abu, his colleagues, and the succeeding caliphs, especially Omar (634–44) and Othman (644–56), inspired the great armies that were to pour forth from the country to conquer the world for Allah. The troops were offered the two-fold inducement of plunder and riches on earth, and eternal salvation in the kingdom of Allah when they died.

The Arab invasions occurred in a series of 'waves', from about 635 to about 800. In these years the size and the efficiency of the Arab armies proved extraordinary. Sweeping over the Near East and the Mediterranean and offering their opponents the choice of 'Allah or the Sword' they marched or rode thousands of miles and conquered nearly all before them.

The first great power to collapse before their onslaught was Sassanid Persia. In 634 Arab leaders began to drive the Byzantines out of Syria, Armenia and Egypt, all of which fell in the space of a few years. After the death of Mahomet, the Arabs crossed the Euphrates in 637 and destroyed the Persian army at Kufah. Then they drove the last Sassanid king, Yazdegerd, out of his empire into India.

No sooner had these tough and almost invincible warriors conquered so huge an area than they settled down and promptly changed their way of life. They built up fine cities at Damascus, Baghdad and Cairo. They adopted existing systems of government and improved them. They developed the land, instituted taxation

The secret of the success of the early Moslem invasions lay in the incredible swiftness of Moslem horsemen and their reckless bravery

10th century gold pitcher from Iran. The chiselled relief decoration includes peacocks, ibex and a winged human-headed creature surrounded by floral motifs

and encouraged industry and trade. At the same time they allowed their subjects considerable latitude in religious belief, in law and in the observance of local customs.

In about 660 the caliphate became a hereditary monarchy, and so like many earlier civilizations Islam had its dynasties of rulers. The first was the caliphate of the Omayyads, from 658 to 750. They ruled the Moslem world from Damascus. Then came the Abbassids, from 750 to about 1100, who governed from Baghdad. In 762 Baghdad was officially made the caliphs' capital. But like earlier civilizations, too, Islam had its periods of internal strife, stagnation, and revival. Sometimes the strife was so bad that no progress at all was made in what was so promising a civilization.

The Arabs began to move in conquest again, towards the end of the seventh century. Their advance was so rapid and extensive that they overran parts of India and even reached the borders of China.

But there they were at last stemmed.

Undismayed by this, the Arabs then turned along the North African coast and conquered as far as Morocco (788). Some branched off south-westwards, through the incredibly long wastes of the Sahara Desert, and reached Senegal, Nigeria and Ghana, and some advanced through the Sudan (then known as Nubia).

The Arabs clashed with Byzantium and there they met their first major defeats. Time and again they tried to take Constantinople but failed. But all the same they overran much of the Byzantine empire, especially the valuable cities and hills of Asia Minor. By the middle of the eighth century they controlled the Mediterranean Sea from Asia Minor and Egypt to Morocco, and beyond. They had achieved one of the greatest efforts of empire-building in the history of mankind.

The Islamic civilization was by no means merely one of conquest and terror. In time it invigorated the decaying world of Europe. It regenerated society and it revived art and literature, science and medicine, law and philosophy. Many of the great treatises of the ancient world of Greece, Persia, India, Rome and elsewhere came down to us by means of Moslem scholars and scribes.

The Moslem advance could not go forever unchecked, and in France the Arabs who had conquered Spain by overthrowing the Visigothic kingdom there in 711–13, were decisively defeated at Poitiers by Charles Martel, chief of the Franks (See page 213) in 732.

Despite setbacks, Islam maintained immense power and influence. The Moslems became very rich as they absorbed the trade routes and the trading stations of their subjects. The secret of silk manufacture, guarded so jealously by the Chinese for more than two thousand years, had been accidentally discovered by a Byzantine merchant, and the Moslems exploited it.

In about 750 the Omayyads were driven out of Damascus by the Abbasids, who then set up their capital at Baghdad. One Omayyad prince escaped to Morocco where he crossed into Spain and set up an independent caliphate with a capital at Cordoba in 755. Towards the end of the century Islam spread within the Abbasid empire, and in Spain and Morocco. This enabled the ripe and vitalizing Arab culture to grow. Ideas and knowledge from earlier ages were spread throughout the world by enthusiastic and highly gifted scholars. In this time the Indian system of numbering with digits from one to ten (which we call Arabic numerals) and many other mathematical theories and methods, were brought to the Near East. Greek geometry, Persian astronomy, and Arabic chemistry were studied everywhere. Islam was in fact responsible,

more than any other influence, for the foundation of modern experimental science.

It seemed as if the Mediterranean lands, the Near East – and even the Far East – were to bask in an era of peace and order, learning and art. But it was not to be. By the middle of the ninth century Europe and the Near East had become victims of fresh invasions, this time by Vikings from Scandinavia, by Langobards from northern Germany, Magyars from Russia, and Arab pirates from North Africa. Islam survived the attacks but in the process was weakened and changed. Much of the zest went out of the Moslem people. And to make matters worse, a further and more terrible danger loomed on the horizon – the Turks from central Russia.

Cairo, a Moslem city founded in Egypt over a thousand years ago, had many mosques for the worship of Allah. This one in the background was built in the 14th century

# Europe in Turmoil

After the collapse of the western Roman empire in the fifth century A.D., to which the eastern Romans had been strangely indifferent, western Europe sank into an age of stagnation. Although the name 'barbarians' is given to the Goths, Visigoths and Vandals who overran the west, it should not be thought that they were savages. For more than a century they had lived near the boundaries of the Roman empire, were familiar with Roman culture, and had already started on the road to civilization themselves.

The barbarians broke up the unity of western Europe and this meant that new forms of government, new centres of rule, and new focuses of loyalty had to be found. In Europe only one uniting factor remained, and that was Christianity, whose Church was still ruled from Rome by the Popes, who at that time were entitled 'Pontifex Maximus'.

The history of western Europe during the next two hundred years or so is confused. It follows a pattern of disorder, invasion, plague, and economic and cultural stagnation, in which the only light seems to be the survival of Christianity against every obstacle. Throughout the West groups of educated and pious men

called monks, fired by the zeal of their faith, formed religious orders, little units of civilization with miniature governments. These orders often built monasteries to house their members and to give them a place to study and to pursue their religion apart from the world. The monks went out among the barbarians and tried to convert them to the Christian faith. They also gave advice on law, provided medicine and care for the sick, and succour for those who were starving or homeless.

The monks pursued studies in all kinds of subjects. Laboriously they copied out ancient texts and manuscripts, and in this way were able to preserve Greek and Roman literature, for the originals were in many cases destroyed in the periods of upheaval. They also grew their own crops, reared their own livestock and manufactured their own wine and ale. Their influence was immense throughout all western Europe, and lasted for centuries. None was more active than the Irish monks, scholars and artists who at this time provided Ireland with a Golden Age of art and literature.

Out of the disorder of the fifth and sixth centuries arose the beginnings of nations. These nations gradually evolved individual languages, based largely on Greek and Latin (except for the British and Scandinavian states), and they each

In earlier centuries, monks in mediaeval Europe undertook a great variety of activities in their community buildings

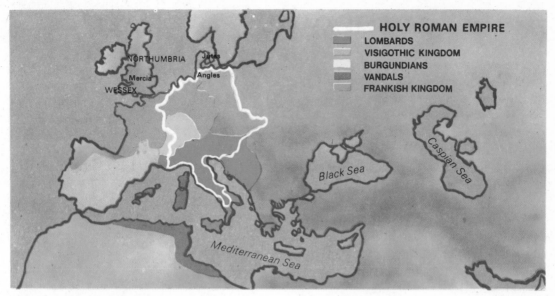

Map of mediaeval Europe

sought a role in the western world. The Franks, one of the most energetic people, formed a new state and gave their name to France. The Franks moved into Gaul from the Low Countries, that is, Holland and Belgium, and from the Rhine Valley, in about 470. Their first great leader was Clovis (481–511), who in 503 accepted Christianity, and prevailed upon his subjects to do so, too. He conquered and welded into one country all Gaul, Belgium and Holland. He was the first of what later became known as the Merovingian dynasty of kings. When he died, the new Frankish kingdom fell apart and it was not united again until Clothaire I became king in 558. It was again split up sometime after Clothaire's death and remained partitioned until 663.

Earlier, the Byzantine emperor, Justinian, had driven the Ostrogoths out of Italy and brought the peninsula back into the eastern Roman empire. This did not last, for in 570 another fierce tribe of Germanic warriors, the Lombards, moved in and overran nearly the whole country. They remained there for nearly two centuries. They left the Church at Rome unharmed and allowed its head to maintain spiritual power over all Christians.

The Visigoths in Spain, meanwhile, conveniently protected in the peninsula by the Pyrenees mountains, settled down with the Roman and the native populations. In time they accepted Christianity, under their king, Recarred I, towards the end of the sixth century. At this enlightened king's court all the arts and learning were encouraged. One book written at this time, the *Etymologiae* by

Bishop Isidore of Seville, a kind of encyclopaedia of knowledge, is said to have had a profound influence upon mediaeval European thinkers.

During these times the British Isles had been subjected to waves of barbarian invasions. The Roman legions had been recalled to help save Italy from another Gothic invasion (408–10) and the British Celts were left to fend for themselves. By the middle of the century the raiders had started to settle in Britain. Jutes from Denmark under two leaders, Hengist and Horsa, landed in Kent in 449, and they overran the south-east of the country. In about 477 another wave of raiders, this time Saxons from northern Germany, under their chief Aella, came and settled in Sussex and Hampshire and founded the kingdom of Sussex. In 496 yet another wave of raiders, also Saxons, came to Southampton Water, under their leader Cerdic, and swiftly occupied the area immediately west of the Test, founding the kingdom of Wessex.

In the next century Angles from Germany crossed the North Sea and landed in Norfolk, Lincolnshire and Yorkshire, established settlements and pushed into the Midlands. Before long the Jute-Angle-Saxon races, who together are called the English, were in possession of nearly all that territory that is now England. The various Celtic peoples, Welsh, Scottish and Cornish, had been driven into the fastnesses of the mountains of Snowdonia, the Brecon Hills, the Highlands and of Cornwall.

The English were great farmers, who preferred the flatter and more arable land of England. There they gradually evolved an ordered way of life in, to begin with, seven kingdoms (Northumbria, Mercia and Wessex, Sussex, Kent, Essex and Anglia) and then later three (Northumbria, Mercia and Wessex). Finally, all

England was united under Ecgbert, king of Wessex (c. 829). The English kingdoms were converted to Christianity early in the seventh century. In the following century, like the rest of western Europe, England was subjected to raids by the fierce Scandinavian warriors called Vikings.

Other areas of Europe were undergoing long periods of turmoil. Then, at the beginning of the eighth century the Arab Moslems successfully invaded Spain after crossing the Straits of Gibraltar. They overthrew the Visigothic kingdom there (711–13) and began to rule the whole peninsula. They moved northwards across the Pyrenees and invaded Gaul. It looked as if all Europe, like the Near East and India, would fall before the sword of Islam. In Gaul the Merovingian kings had

whom historians have called Charlemagne (Charles the Great) came to the Frankish throne in 768. In many respects he was a remarkable man.

A man of little learning himself, he organized schools and universities and welcomed scholars from many countries at his court. Some came from Wales and Ireland. Although not deeply religious, he championed the Church, helped monasteries in his lands, and enlarged his father's gift to the Church which had enabled it to set up a small sovereign state (the Papal State) in Italy, after he had annexed the Lombard kingdom. (Pope Hadrian I had requested his aid against the Lombards in 773.)

In 800 Charlemagne made a pilgrimage to Rome where, with the blessing of Pope Leo III, he was crowned emperor. This gave western Europe the symbol of unity it had lacked since the collapse of Rome nearly four hundred years before. By the time of his death in 814, Charlemagne's territories, known as the Holy Roman

Charles Martel (top left), mounted on horseback, leads a Frankish army to victory against the Moslems at Poitiers in 732 A.D. His grandson, Charlemagne (below), was one of the most famous rulers of all European history. Although uneducated himself, he welcomed scholars at his court and encouraged learning throughout his dominions

proved ineffectual and unable to resist the advances either of Islam or of their more immediate neighbours. One Frankish chief, Pepin, who came from Germany, had seized control of Gaul, although he did not expel the king. His son, Charles Martel (717–41) met the Moslems in a great battle near Poitiers in 732, and inflicted the first serious defeat Islam had sustained in Europe. This victory saved Gaul and the rest of western Europe. The Moslems retired behind the Pyrenees.

Charles Martel's son, Pepin III, deposed the last Merovingian ruler in 751, united the Franks in Gaul and elsewhere, and founded the Carolingian dynasty when he was elected king in 768. Pepin was succeeded by his son Charles, destined to become one of the greatest rulers Europe has ever known. Charles,

Empire, included what are now France, Belgium, Holland, northern Spain, Germany, Italy, Austria, Czechoslovakia and Poland. What is more, Christianity had become the religion of western Europe and people were now willing to fight to defend the faith. It was Charlemagne who pulled western Europe out of the stagnation in which it had languished for so long.

After Charlemagne's death the empire passed through a long period of division and faction. He had one surviving son, Louis I, the Pious (814–40). Louis was deposed in 833, but restored a year later. In 840, when Louis died, one of his sons, Lothair I, became emperor. He quarrelled with his brothers and was defeated by them at Fontenoy. By the treaty of Verdun (843) the empire was divided thus: Lewis the German obtained Germany, Charles the Bald obtained France and Lothair retained Lotharingia and Italy. In 875 Charles the Bald was crowned emperor, but it was not the united empire of Charlemagne's day. A host of small states had grown up within the empire

and their rulers had become powerful and often quite independent of the emperor or the kings of the constituent countries. In this atmosphere feudalism (*See* page 253) was bound to flourish.

The divided empire was threatened by Viking raiders who had ravaged England, Scotland, Ireland and Wales, and also by a massive invasion of Magyar people from Russia who poured into the Balkans and settled in what later became Hungary. It is said that their ravages were as violent and sweeping as those of the Huns of five hundred years before. Like the Huns, the Magyars destroyed all crops and livestock, burned buildings, especially churches, and killed off all the men and the children.

One of the main dangers to the empire of Charlemagne and the lands of his successors was the Magyar race, a collection of tribes from Russia who, for years, inflicted terrible damage to the empire's outposts, lines of communication and crops

They seized the womenfolk for themselves. They raided Italy, France, Switzerland and Germany. Their progress seemed unstoppable until a great king of Germany, Otto I (936–73), defeated them at Augsburg in 955.

Otto had become king of Germany in 936. At once he set out to restore the power of the emperor of the Holy Roman Empire as it had been in Charlemagne's day. He crushed the powerful and quarrelsome landowners. Then he moved into Italy and had himself crowned Emperor of the Holy Roman Empire at Rome in 962. His empire, however, was not easily held together by his successors as fresh invasions of Vikings threatened any attempts at stabilizing national frontiers.

In England, meanwhile, Ecgbert, king of Wessex (809–38), defeated the rival Mercian king Beornwulf in 825, and three years later became first effective king of all England. Ecgbert crushed a Viking army at Hingston Down in 836. His grandson, Alfred (871–900), destined to become the greatest king ever to rule in the British Isles, crushed another powerful Viking force, under Guthrum outside Chippenham in Wiltshire in 878, and then persuaded the defeated survivors to accept Christianity.

Alfred was a scholar, an inventor, and a law-giver, as well as a tough and brave military commander. He started the *Anglo-Saxon Chronicle,* the main source of information about England of those

Four scenes from the Bayeux Tapestry, a needlework narrative of the Conquest, over 230 feet long. Top left: Harold swears to support William's claim to the English throne. Top right: Norman cavalry

times, and he codified the laws of the country. After he died in 900, England was fortunate in that for the next eighty or so years his successors proved almost as able as he was. In this period England moved ahead in the development of agriculture, learning, art and building to a remarkable degree.

The century of good government by Alfred and his descendants in England was brought to an end by the weak and cowardly Aethelred the Unready (979–1016). When the Vikings saw England divided between supporters and opponents of Aethelred, they began anew their fearsome raids. Aethelred tried to buy them off with gold but they only took the bribes and then returned for more.

charging at Saxon spearmen plunge headlong into a ditch. Bottom left: Odo, Bishop of Bayeux, says grace at a feast before Hastings. Bottom right: After a last heroic stand, Harold is struck by an arrow and killed

In 1014 the Danish leader Sweyn Fork-beard drove Aethelred off the English throne and assumed it himself. He died shortly afterwards and was succeeded by his able son, Canute, whom the English at first would not accept. They invited Aethelred back and when he died in 1016, his son Edmund, the bold and dashing commander who was called Ironside on account of his bravery, was elected. So Edmund and Canute fought it out in the year 1016 and finally agreed to divide the kingdom. Edmund died in November, and Canute was then generally accepted as king.

Canute reigned for nineteen years and showed himself to be a wise, able and generous ruler. He reformed the law;

Alfred of England (871–900), the only English king ever to be called The Great. Soldier, statesman, scholar, lawyer, inventor, he more than earned the title

he filled the highest offices of government not with fellow Danes but with English nobles; encouraged a revival of learning and instituted a programme of building. He died in 1035 and was succeeded by two worthless and cruel sons. The second, Harthacanute, died in 1042, whereupon the English Council, called the Witanagemot, chose the pious younger brother of Edmund Ironside, Edward. Called the 'confessor', for his devotion to God, Edward had spent most of his life in Normandy in exile and did not understand English ways. He filled his government with Norman friends, although he did retain the services of the Saxon Godwine, Earl of Wessex, as chief adviser. Godwine, an able and popular statesman, struggled to limit the influence of the Normans in England. Edward left the business of government to his ministers and devoted his life to prayer and to glorifying God, principally by starting to build Westminster Abbey.

Godwine died in 1053 and was succeeded as chief minister by his equally able and popular son, Harold. During his term of office Harold is said to have been compelled, when rescued by Normans in the English Channel from a shipwreck to swear an oath to William, Duke of Normandy, that he would ensure William's succession to the English throne on Edward's death. But when the king died in 1066, Harold was elected successor by the Witanagemot, and so he declined to honour a promise which he claimed had been extracted by force.

In September Harold went northwards to Yorkshire to deal with a large invasion of Vikings under Harald Hardrada, the seven-foot tall Norwegian chief, and at Stamford Bridge he crushed them. While on his triumphant return to the south, Harold heard that William had landed near Hastings in Sussex. Hastily assembling troops in the south, the king met William in battle on October 14th and was defeated. He and most of his nobles around him were killed fighting.

William of Normandy obtained by conquest what he claimed he should have had by right. On December 25th he was crowned king of England. This was the signal for a profound change in the structure of English society.

William the Conqueror was crowned in Westminster Abbey on Christmas day 1066

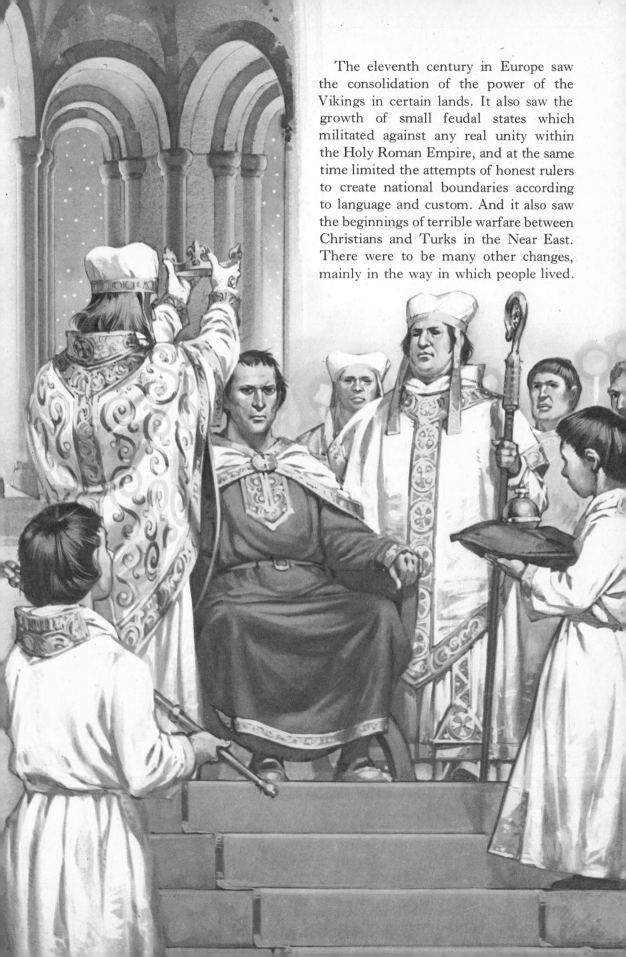

The eleventh century in Europe saw the consolidation of the power of the Vikings in certain lands. It also saw the growth of small feudal states which militated against any real unity within the Holy Roman Empire, and at the same time limited the attempts of honest rulers to create national boundaries according to language and custom. And it also saw the beginnings of terrible warfare between Christians and Turks in the Near East. There were to be many other changes, mainly in the way in which people lived.

# The Celts in the British Isles

When the Roman Legions gradually began to abandon Britain in the first half of the 5th century A.D., the British Celts in southern Britain had to fend for themselves. Before many years had passed they had to deal with major invasions of Saxons, Angles and Jutes in what is now England. Within one hundred and fifty years the Celts had been driven out of England and had joined their kinsmen in Wales and Scotland. The Gaelic Celts in Ireland, meanwhile, unaffected either by Roman or Anglo-Saxon invasions, were about to enter a golden age of art and literature.

How did these Celtic peoples fare in the years between the collapse of Rome and the conquests of the Viking Normans?

The British Celts were descendants of the earlier European Celts who had emigrated to Britain over the centuries from about 700 to 100 B.C., and formed communities in many parts of England, Scotland, Wales and Ireland. They resisted the Roman invasion with fanatical determination, but were eventually overcome, and then accepted the protection of Rome and the benefits of its civilization and organization, eventually becoming Christians. The Welsh remained Christians ever afterwards.

We have seen that the Celts in Gaul were seldom able to unite and spent as much time fighting each other as they did their common enemies. This was no less true of the Celts in Britain, and when they were driven into Wales they continued this fruitless quarrelling. Indeed, had they been able to join forces it is possible they could have beaten off the Anglo-Saxon invasions altogether.

## Wales

In the sixth century there arose in Wales a strong man who tried to unite the people. He was Maelgwn, and throughout a bloodthirsty career of murder and warfare he succeeded in making a kingdom out of Gwynedd, that is, Anglesey, Caernarvon, Merioneth and part of Denbigh. No sooner had he died, however, than his dominion broke up into small tribal factions. For the next three hundred years the story of Gwynedd, like that of the rest of Wales, is very confused. Constant civil war weakened the kingdom and rendered it easy prey to raiders from England. Then towards the end of the eighth century the Welsh, like everyone else in western Europe, were subjected to Viking raids that became increasingly severe as time went on. Once again the Welsh had a common enemy, one that could only be resisted if they were united

under one leader. Such a leader was Rhodri Mawr (Roderic the Great) who had himself made prince of Gwynedd in 844.

Rhodri was a descendant of Maelgwn. In little more than ten years he established himself as prince of all Wales, either by conquest or by compelling other princes to recognize him. Then he turned on the Vikings and in a series of battles dealt them many severe blows. One engagement off Anglesey in 856 resulted in total defeat for the Vikings and the death of their chief, Horm. This is commemorated by the name given to a promontory near Llandudno, Great Orme's Head.

Rhodri's grandson, Hywel Dda (Howel the Good) was a great law-giver. He had travelled in Europe and learned much of the ways in which the nations were governed. When he returned he called a meeting of princes and government officials, discussed the country's existing laws and obtained agreement on a new code of law. This was a most enlightened and humane code, which included the abolition of the death penalty (a thousand years before the English passed a similar law, in 1967).

Succeeding princes of Wales fought the Vikings, the Anglo-Saxons and rival

The Gaelic Celts in the Scottish Highlands used to cover their faces and other parts of the body in battle with blue dye, presumably to frighten the enemy. The Romans called them Picti, or painted men

claimants to their positions, with varying results, until a really strong man emerged – Gruffydd ap Llywelyn ap Seisyll (1039–1063). This great prince put down all opposition, welded the Welsh into a nation, and dealt several crushing blows on the English. He is referred to as king of Wales in the *Anglo-Saxon Chronicle,* which is an indication of his power and influence.

·Gruffydd was murdered, and in the reign of his successor Bleddyn (1063–1075) Wales endured the first of the Viking-Norman invasions. The Normans who invaded England under Duke William of Normandy in 1066, and conquered the Anglo-Saxons, overran huge districts of south Wales, establishing small 'kingdoms' which came to be called the Welsh Marches. Only Gwynedd and central Wales escaped this occupation, and Wales was not to become a nation again until the time of Owain Gwynedd (1137–1170).

### Scotland

When the Romans first came to Britain the inhabitants of Scotland were for the most part Gaelic Celts who had come over as emigrants from central and west Europe several hundreds of years earlier. They proved a constant source of nuisance to the Roman occupation forces, who called them *Picti*, or painted men, because of the blue dye they smeared over their faces in battle. Two emperors, Hadrian and Antoninus Pius, had to build strong wall fortifications across the country to keep them under control. The Picts were confined to the Scottish Highlands above a line between the River Forth and the River Clyde (the Antonine Wall from the Forth to the Clyde was built in 141–146).

When the Romans left Britain the Picts charged down into the south and attacked the British Celts.

The story of Scotland over the next two hundred years or more is almost unknown as no records have survived. It seems that the Picts, like the British in Wales, continually fought with each other. In the sixth century a huge gathering of families of Gaelic Celts from Ireland emigrated to western Scotland and the Western Isles. These Gaels

The Tara Brooch, one of the most famous examples of Irish Celtic jewellery

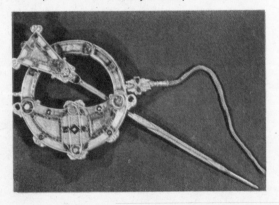

were also known as Scots, and this is where the name Scotland originated. The emigrants were Christians and they settled down side by side with the still pagan Picts with whom they quarrelled constantly.

In the middle of the sixth century (563) a Gaelic missionary from Ireland, Columba, sailed to the island of Iona, off Argyll, and there set up a monastery. From this place he and his workers set out to convert the Picts to Christianity, and before the end of the century they had largely succeeded.

The Scots and the Picts, racked with internal strife, were attacked by the Vikings in the eighth century. Considerable damage was done to monasteries and other buildings and crops were destroyed. Clearly a national leader was needed, and in 834 they found one in Kenneth McAlpine.

Kenneth became king of the Scots in the west in that year, and at once prepared an army to deal with the Vikings.

At first the Vikings did little more than sack and plunder coastal towns and up-river monasteries in Britain, only settling later on

In seven years he cleared them out of his kingdom, and then he marched into the Pictish kingdom and expelled them from there. By 843 he was master of all Scotland above the Forth-Clyde. To make his position as first king of Scotland more secure he moved his capital from Argyll to Scone in Perthshire. All succeeding kings of Scotland were crowned at Scone.

Kenneth died in 860, and for the next one hundred and forty-five years his descendants had to devote their reigns to beating off fresh Viking raids. Some also tried to enlarge Scotland by bringing in the kingdoms of Strathclyde and Lothian, between the Forth-Clyde line and

Hadrian's Wall. None succeeded until Malcolm II, who became king in 1005. This great Scotsman annexed Strathclyde and Lothian and laid the foundations of the Scottish nation. He had to accept Canute of England as overlord, but this was no more than lip service for it is unlikely that the Dane would have been able to enforce such fealty even if he had wanted to.

### Ireland

While the story of the Celts in Ireland in this period has some points of similarity with Scotland and Wales, it is in most respects very different. To begin with, the Gaelic Celts, who had populated the island in the sixth century B.C. and gradually absorbed the more barbarous natives they found there, were not to any extent influenced by their Brythonic kinsmen in Britain. Moreover, when the Romans occupied Britain, they never

St Patrick is the patron saint of Ireland. He converted the Irish to Christianity in the 5th century A.D. He is also said to have put the curse of God on snakes in Ireland, banishing them from the island forever

ventured to Ireland except on peaceful trade missions.

The Gaels therefore had centuries in which to develop their own civilization and to adopt such aspects of Roman culture as they wanted through contact with the traders who visited their shores. These Gaels were talented and imaginative people. They combined their own inventive genius with that of the Romans, and in time developed a culture that was to shine in a Europe rendered stagnant and gloomy by the collapse of the Roman empire in the west.

Soon after that event, which hardly affected Ireland, bands of pirates landed in south Wales and kidnapped a number of people. One was a boy, Patricius, son of a Roman-British army officer. Patrick, as he became known, spent some years in an Irish prison, and during that time he dreamed of escaping, entering a monastery and learning enough to bring the Irish people to Christianity. One day he did

escape and eventually reached a French monastery. A few years later he returned to Ireland with the Pope's blessing and in twenty years had converted the Irish.

He was not able, however, to cure the Irish of their fondness for war and inter-family feuding, which was as bad in the ruling houses as it was at the humblest level. For centuries no one emerged as real and effective king of all Ireland, though many claimed the title.

In these years of civil strife, conditions must have been as difficult as they were in Europe. Yet Irish craftsmen were the most skilful in Europe in metalwork, enamelling, jewellery-making and stained glass-making. They produced exquisitely illuminated manuscripts, like the *Book of Kells*; they wrought wonderful bronze, gold and silverware such as the Ardagh Chalice; and they carved magnificent stone crosses which can still be seen all over the country. They wrote poetry and heroic legends. They built many monasteries in which scholars studied and then went to Europe to take education and art to their European colleagues who were struggling to keep the flame of learning alive in a 'Dark Age'.

Ireland also suffered from Viking raids and also lacked any leaders strong enough to break their power. Then in 984 Brian Boru, king of Munster, invaded Leinster, conquered it and began the task of establishing himself as king of all Ireland. This great ruler succeeded in his aim and had the title accepted by the Archbishop of Armagh, head of the Irish Church.

Brian dealt the Vikings many blows. By 1014 the Vikings were confined to the area of Dublin, and in that year they fought a battle with Brian at Clontarf on Good Friday. By the evening, the Vikings were on the run, utterly crushed. But as they fled, two or three dashed into Brian's

Detail of the initial letter of the Gospel of St Matthew from the Book of Kells, a famous 8th century Irish manuscript

observation tent and cut him down. It was a great tragedy for Ireland. Even today he is the best known and the most revered of all Irish kings.

Upon Brian's death, Ireland relapsed into internal strife and rivalry. In Chapter Forty-six on Britain in the Norman and Plantagenet periods we shall see how this division was exploited by the Normans and what happened to the Irish people.

# The Sassanid Empire in Persia

The Parthian kings whom we mentioned in Chapter Twenty-one were not real Persians. Strong as some of them were they only remained on the throne if they had the loyalty of their Persian subjects. In their relations with Rome they were generally on the defensive. While up to the time of Trajan the Romans had not succeeded in making any serious inroads into Parthian territory, the Parthians were unable to make any sizable conquests in Roman territory in Asia Minor. This was a sort of stalemate situation, for even when Trajan invaded Mesopotamia and took Ctesiphon, his successor Hadrian withdrew Roman forces from these areas. Septimius Severus was the last Roman emperor to have any real success against

Example of Sassanian art, a silver gilt vase of the 6th century decorated with cocks and birds (4½ ins high)

Parthia when he captured and annexed northern Mesopotamia (195–199) and set Ctesiphon aflame.

In about 226, Ardashir, the strong and fearsome grandson of the Persian chief, Sassan, organized a revolt against the Parthian government and assassinated the king, the last of the Arsacid dynasty. He then seized the throne for himself, and so began the famous Sassanid line of the kings of Persia, one that was to last, despite Hun invasions, until the arrival of the Arabs in about 640 A.D.

The Sassanid kings were much more enlightened than their Parthian predecessors, and their Neo-Persian empire became much stronger, and was better governed. Although they raised severe taxes, they also granted large landowners limited powers in local government, and encouraged the development of towns. Like their contemporaries, the Romans and the later Han Chinese, they also developed a highly efficient civil service machine for the everyday administration of the empire.

Before long the Persians were strong enough to take the offensive against Rome, especially as this revival of strength coincided with a particularly weak period of rule in the Roman empire.

Ardashir himself recaptured northern Mesopotamia. His son Shapur I (c. 240–272) captured Dura and even besieged Antioch, in Roman Syria. In 260, the Roman emperor, Valerian, was captured

Marching against the Persians, the Romans – led by their emperor, Valerian – were defeated at Edessa, and Valerian was captured and tortured to death

A miniature depicting a Persian doctor
bandaging the hand of a patient (1609)

reconstructed the army and forged two very powerful war arms, heavy armed horsemen and mounted archers, the latter acquired from their Parthian predecessors.

But, despite this great Sassanid resurgence, Persia was continually concerned about the mounting pressure of the barbarians on its northern borders – and later of Arab pressure in the south. From time to time Persians and Romans actually combined forces to keep the barbarians out, but the two powers weakened each other by profitless wars along their mutual borders.

The Sassanid era was perhaps the greatest in the long history of the Persians. Irrigation and agriculture were brought to a high peak of efficiency. Trade and industry flourished, and merchants ventured as far as China and Spain. The law was reformed and became as fair as its Roman model. Universities were established, and the special study of medicine resulted in Persian doctors being the most eagerly sought after in the world.

But Sassanid power could not last for ever. After the division of the Roman empire and the collapse of the western half, Persia became involved in a series of indecisive wars with Byzantium. Constantinople was impregnable, and the Persian army grew less and less effective.

From about the middle of the fifth century Persia was subjected to continuous raids by the fierce Huns, who in 485 succeeded in slaying the Persian king, Peroz, in battle. Thereafter, for more than a century, although the Sassanids were allowed to rule in their own right, they were in fact no more than dependent kings subject to the barbarians.

Then, at the beginning of the seventh century, under Chosroes II, the Persians once more regained their supremacy for a brief period. In five years, 613–618,

by the Persians in Syria and humiliated by Shapur.

Shapur also moved eastwards into Afghanistan and defeated the Kushan Indians in several battles.

The revival of Persia was not only a military one; there was, at the same time, a great resurgence of learning and art. Greek plays, poetry and writings were translated and published. Indian treatises on science and mathematics were also translated. Old Persian art forms from the times of Cyrus and Darius were revived and embellished. You can see from the picture how exquisite were the skills of the craftsmen of the time. In architecture they introduced the use of the dome for large buildings, a practice which spread to the West.

The Persians revived something of the splendour in which their ancient kings had lived and held court. They also

Chosroes conquered Syria and captured its capital Damascus, stormed Jerusalem and stole the Holy Cross which he brought to Ctesiphon. Then he overcame Asia Minor and Egypt.

Chosroes was succeeded by his son, Kavadh, who was forced to return much of the territory to the Byzantines, and when he died Persia fell into anarchy, an easy prey to the Arabs.

The destruction of Persian power by the Arabs was swift and permanent. But the influence of Persian civilization proved indestructible. Persia had enabled China and India to maintain contact with Rome and Byzantium; it had also helped to protect the Great Silk Route. The Persian empire had, in fact, carried Eastern civilization to the West and brought Western ideas to the East. It was perhaps no coincidence that the Persians occupied the best part of the Fertile Crescent where man had first become civilized, in the fifth millenium B.C.

Chosroes II, known as the 'Victorious', plundered Jerusalem and seized the Holy Cross

# The End
# of Ancient India

When Asoka, the great king of India, died in 232 B.C., India disintegrated into warring factions, and for many years no clear picture of the country's history can be traced. This is similar to the older period when the Harappa and Mohenjo-daro civilization in the Indus Valley (*See* Chapter Seven) disappeared and left no trace before the Aryan invasion.

What we do know of India in those early times is very scanty. Some independent Greeks living in Bactria moved down into the Punjab and set up a kingdom there, with a capital at Kabul in Afghanistan. This kingdom lasted for about two hundred years, and in that time the Greeks appear to have influenced Indian civilization markedly, for there are traces of Greek science and medicine, as well as art, in the culture of the time.

In about 100 B.C. a horde of semi-civilized people, the Sacae, came down

Kalidasa, the most famous poet of Sanskrit literature (c. 400 A.D.)

from Russia and overran Bactria and the Greek kingdom in the Punjab. They set up a new kingdom of their own, called the Kushan kingdom. We know very little of these people save that, as time went on, they expanded their dominion into central India. The greatest of their rulers was Kanishka, who probably lived in the first half of the second century (100–150 A.D.). He is believed to have adopted Buddhism as the national faith and helped to spread it. He also opened up trade routes to the Roman empire and made contact with China. At about this time, Buddhism began to reach the Chinese.

After 200 A.D. the Kushan kings ran into trouble with the great Sassanid kings of Persia, and before the end of the century the Kushans had been displaced by the Gupta dynasty. The first Gupta king was Chandragupta I (320–336). This dynasty created and maintained a well-organized government which lasted for nearly two hundred years. It was a time of comparative peace and prosperity for India. Even the highway robbers – always a problem in India – were kept down, and people felt safe to travel from one city to another.

The Gupta rule brought in a Hindu renaissance, that is, a resurgence not only of the Hindu faith and the caste system, but also of learning, art and science. Certainly the sculpture and painting of those days was vigorous and exciting. Poetry and playwriting also flourished and one of India's most famous poets, Kalidasa, produced works in that period that have been admired ever since.

Chandragupta and his successor Samudragupta (336–385) expanded their dominions as far east as the Bramaputra River and southwards as far as Ceylon. But ever present was the menace of the barbarians from central Asia pressing down on the empire's borders, just as they threatened the boundaries of the Roman empire – and of China, too.

By the end of the fifth century the Huns had poured into Sassanid Persia and across into India. These invasions were a turning point for India. Centuries of tradition disappeared as the Huns absorbed the native populations. From then on India itself never again produced a great dynasty. It was to be ruled by one invading dynasty after another until, when the British left in 1948, it at last achieved full independence.

The Huns overran India, sacked its towns, massacred whole populations and destroyed as much as they could of Indian art and culture. But they do not appear to have remained very long in India, possibly because, coming from the cold regions of Russia, they could not endure the hot Indian climate.

Following the Huns came another invading horde, the Turks, who originated, not as one might suppose in Turkey, but in central Russia, north-east of the Caspian Sea. They were kinsmen of the Mongols (*See* Chapter Thirty-nine) and were fierce, savage, uncultured warriors who lived a roving life in the saddle, sometimes even sleeping on horseback. They never bothered with agriculture, and had no urge to learn or to better their way of life by following the examples of the more civilized people they conquered. When they overran a country they sacked the towns, burned the cornfields and blocked the irrigation systems. Then they took what plunder they could and returned to central Russia.

Fragment of a 5th century sandstone frieze with a lion and two warriors from Uttar Pradesh

For a long time India was in a state of complete anarchy. Nothing remained of the old order. There was a short revival of order under a chief called Harsha, in the middle of the seventh century, but when he died his dominion broke up. In about 700 the first Moslem Arabs (*See* page 205) invaded India and settled in the west. But for the next three hundred years India was really no more than a vast sub-continent populated here and there by small village communities, speaking different dialects, and owing loyalty to no central government. As such the Indians did not progress very far in these times.

In about 1000 A.D. fresh Moslem invaders were to make deeper and more permanent settlements in India.

# China and the Barbarians

When, at the end of the second century A.D., the able general Tsao put an end to the once-great Han dynasty, and China also suffered a dreadful plague, the country almost immediately split up into three separate kingdoms. These were the northern kingdom of Wei, the western kingdom of Chu and the eastern kingdom of Wu. Before long the kings were fighting for supremacy, and by about 250 A.D. the Wei kingdom had triumphed.

Unity was restored for a time, but it was not to last as the pressure of the barbarians on the Chinese borders was building up. The Great Wall of China was to prove ineffective against these fierce wandering people who were to become the scourge of all civilization.

The Chinese emperors made the great mistake of inviting some barbarian chiefs to help defend the borders against other barbarians. It was a mistake that the

Nanking, enlarged under the Tang dynasty, seen during an eclipse of the sun. People in the streets brandished torches to drive away the dragon which they believed was devouring the sun

Map of China in 250 A.D.

Romans had also made, and it had the same result — the barbarians became the masters.

A varied collection of these barbarians, Turks, Mongols and Huns, from central Russia, moved into China and after the usual pillage and destruction, tried to absorb the advanced civilization they found there. In particular they seemed to respond to the teachings of Buddhism which had been introduced to China at the end of the Han dynasty. This was a very important factor in the future development of China, for it ensured a

A horse and rider in glazed earthenware (Tang dynasty)

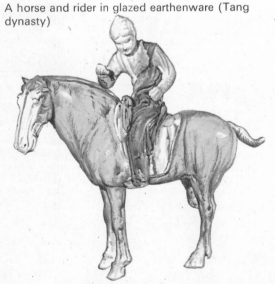

kind of continuity of thought and culture that enabled China to develop in an age when other civilizations were lying dormant or, like India, had vanished.

At the beginning of the seventh century the Tang dynasty seized power in China, and a new age in Chinese civilization began. There were many inventions, such as the water mill and wheel-barrow, movable printing type, and fine porcelain, a considerable improvement on pottery. Some of the Tang porcelain figures are particularly beautiful. The capital city of Nanking was enlarged and adorned with many splendid buildings.

The Tang period is also renowned for the beauty of its sculpture and painting. Like the early Egyptians the Chinese carved huge statues for their tombs. They also introduced the painting of pictures with brushes on silk. In these fields the development of their skill was greatly in advance of anything else in the world at the time.

One of the Tang emperors, Li Shihmin, also introduced an extensive programme of reform, aimed at easing the condition of the peasants and at regulating taxation. The old civil service machinery developed by the Han dynasty was improved by the setting up of an efficient secretarial service which co-ordinated all the different state departments. The army was also reformed.

In this great period of Chinese history, Chinese ideas spread to Japan, Korea, South-East Asia and as far west as Tibet. Japan had already begun to emerge from primitive conditions into the kind of localized units of society that characterized the early civilized days of Egypt, Sumer and India. Gradually, the archipelago became united under the Soga family of kings. The spread of Buddhism helped the Japanese to develop a firm standard of behaviour and the ideas of the Chinese civil service were adopted almost wholesale in Japan. They also borrowed the Chinese script, styles of dress and social habits. The picture was much the same in Korea, Indonesia and Vietnam.

But despite this great era in China, there was constant danger of further invasion by Turks and Mongols and in about 900 the Tang were no longer powerful enough to resist the pressures. Their great empire began to fall apart as one province after another either succumbed to the barbarians or broke away to form separate kingdoms. One of these

A scene from Japanese court life, of about the 11th century A.D.

A crescent jade plaque of the Sung period, the ends of which are carved in the shape of dragon heads

Greyish nephrite bowl of the Sung period, decorated with a regular geometrical pattern of spirals

was the Sung province in the south which retained and developed the best elements of Chinese culture over a long period of time. This small province grew under a series of very able rulers. Tai-tsung (975–1000) and Shen-tsung (1000–1022) methodically occupied the other kingdoms of China, one by one, which were south of Peking.

One of their successors, Hwai-tsung, who was a man of considerable artistic achievement, encouraged all manner of arts and crafts. He himself collected coins, wrote poetry and was skilled in painting on silk. Under his patronage, porcelain manufacture developed greatly (perhaps the most highly valued of early Chinese porcelain is from the Sung dynasty period), and printing became widely used. Green jade was used for some exquisite figure carving.

Another Sung emperor, Wang Ngau-Chi, who ruled in the middle of the eleventh century (about the same time as William the Conqueror in England) introduced a programme of social reform that was centuries ahead of the Western world. He stabilized prices, fixed wages and organized farming so that small farmers could make a living, with the help of government subsidies.

While Chinese culture was being preserved and enriched under the Sung dynasty, interesting developments were also taking place elsewhere in the Far East. In Japan, the king's court became a centre of art and learning. Buddhism was adopted, with modifications, as the state religion. In the country districts, however, Japan suffered the same conflicts as early China; strong local landlords oppressed the peasants and central government proved incapable of stopping them. Indo-China broke away and became a kingdom on its own, developing a culture modelled on Chinese civilization.

The whole fabric of Chinese civilization and the off-shoot cultures in Indo-China, Indonesia and Burma, however, were once again threatened with extinction when the great Mongol leader, Genghis Khan, began his series of marches and conquests which were to make him one of the most famous military adventurers of all history. At the beginning of the thirteenth century Genghis Khan looked towards China and prepared for invasion.

The Sung Emperor Wang Ngau-Chi with his retinue, visits a pottery factory outside Peking

# Ancient Civilizations in the Americas

About twelve thousand years ago Palaeo-lithic Man found his way from the Russian steppes across the Bering Straits into Alaska and then downwards into North, Central and South America. By about 2000 B.C. the inhabitants of Central and South America had ceased to hunt for food and had begun to cultivate a native plant called maize (or corn). Soon, village communities like those that had sprung up in the Fertile Crescent in the Near East grew up, and it was not long before great eras of American civilization followed. The Maya in Central America was perhaps the greatest. Later on, two more splendid civilizations arose, the Aztec in Mexico and the Inca in Peru. All these civilizations were, in many respects, as advanced as those of early Asia. The Incas, for example, managed to run a huge empire with a standard of efficient organization that compared favourably with that of ancient Rome. The Mayas built remarkable structures that, through sheer size and architectural skill, have lasted for hundreds and hundreds of years.

In the Guatemala and Honduras regions of Central America the Mayas, already civilized for several centuries, entered their golden age in the fourth century A.D. approximately when western Europe was about to be plunged into the Dark Ages. They built huge, shining temples and tombs, similar to Egyptian pyramids and monuments, out of stone and cement. The cement was made by rubbing two flat stone surfaces together, with sand and water in between. On these buildings they carved exquisite sculptures and painted vivid wall pictures. They developed a strange type of pictograph writing that is so complicated that it has not yet been properly deciphered. A chronological history of events for these

Maya ceramic figure from Campeche, Mexico (11 ins)

great people cannot be written, for their records have not yet been interpreted.

The Mayas invented a calendar that was more precise than the Julian calendar of the Roman world. They made great strides in astronomy. They developed an intensely individual style of architecture, specializing in friezes of stone on sloping roofs. Many of their bigger cities appear to have been centres of religion rather than residential towns. Most of the buildings were for religious use, such as temples, granaries for the gods, and observatories for astronomers to study the stars. The Mayas believed in a variety of gods, and they related their beliefs to the stars in the sky at night.

The priests also put forward many theories and principles for mathematical science. They devised a numeral system counting in twenties, not in tens, by a method of dots and bars; a bar equalled five and a dot equalled one.

The Mayas were peaceful people on the whole, and for much of the time they enjoyed good government. Clearly their society was well-ordered because they could put up huge buildings and monuments with such technical skill. They also cleared away huge areas of forest and cultivated the soil, areas that have since been allowed to decay and become desert.

Their achievements are all the more remarkable when it is remembered that they had no metal tools and did not understand the use of the wheel for transportation.

The cultivation of maize was their principal occupation, for its products supplied their main diet, bread and cakes. They grew all manner of other plants (including cocoa beans for making a type of cocoa drink). It is thought also that they grew tobacco and smoked it in clay pipes. The Mayas fashioned some very beautiful pottery and in many cases the

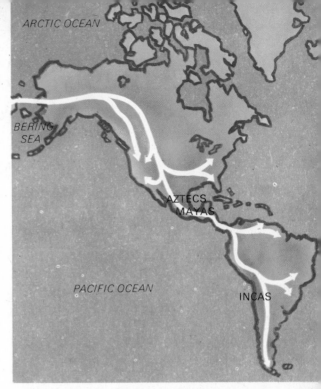

Map showing the principal routes of early Americans who migrated southwards

decoration on the items told some story or other, either about their gods, or about their way of life.

The ordinary Maya man lived in a thatched timber-walled cottage, either in the middle of his maize fields or on the outskirts. He grew enough crops not only to feed his family and entertain his friends, but also to trade with neighbouring villages, and to provide food for the priests and the chiefs.

The Maya civilization began to decline after about 900 A.D. Later on, Maya culture appears mingled with another Central American culture, the Toltec, which began in Mexico. The blend was a most successful one, and at Chichen Itza Maya architecture and sculpture had a splendid revival. The Toltecs brought with them their own gods to add to those worshipped by the Mayas. The most respected was Quetzalcoatl. But at this time the Toltecs believed in human sacrifice to their gods. Remains of one particular sacrifice of Toltec days have

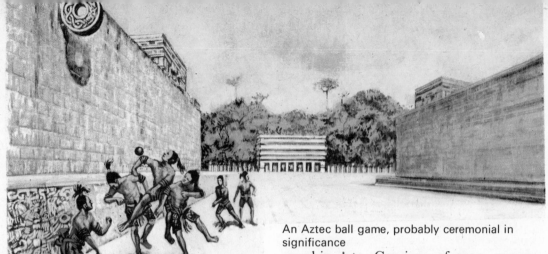

An Aztec ball game, probably ceremonial in significance

been found at Chichen Itza; some children's skeletons were discovered in a well 130 feet deep.

In time, the Toltecs succumbed to pressure from a wandering race in Mexico, the Aztecs, who were the fiercest and bravest people to appear in Central America. Their history is told in Chapter Forty-eight.

Meanwhile, in South America, Man had been advancing as rapidly as in Central America. In the shadow of the Andes mountains on the west coast in what is now Peru, the first civilized people appeared. In about 2500 B.C. they were already growing peppers, gourds, beans, cotton, and erecting great stone buildings. Thereafter, they progressed in stages which have been clearly established by archaeologists.

The first was the Chavin de Huantar culture which flourished in the northern highlands of Peru from about 1300 to 400 B.C. Like the Mayas, these Chavin people's lives were surrounded by religion and nearly everything was devoted to the fostering of belief in and the comfort of the gods. At Chavin, a most magnificent temple, well over three thousand years old, has survived. The sculpture and reliefs carved into the pillars of the building tell a great deal about the Chavin people, especially how they appeared to worship cats. Carvings of men, women and even other animals have cat faces or cat tails. Possibly they believed that the cat was a representation of a god in animal form, and this is more easy to understand when it is remembered that in ancient Egypt, too, the cat was revered as a sacred animal. In recent years it has been suggested that some Egyptians set out across the Atlantic Ocean in boats made of papyrus. If it is true, it could explain how the earliest Peruvians had characteristics similar to those of the ancient Egyptians.

The second stage of Andean culture was the Paracas, from 400 B.C. to 400 A.D. These people came from further south towards Chile. They knew the craft of textile weaving and produced clothing and rugs that have seldom been improved upon in Europe or Asia. Once again the cat dominated their designs and patterns.

The third Peruvian stage was the Nazca culture which produced very skilled potters and sculptors. The Nazca people painted and decorated their wares in gay colours with crude but expressive designs indicating something of their way of life. The Nazca people declined when they were invaded by the Mochicas from the north.

The Mochicas were a much more warlike and more scientific people. They built roads, and constructed viaducts and aqueducts in the gorges of the Andes. They had a rigid class structure, in which the priests and the scientists were prominent. The Mochicas dominated civilization in South America from about 400 to 700 A.D. Their original ideas were later to be adopted and improved by the Incas. They depended very largely for their great building programmes on slave labour, usually native and primitive Indians from the plains or from as far away as Bolivia and Brazil. One structure they built – it must have taken thousands of men many years – was the Pyramid of the Sun, near Trujillo, which is said to contain more than 120,000,000 bricks, and it compares in size with the Great Pyramid at Giza in Egypt (*See* page 29).

In about 1000 A.D. the Tiahuanaco began to flourish in the plains south of Lake Titicaca, some 12,000 feet above sea-level, the world's highest lake. There, the Tiahuanaco city still stands, once a great religious centre like Chichen Itza. Huge structures tower over the plains, evidence

Stone of the Sun, an Aztec device for calculating the date, carved in 1479

of a vigorous and determined people. One building is particularly stark and impressive, the Gateway to the Sun, which is a doorway carved in a ten-foot block of stone with a highly-decorated frieze. The Tiahuanaco designs are found on metal, pottery and wood all over Peru, so at some time they must have been the ruling civilization. They were followed by the greatest of all Peruvian civilizations, the Incas (*See also* Chapter Forty-eight).

Meanwhile, in Central America, three other civilizations flourished in isolated regions at about the time of the Maya Classic Age. These were the Teotihuacans, whose city was built where modern Mexico City now stands, the Zapotecs of Oaxaca, and the Olmecs of Vera Cruz. They were all maize-cultivators, they all understood the same scientific and astronomical data, and apparently had much the same sort of religion. They differed, however, in art, language and customs.

Some of the sculpture is very vigorous and beautiful. Stone work and jade were especially fine, and so was their carving in porphyry. Again the cat faces intrude in the art of these civilizations.

The Teotihuacans built on a grand scale. One pyramid to the sun, some 700 feet square at the base and 200 feet high, has a temple on its summit. The stone panels of this temple, in particular, are a fantastic creation.

In the thirteenth century the Aztecs in Mexico and the Incas in Peru were beginning to make themselves felt among their more cultured neighbours, and before long they were to take over the best aspects of these civilizations and improve them to such an extent that they astonished the greedy Spaniards who discovered them in the sixteenth century and who, to the shame of all Christendom, destroyed them.

# Mediaeval Europe

The Vikings from Scandinavia had begun to raid and plunder their more immediate neighbours in the British Isles towards the end of the eighth century. In the ninth century they were severely defeated by Alfred the Great of England and Rhodri Mawr of Wales, but this did not stop them extending their raids further afield. They went to northern France, to Spain, to Morocco, to Majorca, landed in the south of France, sailed up the Rhone, and even sacked the Italian city of Pisa. They also marched through Russia down to the Black Sea.

In the eleventh century it was Canute, king of England, Denmark and Norway, who brought Scandinavia into the European orbit. He occupied parts of Poland, and other states bordering the Baltic Sea, and both Iceland and Sweden recognized his power over them. From his time on, the Scandinavian countries began to play their part in the development of Europe.

The Danish kings who followed Canute wielded considerable power and their influence reached into Germany. For about fifty years, c. 1180 to c. 1230, they also dominated the Baltic, but by the latter year King Waldemar II had been severely beaten by the Germans. The Swedes, meanwhile, had expanded eastwards, conquered Finland and established settlements in north-eastern Russia as far as Lake Ladoga.

The lands of Otto the Great of Germany had grown so extensive that he had had to give much of them to vassal dukes and bishops. But this led to serious quarrels between the empire and the Papacy. Popes had always appointed bishops and had invested them with the robes and other paraphernalia of office. Now the German kings wanted people of their own choice to succeed to vacant bishoprics. In 1073 Pope Gregory VII, an able and very determined man, seeing

Trade map of Europe showing the Vikings' routes of invasion from the 9th century onwards

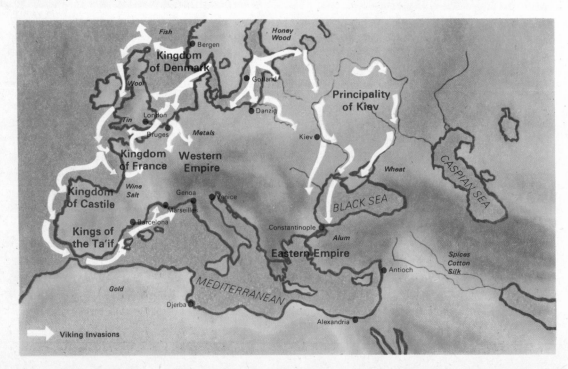

that the authority of Rome was in danger, announced that any bishop appointed anywhere in Europe must be invested by the Pope, and any king, prince or duke appointing and investing a bishop himself would be excommunicated from the Church. The king of Germany, Henry IV, defied the Pope and invested a bishop. He was promptly excommunicated, and as that sentence meant that the king's people would lose many privileges such as Christian burial, solemnization of marriage, etc., not many of Henry's subjects elected to support him. So he had to beg the Pope's forgiveness at Canossa in 1077.

In a few years, however, Henry again offended the Pope and was again excommunicated. This time he assembled an army, invaded Italy and captured Rome, driving the Pope into exile in the south.

This quarrel between the Papacy and the German kings racked the empire and Rome for years until in 1122 a compromise was reached. Rulers were allowed to keep feudal power over the bishops, that is to say, the bishops had to obey the laws of the country in which they lived in secular matters, but the Popes kept full spiritual power and retained the investiture rights. Thirty years later the quarrel opened up again when Frederick Barbarossa, the handsome and bold king of Germany from 1152 to 1190, decided to ignore the 1122 arrangement. He invaded northern Italy and entered Rome where he expelled the Pope and installed a new one. For a while it looked as if Frederick would rule the whole Christian Church, but the Italians rebelled against the harsh behaviour of his troops and defeated them in battle. Frederick confessed his wrongs to the real Pope, whose name was Alexander III, restored him to Rome and retired to Germany. He ruled well for the remainder of his reign, and

The Emperor Frederick Barbarossa was drowned during the Third Crusade

was drowned in 1190 while accompanying other leaders of the Third Crusade to the Holy Land.

Barbarossa's descendants continued to quarrel with the Popes. His grandson, Frederick II, who was king of Sicily, wanted to be Emperor of the Holy Roman Empire. Most of the German dukes and bishops were against this as he did not know much about Germany and its problems. The Pope, Innocent III, a wise and capable lawyer, supported Frederick's candidature. War followed and Frederick's party was successful, whereupon he was elected emperor.

Frederick II, however, quarrelled with later Popes. He was a strange man and few people really understood him. His gifts were such that to some he seemed of superhuman intellectual power, and to others he appeared insane. They called him 'Stupor Mundi', the Wonder of the World. Frederick wanted to bring all Italy into the empire and to subject the

Popes to his will. A new Latin empire was to dominate Europe, and Rome was to be its capital.

The Pope of the time, Gregory IX, resisted, and when Frederick marched through Italy and failed to take Rome, Papal forces and allies defeated him at Parma. His sons continued the struggle but without success. Eventually, the kingdom of Sicily was given a French prince, Charles, brother of Louis IX of France. This was not a wise move on the Pope's part for it encouraged France to be as aggressive as Germany had been. Moreover, the continual dabbling of the Popes in secular matters weakened their authority and they were later on treated as no better than vassals.

German attention, meanwhile, was focused eastwards and the kings, sometimes in co-operation with their vassal dukes, made inroads into Poland, Hungary and Bohemia (now known as Czechoslovakia), settling people there and fighting with the Slav people who had been there for centuries.

Those Vikings who had come to the Mediterranean to sack towns for plunder did not stay, to some extent because the climate was unsuitable. But after Canute had made them powerful in the eleventh century they began to take an interest in Italy and Sicily. Italy was then an assemblage of states which were not united and which had few aims in common. The south, for example, was much influenced by Islam, for Moslems had been in Sicily and the toe of Italy for centuries. The north, on the other hand, was under the influence of the Germans and the French. In the centre was Rome, the home of the Popes.

The Vikings who had settled in Normandy (called Normans, a shortened form of Norsemen) began to move into the Mediterranean area. Robert Guiscard,

St Louis IX of France built the Sainte Chapelle in Paris to house Christ's crown of thorns

a Norman chief, descended on southern Italy and captured the major ports of Taranto and Brindisi. By 1070 he was established there and soon came to terms with the Popes who believed they could use the Normans for the Crusades. In the north, the sea towns of Pisa, Genoa and Venice had already begun to build up vast wealth from Mediterranean trading, and while doing so wanted to remain completely independent of any power group. So they resisted all attempts at unification in Italy. As they were for centuries among the wealthiest communities in the whole peninsula, their opting out made unity impossible.

This lack of unity was in many ways damaging to Italy as a whole. The struggles between the empire and the Popes were more often than not fought out on Italian soil. Armies ravaged the fertile countryside in the northern and central parts. Rome itself changed hands

several times, and a few more priceless remains of antiquity were destroyed each time. Small states changed sides as it suited them. National loyalty meant nothing. Even the rich sea towns fought each other for a variety of trivial reasons and gained little. Had any powerful empire of determined warriors and crusaders like the early Moslems been active in the Mediterranean at the time, they could have overcome the whole peninsula and become very rich.

In this very unsettled condition Italy became the home of the great Renaissance of art and learning (*See* Chapter Forty-two). Rulers of small states vied with each other in the ownership of works of art and in the construction of buildings and civil engineering work, and so the artists and craftsmen were given a splendid stimulus to reach new heights of creative work. The growing financial strength of the commercial cities released resources for this art and building,

although the artists and builders themselves were by no means always well rewarded.

Although unification was out of the question, after the fall of Constantinople in 1453, Italy became a very important theatre of activity, for it was thereafter the sole fountainhead of the Christian Church, except for the Eastern Orthodox Church which Rome did not recognize. In Chapter Fifty-eight we shall see what happened to Italy.

In Chapter Twenty-nine you will remember that Spain and Portugal had been largely in the hands of the Moslems under the Omayyid caliphate. By the beginning of the eleventh century the Moslems still occupied the southern and eastern parts of Spain and some of Portugal. But the rule of the caliphs had begun to decay because of their incessant quarrelling with their kinsmen in Morocco. This was an opportunity for Christian armies to try to recover the peninsula. In the eleventh century Alfónso VI, king of León and Castile, a state in Spain, moved southwards into the Guadarrama mountain range and took Toledo, some seventy miles south of Madrid. Gradually, the Christians recovered the bulk of the peninsula, but it took centuries because the countryside is

Map showing the struggle to oust the Arabs from Spain and Portugal

for the most part not suitable for open warfare, and the Moslems were so determined to hang on to the country that they fought desperately for every mile. Sometimes they recaptured districts which had to be fought for again. And for many years, too, the kings of Aragon were involved in major struggles with France, which took up all their resources.

In 1340, Alfonso XI, king of Castile, defeated the Moslems in open battle on the River Salado, and drove them southwards. They retained but a fragment of their former dominion, the small state of Granada. They were not dislodged from this for another century and a half.

Alfonso was succeeded by Pedro the Cruel (1350–62), in whose reign a bitter civil war broke out. This lasted for years, right into the time of his successor Henry.

In Portugal, the wise King John (1385–1433), started to attack the Moslems in their own lands in North Africa. Raiders descended on the Moroccan coast and sacked the splendid towns and ports which were rich with centuries of accumulated plunder. The Portuguese, a nation of sailors toughened by the rigours of the Atlantic winds, proved almost invincible at sea. In 1415 John launched a combined land and sea attack on Ceuta, on the north

Alfonso XI led a Spanish army to victory against the Moslems on the River Salado in 1340

coast of Africa opposite Gibraltar. After a long siege the Portuguese captured it, establishing their first foothold on African soil. This was to be of immense value. Casablanca and Tangier were then captured, and this dominance of the North African coast was to help Portugal in its pioneering days of discovery.

In the time of Otto the Great of Germany, France was little more than a collection of states, duchies and counties. Large parts were held by the Normans. There were kings of France but for a long time the majority of people in France did not accept them. William of Normandy, who conquered England in 1066, certainly refused to accept the French king as his master. For four hundred years of French history, much of the time was taken up in fighting between the kings of England and France as to who should own what areas of land in France.

When Henry II of England came to the throne in 1154, he was already the landlord of vast domains in France, Anjou, Touraine, Maine, Aquitaine and Normandy. These were as large as (if not larger than) what remained under the kings of France. In 1180 the French throne passed to Philip Augustus, a shrewd and capable ruler who set out to make France united and strong. He determined to drive the English out of all those states so he began by playing the sons of Henry II against their father. Then, when John became king of England in 1199 and showed little interest in maintaining the extensive dominions in France, Philip attacked the English on several fronts at once. In a short campaign he won huge areas and captured several big towns.

Most of these acquisitions remained in French hands until the time of Edward III of England (1327–77). Philip's son, Louis VIII, extended French rule to the

south of France and in the reign of his son Louis IX, the French people began at last to feel a real sense of national identity.

This extraordinary king was only twelve when he succeeded. He grew up to be a man of gentle disposition, wise and scrupulously fair. He was devoted to religion and was filled with compassion for anyone less fortunate than himself. You would not think these qualities would stand him in good stead in a violent and warlike age, but as he was also courageous, daring and inspired, he turned out to be one of the greatest kings of French history. By the dignity of his manner and the generosity of his spirit he succeeded in wielding a degree of authority over his vassal dukes and counts that more violent people like Philip Augustus could never have done.

Louis introduced important reforms in France. Perhaps his best idea was the system whereby anyone, exalted or

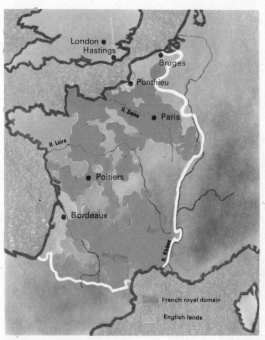

Map of France in 1328

On the next page: Joan of Arc attends the crowning of the Dauphin at Rheims

humble, could bring a grievance before him in person for settlement. To get this system to work he organized a government department with provincial agents whose job it was to carry out his wishes in these matters.

France was at peace for much of his reign and in that time flourished in many respects. It was an age of great architecture, cathedral building, road construction, and educational advancement. The University of Paris, already instituted, became a European centre for the study of philosophical subjects. Thinkers and writers of many countries assembled often in Paris for discussions which were to be regarded as very important in the development of learning in general.

Louis's successors were not so wise or gifted; and they were more aggressive. They quarrelled with the Popes, with their neighbours, and with England. In 1302 Pope Boniface VIII unwisely announced that Popes had full spiritual control over all kings and princes, which was the same as saying that they had authority over all acts of government. Philip IV of France objected to this and sent a detachment of troops to arrest the Pope. All Christendom was horrified. Boniface was released, but he died immediately. His successors bowed their heads to Philip and so became little more than subjects of the French crown. The Papal See was moved to Avignon in southern France, where it remained for seventy years.

The Popes finally returned to Rome in 1377 in the time of Gregory XI. When he died the next year Urban VI was elected by the usual system of votes cast by a conclave of cardinals. But the French refused to accept him and promptly elected Clement VII, and installed him at Avignon. There were now two Popes, a disgraceful situation, and the support for each among European princes was

about equal. This distressing state of affairs lasted several years and it severely damaged the prestige of the Church.

In 1412 agreement was reached when all parties accepted Martin V as Pope, in Rome. France, meanwhile, had endured a number of military defeats, at Crécy (1346), Poitiers (1356) and Agincourt (1415), all at the hands of the English. Henry V, the victor at Agincourt, forced the French to accept the Treaty of Troyes whereby he was to become king of France on the death of the French king, Charles VI. When Henry died in 1422, his baby son, Henry VI, became heir to both thrones. Henry V's brother, the Duke of Bedford, fought to maintain the gains and to begin with, succeeded. Then, in 1429, a young French country girl from Domrémy, Joan of Arc (Jeanne d'Arc), who believed she was sent by God to deliver France from the English conqueror, succeeded in persuading the eldest son of Charles VI, the Dauphin

Pope Boniface VIII was imprisoned by Philip IV of France for trying to exercise control there

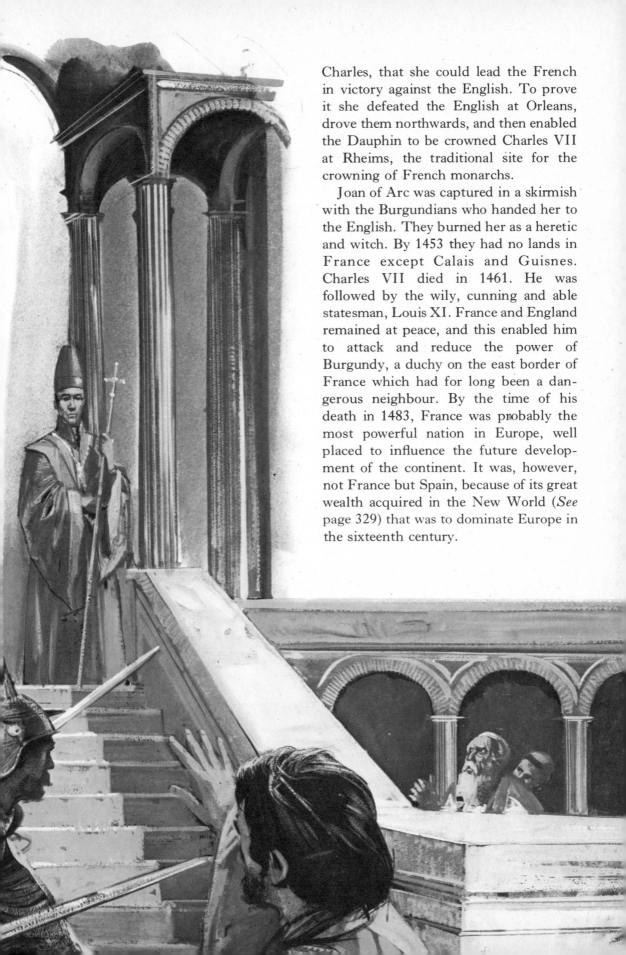

Charles, that she could lead the French in victory against the English. To prove it she defeated the English at Orleans, drove them northwards, and then enabled the Dauphin to be crowned Charles VII at Rheims, the traditional site for the crowning of French monarchs.

Joan of Arc was captured in a skirmish with the Burgundians who handed her to the English. They burned her as a heretic and witch. By 1453 they had no lands in France except Calais and Guisnes. Charles VII died in 1461. He was followed by the wily, cunning and able statesman, Louis XI. France and England remained at peace, and this enabled him to attack and reduce the power of Burgundy, a duchy on the east border of France which had for long been a dangerous neighbour. By the time of his death in 1483, France was probably the most powerful nation in Europe, well placed to influence the future development of the continent. It was, however, not France but Spain, because of its great wealth acquired in the New World (*See* page 329) that was to dominate Europe in the sixteenth century.

# European Society in the Middle Ages

The barbarian invasions of western Europe in the fifth and sixth centuries destroyed the unity of the Roman empire, and in doing so they also altered the structure of society itself. Under Rome even the small farmer or provincial government official enjoyed a measure of stability. Prices might rise, or towns might be attacked by wild tribes on the empire's borders, but behind the citizen was the power and majesty of Roman law and justice.

The barbarian invasions changed this, and for a long time to come the ordinary man was left to fend for himself. He could still make a living out of a small farm or vineyard, or as a weapon-manufacturer, or he could join one of the wandering bands of raiders who never settled down to a peaceful way of life. But he really needed more than this, for stability is always Civilized Man's ultimate goal. So out of the disorders of the time a new system of society – feudalism – developed.

When the barbarians overran a country the chief would apportion lands to the bravest of his commanders as a reward for services rendered. But there were dangers in this practice. A particularly aggressive commander might try to capture his neighbour's land and then, more powerful than before, turn on his chief and overthrow him. This, in fact, happened quite often.

Eventually, when the Franks began to build their empire in the sixth century, the kings modified the system by attaching conditions to the land gifts. A territory would be awarded to a commander or lord in usufruct (from the Latin: *usus* = use, *fruor* = I enjoy), which meant that the lord had full rights over the land provided he swore allegiance to the chief or king and fought for him

A mediaeval European castle with a village outside the walls. Villagers supplied the castle inhabitants with most requirements

one man to manage, so he divided the territory into smaller units, or estates, some of which were further sub-divided. This meant, in effect, that each lord owed his loyalty to the one immediately above him who held slightly more land, but there, too, was an inherent danger. If lord A wished to overthrow the king, he could demand the loyalty of all sub-divisions below him. The danger was increased when, after the time of Charlemagne, the lords were empowered to raise taxes on their own account and to forbid men from leaving their lands. By the end of the ninth century the lordships, whether dukedoms, marquessates, counties or baronies, were made hereditary, as were the estates that went with the titles. Only a strong king like Otto the Great of Germany (*See* page 215) or Louis IX of France (*See* page 247) could keep the lords under some sort of control.

This system, called the feudal system (from the Latin: *feudum* = fief; fief is land held in tenure), had spread to England by the time of the invasion of William, Duke of Normandy. But William modified it in a most effective way. All ranks in the system were compelled to swear allegiance to him first and to the lord immediately above them secondly. So if Lord *A* wanted to rebel, his tenants and sub-tenants were

whenever asked. The lord had to supply an army of men from his land, provide them with arms and other equipment, and feed them. What is more he was expected to give the king a share of the profits from the farms and industries on the land.

This did not eliminate the dangers of lords seizing power for themselves, but it certainly reduced them. The system of landholding in return for services or profit-sharing gradually extended. The original grants were often too large for

obliged to support the king. The chances of success of a rebellion were rendered even less likely by William's careful allotment of lands. He might give to Lord *A* ten thousand acres in England, but it would be split up into a number of small pieces, say, one part in Devonshire, one in Sussex, and one in Yorkshire. It would, therefore, be extremely difficult for Lord *A* to assemble his total military force in one place without either crossing land belonging to another lord who did not sympathize with him or actually having to meet the king himself in battle. This, of course, presumes that Lord *A's* tenants and sub-tenants were willing to risk breaking their oath of allegiance to the king, as well.

The feudal system enabled the Norman kings to keep a very tight hold on England after the Conquest in 1066.

But what of the people lower down the social scale? The feudal system provided the stability to grow crops and to trade that the ordinary man needed. But he had to pay for this by remaining subservient to the upper classes or lords. Neither a serf (a slave with few rights) nor a small-holding freeman ever had a chance to better himself. Under a generous lord — and there were few of them — serfs might become a little richer and so enjoy a few comforts such as fine clothes or a larger house. But whereas today a person from the humblest birth can, by hard work, become head of a big company, no such advance was possible under feudalism.

While it is tempting to decry this order of society, it needs to be recalled that European Man of the Middle Ages had really had to start again from the beginning after the collapse of Rome, and that compared with his contemporaries in Byzantium, Persia or China he was not very civilized.

Although the feudal system lasted for centuries in Europe, its effectiveness was limited to country districts, because it was based on land holding. In the early days this meant nearly all of a nation was run on feudal lines, for there were few towns. But once the Crusaders had begun their expeditions to the East, and a lively trade between East and West had resulted, the need for towns became more pressing. New industries evolved to cater for traders and travellers and these could not be accommodated in rural areas. The kings had to grant the new towns that grew up some form of self-government, as the feudal lords were not equipped to organize and run thriving city affairs. Merchants and craftsmen, however, were ready to run towns. Charters were granted to towns by

Markets and fairs were held regularly in the squares of many European towns in the Middle Ages. This one is in a Dutch town in the 15th century

favour of a king, and for a long time a city's most prized possession was its charter.

Naturally towns became more and more important in the life of a country for they acquired greater wealth and their prosperity was less affected by bad weather than were the seacoast estates whose wealth depended upon fields of corn or hillsides of cattle or sheep. Towns in particular, such as the famous Hanseatic towns in Germany and the Italian trading cities, assumed international importance.

Feudalism not only depended on land; it also depended on labour to maintain the system, especially the serf population, out of which the lords extracted much hard work in return for very little reward. As long as the serfs were loyal and peaceable, the landlords remained strong and influential, but when serfdom was more or less abolished in England soon after the Peasants' Revolt of 1381 feudalism decayed. In its place rose a mercantile society.

On the continent, however, feudalism persisted for many more years, and this inhibited the development of continental civilization and allowed the British to rise to the forefront of Europe. Indeed, the persistence of feudalism in France into the eighteenth century was one of the major causes of the French Revolution of 1789.

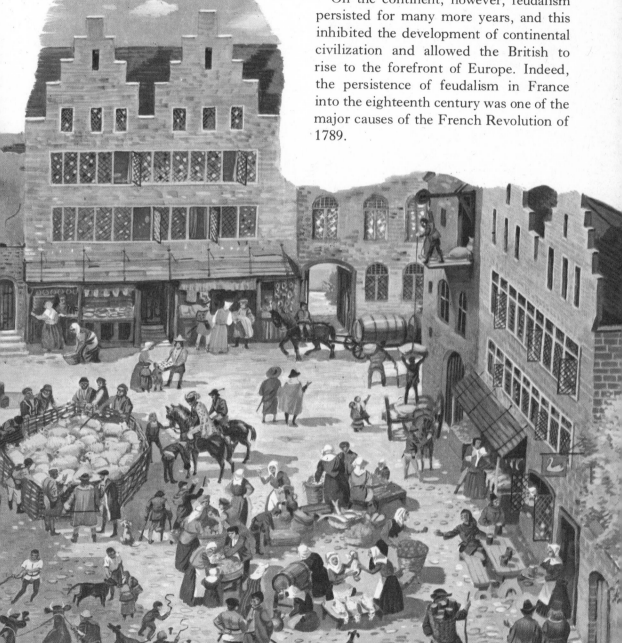

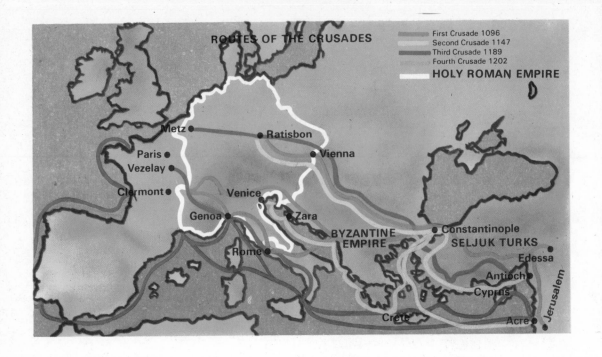

ROUTES OF THE CRUSADES

First Crusade 1096
Second Crusade 1147
Third Crusade 1189
Fourth Crusade 1202
HOLY ROMAN EMPIRE

Metz • • Ratisbon
Paris • • Vienna
Vezelay •
Clermont • Venice
Genoa • • Zara
Rome • BYZANTINE • Constantinople
EMPIRE SELJUK TURKS
• Edessa
Antioch •
Cyprus
Crete Acre • Jerusalem

# Islam and the Crusades

After about three hundred years of almost uninterrupted progress Islam, in the tenth century, relapsed for a while into stagnation, and its influence and power waned. Its culture remained strong and vigorous, as may be seen in the buildings of the time almost anywhere along the Mediterranean coastline, but its military strength and energy were sapped. There were fierce uprisings among the Arab and Turkish believers in the Islamic faith, and the now militant Christians moved in and took advantage of the disarray. Corsica, Sardinia, and part of Sicily fell into the hands of the Normans or French.

Meanwhile, Turkish tribes from central Russia had begun to infiltrate Islamic territories in the Near East and India. The Ghaznawids occupied what is now Pakistan and Afghanistan. In about 1000

they advanced into India and crossed the River Indus and headed for the Ganges. The towns of Lahore and Peshawar fell and the Moslem faith replaced the Hindu faith. This laid the foundations for the divisions between Hindu and Moslem that ever after affected the unity and peace of India, and which have now only been partially smoothed over by the creation of the two states, India and Pakistan.

Another more terrifying Turkish tribe, the Seljuks, came down from Russia in hordes and attacked Persia and the Ghaznawid dominions and very swiftly overran them. Baghdad was captured and the Turkish leader Tughril seized power as the caliph, or sultan, as he called himself. Tughril advanced into Armenia and his successors chipped away the Syrian cities and plains. By about 1050 the

Seljuks were in control of land stretching from western Asia Minor to the Ganges.

West of the Mediterranean the Moroccan Moslems expanded southwards and took Islam right into the heart of Africa. They also invaded Spain and Portugal and crushed several European armies sent against them. They captured Seville, Saragossa and Valencia in Spain and almost reached the Pyrenees.

Christian Europe, however, was determined not to allow the advances of the Turks to continue so successfully. The cruelty practised on the Christian pilgrims who journeyed to the Holy Land of Palestine by the Turks drove the European princes and kings to forge alliances and to make war. In 1095 the Pope, Urban II, invited the Christian leaders to bury their differences, raise a huge composite army, and set out for the East to recover the Holy Land from the Turks. Crusaders, led by Peter the Hermit, a popular wandering preacher, left for the Holy Land, but perished in Asia Minor. Then Godfrey of Bouillon, Duke of Lorraine, set out with an army. This was the First Crusade, and to show that the campaign was being waged on an international and Christian basis, all the knights and soldiers wore a red cross on their uniforms. The leaders were sons of kings or princes, or dukes of small states, and besides Godfrey these included Robert, Duke of Normandy, the eldest son of William the Conqueror, king of England.

The great army marched eastwards and arrived in Constantinople where it was given a very cold welcome by the Byzantines. The cultivated Byzantines distrusted the western Europeans, and despised their tough and not very attractive behaviour. The western Europeans, for their part, derided the luxurious and oriental style of living they found in what was supposed to be a bastion of Christendom. In this mutual antagonism were nurtured the seeds of future disaster.

The crusaders pressed on through Asia Minor and encountered surprisingly little resistance from the Seljuks whose great burst of energy seemed to have evaporated. In 1099 the crusaders captured Jerusalem. Baldwin, count of Flanders, was put on the throne as king of Jerusalem (1100–1118). It was a great triumph for Christendom. Several small

One of the greatest figures in Moslem history, the Sultan Saladin, wearing battle dress

Christian provinces were founded in Asia Minor, including states centred at Edessa, Antioch and Damascus.

Within fifty years, however, Islam was revived, and the Europeans were driven out of some of these states and from Edessa, in 1144. This prompted the proclamation of the Second Crusade, by Pope Eugenius III in 1145. This crusade began in 1147 and was led by Louis VII of France and Conrad III of the Holy Roman Empire, but it only got as far as Damascus where in 1149 it was beaten off by the Moslems.

Islam was on the march again. In 1171, Saladin, a tough, brilliant, but kind and generous soldier from Iraq, who had been appointed viceroy of Egypt by the caliph, overthrew his master and seized

power. He aimed to build up a new Moslem empire, united and strong, well able to resist the onslaughts of western Europeans and the Byzantines. In the space of a few years he conquered Egypt, Palestine, Syria, Libya and part of Asia Minor. In 1187 he captured Jerusalem.

In 1189 the rulers in western Europe got together to form a Third Crusade, the guiding light of which was Richard I of England. Together with Philip Augustus, king of France, Richard mustered a large army, bleeding England by taxation to pay for it. In 1191 the crusaders captured Acre, but on the way to Jerusalem the two leaders fell out. Philip returned to France and Richard abandoned the campaign and set out on his return journey, during which he was captured and held to ransom (*See* page 291). But before leaving the Holy Land Richard had come to terms with Saladin. The cultured Moslem leader, unlike the savage Seljuks, allowed the Christians to continue to visit the Holy City, and other religious shrines were unmolested. This was typical of Saladin's generosity.

There were five more crusades: the Fourth, from 1202–1204, was particularly catastrophic for Christendom. The leaders of western Europe started off with good intentions, that is, to recapture the Holy Land, and they were backed financially by the bankers from Italian cities like Venice and Genoa, which had become immensely prosperous owing to increasing trade in the Mediterranean. The crusaders sailed towards Constantinople on the first leg of their journey. But on the way they gave up the idea of advancing into Moslem territory. Instead, for motives which are not really clear, they turned on Constantinople itself, captured

After the capture of Acre, Richard I of England marched on Jerusalem, but decided not to attack the Holy City it and looted its precious buildings. Then for the next fifty years western Europeans established and administered the Latin empire, what they regarded as a new Roman empire in the East.

The Italian cities benefited enormously from this turn of events, for it enabled them to move into the Aegean Sea area and set up new ports and trading stations. Though they did not retain these for very long, it was long enough for them to get very rich indeed and put the profits into enterprises elsewhere. In the fourteenth century, for example, the Italians were able to lend money on a large scale to European leaders who had wars to wage. One who borrowed extensively – and incidentally bankrupted the lender – was Edward III of England, who claimed the throne of France and set out to obtain it by force (*See* page 293).

Byzantium eventually recovered its lost capital, Constantinople, in 1261 and overthrew the Latin empire, and the emperor returned to power. But the fruitless war made it in the long run easier for the Turks and Moslems to move into Europe. All the same, Islam had sustained severe damage, and its strength in the Near East was not what it had been. When the Moslems, in the early years of the thirteenth century, were faced with the threat of the armies of Genghis Khan, Islam could not rise to overcome the invaders. (*See* page 266.)

The last crusades were indecisive and, at the end of this long series of Holy Wars, the Holy Land still remained in the hands of the Moslems. But in other respects the wars proved important in the development of European civilization. To begin with, trade expanded for the Italian cities and other merchandising centres and so brought a lot of wealth to western Europe which had not been very prosperous before. The continuing antagonism

between Christianity and Islam affected greatly the prices of goods obtained from the Far East for these had to be transported on the overland routes across Moslem and Turkish territory. Naturally, the goods were taxed on the way, and when they arrived in European markets they were expensive indeed. So Europeans began to seek new markets and new ways to get to the old-established trading centres in the Far East.

The leaders of the Fourth Crusade (1202–4) abandoned their journey to the Holy Land and turned against Constantinople, for political reasons, and sacked it

# Genghis Khan
# and the East

The Far East in the twelfth century was as unsettled as anywhere in Europe and the Near East. While the Sung dynasty in China continued to nurture the ancient and highly developed Chinese civilization, various races on the borders of China were in continual turmoil, thus endangering the peace of the Sung. On one occasion, after an emperor had employed one of these tribes, the Kin, to help him deal with other tribes, the Kin turned on the Sung empire and overran a large part of it. They left only after a long period, and then set up an empire of their own in the Peking province. The Kin absorbed Chinese culture as completely as previous invaders of China had done. Meanwhile, the Sung settled down again, strengthened their defences, and continued the development of their arts and industries.

Suddenly, early in the thirteenth century, China was attacked by Genghis Khan, one of the greatest warriors and conquerors of history.

Genghis Khan, whose Mongol name was Temujine, was born in 1162, near Lake Baikal in Mongolia. His father, a Mongol chieftain, died when he was young and so Temujine had a hard life in his youth; it was no less severe in his early manhood. Succeeding to his father's

Genghis Khan (1162–1227), conqueror of most of Asia in the early 13th century, made plans for organizing his huge domains into a permanent empire. Unfortunately, he died before they could be put into effect.
On the following page, Genghis Khan's fierce warriors breach the almost impregnable Great Wall of China in their raids eastwards

chieftainship, he was forever fighting with a variety of neighbours, all of whom wanted to be the leading Mongol chief. Temujine aspired higher than that. He envisaged no less than a united and well-disciplined Mongol army which would invade all parts of the world.

By the beginning of the thirteenth century, Temujine, who was king or 'khan' of the Mongols and who had added the name Genghis, which means 'Lord Absolute', was ready to move beyond the borders of Mongolia. Out of its scattered and fractious tribes he had moulded a well-organized and powerful military force. This consisted almost entirely of cavalry, brave men who were extraordinarily skilled on horseback and who could manoeuvre with astonishing speed. It was this speed, more than anything else, that frightened the Europeans – and the Moslems, too, who were no strangers to the skill of fast riding.

Genghis Khan launched his first attack on China in 1206. Marshalling his fierce warriors in their cavalry squadrons, he addressed them saying: 'The emperors of China have done much injury to our ancestors and to my relatives. Now the great God assures me that the victory will be mine. In this kingdom of China he gives me the opportunity and the power to vindicate my ancestors.' (Genghis Khan's relatives were the rulers of the Turkish peoples along the great central Russian belt from the Black Sea to Mongolia.)

The rulers were quite unprepared for Genghis Khan's onslaught, and the Great

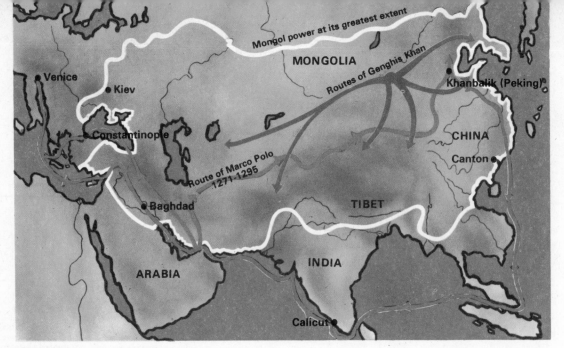

Map of Genghis Khan's empire

Wall of China was breached in three places. Through these openings the Mongolian chief poured three armies and by 1217 all northern China was in his hands.

The tale of his conquest spread quickly throughout the world. Some of the Moslem leaders in the Near East refused to believe it until one of Genghis Khan's ambassadors showed them a superb jewel that was known to have belonged to the Kin emperor.

Genghis Khan left the completion of the conquest of China to an able lieutenant, Mukhuli, and gave him full military authority. This enabled him to embark on his next adventure – the invasion of Khwarezm, an Islamic dominion embracing north-western India, eastern Persia and Afghanistan. In three years he conquered that area and captured its principal cities, Bokhara and Samarkand. Genghis Khan agreed not to plunder the latter, a most beautiful town with many splendid buildings, on payment of a tribute of two hundred thousand pieces of gold. But several thousand inhabitants, mainly skilled artists, writers and craftsmen, were deported and sent to work in Mongolia, in northern China and in northern Russia. China and Mongolia were thus brought closer to the more westerly civilizations.

By 1225 Genghis Khan was master of all Asia, except for India and the Sung empire, but even in those places his power was such that their rulers bowed to his wishes in many respects. His empire now stretched from Persia to Peking, from Siberia to the Indus, and he is said to have admitted that it would take two years to travel across his domain from one end to the other.

In 1227 the great Mongol leader, who was by no means as savage or as barbarous as one might suppose, was taken ill while on a journey of inspection in China, and he died in the province of Shan-Si. He was succeeded by his son, Ogdai, whose unenviable task it was to organize the vast territory left in his care. It seems that his father had worked out some ideas of how to organize the empire, and these were remarkably far-seeing and practical.

Ogdai was an insignificant man who was far too fond of wine; some of the time he was quite unconscious from drinking. Genghis Khan's close friend, the Chinese statesman Ye-le-tchutsai, brought to the Mongol empire many benefits of Chinese civilization. Taxation was based on a percentage of livestock or land produce. Irrigation was improved in dry or desert areas. Wells were sunk along the main highways at regular intervals. A system of relays of horses for postal services throughout the empire was established, and so anticipated by two hundred or more years the introduction of a similar system in England by Richard III. The capital of the empire, Karakorm, was enlarged.

Ogdai, meanwhile, tried to reform himself, and also busied himself with military expeditions. He advanced through the wild wastes of Russia and reached Moscow, which was then not much more than a small town. He moved further westwards into Europe itself and overran Poland, Rumania, and Hungary. All Europe waited to see if he would cross the Danube and surge into Germany and France.

But Ogdai died in 1241, and almost at once his armies began to recede back towards Russia where they took up positions along the Volga. We do not know why this happened. Perhaps the lines of communication were too far extended for safety, and certainly there was trouble of one sort or another brewing at home.

For the next twenty years the picture of Mongol dominion is not clear. The children and grandchildren of Genghis Khan engaged in ceaseless wars with one another. The territories in the West paid less and less attention to the government in Mongolia. Then Khubilai Khan, one of Genghis Khan's grandsons, set himself up in Peking as king and swiftly adopted all the outlook and trappings of a Chinese

Khubilai Khan, grandson of Genghis Khan, was a great ruler

emperor. Chinese writing was learned and used by his staff, he adopted Buddhism as his faith, and Chinese rites were followed at court.

Some time after 1250 Khubilai Khan invaded Sung China and in a long drawn-out campaign conquered the whole empire. He then became emperor there in 1260 and founded the Mongol Yuan dynasty. He ruled the whole of China as well as the other Mongol territories which stretched from Russia to the China Sea. But just like the other invaders of China, he soon became more Chinese than the Chinese. His court was filled with the best educated Chinese servants and courtiers he could find. The splendour and richness of the buildings, the diversity of industry and craft, the wealth of the markets and shopkeepers, all made a great impression on the famous Venetian traveller and merchant, Marco Polo, who visited the court of Khubilai Khan at Peking in 1275.

Khubilai Khan died in 1291. Already the extensive Mongol empire was disintegrating, for the distances were too great for the emperor to maintain order throughout. There were not enough deep-seated and native traditions to make Mongol rule attractive. The Turks in the western part of the empire had little in common with Khubilai Khan, who had become a natural successor to the Chinese rulers.

Although the Mongols reached Hungary and Poland and then turned back, the effect of their invasions was permanent. The great wealth of China and its astonishing advances in civilization were, for the first time, properly appreciated by the Western world. Hitherto, first Persia, then Parthia, then Persia again and finally Islam, had either blocked or restricted intercourse between China and the West. The trade routes had been extremely hazardous. Although the Romans had been aware of the Far Eastern empire and had bought great quantities of Chinese silk and other goods, very little of the nature of Chinese civilization had been understood. Now the enterprising merchants of the West saw opened to them a whole new realm for trade and business, and before the thirteenth century was over Europeans had begun trading on Chinese soil.

This peaceful intercourse between western Europe and China posed a dangerous threat to the Islamic nations who, at this time, were in one of their periods of decline (*See* Chapter Thirty-eight).

Although the great Mongol empire fell apart soon after the death of Khubilai Khan, many parts of it remained in the hands of descendants of Genghis Khan. But there were few points of common interest with which to cement the very different peoples together, and for about

Marco Polo's visit to Khubilai Khan helped to improve communications between China and Europe, and new trading opportunities resulted

eighty years the khanates created by Genghis Khan pursued their own ways with varying fortunes. The khanate of Jagatai, for example, failed to conquer India, and the khanate of Jiji held on to its valuable Russian lands only with the greatest difficulty.

Then, in 1369, Timurlaine, a descendant of Genghis Khan, who was born in 1336 in what is now Turkestan, seized power there and had himself declared ruler at its capital, the splendid city of Samarkand. He had already conceived the idea of rebuilding his ancestor's empire.

Timurlaine constructed a large, highly mobile army, welding it into a great fighting force by the sheer magnetism of his character and the ease with which he won men's hearts. With this army he launched out on a path of conquest that was to stand comparison with Genghis Khan's. Persia and central Asia fell. Then he stormed into Russian territory, reaching Moscow which already lay in ruins as a result of the attentions of an earlier conqueror. He attacked the Ottoman Turks in Syria and then marched into India in 1398, where he captured Delhi.

Posing as the defender of the orthodox Islamic faith (he was almost certainly an unbeliever), he cut down his enemies in huge numbers. At Ispahan in Persia he piled up the skulls of some 70,000 victims in mounds all round the city walls.

In 1402 Timurlaine defeated the Ottomans again under Bayazid II at Ankara which gave the crumbling Byzantine empire a brief respite from the fate which was ultimately to engulf it. Soon afterwards Timurlaine began preparations for an invasion of China, but he died in 1405 before he could set out.

At once his loosely assembled empire broke up, but his name had become famous throughout Europe and Asia. And

Timurlaine, descendant of Genghis Khan, attempted to rebuild the huge empire of his ancestor. To some extent he succeeded, but his dominions broke up soon after his death

in the sixteenth century a descendant of his, Babur, was to found the great Mogul empire in India.

The death of Timurlaine, and the decline of his power gave Islam the chance to move forwards towards the splendid age in which it became the dominant power in the Near East.

# The End of Byzantium

By the end of the tenth century the Byzantines, under the emperor, Basil II, occupied nearly as much territory as Justinian had four or more centuries earlier. Islam was weak near the borders of the empire and Byzantine influence was felt even in the Fertile Crescent itself. The empire had succeeded in confining the Bulgarian raiders within their own lands and also in controlling the Arab pirates off the coasts.

Internally, Byzantium enjoyed a measure of sound and stable government. The monarchy had become hereditary

Timurlaine defeated and captured the Ottoman sultan, Bayazid II, at Ankara in 1402

and the emperors were surrounded by a military splendour and protocol that would have pleased Diocletian and Constantine I. This stability brought about an expansion of trade. But most of the wealth found its way into the hands of the few, emperor and court, nobles and merchants, generals, and admirals of the fleet.

In the next century, however, the Byzantines were attacked by the Seljuk Turks, driven out of the Fertile Crescent, and left only with Greece and part of Asia Minor. It was then that the pilgrims from Europe first met with the harsh cruelty of the Seljuks and, since the Byzantines were not strong enough to control the Seljuks, they turned to western European princes for help. The Byzantine emperor, Alexius, sought help from Pope Urban II in 1095. Thus arose the crusades, as we saw on page 257.

Constantine XI. The Christian Roman empire, from the first to the last Constantine, lasted about 1,100 years

The thirteenth and fourteenth centuries were, so far as Byzantium was concerned, one long period of fighting, against an endless stream of outside combatants – Bulgarians, Italians and Turks – and also of civil strife. Emperors were elected and then dethroned with considerable frequency. Occasionally strong rulers like Michael VIII and Manuel II restored the empire to a semblance of unity and peace. But the raids, the slackening off of investment by foreigners, and the increasing torpor of the ruling classes, all undermined the very fabric of Byzantine society. Unwilling to advance out of a rut of tradition, the Byzantines seemed to stand still while the rest of the world passed them by. For centuries the emperors managed to preserve the city of Constantinople from significant harm, but the day of reckoning was close at hand.

At the end of the fourteenth century the great Ottoman Sultan Bayazid II chipped away at some of the remaining Byzantine possessions in Europe, Bulgaria, and northern and central Greece. Then, in 1402, he was defeated and taken prisoner by Timurlaine at Ankara (*See* page 270), and this gave Byzantium a respite from the attacks of the Turks.

No sooner had Timurlaine died, however, than his extensive but ill-organized empire disintegrated. At once the Ottoman Turks regenerated their armies and continued attacking the Byzantines. By 1453 the Sultan Mahomet II was ready to deliver the final assault on Christian Constantinople.

For eight weeks, more than one hundred Ottoman cannons, ranged around the hitherto impregnable fortress, pounded the city walls and temples, bringing fearful slaughter and damage. Then, at the end of May, the Emperor Constantine XI was killed. Almost immediately his generals agreed to surrender and the great city fell. The Byzantine empire was at an end.

Miniature from an 11th century manuscript showing the Emperor Nicephorus III Botaniates standing between St John and the Archangel Michael

A small wooden casket covered with beaten gold and set with gems and enamels. Pepin of Aquitaine presented this reliquary to the Abbey of Conques in the 9th century ($7\frac{1}{4} \times 7\frac{1}{4} \times 3\frac{1}{2}''$)

What had enabled this empire to last so long against so many attacks? What was the measure of Byzantine contribution to world civilization? First, the Byzantines never abandoned the tradition of Imperial rule and power. Nor did they for once waver in their belief in Christianity as the only true religion. Secondly, when all around them the fruits of Greek and Roman learning were being engulfed by the overwhelming barbarian forces they preserved and embellished the rich cultural heritage bequeathed them.

Among their invaluable literary achievements were the copies they made of early Greek and Roman books, plays, philosophical writings and scientific treatises. They also produced original works themselves, and spread these throughout their territories and further afield when the opportunity arose. In art they excelled in painting and in mosaic illustration, as you can see from the pictures. They built the most splendid cathedrals, libraries, aqueducts, public places of entertainment, offices and palaces. Their skills combined the best of the Oriental and the Western worlds, and when the great city of Constantinople fell, the Byzantines fled in droves to the West where they played a vital part in the Renaissance (*See* page 276).

The Beresford Hope Cross, 9th century. The colourful inlays of enamel were a favourite form of decoration in Byzantine precious objects

5th century mosaic from Santa Maria Maggiore, Rome, of Abraham receiving angels (above) and (below) his wife, Sarah, preparing cakes for them. It is the story of God's promise to give him and his wife a son

# Islam and the Ottomans

At the time when Genghis Khan was leading his invincible horsemen across Asia (1206–1225) Islam was in the throes of one of its periods of decline. The Moslem Turks had sustained severe defeats at the hands of Christian Europeans, not only in the West but also in the Near East in Asia Minor and Syria. Thus the Turks were unable to resist the great Mongol chief, except in India where, most probably, the warm climate proved too much for the Mongols who were used to the Russian cold.

The Moslem Turks lay quiet for some years, but towards the end of the thirteenth century, when it was clear that Khubilai Khan's vast empire could not remain intact, they began once more to revive the missionary spirit of Islam which carried them along so swiftly in conquest.

They overran India between the Indus and the Ganges Rivers. But in doing so they severely damaged the ancient Indian way of life. Agriculture and tillage had been carefully pursued by the Indians even after they had ceased to be a great empire under Asoka and Harsha, and India was a vast area of small village farming communities. The Turks devastated the farms and turned the fields into grassland for their horses. For the Indians, with so long a heritage of civilization, times were indeed hard, and they were not to be relieved until the sixteenth century when Babur, the first of the great Mogul emperors, set up an empire that lasted down to the middle of the eighteenth century.

The Moslem Turks also spread the Islamic faith to south-eastern Asia including part of Indonesia. But Islam's greatest achievement at this time was the foundation of the Ottoman empire.

The Seljuks were unable to resist Genghis Khan, but when the iron hand of his rule was removed after his death, another Moslem branch in Asia Minor rose up and assumed the leadership of all Moslems in the sub-continent. Steadily, over the years, they crushed all opposition and also won victories against the Byzantines, establishing their first territorial gains in Europe. This was in the time of their Sultan, Orkhan (1326–59), who is credited with remodelling the Turkish army and building it into a superb fighting force. Orkhan was succeeded by Muradh I, who ruled for thirty years (1359–89), and founded what is called the Ottoman empire, named after Orkhan's father, Othman I (1299–1326).

Muradh was a dashing and successful commander in the field. He was also a skilful negotiator and wherever possible

Map showing the growth of the Ottoman empire from 1350–1700

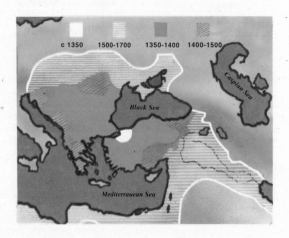

c 1350   1500-1700   1350-1400   1400-1500

Caspian Sea

Black Sea

Mediterranean Sea

Mahomet II, the Ottoman sultan who captured Constantinople in 1453

followed by his remarkable son, Bayazid, who continued making inroads into Europe. Bayazid conquered much of Greece and threatened Constantinople itself, but he was called back to Asia Minor to meet the advance of Timurlaine.

Timurlaine invaded Asia Minor on behalf of his ally the emir of Sivas, who had been attacked by the Ottomans. At Ankara, in 1402, Timurlaine utterly defeated Bayazid, destroyed his army and took him prisoner; Bayazid died within a few weeks. Asia Minor was ravaged and then annexed, and Ottoman power was eclipsed.

Bayazid's successor, Mahomet I, agreed to reign in peace in what was left of the Ottoman dominions, but in 1421, his successor, Muradh II (1421–1451), renewed the war against the Byzantines. Timurlaine's empire had disintegrated when the great chieftain died in 1405, and so posed no danger. Muradh reoccupied Greece and part of Bulgaria, and brought his forces to within a few miles of the Bosphorus. Two years after he died, his successor, Mahomet II, captured Constantinople itself and so brought the Byzantine empire to an end, more than a thousand years after its creation.

The capture of Constantinople was one of the most important events in history. Thereafter, for nearly five hundred years, the Ottoman Turks dominated the Near East and the eastern Mediterranean. They were not dislodged until the end of the First World War in 1918.

It was ironic that the captor of Constantinople should be called Mahomet, the name of the prophet whose teachings were the basis of Islam, and that the emperor of the city, killed in the siege, should be called Constantine, the name of the Roman emperor who founded the city and who made Christianity the religion of Rome.

satisfied his territorial ambitions by discussion rather than war. In his time the Ottomans extended their hold in Europe. Adrianople and Salonika, two important Byzantine cities, were captured and Constantinople itself was more than once endangered. So the emperor decided to negotiate with Muradh and recognize him as overlord.

Muradh was killed when the Serbians defeated the Turks in a battle, and was

# The Renaissance in Europe

In the fourteenth, fifteenth and sixteenth centuries A.D. there occurred in Europe a marked upsurge of artistic achievement and a great revival in learning. It came about at a time when the nations of Europe were beginning to find their roles in civilization, when men began to rediscover the ancient Greek and Roman ideas and culture that had made classical days so exciting and adventurous. This upsurge came to be called the European Renaissance, and it began in Italy.

Illuminated page from the breviary of the Duke of Bedford (regent for the English crown in France in the 15th century) showing the death of St Edward the Confessor

The rich literature and thought of Greece and Rome had been submerged in the West by the barbarian invasions. Here and there, chiefly in Irish monasteries, scholars copied out many texts of the works of these ancient writers, but because their lives were devoted to the service of God they tended to ignore or give scant treatment to any manuscripts that were not by Christian writers or which did not fall in with Christian ideas. The philosophers like Plato, Aristotle, Lucretius and Seneca were considered pagan and so likely to undermine Christian doctrines. In time much of this literature disappeared.

Then, in the fourteenth century, when the Roman Catholic Church itself was bitterly rent by what is called the Great Schism, when there were two Popes reigning at one time, men of learning became increasingly sceptical of the faith as it was being practised and they looked about for support for their ideas. They found them in the ancient manuscripts copied out and stored in the monasteries. As Latin was the language of the Church they had little difficulty in translating the classical works, and Greek scholars from Byzantium helped with the Greek renderings. To their delight they unearthed precedents for their ideas. They discovered that the ancient Greeks and Romans had believed above all in the dignity of man, unlike the mediaeval Christians who regarded life on earth as but a step to the next life.

These men of learning came to be known as humanists. They believed that

One of 62 existing self-portraits of the Dutch painter Rembrandt van Rijn (1606–1669)

their ideas were perfectly in harmony with the essential teachings of Christ, and they were supported by large sectors of the Church. Only the hierarchy, the bishops and their courts, which had everything to lose by allowing the new ideas to spread, organized opposition to the new humanism. After the fall of Constantinople in 1453 (*See* page 272) many more Byzantine scholars came to western Europe, and they brought with them a great variety of ancient texts. One of the most important was the New Testament in Greek, and when it was translated it was found that Christ's teachings were very far removed from the interpretation placed on them by the Church for so long.

These translations and learned works on other subjects, including science and astronomy, were publicized all over Europe by means of the recent introduction of printing into Europe (in about 1440). Soon, printed books were available to literate people, although they were not cheap. These were increasingly published in the languages of the countries in which they were sold. The relatively small percentage of people who hitherto had been able to read at all was now increased by leaps and bounds. Original works of philosophy, adventure and history were published.

There is not room to mention more than a few of the very famous literary people of the Renaissance period. Among these were Rabelais the French physician, who wrote *Gargantua*, Cervantes the Spanish knight who lost an arm at Lepanto (*See* page 329) and wrote *Don Quixote,* Machiavelli the Italian diplomat whose *Il Principe* (The Prince) is a brilliant discourse on statecraft, Camoëns, the Portuguese poet who immortalized the voyages of Vasco da Gama (*See* page 283) in the *Lusiads,* Sir Thomas More, the English Lord Chancellor who wrote *Utopia.* Shakespeare, the greatest playwright-poet of all time, though writing as late as the seventeenth century, is regarded as the leading figure of the English Renaissance. It is not easy now in an age of mass communication to appreciate what a marvellous thing it was to be able to read these and many other works for the first time in print rather than in hand-written manuscripts.

Along with this great revival of learning and writing there was a most splendid flourishing of art in all its forms – painting, drawing, sculpture, architecture. Again this revival began in Italy. Up to the fourteenth century western European

St Francis renouncing his inheritance – a fresco from the immensely influential School of Giotto

art was stiff and formal, with little thought given to the three-dimensional aspect or life-like representation. Then the Italian painter Giotto began to paint in natural colours and form and so opened the world of painting to the wonderful representativeness that characterized Renaissance pictures. For three or more centuries the Italians, whether Florentine, Venetian, Tuscan or Roman, produced a stream of artists of genius. Brunelleschi, the architect, rediscovered and developed the principles of the architect Vitruvius

St Peter's, Rome – Michaelangelo's magnificent concept of the baroque style in which all the design elements are merged into a unified whole. The brilliant sculptor, Bernini, designed the vast square and enclosing colonnade

who lived and worked in the reign of Augustus (*See* page 180). One of his greatest emulators was Palladio who in turn influenced England's Inigo Jones. The painting and sculpture of Leonardo da Vinci and Michaelangelo is probably the most magnificent in the world, though scarcely less exquisite was the work of such artists as Fra Filippo Lippi, Donatello, Botticelli, Titian, and Raphael. Leonardo and Michaelangelo, moreover, were also architects, scientists, inventors and poets, and have probably never been equalled for many-sided genius, except perhaps by Isambard Kingdom Brunel in nineteenth century England.

Outside of Italy there was no shortage

of men of genius; the Dutch produced one of the finest schools of art, and among the most notable painters was Rembrandt. Spanish painters included El Greco and Velasquez, while Dürer and Holbein represented Germany.

The revival of learning and the renaissance in art were accompanied by a new enthusiasm for science, especially experimental science. This was perhaps the most far-reaching aspect of the age. For centuries scientific experimentation and investigation had been discouraged, even stifled, by the Church, largely through fear and ignorance. Roger Bacon the English friar who discovered the explosive properties of gunpowder and interested himself in many other scientific things, was prohibited from continuing his experiments by the Pope at the request of frightened monks. Gunpowder proved decisive in the making of the new nation states, for if the monarch monopolized it (as Henry VII of England did) he could control all sources of rebellion. Even when Copernicus the Polish astronomer suggested that the earth moved round the sun and was global in shape the Church threatened his life and those of others who dared to repeat such things. One very great mathematician and astronomer, Galileo Galilei, actually proved Copernicus was right, but recanted his discoveries when the Church accused him of heresy.

This new spirit of enquiry embraced a variety of scientific subjects such as astronomy, chemistry, physics, biology, anatomy and medicine. Plants and animals were examined, grouped and written about. Vesalius dissected an entire human body, despite severe Church objections on the grounds that the human body is sacred after death, and drew up a complete series of anatomical drawings. This led to explanations for a number of

Galileo Galilei (1564–1642). As the first man to use the telescope to study the skies, he proved that the earth revolves around the sun

human functions, ailments and deformities and it opened up a new era in surgery and medicine. Alchemists continued to try to convert base metals to gold, but more advanced chemists showed that this was in fact chemically impossible.

One prominent feature of the Renaissance was a new freedom for men, a liberation of the spirit and the mind expressed in thought, writing, painting and building. This was a breakaway from the narrow and confined intellectual disciplines of the dominant Church, although it was by no means anti-religious. Indeed, the very best of the painting was invariably representative of subjects from the Scriptures or from Christian tradition. Above all, the Renaissance was the beginning of a stage of progress in the development of mankind which now seems to be almost limitless in regard to the possibilities of the future.

On the next page are examples of Leonardo da Vinci's work – a self-portrait as an old man, a giant crossbow operated by a treadmill, studies of the lifting power of a wing, a carriage equipped with flailing scythes, and his painting the 'Virgin of the Rocks'

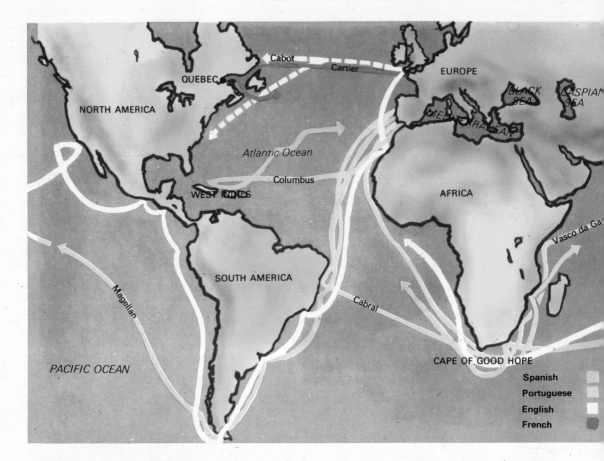

Spanish
Portuguese
English
French

# The Age of Discovery

By the beginning of the fifteenth century the Ottoman empire was so strong that it controlled the great part of intercourse between western European countries and the Far East with its great riches. The Ottomans allowed trade between East and West to continue, but in doing so exacted stiff taxes on goods in transit. These charges were so high in so many cases that the products, when they were sold in Venice or in other trading cities in western Europe, were many times the price originally paid in the Far East. This particularly applied to spices which the West needed both in quantity and variety, to preserve food and to help disguise the taste of meat and other things which

suffered from long storage. The Ottomans also ran lucrative businesses themselves, taking advantage of the control they exercised over the overland caravan routes across Persia into India and China.

The visit to China (1271–95) of Marco Polo and the descriptions of the wealth and culture he found there had astonished all western Europe, and enterprising men became ambitious to find new ways to the Far East to gather up these riches without paying the taxes levied by the Turks.

In 1415 combined naval and military Portuguese forces attacked and won the town of Ceuta in North Africa from the Moors. This decisive achievement established the first real European foothold in

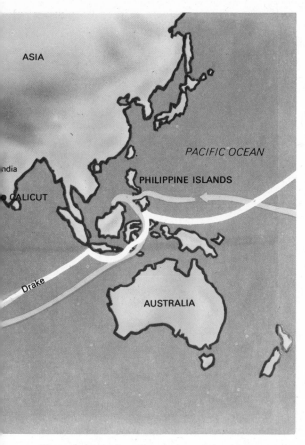

ASIA

PACIFIC OCEAN

India

CALICUT

PHILIPPINE ISLANDS

Drake

AUSTRALIA

Map of the major discoveries of the fifteenth and sixteenth centuries

North Africa for hundreds of years. It was also the beginning of a programme of exploration and discovery by Portuguese sailors to find new ways to reach the Far East without encroaching upon Ottoman territory or interests. Led by Prince Henry (1394–1460) who set up a school of navigation at Sàgres where sailors could study astronomy, map-making and geography, Portuguese mariners set out on a schedule of voyages.

Although the north-western coast of Africa was known to Portuguese sailors, it was generally believed that no advance could be made beyond a certain point because there the waters boiled and flames rose from the sea. Henry, called Henry the Navigator, urged the Portuguese captains to bury their fears and sail

southwards, and he provided the money for the voyages. Gradually the captains overcame their fears and sailed slowly southwards, year by year.

Then, in 1433, Gil Eannes finally rounded Cape Bojador and sailed into the waters of the Gulf of Guinea and thus destroyed the superstitions about the boiling seas. Encouraged by this, other Portuguese navigators ventured further towards and across the equator. Prince Henry died in 1460 before a route to India was found. Then, in 1487, Bartholomew Diaz reached the Cape of Good Hope and rounded it, landing on the south-eastern coast of Africa. He was anxious to go on, but his sailors threatened mutiny and he had to return to Portugal. The king was most excited about the voyage. When Diaz described the dreadful weather he met at the Cape, calling it the Cape of Storms, the king replied that he should be optimistic and call it the Cape of Good Hope, a name which has stuck ever since.

Ten years later Vasco da Gama rounded the Cape, sailed up the east coast, crossed the Indian Ocean and made a landing at Calicut in 1498. A sea route to the Far East had at last been found. Although it took many months the voyage was of the greatest importance to the development

Prince Henry the Navigator encouraged Portuguese sea captains to explore the coast of West Africa, early in the 15th century

of western European economy. Even a journey of a year to bring back shiploads of spices at cost price from the Far East meant cheaper spices for the consumer in the end.

Meanwhile, other sailors had thought of sailing due westwards and reaching China and Indonesia directly. One of these was a Genoese called Christopher Columbus. He tried to interest the Portuguese court, but failed. So he went to Spain where the queen and king, Isabella of Castile and Ferdinand of Aragon, were anxious to join in the race for a route to the Far East. They helped him to fit out his ships and in the summer of 1492 he set out westwards. Early in October he sighted land, closed in, dropped anchor and stepped ashore with a few colleagues. On the seashore he knelt down and gave thanks to God. He believed he had found China or the East Indies, but in fact had only found an island, San Salvador, in what came to be known as the West Indies. This island was one of the Bahama group and far

Christopher Columbus failed to get Portuguese support for his voyage westwards towards China, so he begged the help of Ferdinand and Isabella of Spain

from possessing cities of fabulous wealth and splendour it boasted only native chiefs decked in beads and golden ornaments. None the less a new world had been found, and others were to follow Columbus's pioneering work.

Within a few years the business of discovery had become extensive. John and Sebastian Cabot, helped by Henry VII of England, sailed from Bristol in 1497 westwards in search of a north-west passage to China and discovered New-foundland. In 1499 Amerigo Vespucci landed in South America, and the whole continent of America was named after him. In 1500 Pedro Cabral, a Portuguese navigator, discovered Brazil; and in 1519 another Portuguese, Ferdinand Magellan, set out on a voyage which rounded Cape Horn and took his crew round the world and back to Portugal, though he was himself killed by natives in the Philippines.

These discoveries – and those which followed – were not only important for the economy of western Europe. They were also a sign of a new sense of Man's strength and power. They opened up not only a new world; they opened men's minds to greater possibilities in science and thought. To some extent they also established the political superiority of western Europeans over the Eastern people because they called for and gave rise to a new concept of war – naval strategy. Thereafter, in reality, Western nations dominated the world by virtue of their naval strength and capability. Though the Ottomans were to be masters of a great part of Europe and Asia for some time, the first serious defeat they suffered was at the battle of Lepanto in 1571 – and that was a defeat at sea.

Ferdinand Magellan set out to sail round the world. At the southernmost tip of South America he had to lead his ships through terrible straits – now named after him – by going ahead in a rowing-boat

# China after Khubilai Khan

Khubilai Khan was succeeded by one of his sons, Timur Khan, as emperor of China. Timur was an aggressive, military man who was far more interested in territorial expansion than in cultural activities. He invaded the state of Burma, which had been created in about 900 A.D. by southern Chinese emigrants. There, these emigrants had evolved an ordered society, ruled by a dynasty of kings, the greatest of whom was Anawrahta, who reigned in the middle of the eleventh century. Anawrahta had built a splendid city at Pagan, and Timur proceeded to sack it.

The destruction of their capital demoralized the Burmese and they degenerated into a collection of small feudal duchies which quarrelled ceaselessly. It was not until the eighteenth century that Burma once more became an ordered kingdom.

A Chinese bronze vessel, shaped like a cock (Ming dynasty, 14th century)

The Chinese had never really welcomed Genghis Khan or his descendants, and although the later Mongol emperors had become completely Chinese in every way, there were still elements in the south who longed to see a return to power of real Chinese rulers. These elements rose in revolt against a kinsman of Khubilai Khan and, led by Chu Yuen-Chang, a Chinese general, they seized Peking in 1368. The Mongol dynasty in China came to an end and a new Chinese dynasty, the Ming, began to rule when Yuen-Chang was elected emperor by his associates. He changed his name to Hung-Wu, for Wu was the family name of a very old Chinese line of emperors.

This new dynasty began to pursue a determined policy of isolation. It was felt that the increasing contacts with the West left China exposed to the greed and envy of other lands. China had for many centuries preserved its culture despite invasion and conquest, and the Ming emperors did not wish to see it decay or become watered-down. Hung-Wu himself set out to obliterate as much of the Mongol influence as he could.

The third Ming emperor, Yung-Lo (1403–24), rebuilt Peking. He also commissioned a vast encyclopaedia of Chinese history, called the *Yung Lo Ta Tien*. This is said to have filled eleven thousand volumes bound in yellow silk, and contained nearly 370,000,000 characters (that is, Chinese pictographs), which is equivalent to about five hundred million words. Only three copies were made and they have all but disappeared, for no more than

The Chinese general, Chu Yuen-Chang, founder of the Ming dynasty, seized Peking in 1368, and had himself made emperor

one hundred and fifty volumes exist. These are in various museums.

Yung-Lo was an exception to the isolationist-minded Chinese emperors, for he invaded Mongolia successfully and then began to plan a series of naval operations against the coasts of Ceylon, southern India and Malaya. But he could get little support for his programme from the government and eventually had to give up these enterprises.

The Ming dynasty was noted for its cultural achievements in many fields. Pottery and porcelain reached new heights of design and gracefulness, and Ming china today is among the most valuable that can be bought in any antique markets or auction sales anywhere in the world.

The territories under Chinese dominion contracted during the Ming dynasty, for the Ming emperors, like those of the Sung, devoted most of their energies to fostering this unique civilization.

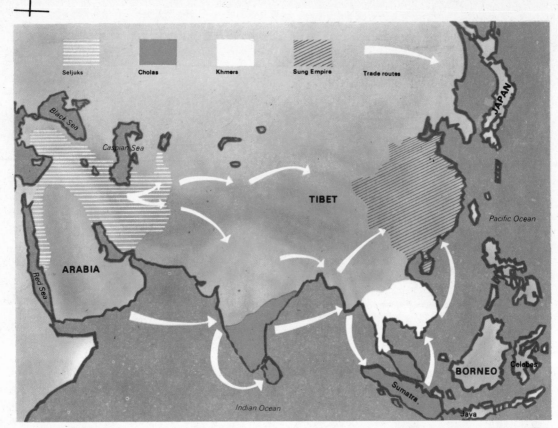

# The Far East: 900–1300

When Chinese civilization enjoyed a new burst of development under the T''ang dynasty many Chinese institutions were adopted throughout the rest of South-East Asia, Korea and Japan. These nations gradually broke away and modified the Chinese way of life to suit their own tastes. Now and again great men came to the front and enlarged their dominions at the expense of neighbours who were in periods of decline.

In Indo-China, for example, which broke away in about 930, a strong race, the Khmers, under a cultured line of rulers, evolved a quite separate civilization throughout the peninsula, which was a mixture of Indian and Chinese cultures. They erected magnificent temples and set up an ordered state structure that was to last for centuries. The natural geographical advantages of many lakes helped the spread of agriculture based on rice crops, and this brought the Indo-Chinese much prosperity. One king, Suriavarman, who ruled for most of the first half of the twelfth century, has left his mark on Indo-China with a splendid temple at Angkor.

The conquests of Genghis Khan did not actually reach Indo-China, but the unrest they stirred up served to undermine the Khmer empire which broke up.

Much of the Khmer territory was absorbed by the neighbouring state of Siam which continued the development of an individual Indo-Chinese civilization.

The Japanese also developed a Chinese civilization, and adapted Chinese culture to their own tastes. But the country was racked for centuries by civil strife between military cliques, as England was during the Wars of the Roses. First one family of military lords would dominate the Japanese archipelago, and then another. These lords were invariably ruthless in the prosecution of their wars, and the peasantry received little consideration.

Japan was invaded by Khubilai Khan, but he did not succeed in conquering the country. His successors did not consider it worthwhile to continue the attacks, and the Japanese were left alone. They seem to have relished this isolation, for the institutions they set up did not alter very much for several centuries, and the Japanese made no impact upon the world until the nineteenth century.

The other people who began to develop their civilization in these times were the Indonesians, who occupied the islands of Sumatra, Java, Borneo and the Celebes. Indonesia had been colonized by southern Indians, in the earliest centuries A.D., who brought with them the two religions, Hinduism and Buddhism. Both faiths flourished in Indonesia and many temples survive testifying to the vigour and creative spirit of the people. In later times Islam established itself in the islands when Moslem Arab sea-traders from the Persian Gulf, and from the Indian coasts, visited them and set up trading stations.

The Samurai in Japan were military guards, with a special code of behaviour and discipline. Occasionally they had duels among each other. After the 16th century they ceased to guard the emperor

ANGEVIN EMPIRE
Henry's paternal inheritance
Under direct rule
Owing suzerainty

Acquisitions by marriage with
Eleanor of Aquitaine (1152)
Under direct rule
Owing suzerainty
Other acquisitions (1169-72)
Kingdom of France
Henry's control by marriage of
Geoffrey and Constance of Brittany

# The Growth of England

After his victory at Hastings in 1066 William the Conqueror swept across England, brought the whole land under his rule, and then introduced his own system of feudalism (*See* page 253). He also divided up the country, retaining some land for himself, giving some to the Church, and the rest to his associates. To assess the value of his possessions – and those of everyone else – he instituted the Domesday survey, a check on the contents of every estate in the land, how much livestock each landlord had, and what acreage of crops was grown.

When William died in 1087 Anglo-Saxon England was firmly in the grip of Norman dominion. His two sons, William II (1087–1100) and Henry I (1100–35) were both tough, able, and, when necessary, ruthless men who kept their father's system working and also did much to blend the Norman with the Anglo-Saxon people. Henry, a scholar and lawmaker, married a Saxon princess and so set an example to his nobles.

The death of Henry I was the signal for an outbreak of fearful civil war. He had left the throne to his daughter Matilda, but the barons would not accept her. They chose his nephew Stephen, and for nineteen years the two claimants fought, and reduced the country to misery. Finally, by the Treaty of Wallingford in 1153, Stephen kept the throne for his lifetime and agreed to pass it to Matilda's son, Henry Plantagenet, who was to become the first king in the longest reigning dynasty in English history.

Henry II, the first Plantagenet, and Eleanor of Aquitaine. Through their marriage England gained vast territories in France (*See* map)

Henry II (1154–89) inherited considerable dominions from his parents; he acquired more by his marriage to Eleanor of Aquitaine. This thick-set, red-haired, grey-eyed man, who had indomitable energy – he was said to have taken meals on horseback so as not to waste time – was quick tempered, but imbued with a strong sense of justice. His reign can be divided into four phases: the restoring of order in England, achieved by pulling down the barons' castles and building better ones of his own, and protecting the people against the barons; the consolidation of his empire and the acquisition of new lands – he overcame Ireland in a lightning campaign in 1171; the reform of the legal system including the introduction of trial by jury and travelling judges; and the quarrel with the Church which, he said, should not have the right to exclude its members from obedience to the common law. This quarrel culminated in the murder of the Archbishop of Canterbury, Thomas Becket, who had once been Henry's friend and then became his chief opponent. The murder was undertaken as a result of some hastily spoken words by the king.

Henry died in 1189 and was succeeded by his son Richard, who became famous as one of the leaders of the Third Crusade. In his insatiable ambition for military glory, Richard I (1189–99) bled England of much of her wealth to pay for his crusade expenses. The crusade was not entirely successful as he failed to take Jerusalem, and was himself captured on the return journey and not released until a huge ransom had been paid by an already overtaxed nation.

Richard was followed by his brother

John (1199–1216), an able and at many times very popular man, who was by nature lazy. John loved England and the English. When he wanted to appoint an English friend as Archbishop of Canterbury, the Pope, Innocent III, refused to ratify it. John persisted, whereupon the Pope excommunicated him and withdrew certain religious privileges from the people, such as Christian burial and the solemnization of marriage.

In 1215 some of the barons forced John to seal a document called Magna Carta. This was supposedly a charter of liberties for the people, but in reality was no more than a licence for the barons to wield more power. The same Pope who had excommunicated him absolved John from his oath to abide by the charter. In the civil war which followed John died and was succeeded by his young son Henry III (1216–72).

Henry's long reign was in many respects disastrous. He had foreign favourites whom he allowed to run the country. Only one of them proved to be of any use to England, Simon de Montfort, who married the king's sister. Henry angered all classes by his extravagance with the nation's funds and by his actions

abroad taken without reference to the Great Council. In the end de Montfort rebelled and forced the king to accept the institution of a Parliament. This consisted, at the first sitting of 1265, of two knights from each shire or county and two burgesses from each city or borough, meeting together to decide the conduct of the nation's affairs. It was a landmark in English history.

Henry was succeeded by his son Edward I (1272–1307), who was tall, handsome and very gifted. Like his great-grandfather Henry II he was a lawgiver, and he was also a soldier-statesman. He

King John of England (1199–1216) studies Magna Carta before affixing his seal to it

aimed to unite the British Isles into one kingdom. His invasion of Wales in 1282 was successful when after the death of Llywelyn the Last, Welsh resistance collapsed. But Edward I failed to beat the Scots, even though he captured and executed one of their leaders, William Wallace.

Edward II's reign (1307–27) was signalized by the crushing defeat of the English by the Scots under Robert Bruce at Bannockburn in 1314. Edward was murdered at Berkeley Castle and the throne passed to his son Edward III (1327–77).

For the first part of his reign Edward III was everything that the legendary King Arthur had been – handsome, courageous, chivalrous, and an inspired leader of men. Conceiving that he had a claim to the throne of France (through descent) he prosecuted a war – known as the Hundred Years' War because it lasted on and off from 1337 to 1453 – which at the start was attended with great success. Smashing the French fleet at Sluys in 1340 and the French army at Crécy in 1346, Edward conducted his campaigns with Arthurian gallantry and splendour. He created a new order of chivalry, the Order of the Garter, as a reward for services rendered by detachment commanders in the field at Crécy.

But this glamorous era was brought to an end by the Black Death, a plague which in 1349–50 killed about a third of the English people. When the worst was over the whole structure of society was in need of reform. Serfs and peasants had been killed off by the thousands and there was an acute shortage of labour. Instead, however, of allowing labourers to move where they wished to get the best wages, Edward, by the Statute of Labourers, forced workers to stay on their farms and to accept a pre-plague wage structure, despite the sharp rise in the cost of living. Misery and discontent were soon widespread, and they were made worse by fresh visitations of the plague.

The king's eldest son, the Black Prince, wore himself to death fighting to keep their possessions in France, while the government at home fell into the hands of the aging king's mistress and her favourites. Edward died unmourned in 1377, a shadow of his former self.

He was succeeded by his grandson Richard II (1377–99), who was only a boy. In 1381 England was rent by a severe and widespread rebellion known as the Peasants' Revolt. The leaders demanded

Part of the recumbent statue of the Black Prince, in Canterbury Cathedral

Insignia of the Order of the Garter

redress for the grievances which stemmed from the Statute of Labourers, but the rising was really a general desire to see the end of the feudal system and the abolition of serfdom. The young Richard made many promises which he did not keep. Then, when he reached manhood he dismissed his advisers and began to rule as a tyrant. By the end of the century he had been forced to abdicate by his cousin Henry Plantagenet, Duke of Lancaster, who seized the throne and ruled as Henry IV (1399–1413).

Henry was a great patron of the arts and building. He also encouraged trade and commerce, preferring the company of craftsmen and merchants to that of the nobles who seemed to be ever wanting to dispossess him of his throne. But he was cruel to a new religious sect, the Lollards, who were followers of the preacher John Wycliffe. Wycliffe had attacked the laziness, extravagance and immoral lives of the bishops and clergy in England and had urged a return to the more simple life as led by Jesus of Nazareth himself.

Henry's son was Henry V (1413–22), a prince of the same stamp as the young Edward III. He reopened the matter of the claim of England to the French throne and at Agincourt in 1415 he crushed a French army five times the size of his in one of the greatest victories of English history. By the Treaty of Troyes he was

John Wycliffe tried to persuade the higher clergy in England to lead better lives. His followers were cruelly persecuted

recognized as heir to the king of France, Charles VI. He then married Charles's daughter and their son became natural heir to the two thrones. Henry died of fever in 1422 when his son was only a few months old.

The reign of Henry VI was tragic in every respect, personally, militarily, and politically. The king himself was a good and pious man all his life, fond of books, devoted to religion, and deeply interested in building. In 1441 he founded Eton College and King's College, Cambridge, and he undertook numerous improvements to cathedrals and public buildings. But he was weak and allowed his headstrong wife, Margaret of Anjou, and his unscrupulous relatives, the Beauforts, far too much power, which they all misused.

His uncle, the Duke of Bedford, a general not much less brilliant than his brother Henry V, continued the war in France, but after his death in 1435 the English were driven out of France altogether, retaining only Calais and Guisnes. At home a series of relatives mismanaged the government so badly that a disastrous civil war broke out in 1453, which is known as the Wars of the Roses. This is because the wars were fought between the two branches of Edward III's family, the house of York whose emblem was a white rose, and the house of Lancaster whose emblem was a red rose.

In 1461 the Yorkists triumphed at Towton. They were led to victory by one of the greatest English soldier-statesmen, Richard Nevill, Earl of Warwick, a cousin of the king and the biggest landowner in the country apart from the Crown. Warwick was immensely popular, especially with his tenants. He was fearless, dashing and supremely self-confident and he had much to be self-confident about. He loved work, particularly the

The French cavalry were cut to pieces by English and Welsh archers, positioned behind stakes, on the field of battle at Agincourt in 1415. The British victory strengthened the hold of Henry V on large areas of France

day-to-day business of government, and so when the pleasure-loving Prince Edward of York became King Edward IV after Towton he was glad to leave the affairs of state to Warwick.

For some years the system worked well, but in 1469 the two men fell out over the king's marriage with a commoner. Warwick transferred his allegiance to Henry VI who had been languishing in the Tower since 1464 and drove Edward off the throne. In 1471 Edward IV and Warwick fought it out at Barnet and the great leader was killed. Henry was returned to the Tower where he died almost at once.

Edward ruled well for the next twelve years. He encouraged trade, art and building. William Caxton first set up his printing press at Westminster in 1474 under the king's patronage. When the king died in 1483 he was succeeded by his young son, Edward V, who was shortly afterwards declared illegitimate and so disqualified from succession. Edward V was deposed and his uncle, Richard of Gloucester, assumed the crown.

This able and courageous soldier-statesman, who had married the younger daughter of Warwick and who resembled him in many ways, governed extremely well. He introduced a postal service by means of relays of horses, and he had all the laws of England written in English for the first time. He founded the College of Heralds, he advanced trade by granting licences to merchants and charters to seaport towns, and he had more statutes passed in his short reign than any previous monarch.

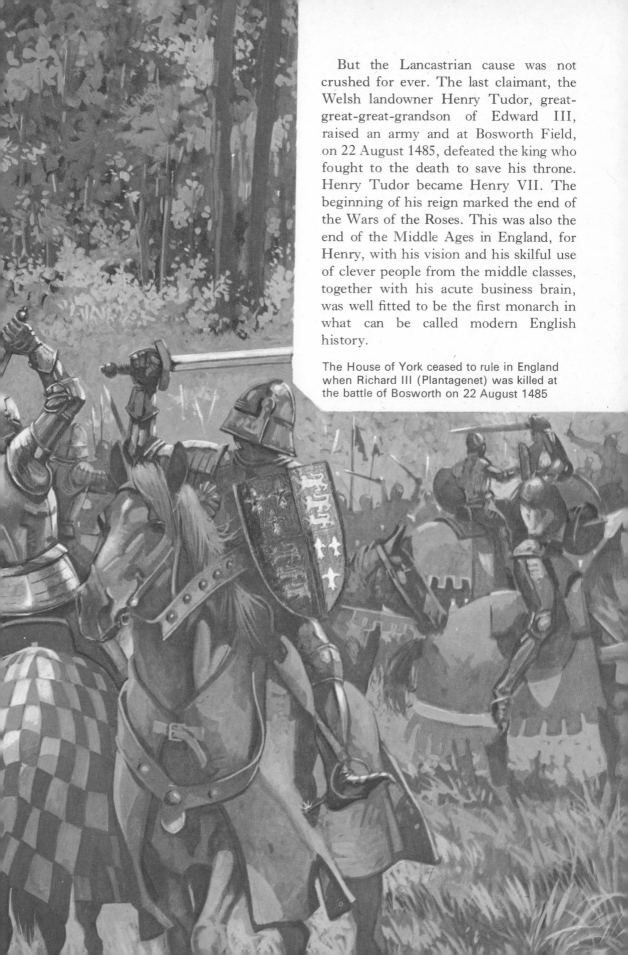

But the Lancastrian cause was not crushed for ever. The last claimant, the Welsh landowner Henry Tudor, great-great-great-grandson of Edward III, raised an army and at Bosworth Field, on 22 August 1485, defeated the king who fought to the death to save his throne. Henry Tudor became Henry VII. The beginning of his reign marked the end of the Wars of the Roses. This was also the end of the Middle Ages in England, for Henry, with his vision and his skilful use of clever people from the middle classes, together with his acute business brain, was well fitted to be the first monarch in what can be called modern English history.

The House of York ceased to rule in England when Richard III (Plantagenet) was killed at the battle of Bosworth on 22 August 1485

# The Decline of Celtic Power

The conquest of England by William of Normandy in 1066 marked the beginning of the end of Celtic independence in Wales and Ireland, though in Scotland the decline was to take much longer. No sooner had William overrun England than he authorized some of his barons to invade Wales. Three of them moved across the border: Hugh of Avranches from Chester along the Dee valley; Roger of Montgomery from Shrewsbury along the Severn valley; and William Fitz-Osbern from Hereford along the Wye valley. In short campaigns the Normans occupied large tracts of Welsh territory and established the Welsh Marches, a string of stone castles built from Chepstow to Pembroke, that no one in Wales was strong enough to resist.

### Wales

When the English king Henry I died in 1135, England dissolved into civil war. This was the moment for the Welsh to strike, and under Owain Gwynedd, son of Prince Gruffydd ap Cynan of Wales, they drove the Normans out of Cardigan, Carmarthen, and Glamorgan. By 1152, Owain, then Prince of Wales, was virtual master of the country. This success was attended by a great flourishing of poetry and music, art and building. Two of Wales's most famous poets, Gwalchmai and Cynndelw, sang and recited at Owain's court. Great abbeys thrust their towers and sharp roofs into the sky at Valle Crucis, Strata Florida, and Tintern. And the first eisteddfods, that is, competitions in music and verse, were held. They still take place annually, in August.

Owain died in 1170 and the next prince of importance was his grandson Llywelyn Fawr (Llywelyn the Great – 1194–1240). Llywelyn was a man of many talents. Skilled as a general, learned, devoted to religion, filled with interest in legal matters, he was an ideal man to give Wales what it needed – unity and national pride. He created a Council of State to act as advisory body to the princes. Courts were set up to deal with land disputes, for the Welsh were notorious for not registering or outlining land claims

Owain Glyndŵr presides at a meeting of the Welsh Parliament at Machynlleth early in the 15th century

in writing. Regions were ordered to provide detachments of troops for suppressing internal disorder and for national defence. And the English were kept out of the country for the rest of his reign.

Llywelyn died in 1240 and was followed by his younger son Dafydd, in whose reign some of the Marcher territories were retaken by the English. Dafydd died in 1246 and was succeeded by his nephew Llywelyn.

This tall, dark and good-looking prince determined to emulate his grandfather and rule all of Wales. He had all the qualities needed to lead a national campaign for independence, courage, military skill, cunning, endurance, and the ability to persuade men to follow him. When Edward I of England returned from the Seventh Crusade in 1274 and demanded Llywelyn's presence at his coronation, the Welshman refused to go, as he did not recognize Edward as overlord. So the countries went to war. The English won, and Llywelyn agreed to peace terms.

A few years later Llywelyn made a last bid to expel the English, but he was again defeated and driven into the mountains of Snowdonia. From there he went southwards to rouse the men of Brycheiniog (Brecon), but one evening in 1282 he was killed by an English sentry. Edward took over Wales, brought it into the kingdom of England and governed it according to English law.

For one hundred and twenty years the Welsh lay prostrate. Then, at the beginning of the fifteenth century, a descendant of Llywelyn, Owain Glyndŵr, rose in revolt, drove the forces of Henry IV out of north Wales, and set up a parliament at Machynlleth. Owain then disappeared from history and the Welsh sank again into subservience to the English.

### Ireland

The Welsh were not the only Celtic peoples to endure Norman invasion and succumb to English conquest. The Irish, who were the most cultured people in western Europe in the Dark Ages, were to bow before the English storm.

After the death of the great Brian Boru in 1014, Ireland dissolved into disorder and strife between kingdoms and for half a century little is known of what happened. By the time William the Conqueror had overrun England, however, Turlough O'Brien (1064–86), Brian's grandson, had risen to be supreme ruler of Ireland, and he kept this position until his death. After that, another period of anarchy followed and by 1094 there were two kings of Ireland, Murtogh O'Brien of Munster and Domhnall O'Lochlainn of Ulster. In 1121 Turlough O'Connor, king of Connaught, overcame his rivals and proclaimed himself king of Ireland. He got the support of

The Rock of Cashel, County Tipperary, was traditionally the seat of the kings of Munster. Cormac's Chapel, a Romanesque church, dates back to the 12th century

the archbishop of Armagh, head of the Irish Church, by a generous gift of gold to St Patrick's Cathedral.

Turlough was an energetic ruler who involved himself in a variety of projects. He had bridges built across the Shannon to enable him to reach points of rebellion quickly, and he built castles and forts along the countryside at strategic points. He endowed monasteries, opened schools, and encouraged all manner of crafts, including metalwork, manuscript illumination, and stained glass-making. He sponsored poets and musicians at his court who sang epic songs about Ireland's past heroes, Cuchullain and Rory, and, of course, Brian Boru.

Turlough was succeeded in 1156 by his son Roderic, who had to fight for the next ten years to establish his position as king of Ireland.

In 1171 Henry II of England, armed with papal authority to invade Ireland and put the Church in order, landed at Waterford and with his army swiftly conquered the south-east up to Dublin. He then summoned a meeting of the Church heads at Cashel and dictated the Papal demands, to which they acceded with surprisingly little argument. Then he appointed a chief justice and government officials with instructions to put Ireland under English law. He had himself proclaimed Lord of Ireland, although he allowed Roderic to remain king of Ireland, laying stress on the difference.

It was one thing to conquer Ireland; it was quite another to hold it down, and for the next seven hundred and fifty years the Irish made it extremely difficult for the English authorities to keep order. The story of Ireland after 1171 is one of constant fighting with the English.

When Henry left, English barons went over and settled, establishing small domains like the Marches in Wales. They took over all the native institutions, except the language, and seized the most fertile lands and the best towns. In the thirteenth century these settlers, some of whom had married into Gaelic families, set up their own Parliament of nobles, clergy and knights, at Dublin. These settlers are called Anglo-Irish.

The Anglo-Irish hold on Ireland was never sure. The Gaelic Irish resented them, hated them for their cruelty, despised them for their lack of culture

William III at the Battle of the Boyne, 1690

and overweening interest in empire-building, and their devotion to a feudal class structure. Wherever the English were heavily involved in major continental wars or in civil troubles, the Irish took advantage and rebelled.

Not until the reign of Henry VII did England really have time or the power to rectify the position. Had the Irish been better organized they might have thrown off English rule for good, but when Sir Edward Poynings was sent by Henry VII to Ireland in 1492 the chance was lost, and it did not really come again until the present century.

The story of Ireland from the time of Sir Edward Poynings is one of the sorriest in history. This great race of Celts, who had been the repository of learning and art in the Dark Ages when much of western Europe had lapsed into barbarism, was systematically oppressed, overtaxed and degraded by the English. Frequently the Irish rebelled against the English government, especially when the English tried to force the Irish to become Protestants and penalized all those who would not.

In 1800, by an Act of Union, the Irish parliament was abolished and the Irish were given seats in both the English House of Lords and Commons at Westminster. This was intended to help all the Irish, but in practice only the Protestants and the Anglo-Irish benefited. In 1844-47 a disease of the potato crop caused terrible famine. Many Irish people died. Many emigrated to America in search of a better life. Towards the end of the nineteenth century, led by Charles Stewart Parnell, and for some time helped by William Gladstone when he was prime minister, some Irish M.P.s pressed for Home Rule. But the campaign faltered after Parnell was involved in a divorce scandal. The Home Rule cause revived again in the early twentieth century, and in 1914 a

Michael Collins led the Irish against their English oppressors and forced the government to grant Ireland (except Ulster) independence

Home Rule Bill was actually passed, though it had to be shelved at the outbreak of the First World War.

In 1916, while Britain was at war with Germany, some Irish patriots rebelled in Dublin. They held out for a week, but in the end surrendered. Not only the leaders, but also other less important men, were shot after a court-martial. The Irish people, many of whom had not sympathized with the rebels during the rising, now swung in favour of independence. They found able leaders in Michael Collins and the American-born Eamon De Valera. There was war between the Irish and British until 1921, when a treaty set up the Irish Free State.

Most of Ireland became free and independent. But the six counties in the north, Ulster, remained part of the United Kingdom. The majority there, Protestant and Unionist, opposed a united Ireland. In 1937 De Valera, by then prime minister, loosened Ireland's links with Britain and in 1949 the country became a republic. From the 1960s a campaign of terrorism, waged by the Irish Republican Army on one hand, and by Protestant extremists on the other, troubled Northern Ireland and also spread to mainland Britain. The Irish Republic joined the European Community in 1973.

Sir William Wallace, leader of the Scots against Edward I of England

## Scotland

The Scots, meanwhile, fared somewhat better. Malcolm II was succeeded by his grandson Duncan in 1034, but in six years this vain and incompetent king angered the nobility, and they elected his cousin Macbeth in his place.

Macbeth (1040–57) was one of the best kings of Scotland. He put down highway robbery, crushed opposition, encouraged trade, and spent large sums of money on the Church. His kingdom was sufficiently quiet to allow him to make a pilgrimage to Rome in 1050.

Scotland was invaded by the English in 1057 in support of Duncan's son Malcolm, and at Lumphanan Macbeth was defeated and slain.

The next king who merits attention is David I (1124–53). He introduced the Norman brand of feudalism into the country, reformed the law, and founded monasteries at Kelso, Melrose, Jedburgh and Dryburgh. He impressed his country's historians enough for one of them to write that 'he was the best of all his kind'.

David's son, William the Lion, a bold but impetuous leader, attacked England in 1174, but was captured and sent to Henry II. He remained in custody until 1189 when Richard I of England, anxious to raise every penny he could for the Third Crusade, sold him his freedom for several thousand pounds.

William's son, Alexander II, successfully put down rebels in the Western Islands, and his son Alexander III (1249–86) utterly defeated the Norwegians at the battle of Largs in 1263. Then he conquered the Hebrides, a Norwegian possession, and added them to Scotland.

Alexander was killed in a fall from his horse and his successor was his granddaughter, Margaret, who was only three.

She died soon afterwards, and Scotland was plunged into disarray as several claimants came forward for the throne. The Scottish nobles then invited Edward I of England to select a candidate, and he agreed, on condition that he (Edward) was recognized as overlord of Scotland. The nobles, to avoid civil war, accepted and John Baliol, a great-great-great-grandson of David I, was elected king.

Baliol foolishly invaded England and was driven off at Dunbar, in 1296. Angered, Edward claimed the throne for himself and sent an army of occupation to Scotland. During the English rule the Scots rose under William Wallace (a knight of Welsh descent) and attacked the English. Wallace was eventually caught, tried and executed, but his cause lived on.

Another claimant to the throne, Robert Bruce, a great-great-great-great-grandson of David I, continued the opposition. Edward died on the way to Scotland to deal with Bruce, and his son Edward II withdrew. Seven years later, when Edward II was prevailed upon by his Council to come to the rescue of English barons in Scotland who were being harassed, he marched with a large army to Stirling, and at Bannockburn was completely routed. This was the greatest victory in Scottish history.

In 1314, Scottish forces under King Robert the Bruce utterly defeated the English at Bannockburn

Bruce now ruled, as Robert I, an independent Scotland until his death in 1329. His son, David II (1329–71), was captured by the English at the battle of Neville's Cross in 1346 and kept prisoner for eleven years. He was succeeded by Robert II whose reign was marked by the defeat of the English at Otterburn in 1388. Robert III was a sickly king who entrusted the government of the country to his brother, the popular Earl of Fife. Fife was promoted to Duke of Albany and governed with the same sort of enthusiasm and justice as Richard Nevill, Earl of Warwick, was to do in England in the 1460s.

Robert's heir, James, was captured by English sailors when on a voyage to France in 1406. He was only eleven. For eighteen years he was kept in England, and for fourteen of these Albany ruled in his place. When the great duke died there was grief throughout the country.

In 1424 Henry VI of England released James and he came home to a great welcome. He was worthy of the support of the people for at once he took over the government and restored order after the chaos that had followed Albany's death. He founded schools and enlarged the University of St Andrews. But he made enemies among the gentry and in 1437 he was assassinated at Perth by Sir Robert Graham.

James II (1437–60), who was only six when he succeeded, grew up to be every bit as popular as his father. England was racked with its own difficulties and this gave Scotland several years of un-interrupted peace and development. Trade expanded rapidly. The great fishing fleets of Aberdeen were patronized by the king and a programme of ship-building was begun. More schools were opened and places were made available to children of poor parents.

John Knox upbraided Mary Queen of Scots

In 1460 James tried to recover the border fortress of Roxburgh from the English. One morning as he was inspect-ing the artillery which was bombarding the stout castle walls, one of the cannons exploded and a fragment of iron killed him. He was succeeded by his son, James III, who was not a ruler of the same quality at all. He was surrounded by worthless advisers and companions, and when he was stabbed to death in 1488 he was not mourned. The nation looked forward to better times under his son, James IV.

James IV was a splendid martial figure who could speak seven languages and knew a lot about science as well as art. He set out to bring Scotland into the modern age. He introduced printing, recon-structed the navy, encouraged industry, especially wool and fisheries, and re-formed the law. He set up the Daily Council at which anyone could bring a complaint to him or his representative. He founded Aberdeen University and rebuilt Edinburgh to make it Scotland's capital.

It was tragic for Scotland when James was killed at the battle of Flodden Field against the English in 1513. He was succeeded by his son James V, a boy only eighteen months old. For twenty years the country was ruled by ambitious members of the Stuart family, to the detriment of the Scots. When James attained his majority and took over the government he ruled well, but in 1542, in another war against the English, he was defeated at Solway Moss and died a few days afterwards.

James's heir was a daughter, Mary, only a week old. Her reign was catastrophic from beginning to end. Her French mother tried to bring Scotland under the rule of France, which aggravated England and led to war. In 1558 this policy seemed confirmed when Mary married the king of France's son. A year later Mary's husband became king, and she was thus queen of France and of Scotland. She was a devout Roman Catholic at a time when a wave of Protestant revolt was sweeping Scotland, championed by the fiery and gallant preacher, John Knox. Scotland was converted in an incredibly short time, but Mary would not change her Catholic faith. In 1560 her husband died and she came to Scotland to rule.

At once she fell foul of the Protestant lords and common people, and especially of John Knox. The rest of her reign was the tale of a struggle between her supporters and her adversaries, who were led by her half-brother, the Earl of Moray. In 1569 she was driven out of Scotland and begged asylum from Elizabeth of England, to whom she was heir. Elizabeth kept Mary in confinement for eighteen years. During that time she became the focal point for several plots against Elizabeth. Time and again Elizabeth did nothing, but after the collapse of the Babington plot in 1586 her patience ran out and she consented to Mary's trial and execution (1587).

When Mary was driven out of Scotland in 1569, the throne passed to her baby son, James VI, and the government was managed by Moray. This remarkable man, tough, shrewd, and very popular, was struck down in 1570 by an assassin, to the great grief of all Scotland. Thereafter, until his mother's execution, James VI ruled through a succession of nobles. As heir to the English throne he conducted himself with discretion so as not to aggravate the queen, and in 1603 when Elizabeth died he became king of England, Scotland and Ireland.

For the next one hundred and four years Scottish history was closely bound up with the English. In the Civil War some of the Scots supported Parliament, and others took the side of the king, Charles I, and were defeated by Oliver Cromwell in a campaign after Charles's execution. When James II (1685–88) was expelled from England, many Scots rebelled against the new king, William III. But in 1707 a group of English and Scottish nobles agreed on terms for a union of the countries, embodied in the Act of Union. Scotland retained its law, its Church and its education system, but it lost its independence.

Mary, Queen of Scots, prepares for her execution for plotting to assassinate Elizabeth I of England

# The Aztecs and
# the Incas

### The Aztecs

The Aztecs were a wandering tribe of tough, fighting people who roamed the jungles and plains of northern Mexico. More backward than the Toltecs and the Mayas, they overran these civilizations and in some ways improved upon them. For example, they discovered the techniques of smelting iron and working soft metals, especially gold and silver, on which they did not set so high a value as did the Spaniards who later conquered them.

When they moved into the great central Mexican valley they adopted many of the ideas of their predecessors, including the calendar, the worship of rain and sun gods, and the preoccupation with death and human sacrifice that differentiated the Toltecs from the more humane Mayas. Despite their knowledge of metalworking, the Aztecs continued to make their weapons of stone and their armour of thick cotton plaiting. They also made fine pottery and erected grand buildings.

All Central American civilizations were deeply involved with religious beliefs, but the Aztecs were probably the most absorbed with mysticism and superstition. It is said that during the dedication of a temple in 1486, not long before the arrival of the Spanish, more than twenty thousand people were sacrificed at one ceremony to pacify the gods. This extraordinary obsession with death is reflected in Aztec art and sculpture.

Early in the sixteenth century the Aztecs were ruled by an emperor, Montezuma II, who had his capital at Tenochtitlan. This great city, whose gold-lined roofs glistened in the sun and could be seen from many miles away, had more

than fifty thousand inhabitants living in well-built homes, both grand and commonplace. Tenochtitlan was a rich city and traders prospered. From his capital, Montezuma, through a well-organized government structure, controlled the whole of Mexico.

In 1519, Montezuma was suddenly informed of the landing at Tabasco of a party of foreign people, speaking a strange language, some of whom were mounted on four-legged monsters (horses) and who brandished weird objects which discharged fire (muskets). These people seemed to be searching for gold and silver. Their leader was Hernán Cortez, a middle-aged adventurer from Spain, who had been in Cuba for some years and who had learned about the riches of the Aztecs from traders.

When Cortez had been on the Mexican mainland for a few days he discovered that many of the native people resented the domination of the Aztecs. He was quick to exploit this and he marched with battalions of these natives straight to Tenochtitlan.

Montezuma, believing that Cortez was the god Quetzalcoatl returning from a long sojourn abroad, made ready to welcome the Spaniard. In magnificent pomp and ceremony he had himself conveyed on a gold and silver decked litter, accompanied by bejewelled priests and officials, out of the city to meet Cortez. The Spaniards had never seen anything like this before.

To the everlasting shame of Spain, Cortez accepted this reverential treatment, and then turned on his host, seizing him as a prisoner. He then ordered the Aztec throne to be destroyed, and the temples, palaces and buildings to

Montezuma, ruler of the Aztecs, welcomes Hernan Cortez outside Tenochtitlan. Cortez responded by making him a prisoner

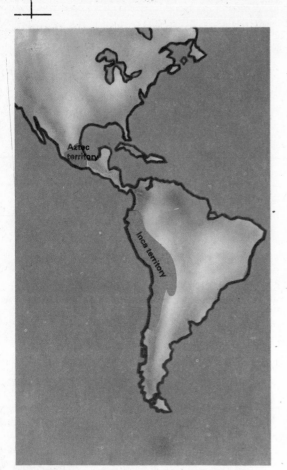

Map of Aztec and Inca territories in Central and South America

population is directly descended from the Aztecs, or from the Mayas, and they are immensely proud of this noble descent. Cuauhtemoc is still a national hero, but no one has a good word to say of Cortez.

### The Incas

The Incas were the last of the great civilizations in South America. They came from the southern part of Peru, from the interior of the Andes mountains, and they were the dominant peoples by the fifteenth century A.D. By this time they had organized the various South American races into one empire, combined the results of the various civilizations, and had done so with the efficiency and thoroughness characteristic of the Romans. The Inca empire stretched from Ecuador in the north to Chile in the south, and included part of Bolivia and the Argentine.

The Incas were splendid engineers. They constructed wonderful roads, some of them very long – in all about three thousand miles. They hewed great tunnels through the mountains along which they piped water for irrigating their fields. They erected huge bridges across the valleys of the Andes, constructed of vast stones of granite which were not cemented and which had not been cut with any metal tools, for they did not understand the use of iron for such work. Many of these stones weighed several tons and they were fitted together with precision. Walls and pillars thus constructed have survived for centuries, and even severe earthquakes have not destroyed them.

The Incas also built splendid monuments, temples and palaces, but as much care went into the building of ordinary houses for the common people as well. The two principal Inca cities were Cuzco and Machu Picchu. Cuzco, the capital, was nearly 11,000 feet above sea-level in

be looted. All ornaments and veneers that bore any gold or silver were melted down, and in three days some two million pounds worth of precious metal were collected.

Some Aztecs rebelled against this appalling behaviour and when Montezuma attempted to restrain them they killed him, and put his nephew Cuauhtemoc in his place. Street by street the Aztecs fought the Spaniards for their capital, until in the end they were forced to yield. Aztec civilization died quickly and was replaced by Spanish government, religion, customs and language.

But the Spanish conquest was not the end of the Aztecs altogether, for even today more than a third of the Mexican

the heart of the Andes, and Machu was 8,000 feet high, sited across a mountain ridge. Cuzco was surrounded by a thick wall some 1,500 feet long. Its streets were planned in an ordered grid pattern.

The Inca empire was organized into groups of people under local governors. At its height, the empire ruled five million people, who were split up into sections of ten thousand, each ruled by a noble. These sections were subdivided into one thousand, and once more into five hundred. The local rulers kept in touch with their superiors by means of relays of couriers. Every section chief was responsible to the Inca – the ruler, himself. The state had a definite class-structure of nobles, traders, craftsmen and artisans. The government organized factories for making textiles, pottery and china, and jewellery. Here and there they built large storehouses which the population had to keep filled in case of emergency or in case the Inca required supplies for himself or for his gods. Ordinary people lived a frugal life, with little freedom, and owned no property, but they had enough to live on. Although writing was unknown, the government officials kept records of accounts by means of a system of tying knots in a set of coloured strings called *quipus*.

The Inca and the nobles dressed richly and were adorned with gold and silver

The Tenochas, the most highly organized of the Aztec tribes, founded the city of Tenochtitlan in the 14th century. It was built on an island in Lake Texcoco and linked by causeways to the mainland (*see* next page)

A page from the Codex Zouche-Nuttal, painted on deer skin, probably representing the ceremony of making new fire. Mexico *c*. 900

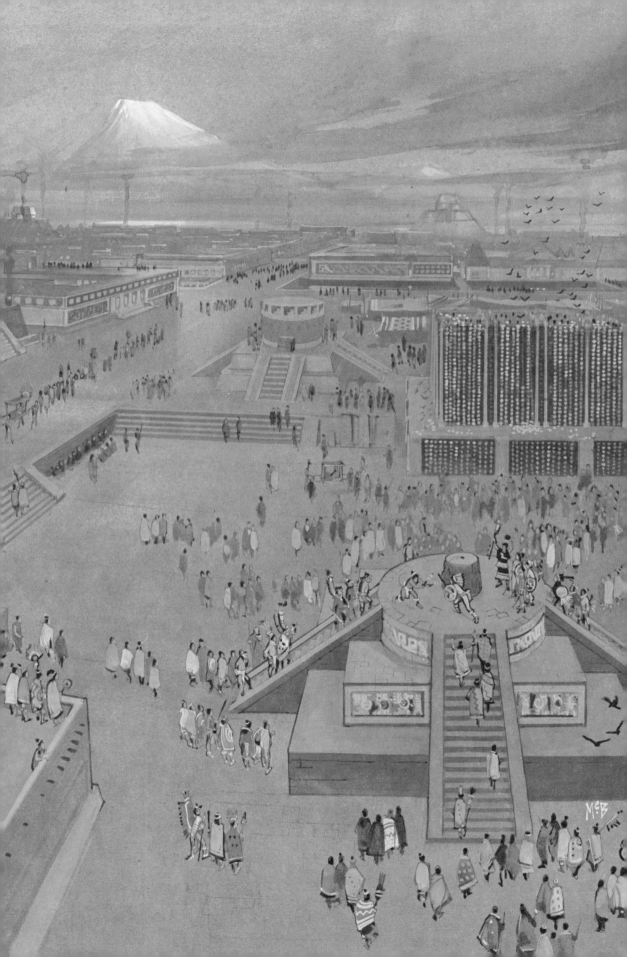

Atahualpa, the Inca of Peru, offered the Spaniards a room full of gold and silverware in exchange for his release. He was ordered to fill the room up to the red line on the wall. This he did, but was brutally murdered, all the same

jewellery. But the ordinary people wore simple, plain garb. Indeed, it was possible to recognize a man's rank by the clothes he wore. The highest nobles, for example, wore brightly coloured earrings.

The Incas learned from their predecessors how to work metal, especially gold. They knew how to hammer, gild, and solder, and they developed the technique of producing metal in large quantities by the use of moulds. This widespread knowledge and use of gold, which they did not value in the same way as Europeans, were the principal attributes that appealed to the first Spanish adventurers that set foot in South America.

The Spaniards behaved in Peru as treacherously as they had in Mexico. The Inca emperor, Atahualpa, while staying at his northern residence in 1532, received news of the approach of a small party of Spaniards, led by Francisco Pizarro. He set out to welcome them, but was immediately seized and put in chains.

Almost at once the government of the Incas began to break down, as the fountainhead had been removed and no one had been designated or trained to succeed. Atahualpa, when he heard that the Spaniards wanted gold and silver, offered Pizarro a room full if he would release him. Pizarro agreed and the amount was collected. Atahualpa was then treacherously murdered and Pizarro set out for Cuzco to take it by storm. The Inca nobility was slaughtered and the empire collapsed.

In twenty years the Spaniards destroyed two of the greatest civilizations of the Americas, both of which were inheritors of earlier cultures reaching far back into the millennia before the birth of Jesus, in whose name the Spaniards inflicted their gross treachery and cruelty.

### Other Peoples in the Americas

When the Aztecs and the Incas were destroyed, only a sort of substratum of primitive peoples remained in the Americas. They were backward people, descendants of those who had probably come across the Bering Strait hundreds of years earlier. Although they were grouped in different tribes, with different characteristics, we still refer to them as Indians.

In the great plains of what is now the United States and Canada these Indians were less civilized than their kinsmen who had moved to Mexico and Peru. But they cultivated maize, and had an organized tribal life. They even built stone buildings, on a much smaller scale (one was recently found on the banks of the Mississippi River, some 35 feet high). These Indians learned much from the Spanish intruders in Mexico. They stole horses from the Spaniards and learned to ride them. This gave them a mobility that they had not known before, and it was not long before they could outride any of the Spanish cavalrymen. Among these Indians were the tribes of the Cheyenne, the Pawnee, the Sioux, and the Comanche.

When the Europeans began to colonize North America they clashed frequently with one or other tribe of Indians. Greedy for land, the Europeans, with their superior weapons (muskets, then rifles and revolvers), drove the Indians westwards and southwards, or broke up their tribal communities and scattered the people. But the resilience of the Indians was astonishing. They stole rifles and other guns and soon learned to use them, generally with deadly effect.

Many of these Indian tribes were well-advanced, in particular, the Cherokee and the Iroquois, who occupied great tracts in the south-east Mississippi basin. But in the end they – and other tribes – had to give way to European rule, and by the end of the nineteenth century it looked as if they might disappear altogether. Fortunately, however, they have been encouraged to continue their existence in reservations in the United States. Indians also survive in Canada, Mexico, Central America and South America. Indeed, the Indians have played a vital role in the development of some of these countries, especially Mexico when the empire of Maximilian was brought down in the 1860s. The rebel leaders may have had Spanish names, but they were really Indian in tradition and in aspiration. In Guatemala and Ecuador, Indian features predominate among the people, despite centuries of Spanish efforts to impose the Catholic religion and the Spanish language.

Chief Sitting Bull, one of the most famous leaders of the great Sioux tribe of Red Indians. The map in the background shows the approximate territories of some of the Indians in North America in the days of Sitting Bull.

# The Greatness and Eclipse of the Ottoman Empire

After the fall of Constantinople in 1453 the Ottoman empire stretched from what is now Rumania to the Euphrates. Its rulers wielded great power, and by 1512 the sultan, Selim I, a cruel but cultivated ruler, was ready to expand the empire further. In a short campaign he won both Syria and Egypt. When he died in 1520 he was succeeded by the greatest of all the sultans, Suleiman I – the Magnificent – (1520–66).

Suleiman was a strange man, for while he did not like warfare at all, his military career was one of almost unbroken success. He reformed the army and made it extremely mobile. He conquered Hungary by crossing the Danube and capturing Belgrade in 1521, and in 1526 destroyed Austro-Hungarian forces at Mohacz. Two years later Budapest fell, and in 1529 he laid siege to Vienna itself. Meanwhile, he conquered Tunis in North Africa and raided towns on the Spanish and Italian coasts, on one occasion actually threatening Rome itself. Before long his fleets dominated the whole Mediterranean.

Western Europe greatly respected this splendid ruler who loved pageantry and ceremonial. He was a law-giver and he brought the laws of his empire much more into line with current practice in the rest of Europe. He also set up educational institutions.

In 1551 Suleiman conquered Persia and added it to his empire, which then stretched from Gibraltar to the Tigris.

Suleiman was followed by Selim II (1566–74), who was an habitual drunkard.

He left the business of government to his grand vizier, Mahomet Sokolli, a bold, wise, and very popular statesman, who had first begun to show his brilliance in the last ten years of Suleiman's rule. This great man continued the expansion of the empire, attacked Venice, Spain and Cyprus and so compelled the Europeans to combine in a league against the empire. In 1571 at Lepanto, near Corinth in Greece, the league's fleet, commanded by Don John of Austria, the illegitimate half-brother of Philip II of Spain, utterly defeated the Ottomans. In the peace talks which followed, however, the Ottomans

Suleiman I (1520–66), known as Suleiman the Magnificent, was the greatest ruler of the Ottoman Turkish empire

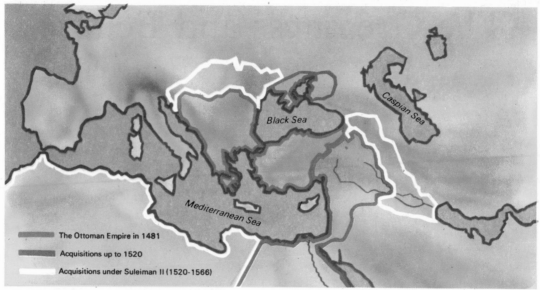

Map of the Ottoman Empire (1481–1566)

obtained much of what they wanted, including Cyprus. This was in large measure due to the skilful negotiating of Sokolli. But Ottoman sea power was dealt a blow from which it did not really recover.

Selim died in 1574 and was succeeded by an equally ineffective ruler, Muradh III, whose principal achievement was the instigation of the murder of the great Sokolli in 1579. It was an act that the Ottomans were to regret, for the decline in Turkish power can, in effect, be dated from that year.

By the end of the sixteenth century the Ottomans were still very powerful indeed, though much more so on land than in the Mediterranean, and no combination of powers in Europe seemed able to break them. What kept them up to strength was their zealous faith, the wandering nature of their people (they were still essentially nomadic like their ancestors), and their magnificently disciplined army which moved with such speed and precision. But as the next century progressed, the quality of the Ottoman leaders declined, and their sultans lived only for luxury and pleasure. Soon rich nobles in the provinces began to ignore the central government and ruled in great state in their own areas.

In 1656 a grand vizier, Mahomet Koprulu, seized power and started a new dynasty of sultans. He restricted the powers of the nobles, and strengthened the machinery of central government. His son, Ahmed (1661–76), was as able and energetic, and he encouraged trade, reconstructed the system of land holding, and embarked upon a number of military campaigns. One of his successes was the capture of Crete in 1669.

Another ruler, Mustapha I, with a large army of over a quarter of a million men, marched on Vienna in 1683, but not far from its gates he was defeated by John (III) Sobieski, king of Poland, and in a short while Mustapha and the Turks were cleared out of Austria-Hungary altogether.

By the late seventeenth century the Ottoman empire was in steady decline. While the Turks were still powerful in parts of Europe they were not really in control. In 1699 they made peace with Austria-Hungary, Poland and Venice, and in 1700 agreed to a truce with Russia. At this time the sultan's court was in continual revolt and an endless succession of grand-viziers rose up to try to restore order. The economic structure of the empire was faulty and it was not helped by the practice of farming out tax-collection as this was inevitably accompanied by corruption. Efforts were made from time to time to reform matters but they consistently failed. It seemed as if Islam was bent on closing its mind to western European ideas and new techniques and so the empire stagnated. The behaviour of the sultans deteriorated, cruelty abounded, immorality was rife. In the provinces the nobles again acted like the feudal lords in England at the time of King Stephen.

Ultimately, the provinces started to ignore Turkey altogether and broke out on their own.

The Turks struggled incessantly with the Russians for domination of the Black Sea, the eastern Mediterranean and even the Balkan countries. Time and again in the nineteenth century tne Ottoman empire was bolstered up by western European powers only in order to prevent its dismemberment at the hands of the Russians. The Crimean War (1854–56) was but one example of Western powers going to the aid of a tottering Turkey.

In the First World War (1914–18) the Ottoman empire joined the central European powers, Germany and Austria, and with German help beat off a British invasion of the Dardanelles, which guarded the approach to Constantinople. But when the subject Arab peoples in the Near East were encouraged by the British to revolt and were supported by arms it was the beginning of the end for the Ottomans, whose empire collapsed in the last year of the war.

The victorious allied powers planned to dismember Turkey after the war, but this was strenuously resisted. Opposition was organized by Mustapha Kemal, a Turkish general who had fought with distinction in the Dardanelles. He founded a nationalist movement and in 1920 he set up a provisional government at Ankara. Then he set out to modernize Turkey. The sultanate was abolished and a republic was declared. Kemal took the name Ataturk and ruled as a dictator till his death in 1938. He eliminated the religious influence in politics, introduced Western

The capture of Sebastopol, the important naval fortress in the Crimea, involved the French and British armies in a long and painful siege in order to save the Turks from the attacking Russians

Kemal Ataturk, founder of modern Turkey

ideas of dress, fashion and manners, and revolutionized transport, public services and the language (by introducing a Latin alphabet). He developed trade and industry, and fostered a sense of national pride in being Turkish rather than Islamic. When he died he was followed by Ismet Inonu, a man of similar stature.

Turkey remained neutral throughout the Second World War, though much help was given to British and Allied servicemen who managed to escape from the Germans across Turkish territory. Since the war the Turks have maintained their friendship with Britain and the West, not the least because through centuries of tradition they have feared the power of Russia, a fear that has been as great in this age as ever before.

### Egypt

Meanwhile, the provinces of the Ottoman empire, as has been said, elected to follow their own paths of destiny. Egypt broke away and was ruled by a succession of dictators. Then in 1798 it was invaded by Napoleon Bonaparte (*See* page 348) who aimed to get at the British in India by cutting off their land routes. In 1802 Egypt was restored to Turkey and three years later the sultan appointed a new khedive (or governor), Mahomet Ali

(1805–49). This remarkable man did much to bring contemporary standards of living to Egypt. He enlisted the help of the French in building a navy and in developing the army. The economy was reformed and invigorated. Then he invaded and overran the Sudan and founded the city of Khartoum.

The next khedive but one, Mahomet Said (1854–63), granted the French facilities to construct the Suez Canal. His son Ismail continued the modernizing process started by Mahomet Ali, but when he abdicated in 1879 all the good that he did was cancelled out by his successor. This was Tewfik, a weak, vacillating man who, in thirteen years, laid his country open to considerable misery. In 1882 British troops moved into Egypt to put down a serious rising there (Britain had purchased a majority of shares in the Suez Canal in 1876 and so regarded the revolt as threatening her

The Suez Canal was constructed over the years 1859–69 under the supervision of a Frenchman, Ferdinand de Lesseps

General Gordon was murdered by Sudanese rebels in Khartoum in January 1885

interests), and from 1883 to 1907 the country was in practice governed by a British administrator, Lord Cromer.

In 1914 Egypt was declared a British protectorate, but in 1922 it was granted independence, with a new ruler, Fuad I, a brother of Tewfik. Gradually the British withdrew, except from the Canal zone, and in 1952 the monarchy was overthrown. Four years later Colonel Gamal Nasser seized power. He ordered the British to leave in 1956 and then nationalized the Suez Canal. Nasser died in 1970, and was succeeded by Anwar Sadat who made courageous efforts to resolve the persisting Israeli-Arab conflict but was assassinated in 1981. The new president is Hosni Mubarak.

### Morocco

Morocco left the Ottoman empire and slid back into a mediaeval condition. In 1905 France attempted to conquer the country, but got involved with Spain, which had interests nearby. In 1956 both nations abandoned their interests and a new nation was formed.

320

## Tunisia

Tunisia was still under the direct control of the Ottomans in the early nineteenth century but the local governor, or bey, was in effective charge. In the 1870s the French moved in with offers of aid for modernization, and in 1881 Tunisia became a French protectorate. Full self-government was given to Tunisia in 1956.

## The Sudan

The Sudan was conquered by Mahomet Ali who valued the province as a supplier of slaves (the Ottomans still had slaves to manage the menial tasks of living). Under a fanatical leader calling himself the Mahdi, the Sudanese rebelled against Egypt in 1883. General Charles 'Chinese' Gordon, sent by the British to try to put down the revolt, was killed in Khartoum in 1885. His murder was avenged when Lord Kitchener led an Anglo-Egyptian army up the Nile towards Khartoum and at Omdurman crushed the rebels in 1898. The Sudan then became an Anglo-Egyptian condominium, and received self-government in 1956. Since the 1980s Muslims in the north and the Christians of the south have fought a bitter civil war.

Saddam Hussein in 1983. The Iraqi invasion of Kuwait in August 1990, began a military action in the Gulf, led by the U.S.A. Iraq claimed that Kuwait was violating its oil quota

## Syria

Syria remained part of the Ottoman empire up to 1918. In 1920 after two years of fighting, it became a French protectorate, but in 1961 it became fully independent.

## Iraq

Iraq, now the nation which lies between the Tigris and the Euphrates, was a Turkish province up to 1918. It then became a British protectorate, and in 1921 the emir, Feisal, was proclaimed king. In 1930 Iraq was granted independence, but during the Second World War British troops occupied the country to protect it from German infiltration. After the war Iraq became independent again, under King Feisal II. He was murdered in 1958 and a republic was set up. Saddam Hussein became president in 1979.

# Persia Lives On

Persia had once had a grand and highly progressive empire, but with the coming of Islam it sank into a state of anarchy in which local lords ruled tyrannically over their people and did nothing for the unity of the country. Persia had been the victim of the Arabs, the Seljuks, Genghis Khan, the Mongols and Timurlaine. In the sixteenth century more Mongols moved in and established a new dynasty of rulers, the Safavids.

The first Safavid king was Ismail (1500 — 24), who called himself the shah (from the name Caesar). He organized the various petty states into one kingdom which occupied the same sort of territory that Parthia had owned several centuries earlier. Ismail, who claimed descent from Mahomet the Prophet, ruled harshly and exterminated all other religions.

Persia was invaded by Selim I of the Ottoman empire in 1513 and had to yield huge areas of land. Ismail's son, Tahmasp, was driven out of Baghdad by Suleiman the Magnificent in 1535, and Persia was reduced to a small state. Despite this, the economy of the Persians was greatly developed and there was a revival of Persian learning, and art and literature. This revival produced some wonderful paintings and sculpture.

In 1586 a descendant of Ismail I, Abbas I, seized power and made himself shah. This tough, ruthless, brilliant organizer drove out Ottoman troops and established the Persian kingdom anew. To hold it together he reformed the army and invited European military experts to train and run it. He also supplied the army with artillery. When he died in 1628 Persia was as great as it had been in the best times of Ismail I.

Unfortunately, Abbas's successors were little more than luxury-loving, cruel and self-indulgent tyrants, and all his work came to nothing under them. The country became an easy prey to Turks, Russians, Afghans and Mongols. In 1722 the Afghans set up their own shah, Mahmoud. He was expelled by Nadir Shah, a central Asian chief, who also invaded India. Nadir Shah had many good ideas about government but never had the opportunity of putting them into operation. After his death in 1747 Persia declined still further until its territory was absorbed entirely by the Ottoman empire. Thereafter Persia remained in the background, making little progress, although it did retain its own language, art and culture.

In the nineteenth century the country was exploited by Britain and Russia for its minerals, oil and textiles. After the end of the First World War Persia obtained independence again, and was modernized by an army general, Reza Khan, who became shah in 1925. He built roads, railways and towns with Western help. He created a new army and reorganized government service. In 1941, his son Mahomet Pahlevi succeeded and ruled Persia, since 1935 known as Iran, until 1979. He made many efforts to modernize Iran and bring social reform, but earned widespread unpopularity because of his use of secret police. He was driven out by an Islamic-motivated revolutionary movement, master-minded by a religious leader, Ayatollah Khomeini, who had been in exile for years. The new government turned away from Western ideas, in favour of a strict Islamic republic. From 1980 to 1988 Iran was at war with its neighbour Iraq.

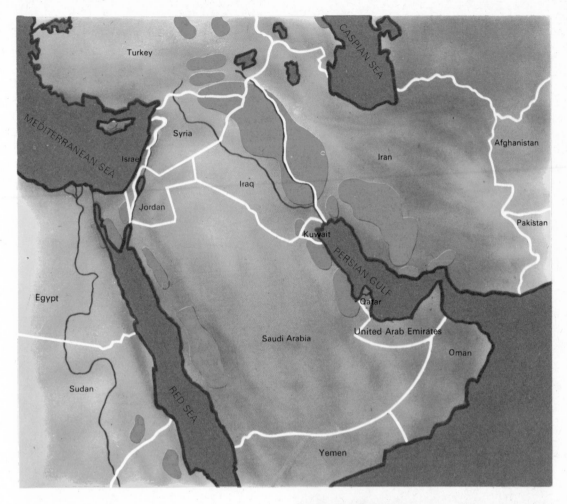

Oilfields have developed with amazing speed since the 1930s in North Africa and the Middle East (*see* map of the principal oil producing countries), and petroleum is, in fact, the chief source of revenue for these areas. On the right is an oil refinery at Jeddah, on the Red Sea

# The Reformation

As Christianity spread and the Church increased its power, much of its original simplicity was lost. In the Middle Ages the Church became corrupt in many ways. The standard of clerical morality was low. Privileges, rank and power were more important than ministering to congregations and to the poor and the sick. The Church was wealthy and priesthood had become a life of comfort without effort. The leaders of the Church were politicians, war leaders, patrons of art, but they were not good shepherds of their flocks. Moreover, the doctrines of the Church needed reform, for they had developed through decisions of Popes and committees and had obscured the original teachings of the gospels.

The need for reform was first pointed out in the fourteenth and fifteenth centuries. Men like England's John Wycliffe and Bohemia's John Huss began preaching and agitating for reform, but their movements were crushed. From time to time the evils of the Church were attacked by scholars like Savonarola (an Italian), Erasmus (a Dutchman), and Colet (an Englishman) who founded St. Paul's School. But it was not until the time of the monk, Martin Luther (1483–1546), that the great revolt began.

Luther was professor of Divinity at Wittenburg in Germany. During this time he visited Rome and was very shocked by what he saw there – the high living of the clergy and the irreligious behaviour of the officials who surrounded the Pope. When he returned to Germany he was in a disturbed state of mind. Then something else happened which stirred him. The Pope, Julius II, anxious to rebuild St. Peter's Cathedral in Rome, was selling indulgences to all who cared to buy them. These were pieces of paper which said that in return for a money payment towards the rebuilding fund the purchaser was forgiven his sins and would be excused punishment for them. These indulgences were sold by 'pardoners' throughout Europe.

Luther believed these to be unlawful according to Church teaching, and he published his objections. These, along with a number of other matters to which he also wanted to draw attention, he included in a document containing ninety-five 'theses', or arguments, which he nailed to the door of the church in Wittenburg in 1517. He had meant the document only to be the starting point of

Map of Europe showing the divisions between Catholics and Protestants

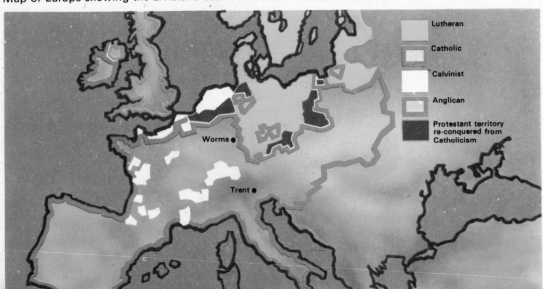

Girolamo Savonarola (1452–98), an Italian monk, preached against high living in certain sectors of the Church. After several warnings which he ignored, he was tried and executed

translated the New Testament into German and this enabled a larger number of people to read the original words of the gospels. Translations were made into other languages (into English in 1525 by William Tyndale), with the same result.

The Holy Roman Emperor, Charles V, viewed these proceedings with dismay. The disagreements about the very fundamentals of Christianity would be bound to lead to strife between states. He tried to get the princes of the empire to come to some arrangement. In 1539, Charles came to a truce with the Protestants at Frankfurt and finally in 1555, by the Religious Peace of Augsburg, it was agreed that Lutheran states would be officially recognized and that the Imperial Chamber would consist half of Catholics and half of Protestants.

Martin Luther (1483–1546), the German religious reformer, nails his 95 theses to the church door at Wittenburg

academic discussion, but in no time at all the news of his action spread throughout Germany. Some of the princes were already opposed to paying German money to the Pope on any grounds, and now they used Luther's arguments to support their own grievances. Luther was ordered by the Church to withdraw his objections, but he would not do so. So in 1520 he was declared a heretic and excommunicated. The Church was thus split into two factions—those who supported Luther and those who did not.

Luther's stand was the signal for other scholars and clergy to press for reform. He had opened men's eyes to a number of awkward questions about the differences between Christianity as preached by the early gospels and as practised by the Church of the time. Luther himself

Meanwhile, in Switzerland, another reformer had set the world of the Church and of scholars talking. This was John Calvin who believed in a return to the strict moral code of the Bible. To make his point he set up at Geneva, in 1541, where he lived, a Church in which the members lived their lives in strict accordance with the teachings of Jesus. All enjoyments were strictly censored and, if necessary, forbidden. This regime had the profoundest effect upon Europe, not least of all in Scotland where one of Calvin's greatest disciples, John Knox, began to preach in 1541. Knox succeeded in converting most of Scotland to Protestantism in a very short time.

By the middle of the sixteenth century the Reformation had a firm foothold in most of western Europe. But it was another hundred years before the Catholic powers would accept that nations had the right to choose for themselves their own brand of Christianity, for they would not accept the Augsburg arrangement. The differences in religion were used by many princes to further their own ambitions. Philip II of Spain sent the Great Armada against England ostensibly to bring the country back into the Catholic fold, but in reality to add yet one more country to his expanding empire. Catherine, the mother of Charles IX of France, had Protestants massacred in Paris in the name of Catholicism, but in reality the act was to strengthen her hold over the king. And Cardinal Richelieu went to the aid of the Protestants in the Thirty Years' War (*See* page 353) so that in the end France would triumph over the other contending nations – which it did.

John Calvin (1509–1564), the French religious reformer, giving a sermon at Geneva. Calvinists did not approve of lavish ornament or decoration in churches and this accounts for the richly carved pulpit being shrouded in sheeting

There have always been disagreements between believers in any religion. Sometimes these differences have resulted in warfare or massacre, and dreadful crimes have been committed in the name of different faiths. This is one of the ironies of history. But in the history of the world no religion has engendered such violence, quarrelling or warfare as has Christianity.

A portrait by Holbein of Desiderius Erasmus (1466–1536), the Dutch religious reformer, who for a while was professor of divinity at Cambridge

# Spain and Portugal

In Chapter Thirty-eight mention was made of the fact that the Moslems retained the kingdom of Granada in southern Spain for a century and a half after being defeated on the Salado by Alfonso XI of Castile in 1340. By 1490 Ferdinand of Aragon succeeded in beating the Moslems and driving them out of Spain altogether. Whether this was a blessing or a curse is open to argument, for the small Moslem kingdom was one of great enlightenment and civilized luxury which eclipsed anything else in the whole peninsula. Granada was, above all, free from the religious bigotry that was to characterize almost every Spanish action in the future, and which was largely responsible for the deterioration in Spanish strength and energy.

Ferdinand had married Isabella of Castile in 1469, thereby uniting all of Spain except Granada. Their grandson, Charles I of Spain, was also Charles V, the Emperor of the Holy Roman Empire, due to the fact that his mother, Joan the Mad, married Philip of Hapsburg.

Spain was a splendid kingdom with a vast empire throughout the sixteenth and most of the seventeenth century. Its people were united under Roman Catholicism, its soldiers were among the best in Europe, and its wealth from the new colonies in the Americas was unsurpassed. But it was partly the empire abroad which helped to bring down the might of Spain, for as time went on, jealous nations attacked the Spanish treasure fleets and made it dangerous and expensive for the riches from the colonies to be brought home. Worse, the Inquisition – a government agency which examined and punished people who did not conform to Catholic doctrines – was extended by Spanish kings to embrace almost anyone who did not think the way they did. This resulted in the stifling of creative thought and scientific investigation.

Despite this, Spain was the dominant power in Europe for most of the period, 1500–1650. Charles V's reign was very successful for Spain.

Charles's son became Philip II of Spain. In his time his half-brother Don John of Austria led a fleet which smashed the Ottoman fleet at Lepanto in 1571, which

Two Spanish Jews are examined by judges of the Inquisition. At right, a masked executioner stands by to carry out whatever sentence is passed, beheading, burning or strangulation

marked the beginning of the downfall of the greatness of Ottoman power. In 1580 Philip annexed Portugal and thus came into possession of further colonial territories in South America, India and the Far East. Spanish art flourished. Miguel Cervantes, who had fought at Lepanto, wrote *Don Quixote*, one of the most famous novels in history. Despite the important events during Philip's reign, Spanish power began to decline. This was tragic because Spain had basically so much to contribute to European civilization.

Philip was a strange ruler. Industrious, extraordinarily patient, and filled with a sense of duty, he spent the best part of his reign in Spain and tried to run a large empire by means of a vast correspondence. Even the progress and the tactics which the commander of the Spanish Armada was to employ against England were carefully set out in a stream of letters taken by fast boat to the admiral while he was sailing up the English Channel in 1588. It is hardly surprising that the Armada was defeated.

Philip's worst difficulties were encountered in the Netherlands, which were,

Miguel de Cervantes Saavedra (1547–1616), Spain's most famous author, lost an arm at the Battle of Lepanto

Map of Spanish colonies in South America in 1828

by 1555, seventeen separate states with their own separate constitutions. They were busy little communities, constructing ships, running markets and engaging in overseas trade. Some of them wished to be Protestant states, but Philip would not allow this. To crush them he sent the Duke of Alva as viceroy, with a large army, to govern the whole area. Alva became unpopular for his crippling taxation.

The northern Protestant-inclined states were led by Prince William of Orange who devoted his whole life to the expulsion of Spain from the Netherlands. Helped by England, he cut the dykes and let in the waters which seriously hampered the troops and baggage trains of Alva's army. Spain poured millions of the wealth, which kept arriving in Spanish ports every year from the Americas, into the Netherlands. A price was put on William's head, and in 1584 he was assassinated. For a while the northern states, which we call Dutch, were in serious danger of collapse, but the destruction of the Spanish Armada brought them a respite. William's son,

Philip II, king of Spain (1556–98) organized the construction of a huge monastery, called the Escorial, about 30 miles north of Madrid. It is built of grey granite. A palace was added in the 17th century. The Escorial is often called the Eighth Wonder of the World

Maurice of Orange, proved to be as great a leader as his father and at Turnhout, in 1597, he completely defeated a large Spanish army in open battle. Thereafter, the Dutch moulded themselves into a nation, pressed on with their trading and commercial enterprises, and began to found colonies in many parts of the world, especially the East Indies.

When Philip II died in 1598, he had lost much of his empire and wasted vast amounts of money in fighting to keep it, but he was none the less still the richest and most powerful ruler in Europe. In the seventeenth century Spain no longer

Simón Bolívar (1783–1830), known as The Liberator. Venezuelan by birth, Bolívar organized movements for independence from Spanish rule in several South American countries

posed the danger she had in the sixteenth. In 1640 the Portuguese won their independence and when, in 1661, a Portuguese princess, Catherine of Braganza, married the king of England, Charles II, a favourable alliance was created.

By the end of the seventeenth century Spain was very much in decline. Her colonies were costing more to run and protect than the wealth extracted from them. The Spanish system of finance was faulty, for taxes were placed on thriving industries to such an extent that they were stifled. All the while the interests of the ordinary people were scarcely ever considered. Religious persecution and the Inquisition continued.

Throughout the eighteenth century Spain languished in a backward condition, dominated for all practical purposes by France (*See* page 349). Napoleon regarded the Spanish as being utterly insignificant and he put his own brother on the Spanish throne. But Spanish pride was not altogether dead. It reasserted itself in a well organized rising in 1808 when the insurgents completely routed the army of General Dupont, who had been sent to put them down, at Bailen. The effect of this Spanish success throughout Europe was profound. It was Napoleon's first major set-back, and revealed that he was not invincible after all. The English came to help the Spanish in their struggle against the French, and with the Duke of Wellington in command, the two nations drove the French right out of the peninsula altogether.

After the end of the war with Napoleon, there was a revolt in the Spanish army. The leaders insisted on a new constitution of a more liberal kind for the country. At first the king gave in, but before long he reasserted his power. The liberal ideas, however, had already spread to the Spanish colonies in South America where

Francisco Franco was dictator of Spain from 1939–1975. As he promised, Spain became a monarchy after his death

Repressive government, meanwhile, continued in Spain throughout the nineteenth and into the twentieth century, despite a number of revolts. In 1931 Alfonso XIII was driven into exile and a liberal Communist government took over the reins of power. For five years this government tried to bring some semblance of modern standards to Spain, but in 1936 a violent civil war broke out led by revolutionary army officers. Their leader was General Francisco Franco who, in 1939, triumphed over his adversaries. He established a right-wing government and remained in power as dictator until 1975.

During the Second World War, Spain was allied with Germany and Italy but did not enter the war in a fighting capacity. On Franco's death the monarchy was restored under Juan Carlos II, and in 1977 Spain had its first democratically elected government since 1936. In 1986 Spain and Portugal joined the European Community.

Portugal developed slowly during the nineteenth century. It had colonies in Africa, the Far East and India, but lost control of Brazil in 1822. There was little progress towards a democratic government. In 1910 King Manuel II was driven out of the country after a revolution, and a republic was set up. In 1926 army officers seized power.

Six years later the minister of finance, Dr Antonio de Oliveira Salazar, became premier and dictator of Portugal. He held power until he had a stroke in 1968, dying two years later. In 1974 Portugal had a revolution and became a democratic republic.

Portugal has given up its colonies, except for the island of Macao off the coast of China. Of its African colonies, Portuguese Guinea (now Guinea Bissau) was granted independence in September 1974, Mozambique became independent in June 1975, and Angola in November 1975.

movements for independence began to grow rapidly.

The principal champion of these movements was a Venezuelan, Simon Bolivar, who had been educated in Madrid and had travelled widely in Europe and North America. Bolivar organized resistance to Spanish rule in Venezuela, and by 1819 had driven the Spaniards out of Venezuela and New Granada and formed a republic called Colombia. Five years later he had driven the Spaniards out of Ecuador and Peru and created new republics, and in 1826 the southern section of Peru was formed into the republic of Bolivia, named after him.

Bolivar aimed to unite all South America under him as a federation of republics (Argentina had become one in 1816 and Chile in 1818, both with the help from British adventurers), but the idea was not popular. In 1829 Venezuela itself separated from Colombia. Bolivar died in 1830, revered by his people.

# The Rise of Great Britain

The victory of Henry Tudor at Bosworth in 1485 and his accession to the throne signalled the beginning of a great age for England, and in varying degrees Wales, Scotland and Ireland as well. Apart from his other qualities Henry VII was an astute business man and had a remarkable understanding of finance (many of the royal exchequer accounts of his reign were personally audited by him and his initials can be seen on the account sheets).

Henry immediately realized that England had far more to gain from commercial and diplomatic agreements with other countries than from endless warfare and hostility. So he negotiated trade

The Welshman Henry VII (1485–1509) was the first practical businessman to occupy the English throne. His supporters often claimed that he was descended from Owain Glyndŵr and from earlier independent Welsh princes

agreements with the Low Countries. He arranged the marriage of his son to the daughter of the king and queen of Spain and of his daughter to the king of Scotland, James IV, and thereby obtained valuable alliances. He also turned his attention to the internal state of the country. To stop the incessant temptation to civil war he broke, once and for all, the power of the barons by forbidding them to have private armies, by monopolizing all manufacture and supply of gunpowder, and by instituting the Court of Star Chamber, a tribunal in which even the grandest lord could neither browbeat the jury nor bully the judges.

His careful nursing of the nation's finances enabled him to leave at his death, in 1509, more than two million pounds in cash to his son, Henry VIII (at least twenty million pounds in today's money).

Henry VIII began his reign well enough. Strong, handsome, cultured, musical, a great dancer and games player, he delighted the nation in the early days with his fondness for pageantry and entertainment. He left the distasteful business of government to Thomas Wolsey, the son of an Ipswich butcher who had, through sheer perseverance and ability, risen to a bishopric. Wolsey loved hard work and was an excellent foreign secretary as well as home administrator. For nearly twenty years he managed the kingdom, earning the greatest unpopularity by his arrogance, greed and lust for splendour and pomp. When he failed, however, to get the Pope to grant Henry a divorce from his wife, Katherine of Aragon, daughter of the king of Spain (Henry wanted to marry a court lady-in-waiting, Ann Boleyn, as Katherine had

Henry VIII (right) with left to right Cromwell, Wolsey and Cranmer. All three served him well and made themselves hated for it

not given him a son), Henry dismissed his minister and would have had him executed had Wolsey not died on the way to London (1530).

Wolsey's successor, the compliant Thomas Cranmer, Archbishop of Canterbury, pronounced the annulment of Henry's marriage to Katherine and enabled the king to marry Ann. The Pope at once excommunicated the king, whereupon Henry broke with the Roman Catholic Church (1534) and declared himself Supreme Head of the English Church. All the same, he did not bring the country to the Protestant faith (*See* page 328), and this made life difficult for the people because they had to deny the supremacy of the Pope (a vital Roman Catholic doctrine), but at the same time adhere to most of the Church's other teachings.

Ann Boleyn failed to give Henry a son, though she bore him a daughter in 1533 who later became Queen Elizabeth I. Ann was accused of infidelity to the king and beheaded in 1536. By that time the king was already in love with Jane Seymour, the daughter of a Wiltshire landowner. Henry married her, but she died the following year giving birth to a son, the future Edward VI.

The rest of Henry's reign was a catalogue of disasters. His new chief minister was Thomas Cromwell, a low-born adventurer of considerable gifts. He superintended the dissolution of the

Mary Tudor married Philip of Spain in 1554

A contemporary portrait of Queen Elizabeth I which hangs in Hatfield House

monasteries, and raised severe taxes. He fell from favour in 1540 and was executed. The king appointed other ministers who had to carry out the unpleasant business of raising money. Eventually, the coinage had to be debased which brought great misery to large sections of the people. When he died in 1547, the nation sighed with relief.

His son, a sickly nine-year-old boy, became Edward VI and, under the guidance of his uncle, Edward Seymour (who had himself made Duke of Somerset and Protector of England), ushered England into Protestantism, to the accompaniment of the smashing of stained glass windows, white-washing of walls and pictures and the destruction of religious furniture and ornaments in churches up and down the country. Somerset ruled with a good heart but with poor judgment. A slight revolt in the West Country was crushed with unnecessary severity and a serious rising in East Anglia was met with weakness. Somerset was ousted from power by

John Dudley, Earl of Warwick, a tough, brave, unscrupulous and very able statesman. He made himself Duke of Northumberland and then ruled harshly. When it became clear that Edward VI would not live, Northumberland tried to ensure that the succession would pass to his daughter-in-law, Lady Jane Grey, a descendant of Henry VII, in preference to Henry VIII's eldest daughter, Mary Tudor. But he got no support, and when Edward died the people of London rose in support of Mary who declined to spare the life of the duke (1553).

Mary was bent on restoring the Roman Catholic faith in England, and in five years she destroyed all the good will of the people by her persecution and burning of Protestants. One of her victims was Thomas Cranmer. She angered the nation by marrying Philip of Spain (soon to become the powerful King Philip II), and she humiliated the nation by the loss of Calais, England's last French possession.

She died in 1558 and was succeeded by her half-sister, Elizabeth.

Elizabeth I's reign was one of the most glorious and productive in English history. The Protestant faith was established along the middle-of-the-road lines, that is, neither imitating Roman Catholicism nor embracing Puritanism. Peace was made with France. Trade was encouraged. English sea-captains were rewarded for their bold attacks on Spanish treasure fleets, coming from Spain's rich empire in South America. The first English trading station was opened in India and the East India Company was granted a charter in 1600. It was a literary age, too. Christopher Marlowe invented blank verse in poetry and penned some of the best poems in the language, and William Shakespeare began to write the first plays of his incomparable output. Other literary men of hardly less brilliance, like

William Shakespeare (1564–1616) a writer of universal appeal, is regarded as England's greatest poet and playwright

Spenser, Jonson and Bacon, also flourished. Traders and public servants who became rich built themselves grand houses in a style that compared favourably with many contemporary styles in Europe.

For years Elizabeth and her government aggravated the patient king of Spain, Philip II, but when the queen signed the death warrant of Mary, Queen of Scots (*See* page 307) his patience ran out. A huge armada of ships carrying troops and weapons was launched against England. The Spaniards were not helped, however, by the fact that it was led by the Duke of Medina Sidonia, a man who had never been to sea. When it sailed up the English Channel, Effingham and Sir Francis Drake attacked the heavy, ponderous and overcrowded ships and drove them off.

Elizabeth never married and when she died in 1603 she was succeeded by Mary Queen of Scots' son, James VI of Scotland, who was her cousin. He became James I of England, Scotland and Ireland. This stuttering, shambling 'know-all' who liked to be known as the 'British Solomon' for his self-confessed wisdom but who only became known as the 'Wisest Fool in Christendom', reduced the prestige of

Heavy galleons of the Spanish Armada were dispersed and set alight by small fire ships sent against them by Sir Francis Drake

and then ruled alone for eleven years. In that time he alienated all classes by his dictatorial behaviour. When he tried to get inland counties to pay Ship Money, a tax first raised in the eleventh century on seacoast counties only for the purpose of providing ships for the defence of the realm, a Buckinghamshire landowner John Hampden refused to pay. The king sued him and Hampden lost, but he became the hero of the hour for his stand.

Charles's chief advisers, the able and ruthless Thomas Wentworth, Earl of Strafford, and the rigid, high-churchman, William Laud, Archbishop of Canterbury, managed the kingdom and earned universal loathing. In 1640, short of money, Charles summoned a parliament, but it would not vote him any funds unless he agreed to moderate his rule. They demanded the head of Strafford, which the king agreed to, in spite of having promised his servant protection. Disagreements between the king and parliament continued and when, in 1642,

the country to its lowest ebb and undermined the stability of government at home. Believing he ruled by Divine Right, he cared nothing for the wishes of parliament or the people. His attitude that his subjects should conform to the Church of England drove the Puritans underground, and many of them emigrated to Holland and to North America from 1620 onwards. When he died in 1625 the nation was filled with discontent. The crass behaviour of his son Charles guaranteed revolution and ensured the triumph of democratic forces in England.

The reign of Charles I (1625–49) can be divided into two parts: 1625–42 and 1642–49. The first was a black period in English history when the king ruled as a tyrant. Having been compelled by parliament in 1628 to agree to the Petition of Right – a document that bound him not to raise illegal taxes or quarter troops with civilians and so terrorize the community – he promptly refused to abide by its terms, dismissed parliament

Charles tried to arrest five leading members of parliament in the House of Commons, this proved to be the flash-point of civil war.

Charles retired to the midlands, and parliament at once secured the support of the City of London, with its bankers and merchants. At first the king had some success, but Oliver Cromwell, the member of parliament for Huntingdon, forged a new kind of army on a professional basis with proper training and regular quarters, and with it defeated the king at Marston Moor and Naseby. After protracted negotiations between parliament and the king, during which Charles secretly tried to get together fresh armies from abroad to restore him to power, the parliamentarians decided to put him on trial. In 1649 he was found guilty of treason to the country and executed.

For the next four years the political situation in England was uncertain.

Parliament ruled but could not agree among its members. Eventually Cromwell, in 1653, now the head of the army and the most respected man in the country, expelled the members and took over the government himself. He had made himself lord-protector.

This remarkable man ruled with firmness and wisdom for five years, and in that time he accomplished much. In war abroad, the English troops won widespread renown for their fighting qualities. The navy beat the Dutch and the Spanish. New colonies were added to the empire, including Jamaica. At home, Cromwell reformed the courts of law, granted toleration of all kinds of Protestant belief, and reconstructed the taxation system. England began to prosper once again, while overseas the name of Cromwell was held in awe.

In 1658 Cromwell died and was succeeded by his son Richard, who had

At the battle of Naseby, in 1645, Oliver Cromwell, a middle-aged country gentleman, proved himself one of the greatest military commanders in all history

no liking for power at all and soon resigned. After a period of uncertainty, Charles I's eldest son was invited to come home and be king, and in the summer of 1660 he was welcomed as Charles II. This tall, handsome and pleasure-loving prince was in many ways an astute ruler. But in his reign of twenty-five years not much was achieved either at home or abroad. The Habeas Corpus Act of 1679 ensured that no man was arrested and detained without trial. Art, the theatre, building, especially after the Great Fire of London in 1666, and science flourished for this was the age of Sir Peter Lely, John Dryden, Isaac Newton, Robert Boyle, and Christopher Wren.

All through his reign Charles resisted the efforts of Louis XIV to get him to bring England back into the Roman Catholic faith, but no sooner had he died in 1685 than his brother James II (1685–88) embarked upon a determined policy of total restoration of the faith. In three years James made himself thoroughly unpopular by his repressive acts against Protestants – he even put seven bishops on trial for refusing to agree to the Declaration of Indulgence granting privileges to Roman Catholics. In the summer of 1688 the discontented elements of the nobility invited his son-in-law, William,

Marshal Tallard (centre) surrenders to Marlborough at Blenheim (1704)

St Paul's cathedral in London was designed by Sir Christopher Wren and built from 1675–1710

Prince of Orange – the champion of Protestants in Europe – to come to England 'to restore her liberties'. William landed in Devonshire and marched towards London. James's forces deserted him and he fled from the country to live out his life in exile.

Prince William became William III of England, Scotland and Ireland, and ruled jointly with his wife Mary who was James's daughter. He had to agree to a number of new rights and liberties for parliament and the people.

William's reign was an important one. Domestically, he granted religious toleration, founded the Bank of England, and gave the press a fair measure of freedom (newspapers were a rewarding and thriving business). Abroad he spent his time thwarting the ambitions of Louis XIV of France by building up alliances with European countries and fighting him. In this he was helped by John Churchill, later to become Duke of Marlborough. When William died from a fall from his horse in 1702 he left England strong, united and well able to resist Louis XIV. By the Act of Settlement of 1701 William had ensured that England would be ruled by Protestant monarchs.

He was succeeded by his wife's sister, Anne (1702–14). Her reign was little more than the story of the career of the great Duke of Marlborough. Anne was on very good terms with Marlborough and, more especially with his wife, Sarah. While this friendship lasted the duke had free rein to display the most magnificent military talents ever possessed by an Englishman. In the War of the Spanish Succession (1702–13) he crushed France and her allies at Blenheim (1704), Ramillies (1706), Oudenarde (1708) and Malplaquet (1709). He was also a skilful statesman and negotiator and might perhaps have ruled England as captain-general. But there was opposition to him, and in 1710 Sarah and the queen quarrelled and the great soldier was dismissed.

# The Greatness of France

The history of France in the sixteenth century presents little more than a long story of civil war over religion. The nation might have become the greatest in Europe, but that role fell to Spain and the events in France at this time were dismal.

At the end of the fifteenth century Charles VIII had dreams of conquering Italy and in 1494 he invaded the peninsula, capturing Florence, Pisa and Rome. But this provoked other European powers to resist him and, led by Austria and Spain, they forced Charles to leave Italy.

His successor, Louis XII, also tried to win land in Italy, with little success, but his cousin, Francis I, who made a great show of crossing the Alps like Hannibal, won a number of victories and forced the Pope to allow the French to appoint their own bishops and clergy.

France went to war with the Emperor of the Holy Roman Empire, Charles V, in 1525. When the Reformation began to sweep Europe and the German states elected to choose for themselves which side they would take, Francis I, although a Roman Catholic, threw in his support for those that elected to accept the Protestant faith, and he sided with them against the emperor. France was defeated, however, at Pavia, in Italy.

By 1560 France itself was torn in two between supporters of Catholicism and followers of the reformed faith, whether Lutheran or Calvinist. At Vassy hundreds of Protestants were massacred by the Catholics, and the war between the two sides went on for thirty years. The monarchy was Roman Catholic, but many of the most powerful nobility were not, and while this situation lasted no peace was possible. The civil war was so intense that French prestige sank and the general development of the nation was arrested.

Protestants in France, called Huguenots, were, to begin with, led by Admiral Coligny. He and the king, Charles IX, were on very good terms and tried to

On St Bartholomew's Day, 24th August 1572, many thousands of French Protestants were murdered by order of the king (left)

Cardinal Richelieu personally conducted the siege of La Rochelle (right)

reach a settlement. But the king's mother, Catherine de Medici, tried to wreck the agreement for she feared that religious toleration in France would bring her influence to an end. On St Bartholomew's Day in 1572, when some thousands of Protestants were visiting Paris for meetings, without the king's knowledge she ordered them all to be murdered. More than eight thousand were slaughtered by troops in a massacre that stunned Europe. Among the victims was Coligny.

It was a fatal mistake, for the massacre alienated France from all her allies. The Huguenots were now supported by Henry, king of Navarre, a cousin of the French king and in the 1580s the heir to the French throne. In 1589 he succeeded to the throne and so hoped to unite the two sides. But his Protestantism offended the Catholic majority, and in order to keep the peace he became a convert to Roman Catholicism. By the Edict of Nantes in 1598 he granted religious toleration throughout France, and thus the long civil war came to an end. Protestants were now allowed to enter universities, take jobs in the government

Henry IV, one of the greatest kings of France, was assassinated by a fanatic named Ravaillac, in 1610

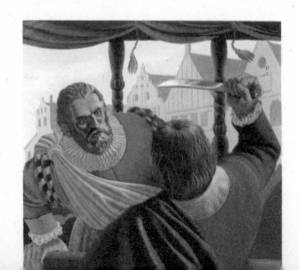

and in the army and even in the law courts. The king then reorganized France with the help of his very capable chief minister, Sully.

Henry was assassinated in 1610 by an insane monk, and his son Louis XIII (1610–43) succeeded him. Louis's reign was a great one for France, very largely because of the career of one of France's greatest men, Cardinal Armand Jean du Plessis de Richelieu, adviser to the queen. This remarkable man became the most influential statesman in Europe. He had one aim: to make France the greatest power in Europe, whatever the cost. He had incredible will power, enormous strength of character, and perhaps the most astute brain in the country.

Richelieu came to power as chief minister in 1624 and remained in power until his death in 1642. His domestic policy was to keep the Protestants under control, with force if necessary (he

343

During his reign of over seventy years, Louis XIV, the 'Sun King', made France the most powerful and civilized nation in Europe

personally led an attack on their stronghold of La Rochelle in 1627). He broke the power of the nobility by blowing up their castles and forbidding private armies. He managed the government of the country through a new class of official, the superintendent, who was drawn from the middle class and therefore not likely to be in sympathy with the aristocracy. These superintendents managed provinces like large local authorities; they had wide powers, and were fully supported by the central government.

Richelieu's foreign policy was directed at making France supreme in Europe. He used every possible device. He supported the Protestants in the Thirty Years' War because their success limited the influence of the empire. He backed the Portuguese who rebelled against Spain in 1640 and declared independence so that Spanish power would be diminished. He encouraged colonial expansion

Thirty Years' War under the two brilliant generals, Condé and Marshal Turenne (perhaps the greatest general in French history apart from Napoleon). Mazarin encountered much opposition at home, and with great difficulty crushed revolts against the government. But he managed to keep French influence in Europe supreme until his death in 1661, in which year the young Louis XIV decided to rule for himself.

Louis dominated France – and Europe – from 1661 to his death in 1715. Known as the 'Sun King' for the splendour of his court and the brilliance of his reign, he was apparently everything that a king should be. He encouraged art, building and science, he managed affairs of government, took a close personal interest in negotiations between France and other nations, and put France on the road to great wealth. Trading companies were opened in America and India, the navy was reconstructed, roads and canals were built, and industry stimulated. Unfortunately, much of his good work was cancelled out by his involving France in

in North America, the West Indies and India.

When Richelieu died in 1642 he was followed by another very able man – a pupil of his – Cardinal Mazarin, who was born in Italy. He, too, was adviser to a queen, the wife of Louis XIII. Louis died in 1643 and was succeeded by Louis XIV, who was only a child. Mazarin virtually ruled France for the next eighteen years. In that time French arms triumphed in the last stages of the

The storming of the Bastille fortress in Paris by revolutionaries on 14th July 1789 was the first major act of violence in the French Revolution. This revolution had a profound effect not only on France but also throughout Europe

wars and by revoking the Edict of Nantes and persecuting Protestants. Many left France to find new lives in other countries like Germany, Britain and the New World. What they gained, France lost, for many were skilled craftsmen.

The two largest wars which nearly crippled France were the war with England from 1689 to 1698, in which a stalemate was reached, and the War of the Spanish Succession (1702–13), in which the English Duke of Marlborough won his splendid victories (*See* page 341).

Louis died in 1715 and was succeeded by his great-grandson, Louis XV (1715–74), who was only a boy. For nearly a century France had led Europe in civilization: now she was to decline, and the decline would be followed by revolution.

Louis XV's reign was filled with struggles to retain the empire and to keep its wealth. Warfare broke out both in Europe and in the French possessions in America, India and the West Indies. The king himself cared little for anything but his own pleasures and was content to

leave the management of government and war to others. The government made the mistake of putting in governors and local commanders in Canada and India, but severely limiting their executive power. This meant they could not always take immediate decisions on the spot, but had to wait for permission to act from Paris. The central government also failed to support these territories with money and troops, and so they were won from France by Britain in the Seven Years' War.

Ineffectual as he was, Louis XV left his name to the furniture which was made during his reign, which was – and still is – undoubtedly the finest and most beautiful in the world. He actively encouraged cabinet-makers in their craft and often discussed intricate mechanisms with them.

His grandson, Louis XVI, was a well-meaning man who wanted very much to arrest the decline of French power, but by making concessions to the restive elements of French society he only hastened the end of the old regime. The country was impoverished. Political power was in the hands of the Parisian aristocrats. The country aristocrats, meanwhile, continued to rule like feudal lords, extracting taxes in mediaeval style from the peasants. These workers were poor, and their agricultural methods hopelessly outdated. The middle class was becoming increasingly aware of its strength and, stirred by such writers as Voltaire, Rousseau and Montesquieu, it began to agitate for radical reforms. The States-General, that is, the French equivalent of parliament, was summoned in 1789. It was the first time it had sat for about one hundred and fifty years. The example of independence and good government set by the United States was in everbody's minds, and revolutionary demands were made.

Bread riots broke out in Paris, and on July 14th an angry mob stormed the Bastille, an intimidating, stone-built symbol of royal tyranny. As it happened there were only four criminals in it. Feudalism was abolished by a vote of the assembly, and a Declaration of the Rights of Man was published.

The king watched these events with some fear. He decided to leave the country but was caught almost on the border. Brought back to Paris he was subjected to what amounted to house arrest and his powers were taken from him.

His wife, Marie Antoinette, an Austrian princess and sister of the emperor, was already unpopular. When Austria declared war on France to try to save Louis, the assembly abolished the monarchy and put the king on trial. He was executed in January 1793, and his wife a few months later.

The Revolution was well under way. The moderates tried to govern at first, but they were overcome by the Jacobins, the leading radical party. Then the Jacobins themselves were divided. Danton and Hébert, two brilliant leaders, were overthrown and executed on the orders of Robespierre, another extremist Jacobin. Robespierre embarked upon a reign of terror for several months; hundreds of people were murdered or brought to the guillotine for execution, generally without trial. Ultimately, Robespierre himself was overthrown by more moderate people and a Directory of Five was appointed to govern the country.

France meanwhile had to contend with invasions along its borders by other European powers, who were appalled at the execution of the king, but the nation held firm. Soon the French would advance across these borders into other lands, under the leadership of a young general born in Corsica, Napoleon Bonaparte.

The Revolution established the supremacy of the middle classes in France in the towns and gave the peasants the greater part of the land in the country. It also established equality before the law.

Queen Marie Antoinette, wife of Louis XVI, was executed by order of the revolutionary government. She had been very unpopular and few Frenchmen regretted her end

Napoleon Bonaparte, one of the most famous generals in the history of the world, entered the French army in 1785, specializing in artillery. He rose rapidly through the officer ranks, even then clearly endowed with amazing military gifts. In his first command, against Austria, he defeated the Austrians and established France as the dominant power in Italy. He had a vivid imagination, excellent administrative ability, and was capable of conceiving great plans and, equally, of absorbing himself in minute details.

He aimed to unite France, govern it from the centre, and establish equality in social and legal matters. He determined to eliminate privilege and conciliate all the classes. Unfortunately, Napoleon had unbounded ambition for power for its own sake, and in the end it destroyed him. Although he was the cause of many good changes in France and Europe, he was the instigator of fifteen years of continuous war which exhausted France and Europe.

In 1798 Napoleon tried to conquer Egypt, but though he defeated the Egyptians at the Battle of the Pyramids his fleet was destroyed at the Battle of the Nile by Nelson, and that kept him locked up in Egypt. While he was there he heard of the general dissatisfaction of France with the Directory and he returned to help overthrow it. The eventual result was that he became first one of three consuls and then sole consul. He also

defeated all of the European armies sent against him, and by 1802 France was the most powerful nation in Europe once again. But Great Britain remained unconquered.

Napoleon turned now to the reorganization of France. He reconstructed local government, simplified and codified the law, and re-established Roman Catholicism as the state religion (the early revolutionaries had turned against religion altogether). He made himself consul for life, and so it was no great step when he had himself declared emperor of the French in 1804. Then he put subordinate kings in other countries. One brother was made king of Holland, and another king of Westphalia.

European powers continued to resist him but he defeated them. At Austerlitz in December 1805 he won a crushing victory against Austria and Russia.

Since he could not break Britain by invasion, he determined to do it by cutting off British trade. By the Continental System he issued orders closing all European ports to British ships and stopped European traders dealing with British markets. But this measure did not work. It only brought great misery to the subject nations for it ruined their trade and made food and raw materials very expensive, because it was more costly to transport goods overland than by sea. Portugal refused to agree to the port closure so Napoleon sent an army to occupy the country in 1807. In 1808 Napoleon deposed the Spanish king and put his own brother on the throne. The Spanish rose in revolt and defeated a French army at Bailen.

Russia did not like the Continental System, and refused to adhere to the terms. Napoleon declared war in 1812, took a 600,000-strong army into that great country and defeated the czar's forces at Borodino. But when he got to Moscow he found it empty, and many of the buildings on fire. All provisions had been removed. So Napoleon could not stay and he made ready to return to France. Then the Russian winter set in and in a few weeks, helped by marauding parties of Russian guerrilla troops, the French army was wrecked. Fuel and food were scarce, the cold appalling, and the roads treacherous. Thousands upon thousands of troops died. When Napoleon returned to France, only 30,000 of the original 600,000 men were with him.

The disaster was a signal for a general uprising in Europe. The Duke of Wellington succeeded in helping the Spanish

Napoleon's invasion of Russia in 1812 was a disastrous failure. Although he defeated Russian forces in battle he was not able to get the czar to surrender. So he retreated, and on the way back, in bitterly cold weather, constantly harassed by guerrilla raids, his 'Grand Armée' was practically destroyed

Louis Philippe, king of France, 1830–1848

were in 1792. Louis XVIII was brought back to the throne again, and in 1824 was succeeded by his younger brother Charles X (1824–30). Charles also tried to ignore the Revolution's achievements and was deposed. A cousin, Louis Philippe, a man of strong democratic feelings, was elected king and remained in power for eighteen years. In his time France developed rapidly. Railways were built, telegraph systems introduced, canals dug, and trade expanded, especially with African lands.

Louis was overthrown in 1848, a year of violent revolutions. After some months of anarchy, Louis Napoleon, Napoleon's nephew, was elected president of the Second Republic. But he was ambitious and did not regard the office as being high enough. He arrested the opposition chiefs and had himself declared emperor following a referendum on a new constitution which he put before the country. He was not at all like his uncle, and for the most part his rule was unsatisfactory. At first he won victories in the field against

The Emperor Napoleon III and his wife, Eugénie, receive the Burmese ambassador. Burma was independent at the time

drive the French out of Spain. At Leipzig Napoleon met a combined army of Russians, Austrians and Prussians and was, for the first time, defeated in a major battle. He abdicated and was granted the island of Elba as a refuge.

Louis XVIII, brother of the executed Louis XVI, then became king, but within three months had made himself so unpopular by trying to reverse some of the achievements of the Revolution that Napoleon, who left Elba and began to march up through France, had no difficulty in gathering support as he went. He fought his last engagement at Waterloo in June 1815, but was defeated by the Duke of Wellington, who admitted that it had been 'a damned close thing'. Napoleon surrendered to the British and was imprisoned on the island of St Helena in the Atlantic Ocean, where he died in 1821. It was an inglorious end to a remarkable career.

After Napoleon's banishment, the Congress of Vienna decided that France's frontiers should be fixed at what they

Austria in Italy, and these were followed by a period of development in France in which Paris was rebuilt. But his gamble in Mexico was a failure, and in the war with Prussia in 1870 he was defeated and captured. The Third Republic was declared and Louis was exiled.

France continued with the expansion of its possessions abroad, especially in North Africa. Towards the end of the century a French detachment nearly came to blows with the British in the Sudan, but the affair was smoothed over by the victor of Omdurman, Lord Kitchener.

In the First World War France bore the brunt of the fighting. It was a war of trench fighting, accompanied by shellfire and devastation, and most of the conflict between the Allies and Germany took place on French soil. Casualties on both sides were very high indeed. Ultimately the Allies triumphed, but the war had all but ruined France.

When twenty years later, the Germans invaded France in the spring of 1940, the whole might of the French army, some 150 or more divisions strong, collapsed — despite the Maginot Line fortifications built between the wars. Part of France was occupied by the Germans until the country was liberated by the Allies in 1944.

After the war no government held power for long. General Charles de Gaulle, patriot and wartime leader of the French resistance, was elected president in 1959, and remained in office until 1969. France prospered as a member of the European Community, developing close ties with its former enemy Germany. Most French overseas colonies became independent peacefully, but there were wars in Indo-China and Algeria. France developed its own nuclear weapons and followed an independent foreign policy. From 1981, France had a socialist president, François Mitterand and he served into the 1990s.

General Charles de Gaulle led the Free French forces in the Second World War. When Paris was liberated by the Allies from German occupation, in 1944, de Gaulle led a triumphal procession down the Champs Elysées. General de Gaulle died in 1970

# The Emergence of Germany

We have seen that the policy of the German rulers of the Middle Ages was chiefly directed at empire-building in the eastern part of Europe. From time to time a ruler would try to unify the states of central Europe within the Holy Roman Empire, but towards the end of the thirteenth century this task fell to the Hapsburg family in Austria (*See* page 362). Thereafter, Germany continued to consist of a number of separate states nominally subject to the Holy Roman Emperor, and most of the rulers of the German state were able to vote for one or other of the candidates for emperor whenever the post fell vacant.

One prominent political feature of Germany in these times was the Hanseatic League. This was the term given to a union of northern German ports and towns – Hamburg, Lübeck, Bremen, Cologne, and others – which formed the League to protect their trading interests. These grew extensively, eventually dominating the Baltic Sea area, reaching as far as Russia and even affecting London.

In the sixteenth century when men were questioning the authority of the Pope, it was a German monk, Martin Luther, who sparked off the Reformation and led what came to be called the Protestant revolt against the orthodox Church (*See* page 324). The German princes were of mixed feelings about the Reformation, and they were more or less evenly divided for and against. The Emperor of the Holy Roman Empire, Charles V, was prepared to tolerate the new religion, but he had a large empire to keep together and could not afford any serious disruption due to religious warfare. So at the Peace of Augsburg in 1555 it was decided that the German princes should be allowed to choose between Lutheranism and Catholicism for themselves. But it was not a permanent solution, largely because a third religious faith had begun to make headway in Europe, Calvinism. After Augsburg, Germany was roughly divided into a Protestant north and a Catholic south.

For a while there was comparative quiet in Germany. Trade and industry flourished, and the German renaissance reached a high point, especially in architecture and interior design.

By the end of the sixteenth century, however, further troubles had arisen when the Protestant states were bitterly divided between themselves, for they were either Lutheran or Calvinist. This was the

One of the 1,282 pages from the Gutenberg 'Bible of 42 lines'. Probably the first book ever printed, it was finished in about 1456

Gustavus Adolphus, king of Sweden during the Thirty Years War, was killed at the Battle of Lützen (1632) before a league of German Protestants under Swedish leadership could be formed

chance that the Catholic states had long awaited and they began to provoke the Protestants in a number of regions. Churches in Bohemia were demolished and the incumbents driven out. This started off riots in Prague and elsewhere. When the emperor's representatives came to Prague to try to sort matters out, the Bohemians threw them out of the window of the discussion room. This event, known as the Defenestration of Prague, 1618, started off the Thirty Years' War, which was conducted with great bitterness and which involved nearly all of Europe. It was fought almost entirely on Germain soil, and it had a brutalizing effect on the Germans.

Frederick, king of Bohemia, was defeated at the battle of the White Mountain near Prague in 1620 by the Imperial general, Count Tilly, and driven off the throne. The leading Protestant nobles were arrested and executed, and their lands confiscated. The Imperial troops then marched north-westwards towards the northern German states which were

being assisted by the king of Denmark. The Imperial army, now led by Count Albrecht von Wallenstein (1583–1634), a brilliant strategist and organizer of troops, defeated the combined German and Danish forces. The victor became a powerful force to reckon with in Germany, and the emperor, frightened that Wallenstein had designs on the Imperial position itself, dismissed him from command.

The interior of the abbey church (1692–1766) at Ottobeuren is a splendid example of the Baroque style

Wallenstein's dismissal coincided with the entry of Gustavus Adolphus, king of Sweden, into the war on the Protestant side (*See* page 396). Gustavus defeated the Imperial troops at Breitenfeld, and the Protestants seemed set to win back all their losses. The emperor recalled Wallenstein and placed him in command again. At Lutzen, the armies of the great adversaries, Gustavus and Wallenstein, fought all day on November 16, 1632. The Swedish king triumphed, but was killed in the hour of victory. Wallenstein thus obtained the initiative, but was shortly afterwards murdered, probably at the instigation of the emperor, who could not control his jealousy.

The war finally ended in 1648, and the result was really a stalemate. The states that had begun as Catholic states continued as such, but the Protestant states were also recognized. The division of Germany was a little more clearly marked: south and west were Catholic, north and east were Protestant. But within these divisions the war had affected everyone. The population had decreased by two-thirds of its pre-war figure, and in many areas there had been extensive starvation.

Out of the ruins of the German states emerged one which was soon to become powerful, Brandenburg. Its ruler, Frederick William (1620–88), was elector from 1640, and it was he who founded the state of Prussia, which was made up of Brandenburg together with additional lands in the region that lies between the Baltic Sea and Bohemia. It was his aim to make Prussia a strong state and enable it to dominate the other German states. He encouraged industry, regulated prices, and initiated the construction of roads and canals.

His successor, Frederick I, became the first king of Prussia, in 1688. It was in his reign that the first signs were seen of

Prince Albrecht von Wallenstein (1583–1634) was one of the most dashing and successful commanders in the Thirty Years War

German militarism; that is, a state run practically on military lines, with an army that was becoming increasingly aggressive in outlook. Frederick was succeeded by his son Frederick William I (1713–40), most of whose reign was spent in improving and glorifying the army. He created a regiment of soldiers who were all more than six feet tall. In 1713 his army numbered about 38,000 men, but by 1740 it had grown to 84,000, and they were all well disciplined, brave, and efficient.

Frederick William I was succeeded by his son Frederick II, who became known as Frederick the Great, one of Europe's most celebrated military leaders. This remarkable man began his reign by invading Silesia (*See* page 363) and holding it. In the Seven Years' War (1756–63), Prussia and Britain were allied against France, Austria and Russia (as main contestants) over who should have the dominions of Austria. These had been won from Maria Theresa in the War of the Austrian Succession (*See* page 363). Frederick demonstrated supreme military gifts. He crushed the French at two battles, Rossbach and Leuthen, in 1757, but later lost to the Austrians and Russians at Kunersdorf, and Berlin was thereupon occupied by the victorious enemy troops. Prussia seemed doomed and was all but impoverished by the military expenses, but suddenly the czarina of Russia died, and her successor, Peter III, who was an admirer of Frederick, withdrew the Russian forces immediately, and the Austrians had to retire.

On the domestic side, Frederick proved to be an industrious and fair ruler. He stimulated agriculture and commerce, and for some time kept the country out of further wars. He granted freedom of religious belief. He encouraged building and art, in particular the design and making of fine furniture, much of it in the French rococo style.

When he died in 1786, Prussia had become one of the dominant states of

Although Frederick the Great of Prussia is remembered as a great military commander, he was also devoted to the arts. He encouraged foreign artists and craftsmen to work in Prussia. Here he discusses with Voltaire (left) one of that great French philosopher's works

Europe, although this was by no means to the liking of many other German states which feared Prussian military might. Gradually Prussian strength declined under the great Frederick's son, Frederick William II (1786–97), an ineffectual king. When Napoleon engaged the Prussians in battle at Friedland in 1807, he not only routed them, he also broke up the state. The western part became the kingdom of Westphalia and the east was made part of the duchy of Poland.

Frederick William III (1797–1840) revived national pride by encouraging men to train in arms secretly and then, when ready, to form divisions and enter into the war against Napoleon. His principal advisers in this were the astute statesman, Heinrich Stein (1757–1831), Gerhard von Scharnhorst (1755–1813), Prussian chief of the army staff who started the reorganization of the army after the battle of Friedland, and August von Gneisenau (1760–1831), Scharnhorst's deputy, who played a leading part in the liberation of Prussia in 1813,

fought at Waterloo, and became a field-marshal in 1825. These men created a fine army, well-fed and cared for, but none the less subjected to the strictest military discipline. Patriotism and honour in battle were the cardinal virtues.

Despite the considerable contribution of Prussia and other German states to the downfall of Napoleon, the Germans considered they were treated ungratefully after the battle of Waterloo. Many wanted union, but they were assembled into a Germanic confederation of some thirty-nine states, under the general supervision of Austria. Of these states Prussia was by far the largest.

The next fifty years of German history were little more than the record of fighting to win – and finally winning – unity, without the protection of Austria. In 1848 the revolutions that convulsed all Europe spread to the German states. The revolt was put down with severity in Prussia.

In 1861 a new king came to the Prussian throne, William I. He was a proud and splendid looking man who believed implicitly in the rights of kings. He wanted to see the union of all the

Prince Otto von Bismarck (1815–98) was principal minister of state in Prussia for nearly thirty years. It was through his policies that Germany was at last united. Here, he reviews Prussian troops before a campaign

German states under Prussia, and he set out to achieve this aided by three very great men. These were Count Albrecht von Roon (1803–79), minister of war, 1859–73, and also minister for the navy, who organized the Prussian army and made it ready to achieve great victories in the Austro-Prussian War of 1866 and the Franco-Prussian War of 1870; Count Helmuth von Moltke (1800–91), chief of the Prussian general staff, 1858–88, who supervised the reorganization of the army on modern lines and sent the troops into battle to defeat Denmark, Austria and France; and the greatest of the three, Count Otto von Bismarck (1815–98), the chief minister of state.

Bismarck, tall, thick-set, with a massive head, was tough, proud, far-seeing and very shrewd. He dominated not only Prussia but also Europe in the years 1864 to 1890. He supported the king in his belief in regal rights, and he kept the assembly of nobles and knights – that is,

Map showing how Bismarck united Germany in three wars

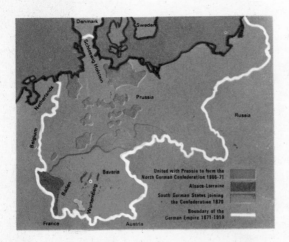

the German parliament – under control. He created the situations in which Prussia attacked Denmark in 1864 to decide who should possess the state of Schleswig-Holstein, Austria in 1866 (the Seven Weeks' War) and France in 1870. All campaigns were successful.

Bismarck also created the union of German states under Prussia that the kings had wanted for more than one hundred and fifty years, and in doing so he made sure that Prussia was the leading power in the union. He provoked the French in 1870 to make war on the German states so that Prussia could intervene and so be regarded as their saviour and thus rise to the head of the Germanic confederation.

The French were defeated in the Franco-Prussian War and the French emperor, Napoleon III, was captured. William I of Prussia was then proclaimed emperor of Germany in the Great Hall at Versailles.

In the last decades of the nineteenth century a united Germany made great strides in industry, science and commerce, and soon took her place among the leading nations of the world. She obtained colonies in Africa and in the Far East.

In 1888 a new emperor acceded, William II, who came to be called the Kaiser (from the name *Caesar*). This headstrong, arrogant and rather stupid man quarrelled almost at once with his leading advisers, especially Bismarck, whom he dismissed in 1890. William decided then to rule on his own. He succeeded in aggravating the nations of Europe, and Great Britain as well, by a series of thoughtless, or deliberately provocative, acts. In 1914, when Austria went to war with Serbia (*See* page 420) the Kaiser intervened on the Austrian side by attacking Belgium. Three days later Britain and France declared war, and so began the First World War which, after four years, was to see Germany brought to ruins and the Kaiser exiled in disgrace.

The stiff terms inflicted upon the Germans at the 1919 Treaty of Versailles stimulated the growth of a nationalist

The German emperor, William II, known as The Kaiser. He was a grandson of Queen Victoria of Great Britain

movement. Organized and led by Adolf Hitler, an impoverished, Austrian-born, water-colour painter who had been a corporal in the trenches in the war, the humiliated Germans began to feel they could once again lift their heads without shame. Hitler, whose magnetic and almost hypnotic personality succeeded in welding the German people into an aggressive and militant throng, solved the unemployment problem by giving everyone a chance to work for the greater glory of Germany by building new roads and making new armaments. At the same time he reconstructed the shattered German army and made it the most efficient military machine in history. In 1938 he began to take the revenge that he considered Germany was entitled to after the 1914–18 war. Austria was annexed. A few months later he seized Czechoslovakia, and in September 1939 he invaded Poland. This brought about the Second World War (*See* page 424).

During his twelve years in office (1933–45) as Führer (leader), Hitler ruled with absolute power. He introduced a number of terrifying policies. In the years of peace (1933–38) it was the Germans who

Cap in hand, Adolf Hitler, Führer (Leader) of the German Reich (state), walks up the steps to a dais at a huge rally of his supporters at Nuremburg in 1937

suffered. His opponents were beaten up and imprisoned and some were even murdered. Catholics and outspoken Protestants were harried. But it was the Jews, whom he believed to have been the cause of the German defeat of 1918, that he persecuted quite mercilessly. Thousands were either put to death without trial or taken to prison camps, there to await whatever fate the authorities saw fit to hand out.

In 1941, when his armies occupied most of Europe west of Moscow, Hitler embarked upon the rounding up and murder of all Jews in Europe. By the end of the war in 1945, no fewer than six million had been packed into concentration camps, herded into specially made gas chambers and killed. It was the most appalling crime in the history of the world.

After the war the surviving leaders in Germany were tried at Nuremberg for war crimes, and crimes against humanity. The majority were found guilty and executed. Perhaps one of the most unpleasant feature of the trial was that all the defendants, except Marshal Goering, turned on their dead leader, Hitler, and blamed him for everything.

One country which suffered terribly at German hands was Russia. After the war, Germany was divided. The east was occupied by the Russians, while the west was under the control of the western Allies, the United States, Britain and France. The capital of Germany, Berlin, was similarly divided between Russia and the west.

The eastern and western parts followed different paths after 1945. The east became a communist state, the German Democratic Republic. The west became a democracy, the Federal Republic of Germany. It rebuilt its industries to become one of the leading countries in Europe. Two of its most able post-war leaders were Konrad Adenauer and Willy Brandt, both of whom

Willy Brandt, one of the ablest figures to emerge in European politics since the Second World War, was elected chancellor of the Federal Republic of Germany in 1969. He was succeeded by Helmut Schmidt in 1974, who was followed by Helmut Kohl in 1983. Brandt campaigned to persuade the Western nations to give more aid to the poorer peoples of the world. He died in 1992.

had opposed Hitler.

West Germany was a founder member of the European Community and worked closely with France. East Germany, loyal to its Communist master Russia, was less prosperous. So many of its people sought a better life in the West, that in 1961 the East German government built the Berlin Wall to shut them in. The East Germans remained shut in until 1989 when a weakening government allowed its citizens to travel freely. The Berlin Wall came down. In March 1990 free elections were held in East Germany, and the Communists were heavily defeated. On October 3 1990 the two parts of Germany were firmly reunited under the government of Helmut Kohl.

# Holland as a Sea Power

The Dutch are by origin part of the ancient German people, and their language is akin to German. They have for centuries occupied the extreme north-west corner of Europe, a land which has been at the mercy of the waters of the North Sea and which is traversed by more than 4,000 miles of rivers, including part of the Rhine and the Maas. They have thus had to endure extreme hardship from climate and from frequent natural disasters like flooding. This has made the Dutch people tough, self-reliant and very patriotic. It has also familiarized them with all the dangers of the sea and made them a nation of seafarers.

At one time the community of Holland consisted of a number of small states with a certain degree of self-government. These states then included what is now Belgium. In the sixteenth century the states became part of the huge Hapsburg empire, which from 1519 to 1556 was ruled by Charles V. We have seen what happened to the Dutch in the second half of the century in Chapter Fifty-two on Spain and Portugal.

After their great successes against the Spanish, the Dutch won complete independence and promptly began to make themselves an important naval power. They had already, from the early seventeenth century, shown themselves considerably adventurous as traders in many parts of the world, and had set up the Dutch East India Company. This organization handled the great majority of products reaching Europe by sea from the East for some time, and had occasionally run into trouble with rival powers interested in the same trading prospects, notably England. This rivalry with England increased during the seventeenth century, and a number of naval wars were fought, with successes to both sides. Early in the reign of Charles II of

formed into a joint kingdom. This did not work, and in 1831 the two countries obtained individual sovereignty. In the East Indies, in the West Indies and in South America the Dutch continued to develop their colonies and expand their trading interests, and Holland became a very rich country. It was said that every household in Holland had some valuable piece or other of Oriental or South American jewellery, painting, sculpture or furniture.

During the First World War Holland remained neutral, but in the Second World War the nation was swiftly overrun by the Germans and held down with great cruelty for nearly five years. Meanwhile, the Dutch colonies in the East were largely overrun by the Japanese and similarly treated. After the war was over, the Dutch granted their colonies independence and concentrated their energies on making their nation the prosperous one it had been before.

### The Netherlands (1559–1609)

England (1660–85), the Dutch admiral, van Tromp, sailed up the river Medway in Kent and set fire to several English ships.

In the seventeenth century the new Dutch nationalism found expression in its wealth through trade and the grandeur of its growing commercial cities, Amsterdam, Rotterdam and the Hague. Some of the greatest painters of all time were Dutchmen of this period, most notably Rembrandt. The Dutch scientists were no less celebrated in history, in particular Leyden, van Leuwenhoek, and Huygens.

In 1688 William, Prince of Orange, chief stadtholder of Holland (the equivalent of king) became king of England, Scotland and Ireland, and this brought Britain and Holland together to resist the ambitions of Louis XIV of France who was anxious not only to extend his dominion in Europe but also to encroach upon British and Dutch trading interests overseas.

In the time of Napoleon, Holland was part of the French empire, but after Waterloo, Holland and Belgium were

# Austria and Hungary

From 1273 the Holy Roman Empire was dominated by the Hapsburg family, who were German-speaking counts, with territories in what is now Austria, in part of Hungary, in part of Poland, in Bohemia and in some of the Balkan states. Most of the Hapsburg rulers of Austria were Emperors of the Holy Roman Empire, and this meant that the other German states were in one way or another subject to them. All the territories were part of the great dominion of Charles V (*See* page 328), and it was his army that was utterly defeated by the Ottoman Turks under Suleiman the Magnificent at Mohacz in 1526. In that battle the king of Hungary was killed, and thereafter the emperor of Austria was also the king of Hungary.

In 1576 Rudolph II became emperor and ruled until 1612. It was his ambition to unite all the Germanic peoples and states into one empire, but he was not able to achieve this. In the Thirty Years' War (1618–48), which was principally a struggle between Catholicism, championed by Austria, and Protestantism, backed by Sweden and France, all went well for Austria at the start. The emperor had two fine generals in Count Tilly and Count Wallenstein. Later, the empire suffered reverses, but at the end of the war gained certain territories outside of the German states. This prompted Austrian leaders to concentrate on developing the empire in these non-German areas.

In the cultural field Austria made little progress; there were no great artistic upsurges, nor were the building programmes very dramatic. But the Austrians had a long run of military successes. It was John Sobieski, the great Polish

Map of the Austro-Hungarian Empire in 1815. The surrounding countries have their modern names, although some of them were not then in existence as independent states.

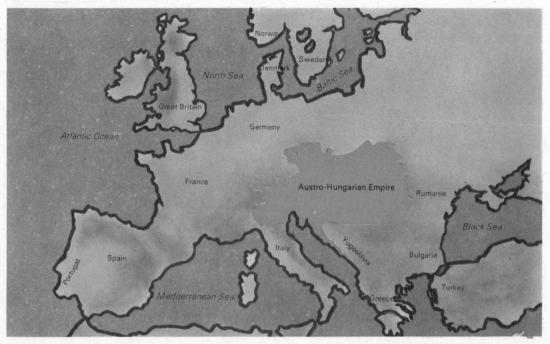

king who, with Austrian and Polish troops, saved Vienna from the Turks in 1683 (*See* page 317). In 1699 the sultan evacuated all Hungary and the country became part of Austria. In the War of the Spanish Succession (1702–13), Austria's Prince Eugene of Savoy proved to be almost as brilliant and successful as the Duke of Marlborough (*See* page 341), and under his command Austrian fighting qualities became as respected as the British.

In 1711 there was a new emperor, Charles VI. He had only one daughter, Maria Theresa, to whom he wished to leave all the Hapsburg dominions; the Imperial title was to go to her husband, Prince Francis of Lorraine. So in 1720 Charles VI drew up a document outlining the details of this inheritance, called the Pragmatic Sanction. Prince Eugene warned the emperor that it would be impossible to enforce adherence to the document, but the emperor persisted.

When Charles died in 1740, Prince Eugene was proved to be right. At once Frederick the Great of Prussia seized Silesia. France then joined Prussia in the war against the empire, called the War of the Austrian Succession. Britain joined Maria Theresa and fought two important battles against France at Dettingen and Fontenoy. Maria Theresa suffered a number of defeats, and so she appealed to her people in Hungary. Visiting them in Budapest, this brave, beautiful, and dignified queen, with a young son on her arm, begged for help. Immediately the Magyar people rose up and responded, and in a short campaign drove the French out of Austria.

In the Seven Years' War (1756–63) France joined Austria and Britain supported Prussia. The results were not good for France, but Maria Theresa emerged in control of her inherited dominions.

Empress Maria Theresa of Austria, wearing the crown of St Stephen, presents her infant heir to her Hungarian subjects

When she died in 1780 all Europe regretted the passing of so noble and devout a woman, who had amazed the whole continent with her patriotism and determination.

Her son, Joseph II, had no easy task when he took up the reins of power. Austria was by now a collection of states, some of which were actively hostile to each other. For example, one possession was the Netherlands, that is, the southern states between Holland and France. These people were Roman Catholics. Another possession was Bohemia, which was Protestant. The languages and customs of many of the states were very different, too. So when Joseph tried to introduce religious toleration for everyone into his dominions his scheme met with the greatest opposition.

During the French Revolution, Austria fought against France in support of the other countries that objected to the deposition of the French king, Louis XVI and his Austrian wife, Marie Antoinette, the daughter of Maria Theresa. At Rivoli in 1797, the young Napoleon (*See* page 348) defeated a combined Austrian and Prussian army and thereby came into possession of many Austrian states in Italy. How Austria fared in the remainder of Napoleon's time is related in Chapter Fifty-four.

Austria suffered very greatly at the hands of Napoleon, but after his defeat it was Austria that played the leading part at the Congress of Vienna of 1815, which was managed by the great diplomatist, Prince Metternich. Austria was deprived of the Netherlands (which in 1830 became the kingdom of Belgium), but she obtained Venice and Lombardy, two rich Italian provinces. This meant that Austrian influence was considerable in Italy, especially in the north.

Metternich was chancellor in Austria from 1821 to 1848. His attitude was essentially anti-liberal and he resisted every attempt by the people to obtain democratic representation. In the revolt in Vienna of 1848, he was expelled from office, and a constituent assembly was formed. At the same time revolt broke out in most of the Austrian dominions, under Kossuth in Hungary, and Mazzini in Italy. The emperor was saved when the Russians offered their help, for they feared the revolutionary movement might spread.

The Italian states were gradually lost during the years 1860–66, and in 1867 the emperor was forced to concede a large degree of home rule to the Hungarians. For the rest of the century science and industry advanced rapidly throughout the empire, and constitutional experiments were tried in one or other of the dominions.

The greatness of Austria was swept away after the First World War when the empire was broken up. Hungary became a regency, Poland a republic, Czechoslovakia a republic under Thomas Masaryk, and Yugoslavia an independent kingdom. Austria itself became a small republic which, in 1938, was annexed, or seized, by the German dictator Adolf Hitler, who had been born an Austrian.

After the Second World War, in 1945, Austria reverted to being a republic. Hungary became a republic in 1946, but in 1949 fell under Communist rule. In 1956 an uprising against the Communist government was crushed with Russian help. However, in the late 1980s Hungary, like other east European states, moved away from Communism, and a non-Communist government was elected in 1990.

When Napoleon was defeated and exiled in 1815, the victors, Great Britain, Austria and Russia, agreed at the Congress of Vienna to 'redraw' the map of Europe, thereby redistributing some of the territories which he had overrun

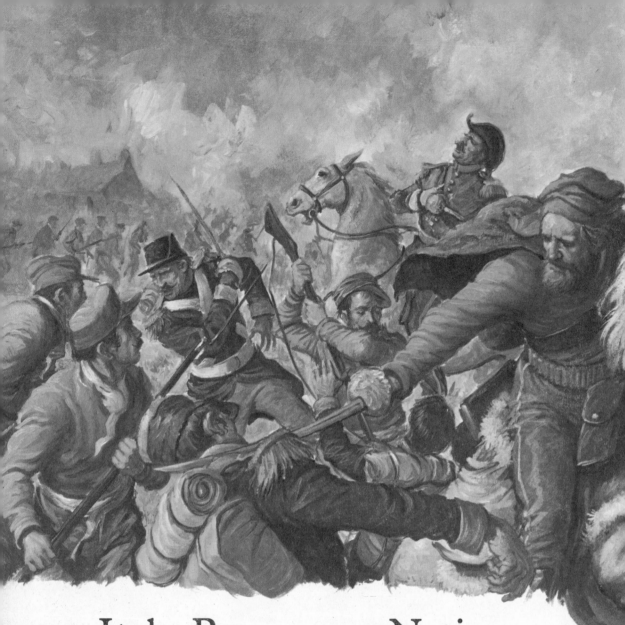

# Italy Becomes a Nation

For centuries after the collapse of the western Roman empire, the peninsula of Italy remained divided between a succession of powers. By the end of the Middle Ages (c. 1500) it was still split up into states which were ruled either by rich local families or by foreign powers. Despite centuries of division the Italian people always longed to be united under one ruler and government. Cesare Borgia, son of Pope Alexander VI (Borgia) who lived at the start of the sixteenth century, tried without success to bring about such unity. After the Reformation, when the power of the Popes was severely curtailed, Italy became a 'mere geographical expression'. As such it still provided the greatest names in the field of art and architecture, but it seemed unable to bury its many differences and become a nation.

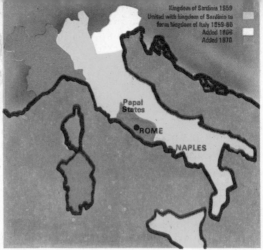

Kingdom of Sardinia 1859
United with kingdom of Sardinia to
form kingdom of Italy 1859-60
Added 1866
Added 1870

Giuseppe Garibaldi (1807–82) and his Thousand red-shirted patriots drove 20,000 Neapolitan troops out of Sicily in 1860 and helped pave the way for Italian unity

Napoleon Bonaparte, a Corsican by birth, tried to unite the peninsula, but he failed, and after Waterloo Austria was confirmed in control of the largest number of states in Italy.

In 1848 Italy was affected by a series of revolts, as were many other countries in Europe. These risings were not successful, and were put down with great severity in the Austrian dominions. One Italian king, Victor Emmanuel of Sardinia (a brave and honourable man and a liberal at heart), who controlled Piedmont, gave his people a fair measure of democratic government. His chief minister after the Year of Revolutions (1848) was Count Camillo Cavour. He was a passionate Italian patriot, and he devoted his considerable energies and talents to building up a nation out of the Italian states. By the time of his death in 1861 his dream had almost come true.

Cavour began by courting the support of Napoleon III (*See* page 350), whom he believed would welcome any plan that offered opportunities of discomfiting Austria. He provoked a war between France and Austria, and in the struggle the French won two great victories at Magenta and Solferino. Piedmont thereby received control of the states of Parma and Lombardy. At the same time the central Italian states agreed to unite, and in 1860 Victor Emmanuel was able to open the first Italian parliament at Turin.

The Papal States, however, were opposed to unity, and Sicily and Naples, ruled by a branch of the Bourbon family, were also opposed.

At that time, an army colonel in Piedmont, who had fought at Magenta, Giuseppe Garibaldi, made plans to invade Sicily and force the Bourbons to accept Italian union. Garibaldi assembled an army of about a thousand men, dressed them in bright red shirts, trained them and then led them southwards by sea to Sicily. With astonishing ease Garibaldi overran the whole island; he then sailed for the mainland and conquered Naples, forcing the Bourbons to leave.

Cavour viewed this success with mixed feelings. Only the Papal States stood between him and Garibaldi. If the latter should attack, what would he do with his gains? Cavour thereupon arranged for an army to attack the Papal States before Garibaldi could get there, and at Castel-fidardo the army beat the Pope's forces. It then moved down to Naples to meet Garibaldi on equal terms. The great patriot brought his conquered lands into the new Italian union of states.

In 1861 when Cavour died, most of Italy was united, and only Venice and the Vatican state itself remained outside the union. Rome was garrisoned by French troops to protect it. Five years later, when Austria was defeated by the Prussians at Königgrätz, Venice received its

The three leading figures in the struggle for Italian unity were (left to right) Count Camillo Cavour, one of the greatest statesmen of all Italian history, Giuseppe Mazzini, a fiery rebel leader who fought ceaselessly for a republic, and Garibaldi

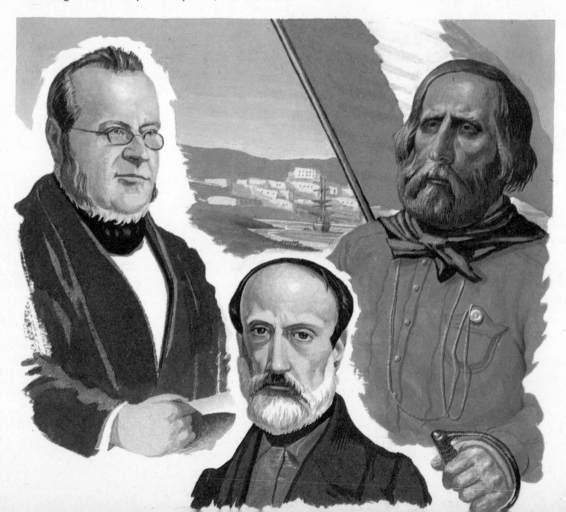

independence and at once elected to join the Italian union. Rome was occupied in 1870 when French troops pulled out in order to help in the Franco-Prussian War.

The capital of the new Italy was very naturally established at Rome, where it has remained. Thereafter Italy moved ahead in developing its agriculture and industry. A modern navy was constructed, and the beginnings of an empire were founded in Africa. In the First World War Italy fought on the side of the British.

After the war Italy was threatened with a takeover by a Communist government. Benito Mussolini, a journalist and revolutionary, created the Fascist party which won several seats at an election. In 1922, King Victor Emmanuel III, terrified of the growth of Communism, appointed Mussolini prime minister. Both the king and the Italian people were to regret this move.

Mussolini assumed dictatorial powers, and in 1928 the government became completely subservient to him. He embarked upon an extensive programme of public works. He also invaded Abyssinia to gain military glory, but succeeded only in earning the contempt of most of the world. In 1936 he made a treaty with Hitler. In 1939 he annexed Albania, and in June 1940 he declared war on Great Britain. His invasion of Greece in October was a fiasco and Italian troops were only saved from disaster by their German allies.

When the Italian and German armies in North Africa were beaten by British, Commonwealth and United States forces, the mainland of Italy itself was invaded and part of it overrun swiftly. This humiliation was more than enough for the Italians. The king dismissed Mussolini and created a new government which promptly surrendered to the Allied

Benito Mussolini, dictator of Italy from 1922–43, tried to imitate Hitler by invading and overrunning other lands. Unfortunately, he got into difficulties nearly every time, and had to be helped by German armies, sent to his rescue by the Führer. His end was squalid. He was caught and executed by Italian patriots and his body hung upside down in Milan

Powers. The Germans thereupon rescued Mussolini, restored him to power in that part of Italy that had not fallen to the Allies. Gradually, however, the Allies forced their way through, and by the spring of 1945 had practically all Italy in their hands.

Mussolini was captured in a hideout in the north by guerrillas who had been supporting the Allied troops, and he was executed. A year later Victor Emmanuel III abdicated in favour of his son, Umberto, who was forced to do likewise a few weeks later. Italy became a republic, and it has been one since. During this time the nation's industry has been regenerated, bringing Italy to the front rank of European industrial powers.

# Britain since 1714

Queen Anne died in 1714 and was followed by her cousin George Lewis, elector of Hanover. George I (1714–27) was a great-grandson of James I and the nearest Protestant descendant living. George spoke no English and his chief minister, Sir Robert Walpole, spoke no German, and so they conversed in Latin. Walpole – an able, cunning and hard-working Norfolk-born squire – managed the kingdom very well. He reorganized the finances, stimulated trade, and kept the country out of war for nearly twenty years. This enabled England to reap the

The *Victory*, in which Nelson led
the British fleet at Trafalgar

benefits of the Industrial Revolution a
generation or more before any other
nation in the world. Agriculture was
revolutionized by the rotation-of-crops
system, textiles were mass produced by
new spinning equipment, and finally
transport was greatly improved by the
cutting of miles of canals.

Britain, as it was now called, because
Scotland had become united to England
by the Act of Union of 1707, took part in
the War of the Austrian Succession with
little success, but in the Seven Years'
War (1756–63) the British covered themselves with glory. Robert Clive won
Bengal in 1757 at the battle of Plassey,
James Wolfe won Canada by beating the
French at Quebec in 1759. Edward
Hawke smashed the French fleet at sea
and made the whole Atlantic almost
trouble-free for British fleets. In other
parts of the world British arms triumphed.

Arthur Wellesley, 1st Duke of Wellington, commanded the allied forces in defeating Napoleon at the Battle of Waterloo (1815)

Over all this fighting ruled the great war minister William Pitt.

The reign of George III (1760–1820) was packed with events, personalities, wars and inventions. Soon after the Seven Years' War, the English colonists in North America (apart from those in Canada) won their independence, (*See* page 381.) In wars against France, Britain's fleet thwarted Napoleon's invasion schemes. Britain's greatest admiral, Horatio Nelson, won victories at Aboukir Bay on the Nile in 1798, at Copenhagen in 1801, and off Trafalgar in 1805, when he crushed the combined French and Spanish fleets. In this last battle, Nelson was killed at the moment of triumph. Napoleon was checked at sea, but went from success to success in Europe. Eventually, however, the Duke of Wellington defeated him at Waterloo in Belgium in 1815.

What had been happening at home? James Watt perfected the steam engine in 1769, revolutionizing factory machinery. Dr Edward Jenner discovered vaccination against smallpox, and so rendered the age-old scourge relatively harmless by 1778. John Macadam invented tar road surfaces and made new roads more comfortable and safe. Thomas Telford constructed a network of roads in Scotland and built the Caledonian canal. In the arts, Reynolds, Gainsborough, Constable and Turner painted some of the most beautiful pictures in the history of British art. Literature flourished, especially poetry, for this was the age of Wordsworth, Keats, Shelley and Byron. The Adam brothers raised architecture and interior decoration to new heights. Parliament was filled with brilliant people such as William Pitt the Younger, who became prime minister at the age of twenty-four; Charles James Fox, the enemy of humbug and privilege;

Isambard Kingdom Brunel (1806–59) acknowledged as the greatest engineer of all time

William Wilberforce, who campaigned to end the evil of the slave trade; Edmund Burke, the clever Irish lawyer, orator and writer; and Richard Brinsley Sheridan, the witty Irish playwright-politician.

As the new century advanced, Britain was transformed by the Industrial Revolution. For many, industrialization brought unemployment and misery, as one machine could do the work of scores of workers. In factory-towns, mills and mines there were jobs, but men had to work long hours for low pay; so did women and children. They barely managed to make enough money to buy food and clothing, and they lived in squalid tenement houses in towns where black smoke filled the air. The landlords and factory owners made fortunes and behaved with cruelty and arrogance to their tenants and workers. Thus the differences between the rich and the poor were aggravated. Meanwhile, the vote was limited to the few people who owned property. Some of the large industrial towns had no members of parliament to represent them at all, while small villages had two or three.

Such conditions could not last without danger of revolt. In 1831 when a Reform Bill was put before parliament extending the vote, and rearranging the distribution of seats more fairly, the House of Lords rejected it. The workers simmered on the point of open revolt. The king, William IV (1830–37), was wise enough to threaten to create enough new peers to get the bill through the Lords, and so upon this threat the bill became law in 1832.

The nineteenth century saw radical changes in British society. Local government acquired new strength. Central government began to concern itself with health and welfare. A penny postage system was introduced which ensured regular and cheap delivery of mail. Criminal law was drastically reformed and the death penalty

Queen Victoria, who reigned for sixty-four years, with two of her many grand-children, Princess Margaret and Prince Arthur, photographed in 1885

was abolished for a wide range of crimes. Public hanging was abolished and imprisonment for debt was curtailed.

In science Joseph Lister revolutionized surgery by introducing antiseptics, Lord Kelvin made possible the first Atlantic cable, Charles Darwin developed his theory that living things had evolved by natural selection over millions of years. Michael Faraday invented the dynamo. In transport and construction, George Stephenson pioneered the steam railway, Isambard Kingdom Brunel built the Great Western Railway, its stations, bridges, tunnels, and a giant ocean-going liner driven by a propeller and paddles.

There was also an upsurge in art and literature, too vast to be described here.

In warfare Britain was involved in only one war until the turn of the century – the Crimean War (1854–56), where she held her own, despite many deficiencies in the out-of-date army system. These were remedied later by Sir Garnet Wolseley.

200 marchers from Jarrow, a town on the Tyne with two-thirds unemployed, took a petition to London in November 1936

The monarch who reigned over this great period of British history, one which included the acquisition of territories that covered a quarter of the earth's land surface, was Queen Victoria (1837–1901), niece of William IV. She set new standards of behaviour in society and did much to restore the morality of the royal family and of people in public life.

Her son, the popular and fun-loving Prince of Wales, became Edward VII in 1901. He forged the Entente Cordiale, a pact of friendship with France. His son, George V (1910–36), had to contend with radical changes in parliament and reform in the House of Lords. In 1914 Britain went to war against Germany. The famous Field-Marshal Lord Kitchener mobilized an army of three million British men to fight in France and Belgium. Kitchener himself was drowned in 1916 on his way to Russia. The war took a dreadful toll in dead and wounded. Women were recruited to replace men in a variety of jobs in factories and offices, and after the war, they at last got the vote.

Britain emerged triumphant from the First World War, but it was severely impoverished. A huge army of volunteers had to be disbanded and work found for the men in civilian life. But there were not enough jobs to go round. In 1926 there was a general strike and the government declared a state of emergency. Volunteers kept essential services going. To make matters worse, the whole world entered a trade depression and by 1930 more than two million people in Britain were out of work. Despite these problems, life for many people improved. New houses were built to replace slums, and people enjoyed new forms of entertainment such as radio and the cinema.

In 1933 Adolf Hitler came to power in Germany and seemed, to some observers at all events, bent on territorial expansion in Europe. Winston Churchill, Britain's First Lord of the Admiralty in the First World War, warned the nation of Hitler's aim, but the government took no notice. When the German dictator annexed

Austria and Czechoslovakia in 1938, Churchill's warnings were understood and the nation began to rearm. In 1939 war was declared against Germany because of the invasion of Poland. Nine months later, when Hitler had surged across western Europe, Churchill was appointed prime minister. Now he directed the nation's war effort against the strongest military power the world had yet seen. Churchill was a statesman of determination and vision, an orator of unequalled powers, and a writer of stirring prose. As Britain's leader during the Second World War he marshalled the forces of Britain and its allies in the darkest days. In partnership with the wealth and military might of the United States, and the brave millions of Russian troops, he helped to destroy the combined might of Germany, Italy and Japan.

Immediately after the war in Europe was over, the British electorate, mindful of the terrible hardships of the early 1930s, returned a Labour government to power with an enormous majority. It seemed the worst kind of ingratitude to Churchill, but the greatest wartime leader does not necessarily make the best prime minister in time of peace.

After the war, Britain struggled to achieve economic growth. Many factories needed to be modernized. The new Labour government nationalized, or took over, key industries such as the coal mines and railways. But later governments reversed this policy. By the 1970s Britain had given full independence to practically all the states of the British Empire, which evolved into a free association of nations, the Commonwealth. In 1973 Britain joined the European Economic Community (the Common Market). Although there were doubts about a possible European government, most people in Britain accepted that their future lay within the European Union. Elizabeth II, who became queen in 1952 on the death of George VI, reigned over a country going through another period of change in its long history.

Mr Churchill greets some of the first New Zealanders to join with British soldiers in 1940. Mrs Churchill is with him

# South and Central America, Mexico

Simon Bolivar's dream of uniting all South America as a federation of republics was never realized. (*See* page 333.) In the nineteenth century there were many quarrels between the new nations. Great landowners and soldiers held power, often at the expense of the poor. The richer nations such as Brazil developed their economies. But the countries of South America seldom enjoyed stable government and for most people life was a struggle against poverty and oppression.

**Brazil** became independent in 1922, with a Portuguese prince, Pedro, as emperor. From the 1840s many European migrants came to settle in Brazil. Rubber and coffee became valuable money-earners. In 1888 slavery was abolished in Brazil. Angry slave-owners turned against the emperor, Pedro II, and he gave up the throne. In 1889 Brazil became a republic.

The continuous destruction of the rain forests in the Amazon region is potentially disastrous for the whole world

The dictator Getulio Vargas ruled as president from 1930 to 1945, and again from 1950 to 1954. In 1960 the government moved to a new inland capital, Brasilia. Brazil has often been ruled by army generals. This was the case through the 1970s and most of the 1980s, but then the country returned to civilian government. Brazil has become South America's most populous and prosperous nation. But its riches are not evenly divided, and many thousands of people live in squalid shanty towns on the outskirts of great cities such as Rio de Janeiro and São Paulo. Settlers have moved into the vast Amazon forest, where roadbuilding, cattle ranching and mining threaten the environment and the few surviving native Indians.

**Argentina** was almost split up in the 1820s, but was held together by two strong leaders; first, Juan Manuel de Rosas, and later by the soldier-president Bartolomé Mitre. From 1946 to 1955 its president was Juan Perón who ruled as dictator, but with the support of most workers. His wife Eva Perón (1919–1952) was equally powerful. Perón returned as president in the 1970s but failed to give Argentina prosperity. Military governments succeeded him and in 1982 generals led Argentina into a brief war with Britain over the Falkland Islands, which Argentina claims. After defeat in that war, civilian government was restored.

Other nations of South America have suffered undemocratic military rule, dictatorship and sometimes violent terrorism. In 1973 **Chile's** elected Marxist president, Salvador Allende, was over-

President Benito Juárez of Mexico, elected for periods between 1861 and 1872

thrown by the armed forces, but democracy was restored in 1990. But by the 1990s the leading nations of South America all had democratic governments.

### Mexico and Central America

Mexico became independent in 1821. In 1848 it was defeated in a war with the United States and lost Texas, California and New Mexico. There followed years of civil war in which France became involved. In 1864 the French made an Austrian, Maximilian, emperor of Mexico but he was shot in 1867. A republic led by Benito Juárez followed, then from 1876 a dictator, Porfirio Díaz, ruled. When he was overthrown by another revolution in 1911, Mexico became a democratic republic.

Central America is a region of small republics. All except **Belize** were once part of Spain's empire. Belize was a British colony from 1638 until 1981. When the Spanish American empire broke up in the 1820s, the Central American provinces became independent. Five of them formed the Spanish Captains General of Guatemala. For a while they were part of Mexico, but then set up a federation. There were many quarrels, and in 1838 the five became the independent countries of **Costa Rica, El Salvador, Guatemala, Nicaragua** and **Honduras**. They have suffered from poverty and dictatorships, and Nicaragua and El Salvador were troubled by civil wars during the 1980s.

**Panama** was part of Colombia until it broke away at the persuasion of the United States government, which wanted to cut the Panama Canal across its territory. The canal was completed in 1914, and the United States controlled a zone either side of the waterway until 1979. In 1990 the United States invaded Panama to arrest its president Manuel Noriega on drugs charges.

### The Caribbean Islands

The islands of the Caribbean include **Hispaniola** (shared by Cuba and the Dominican Republic), **Haiti** and the islands of the West Indies. In the sixteenth and seventeenth centuries, Europeans killed off most of the native Indians and brought in black slaves from Africa to work on sugar plantations. **Cuba** was Spanish from 1511 until 1898 when it gained independence after a war between the United States and Spain. In 1959 Communists led by Fidel Castro overthrew the dictator Fulgencia Batista.

In the British West Indies, attempts to form a federation of island states failed. **Jamaica, Barbados**, and **Trinidad and Tobago** became independent. Some small islands are still governed as colonies.

President Fidel Castro Ruz, Head of the State of Cuba

# The Birth of the United States

Not long after the Spanish had overthrown the Aztec and Inca civilizations in Central and South America respectively, built up an empire and organized the regular shipment to Europe of the riches from the American mines, other western European nations sought to establish colonies in the New World. Among these were England, Holland, and France (Portugal had already settled in Brazil). By about 1600 England had a small settlement in Virginia, and Holland had one around New Amsterdam (which later became New York). There was no gold there, but riches could be obtained from cotton and tobacco growing on the south-eastern side of the continent, and to work those plantations the early settlers at first employed native Indians. Occasionally they did it themselves.

Soon, however, the plantations became so extensive that there were no longer enough people to work on them. A fresh labour force was required. Some traders from Europe obliged by introducing a work force from Africa. These were native people of the western coast of Africa. They were seized by gangs of European sailors, pressed into ships in numbers much greater than the ships could reasonably hold, roughly transported across the Atlantic; and sold to white landowners and plantation bosses. The Africans, in fact, became slaves and

The Pilgrim Fathers landed on the coast of Massachusetts in North America in 1620, and immediately founded a settlement. It was called Plymouth, after the harbour in England from which they had sailed

endured a great deal of misery for a very long time.

The French, meanwhile, who had established themselves in Canada, were also settling in the fertile area of the Mississippi River Valley in what was later called Louisiana.

The population of the English colonies expanded rapidly, not least because of the persecution of Puritans in England, shiploads of whom came to make a new life and to worship God in their own way. In time they absorbed the Dutch settlements. They began to build up a prosperous community of colonies, but it must never be overlooked that the early years were very hard indeed. Immigrants often arrived with little more than the clothes they stood up in, and they had to begin from scratch to build houses, and furnish them. They built usually from timber, which was plentiful.

By 1732 there were thirteen colonies, which later formed what was called the Union, and these became the nucleus of the United States. They were New Hampshire, Massachusetts, Rhode Island, Connecticut, New York, New Jersey, Pennsylvania, Delaware, Maryland, Virginia, North Carolina, South Carolina, and Georgia. These colonies had their own governments, under governors sent out from Britain or appointed by the British government. But the rapidly growing prosperity of the colonies and the stories about them that were spread around in Britain attracted the attention of the government in London. Here was a new source of wealth for the national

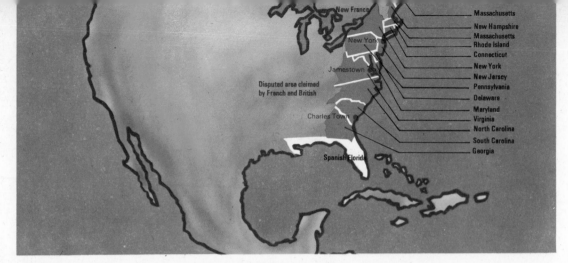

Map of the east coast of the United States showing the thirteen original states

exchequer. Restrictions were imposed upon trade and a variety of taxes were levied on the colonists. They were not allowed to embark upon industries that competed with those at home; they were compelled to provide troops and supplies for British armies which were engaged in fighting the French in Canada. They also had to pay duties on a host of consumer goods, including tea, glass, paper and molasses.

Then, in 1765, the British government passed the Stamp Act. This put a tax on all documents, newspapers and pamphlets, and it was to include the colonies. The Americans, as we can henceforth call them, were incensed. So the tax was repealed, but the bitterness remained because of the fact that the home government had even tried to raise the tax. Matters were made no better when it was remembered that the Americans had no representation in parliament, which meant that their grievances against the mother country could not be heard. In all this lay the seeds of revolt.

Discontent grew increasingly after the Americans provided substantial help to the British in their efforts to win Canada from the French in the Seven Years War (1756–63) and the British demonstrated their ingratitude by failing to give the Americans the redress they sought for their domestic grievances. Finally, in 1773, when a fresh tax on tea was imposed, some Americans, dressed up as Red Indians, boarded tea-ships lying in Boston Harbour, bound for England. They tipped the tea into the water, an event subsequently known as the Boston Tea Party. The British retaliated by closing Boston's harbour and removing the

Angry Americans, dressed as Red Indians, tip chests of tea into Boston harbour as a protest against British-imposed taxes, 1773

city's charter. The Americans, in turn, issued a Declaration of Rights which, among other things, prohibited the importing of any goods at all from Britain until Boston's civic rights were restored. Open war between the Americans and British could not be postponed much longer, and in 1775 incidents at Lexington and Concord in Massachusetts were the signal for the outbreak of hostilities.

The Americans were commanded by a Virginian landowner, George Washington, whose grandfather had been born in England. At first all did not go well for the rebels, despite the fact that the British commander, General Howe, was driven out of Boston. This did not prevent the Americans making plans for establishing their independence and for organizing their own government.

In 1776 a few of the leading intellectuals among the Americans got together to work out a formal declaration of independence. Among these were John Adams (1735–1826), a Massachusetts lawyer, and Benjamin Franklin (1706–1790), a Boston-born statesman, writer and scientist, who had invented, among other things, the lightning conductor. Another was Thomas Jefferson (1743–1826), a Virginian lawyer and the main author of the Declaration of Independence, which was officially issued on July 4, 1776 at a meeting of leaders held in Philadelphia. The event was the most important in American history, and the document provided the basis for the written American constitution which followed eleven years later.

This famous declaration stated, among its clauses that 'these United Colonies are, and of right ought to be Free and Independent States'. It also stated that 'all men are created equal, that they are endowed by their Creator with certain unalienable rights, that among these are life, liberty and the pursuit of happiness'.

In 1777 the turning point of the war

came when the British general, John Burgoyne, who attempted to cut off the northern states from the southern ones, was defeated and forced to surrender at the Battle of Saratoga. Thereafter, the Americans went from victory to victory. The British discomfiture was made worse by the intervention of European powers on America's side, in particular, France. In 1781 General Cornwallis, sent out by the British to command their forces, was trapped with his army at Yorktown and compelled to surrender. The major part of the fighting was over. Two years later, Britain recognized the independence of the American colonies and the new United States of America was acknowledged as a free republic. The western limit of its territory was accepted as the line of the Mississippi River.

In 1787 a meeting of the leading political men of the thirteen states called a Convention and approved the draft of the American Constitution. This document, to which there have been only a handful of amendments in the past two hundred years, thus firmly established the form of government of the United States. This is based on the federal system, in which the member states combine under a central government which is granted certain overriding powers, each member state retaining certain individual powers. Executive power is placed in the hands of a president who is elected every four years. He selects the heads of government departments. Legislative power lies with Congress which consists of a Senate (that is, two members from each state elected by popular vote for six years) and a House of Representatives (that is, delegates elected every two years on a proportional population basis from all the states).

George Washington, commander-in-chief of the American forces, succeeded in crossing the Delaware River to the other side, held by Hessian troops in the service of the English—24,000 men and 18 cannon, with the loss of only four Americans

Three leading Americans who framed the Constitution of the United States: left to right, John Adams, Benjamin Franklin, and Thomas Jefferson

The federal government is responsible for the republic's foreign policy, customs, currency, income tax and postal services, among other things. Each state has its own legislature which is responsible for civil and criminal law, rights of voting, marriage and divorce, and education. Laws enacted by the legislature vary considerably from state to state. The death penalty, for example, is accepted in a few states today, but has been abolished in the rest.

As a constitution the American version was probably the most enlightened and democratic since the days of ancient Greece, and it owed much to the experience of the British in their constitutional development. It was soon to have a great influence in France where, in 1789, a cataclysmic revolution broke out which ultimately changed the face of western Europe.

The delegates at the Convention elected George Washington as first president, and he took office in 1789, being re-elected for a second term (1793–7). This quiet, dignified and courageous man had won the admiration of the majority of Americans during the recent war and his election was an apt tribute to his leadership. He had also contributed greatly to the framing of the Constitution. Much of his time as president was spent trying to reconcile the thirteen states which had widely differing views on many matters.

When the second term expired, Washington declined to stand again. His successor, John Adams, was elected in 1796, for office in 1797 (presidents are elected at the end of a year and take office in the next year). He was an able statesman, but he failed to get re-elected in 1800. The successful candidate then was Thomas Jefferson, possibly the greatest statesman ever to emerge in the United States. This remarkable man, who had been appointed governor of Virginia during the War of Independence, was not only the main author of the Declaration and the Constitution. He had devised a decimal monetary system, and had been the republic's ambassador to France (1784–89) during which time he had actively helped the French intellectuals (who led the revolt in 1789) in the shaping of their Declaration of the Rights of Man.

Jefferson was an excellent administrator. He negotiated, in 1803, with Napoleon, first-consul (later emperor) of France, to buy the French territory of

General Andrew Jackson's defeat of the British at New Orleans during the War of 1812 avenged the British seizure of Washington, during which the Capitol was burnt

Louisiana for about £3,000,000 of British money of the time. He encouraged expansion westwards beyond the Mississippi, and prohibited the importing of slaves for the plantations. Jefferson was elected for another term in 1804.

American territory was expanded swiftly under a number of able and hardworking presidents. In 1817 the fifth was the Virginian lawyer, James Monroe (1758–1831), who had held a number of high offices in the time of his predecessors. In 1823, during his second term, he outlined the famous Monroe Doctrine. This was a policy which in effect meant 'America for the Americans'. The American continents, north and south, were not to be regarded as prey for future conquest or interference by European powers. Americans, for their part, would not interfere outside their own sphere.

This may have been a reasonable plan at the time but it led to the development of a policy of isolationism—that is, avoidance of governmental action anywhere outside the Americas which might provoke international trouble. Sometimes this was right, but sometimes it meant turning a blind eye to affairs where American influence might have been helpful. Many American administrations were basically isolationist in their thinking, even up to the 1930s, and today, although America is a major participant in world affairs, there is still an undercurrent of such thinking in the United States.

In 1829 the seventh president was the South Carolina-born Andrew Jackson (1767–1845) who had a distinguished military career and had become the national hero of the 1812–14 war against Britain. This was a strange war supposedly about the seizure of American sailors by British ships and the violation of neutral rights, which resulted in a complete stalemate, both sides claiming to be victorious. Jackson was the first president to represent the newly formed Democratic Party, which was in opposition to the Republicans. Though he held office for two terms, his administration was marked by several controversial features, including the encouragement of states to resist the controls of federation. There were continuing wars with American Indians, waged in the interests of American expansion westwards.

One of the greatest issues of argument

they failed to deal effectively with the problem of slavery which was gradually threatening to break up the Union. The northern states on the whole did not approve of the use of slaves, nor, indeed, did their agriculture or industries really need them. The southern states, on the other hand, whose climate was warmer and more sultry, claimed they needed slaves (who provided cheap labour), to work their plantations because they were better able to stand the heat. Industrialization had not reached anything like the same level in the south, and the economy was largely agricultural.

The southerners were often needlessly cruel and severe to the slaves. This outraged many northerners, and before long the whole matter became explosive. The south resented the efforts of the north to get better conditions for the slaves, and eventually they threatened to secede, or break away, from the Union and form a confederacy of their own.

In this turmoil a new figure came to

As late as 1860 slaves were sold at slave markets in some states in America. The Civil War was fought largely on the issue of whether slavery should be allowed or not

in the years after Jackson's retirement (1837) was that of slavery. Slavery had been abolished by the British parliament in 1833 after a lifelong campaign by William Wilberforce. This campaign had extended its momentum to the United States, and in 1833 the Anti-Slavery Society was founded in America. For years the members campaigned to get slavery abolished. A number of things happened to help them. One was the publication in 1852 of Harriet Beecher Stowe's novel, *Uncle Tom's Cabin*, which exposed the horrors of slavery and did much to advance the cause of abolition. Another was the Dred Scott case. This was to do with Dred Scott, a Negro, born in Virginia who, in 1848, tried to obtain his freedom on the grounds that he lived in Illinois, a state that did not allow slavery. After several years of fighting in the law courts he lost his case when the Supreme Court said, in 1857, that he was not a citizen of the United States and so had no rights. It seemed a monstrous injustice, and Americans argued fiercely about it for a long time.

Throughout these years America had a succession of presidents who were, on the whole, weak and unimpressive, and

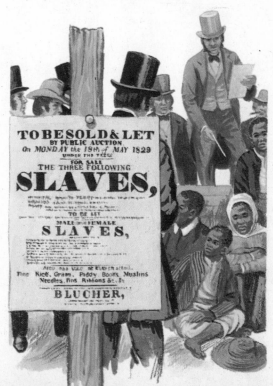

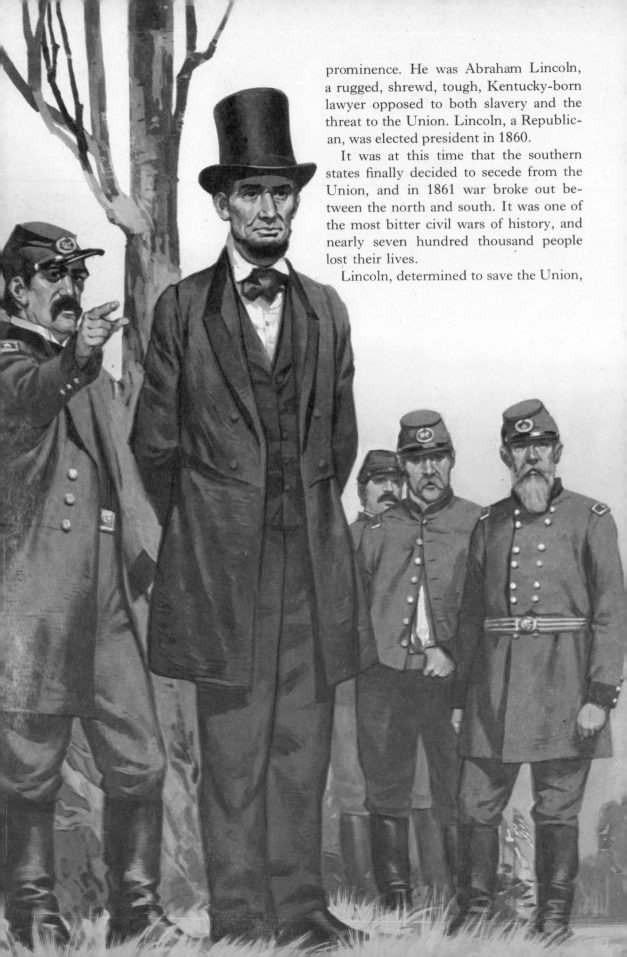

prominence. He was Abraham Lincoln, a rugged, shrewd, tough, Kentucky-born lawyer opposed to both slavery and the threat to the Union. Lincoln, a Republican, was elected president in 1860.

It was at this time that the southern states finally decided to secede from the Union, and in 1861 war broke out between the north and south. It was one of the most bitter civil wars of history, and nearly seven hundred thousand people lost their lives.

Lincoln, determined to save the Union,

prosecuted the war with the sole aim of forcing the south to surrender completely and break up their confederacy. The southerners, on their part, fought with fanatical determination and courage, and at first scored a number of successes under their superior generals – Robert E. Lee and 'Stonewall' Jackson. But the resources of the north were far greater and in the end they prevailed. Lee surrendered to the Union general, Ulysses S. Grant, at Appomattox Court House, Virginia, on April 8, 1865.

The war had been fought mainly on southern soil and the result was impoverishment for the southerners. Slavery had been abolished by Lincoln in 1863 and the slaves in the south abandoned their masters.

Five days after the surrender, Lincoln was assassinated in a theatre in Washington by a lunatic southern actor, John Wilkes Booth, who imagined he had a grievance against the northern victors. It was a tragedy for the south for the hand of conciliation and compassion in the north had been removed.

Abraham Lincoln watches troop movements with General Grant (third from right), and other officers of the Union army

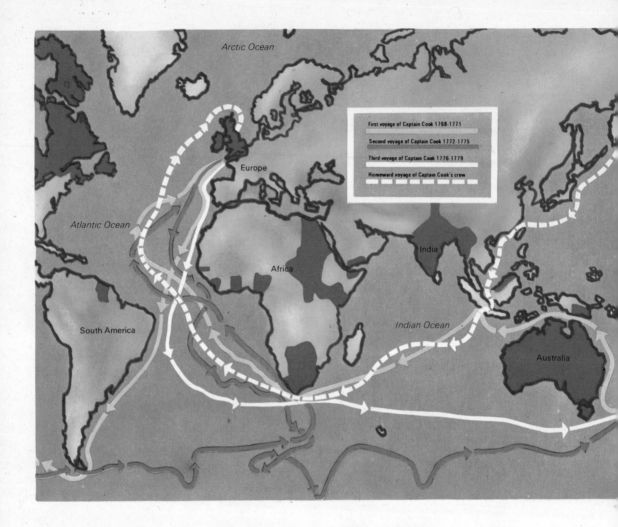

# From British Empire to Commonwealth

Like other western European nations, Britain embarked upon a policy of colonial expansion. The main areas of empire-building were Canada, Australia, New Zealand, South Africa and India. By the nineteenth century, Britain governed all these lands, which were very different in their history and peoples. They were important parts of the British Empire. In time they became independent members of a free Commonwealth of Nations.

### Canada

This huge country, large parts of which are permanently under snow, was first discovered by John and Sebastian Cabot who sailed from Bristol in 1497 under the patronage of Henry VII of England. They landed at Newfoundland and laid claim to the eastern shore. At that time they had no idea of the size of Canada. In 1535, the French sailor Jacques Cartier navigated a ship up the St. Lawrence River, but no

Map showing the routes of Captain Cook's voyages, and Britain's colonial empire in 1914

The French ran into trouble with the English who had set up posts in Hudson Bay, following the pioneering voyage of Henry Hudson, and early in the eighteenth century the British annexed large surrounding areas. In 1759 General James Wolfe defeated the French under General Louis Montcalm at the Heights of Abraham near Quebec and thus won all Canada from France. British rule was not popular everywhere, and a Canada Act shortly afterwards divided the country into two provinces, Ontario (or Upper Canada) and Quebec (or Lower Canada). The latter was largely French-speaking and was partially self-governing.

In 1867 the Dominion of Canada was formed, and soon afterwards the remaining territories joined the dominion.

In both World Wars, 1914–1918 and 1939–45 Canadian forces fought alongside the British, and distiguished themselves in land, sea and air battles. Since 1931, Canada has been an independent dominion. It is governed as a federation of provinces. The French-speaking province of Quebec has a separatist movement seeking self-government. Canada has made great advances in industry and agriculture. It has attracted emigrants from Europe, Asia and the Americas, and plays a leading part in world affairs.

permanent settlements were made at that time.

In the early seventeenth century another Frenchman, Samuel de Champlain, set up a trading station at Quebec on the St. Lawrence, and he made friends with the Algonquin Indians. These Indians had at one time occupied territory that is now the north-east of the United States, but had been driven out by the warlike Iroquois and Mohawks. Champlain called the territory around Quebec 'New France'. In the time of Louis XIV a colony was established there, and along the banks of the river a great many prosperous farms could be seen.

### Australia
Australia, which is a vast continent, was completely unknown until the seventeenth century. Far as the Moslem Arab sailors had ventured in the Indian Ocean and the Pacific, they do not appear ever to have touched Australia. It was populated by aborigines, of whom there are still survivors. The aborigines were in many ways still people of the Stone Age. They lived by hunting and gathering food. Today they are playing their part as citizens of modern Australia.

Jacques Cartier discovered the St Lawrence River in Canada in 1536. Here he met friendly Indians

Dutch sailors made landings on the northern tip of the continent in the early 1600s, and by 1650 the whole northern coast had been charted. The first British ships did not land there until the end of the century when the navigator William Dampier reached the north.

About seventy years later the east coast was charted by Captain James Cook, who discovered and named Botany Bay. Cook was accompanied on the expedition by Joseph Banks, who collected there a vast range of previously unknown botanical specimens. Colonization began swiftly after this discovery, and the British government decided to use the new settlement as a penal colony; that is, when men in Britain were convicted of crimes they could, instead of receiving the death sentence, be transported to Botany Bay for life. It should be realized that some of the crimes committed were political or religious, and it is quite wrong to assume that Australia was founded upon a colony of hardened gangsters. The founding of the New South Wales colony in 1788 marked the beginning of European settlement in Australia.

Life in Australia was very hard and expansion was slow. But by the middle of the nineteenth century there were half a million people of European nationality living there, ninety per cent of whom were British. The six colonies were New South Wales, Queensland, Western Australia, South Australia, Victoria and Tasmania. In 1860 gold was discovered and soon the population doubled as prospectors came out in their hundreds. Soon the need for proper government arose and this was organized with British help. In 1901 the six colonies, now known as states, with some self-government, were combined to form the Commonwealth of Australia. Australian troops fought gallantly in both World Wars. The country is an independent federation of states and territories. Some Australians want a republic, ending the ties with the British crown. Australia has increased its commerce with its Pacific and Asian neighbours. The same can be said of New Zealand, a country with an equally proud tradition of friendship with the United Kingdom in peace and war.

## New Zealand

New Zealand, so called because it was first discovered in 1642 by a Dutch sailor Abel Tasman, who came from Zeeland in Holland, was originally populated by Polynesians who probably arrived from Tahiti in the thirteenth century. These Polynesians, who are known as Maoris in New Zealand, are still there and they have mingled with the European settlers.

Tasman did not establish settlements, and it was not until Cook sailed round the islands that British people became fully aware of the existence of this new territory. Australians ventured there early in the nineteenth century, and in 1840 the British government took over direct control of the islands.

New Zealand has an excellent climate for farming and it is essentially an agricultural country producing some of the best lamb in the world. It is an independent

Lord Rutherford, the New Zealand-born atomic physicist, who split the atom in 1919

Commonwealth member with a parliamentary system of government, and still sells much of its lamb and dairy produce to Britain. A famous New Zealander was Ernest Rutherford (1871-1937), who became Lord Rutherford. He was a great scientist who revolutionized the world's

Captain James Cook lands at Botany Bay in Australia in 1770 after charting the coastline of New Zealand

idea of matter, when he split the atom for the first time, in 1919.

## South Africa

South Africa's coast was discovered and charted by the early Portuguese mariners who ventured south across the equator in the middle of the fifteenth century. Bartholomew Diaz rounded the Cape of Good Hope and a Portuguese landing was made near the Cape shortly afterwards. But, as with so many of their landings in Africa, the Portuguese used them as stepping stones to the next port or to India and the Far East, and it was not until the seventeenth century that Europeans began to settle Africa in earnest. It was the Dutch emigrants who began to make a new life for themselves in South Africa, and they founded Cape Town. Over the next one hundred and fifty years Dutchmen arrived in considerable numbers. They were mostly farmers by trade, and they soon made themselves prosperous, for they found a healthy climate and good farmland.

In 1820 the first British settlers arrived at Algoa Bay (Port Elizabeth) and in less than a generation they colonized the area. This led to friction with the Dutch, and the British tried to drive out the Dutch farmers. In 1836, tired of the incessant arguments with the British administration at the Cape, the Dutch (known as Boers) set out on a march across the mountains to establish republics of their own: Natal, the Orange Free State and Transvaal. This march was called the Great Trek.

In their new settlements, the Boers came into conflict with the Bantu African peoples already living there. The fiercest of these were the Zulus. For a long time, the warlike Zulus made life very dangerous for the Boers, for they resented European intrusion into lands which they had fought for. Eventually the Boers appealed to the

British for help, in return giving up some of their independence. When the Zulus were at last beaten, after a difficult struggle, the Boers expected that the British would give them back their independence. It was in vain. They rebelled, and in the First Boer War had some successes. Britain's Prime Minister Gladstone gave the Boers independence, which was later retracted. There were more quarrels between Boers and British, and in 1899 the Second Boer War began.

At first the Boers were successful. They trapped British armies in three towns, Ladysmith, Mafeking and Kimberley. But when Lord Roberts and Lord Kitchener were sent out to take command of the British forces, the Boers were defeated. The peace treaty led to the Boer territories being united with the British provinces. A Union of South Africa was formed, within the British Empire.

Boer troops ambush a British detachment near a railway line during the South African War (1899–1902)

Field Marshal Jan Christiaan Smuts (1870–1950), one of the greatest South African statesmen of that country's history

In the First World War, South Africans were divided about which side to support. One of the Boer commanders who fought against the British was Jan Christiaan Smuts. He joined the British. Another Boer leader, Christiaan de Wet, supported the Germans. In the Second World War, Smuts led the South African forces, who fought alongside Britain and its allies. In 1939 Smuts had become prime minister, but his party was defeated in an election of 1948, and he lost his seat in parliament. By then the ruling all-white government had declared a policy of apartheid — that is, separate development of the races. Whites, blacks, and people of Asian and mixed origin were to live and work separately. Only whites could vote and govern. This policy made South Africa an outcast in world affairs. In 1961 it left the Commonwealth and became a republic. In 1989 F.W. de Klerk became president and began reforms. Apartheid was ended. Black leader Nelson Mandela was freed from prison. People of all races faced the challenge of moving South Africa forward to a new era of multi-racial democracy.

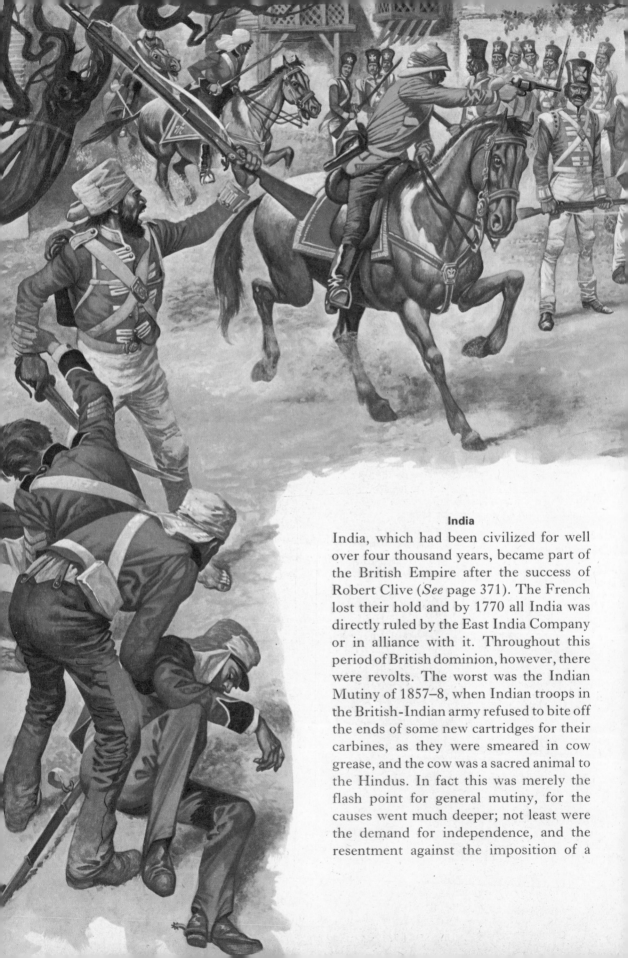

### India

India, which had been civilized for well
over four thousand years, became part of
the British Empire after the success of
Robert Clive (*See* page 371). The French
lost their hold and by 1770 all India was
directly ruled by the East India Company
or in alliance with it. Throughout this
period of British dominion, however, there
were revolts. The worst was the Indian
Mutiny of 1857–8, when Indian troops in
the British-Indian army refused to bite off
the ends of some new cartridges for their
carbines, as they were smeared in cow
grease, and the cow was a sacred animal to
the Hindus. In fact this was merely the
flash point for general mutiny, for the
causes went much deeper; not least were
the demand for independence, and the
resentment against the imposition of a

Mangul Pandy, an Indian sepoy who tried to lead an insurrection of the native guard at Barrackpore against the English, in February 1857, was arrested and hanged

foreign class structure upon a society that was already beset by a strict caste system.

After several severe defeats and massacres, the British restored order, and gradually learned not to trample over the age-old religious and racial feelings of a subject people. The British built up a fine army in India, and this helped to keep the peace in the south Asian region. The Indian forces fought magnificently on the Allied side in both World Wars.

In the 1920s the movement to obtain independence revived, championed by Mohandas Karamchand Gandhi, a Hindu lawyer of exceptional gifts who had lived in both Britain and South Africa. Gandhi advocated passive resistance rather than violence. In the 1930s the British government was actually discussing independence arrangements when the danger of war postponed India's freedom.

Immediately after the Second World War, the Labour government in Britain decided that India must become independent without delay. India's Moslems wanted their own country and in 1947 a partition of India between Hindus and Moslems was made. The Moslems, who were led by Jinnah, obtained northwestern India, and Bengal in the east. They called the new state Pakistan. The Hindus, led by Jawaharlal Nehru, kept the rest. Partition caused considerable violence and bloodshed, and left a legacy of mistrust between Pakistan and India. In 1966 the two countries went briefly to war, neither side winning.

Both India and Pakistan modernized their countries, through industrialization, improved farming methods and education. India's prime ministers after Nehru included his daughter Indira Gandhi and her son Rajiv, both of whom were murdered.

In 1971 civil war broke out between the two halves of Pakistan, East and West. East Pakistan broke away to become the independent state of Bangladesh.

Jawaharlal Nehru, first prime minister of independent India, believed his country should be a force for world peace

# Scandinavia, the Baltic Lands and Poland

The lands around the Baltic Sea are less fertile than those around the warmer Mediterranean. For much of the year the Baltic harbours are blocked with ice. In the sixteenth century most of the land belonged to Denmark whose king, Christian II, was ruler of three separate countries, Denmark, Norway and Sweden.

The Reformation (*See* page 324) broke up the Danish kingdoms because they did not all wish to remain Roman Catholic. Sweden, in particular, resisted the king's attempts to force Roman Catholicism on the country, and in 1523 a Swedish noble,

Charles XII of Sweden (1682–1718) was an energetic military leader who at first had much success against Russia and Poland. He was killed on an expedition against Norway

Gustavus Vasa, seized power and set himself up as independent king of Sweden. He was founder of a great dynasty of rulers who were, for the most part, able and proud monarchs.

Indeed for some time Sweden played a role in European history far out of proportion to its size and population. Although the country was poor, and the population small, the Swedes were tough, hardy farmers — good material for an army which was for long regarded as one of the best in Europe.

In 1629 Gustavus Adolphus joined in the Thirty Years' War on the side of the Protestants, for two reasons. First, he was a devout Protestant and wished to see all nations in Europe able to choose their religion. Secondly, he wanted to control the Baltic Sea and its trade, and also wished to keep under control some of his Vasa cousins who were ruling in Poland.

Gustavus was one of the greatest generals of European history. He was an expert in the use of artillery, then a comparatively new method of warfare. At Breitenfeld he destroyed the army of the Holy Roman Emperor and overran Bavaria. In 1632 he defeated Count Wallenstein at the battle of Lutzen, but to the grief of his Protestant supporters he was killed by a stray shot an hour or so after the victory.

The Thirty Years' War made Sweden powerful. She obtained control of Bremen, the most important port on the Weser River in Germany, which affected the wealth of the Hanseatic towns. Sweden also became the dominant nation on the Baltic Sea and she controlled Finland and

Map of the Baltic area

Estonia. This did not please the Russians, who had no port on the Baltic Sea.

In 1697 young Charles XII came to the throne of Sweden. He was, like Gustavus, a great soldier, and in the first years of his reign scored a number of important successes. When Denmark, Poland and Russia joined forces to attack Sweden, Charles attacked the Danes, defeated them at Copenhagen and received a huge war indemnity, or money compensation. Then he turned on the Russians and defeated them at Narva, near the Gulf of Finland, in 1700. The Russian army was five times the size of his small force. He invaded Poland, captured Warsaw, and obtained excellent terms in a peace treaty in 1704.

Then Charles made the fatal mistake of marching on Moscow. His army got bogged down in the wastelands and, when he was at last able to fight, the Russians defeated him at Pultova in 1709. That was the end of Swedish greatness, and most of her conquests were divided between Sweden's enemies. Russia obtained the Baltic states and the river outlets which it badly needed for trade.

Sweden then declined into a third-rate power. In 1810 one of Napoleon's marshals, Bernadotte, was elected heir to the Swedish throne and in 1818 he became Charles XIV. In the territorial settlements after the Napoleonic Wars, he obtained Norway from Denmark, but the Swedes allowed the Norwegians considerable self-government so that when they voted for independence in 1905 they were ready to launch out on their own. They already had one of the world's largest fleets of merchant ships. During the Second World War, Norway was occupied by German forces. King Haakon VII led a government in exile in Britain.

After the war, Norway flourished from trade and shipping, and also from the sale of oil and gas extracted from beneath the North Sea. Its people enjoy a high standard of living.

Since the time of Charles XIV, Sweden has stayed neutral, avoiding involvement in European wars. Today Sweden is one of the leading technological nations in Europe.

In 1864 Denmark lost a further part of its territory when the duchies of Schleswig and Holstein were made part of Germany

Trygve Lie (1896–1968) fled with the Norwegian government to Britain in 1940. He was secretary-general of the U.N. from 1945–52

after a short war. Denmark became a true parliamentary democracy in 1915 during the reign of King Christian X. Like Norway, it was invaded by Germany during the Second World War. Afterwards, the Danes modernized their industries and farms. In 1973 Denmark joined the European Community. Greenland, which Denmark ruled as a province from 1953, became self-governing in 1979.

Finland, which was a duchy within the empire of Russia from 1809, became a democratic republic in 1919. The Finns went to war with Russia in 1939 and despite the tiny size of their army, under overall command of Field-Marshal von Mannerheim, inflicted upon the Russians severe defeats. Although they joined the Germans in the attack on Russia in 1941, they were not penalized by the Allies, and they have retained their independence since the end of the war. Finland has stayed neutral in foreign affairs, but prospered economically.

On the eastern shore of the Baltic are three small countries called Latvia, Estonia and Lithuania. In their long history they have been ruled by Germans, Danes, Swedes and Poles. From 1721 Estonia was ruled by Russia, and Lithuania too came under Russian rule in 1795. Latvia, which during the Middle Ages was run by German crusaders called the Teutonic Knights, was held by Russia from 1800.

All three countries seized their chance of freedom after the Russian Revolution of 1917. They became independent, but were too weak to prevent the Russians regaining control during the Second World War. Latvia, Estonia and Lithuania were made Communist republics within the Soviet Union. However, in the 1980s Latvians, Estonians and Lithuanians elected parliaments opposed to Communist rule and demanded to be free again. In 1991, as the Soviet Union broke up (*See* page 405), all three republics gained their independence.

Poland has had a tragic history. It was a great Christian nation in the Middle Ages, intensely religious, liberal for the time in its government, and proud. For a while it was ruled by the Jagellon dynasty of kings, but after 1570 the throne became elective, votes being cast by the nobles and the gentry. This proved to be a weakness, for it encouraged the growth of feudal power, which was dying out in other parts of Europe. The greatest Polish king was John Sobieski, the man who saved Vienna in 1683 by crushing the huge army of Turks under Mustapha (*See* page 318) and driving him out of Hungary.

In the eighteenth century Poland was once more reduced to the status of a small power, and in 1772 Frederick the Great of

Field-Marshal von Mannerheim (1867–1951), commander-in-chief against the Russians in the war of 1939–40, and president of the Finnish Republic

Prussia proposed that the country should be split up between its neighbours, Prussia, Russia and Austria. There were three partitions, and each time Russia obtained a little more territory at the expense of the other two. In the time of Napoleon, western Poland was absorbed into the kingdom of Westphalia which he created for one of his brothers. After Waterloo in 1815, Poland was once more divided up, and remained so until the end of the First World War, despite many revolts.

In 1919 Marshal Joseph Pilsudski was in command of the Polish armies that had been formed by the Austrians to fight the Russians in the Great War (*See* page 420) and had now turned on the Communists who had seized power in Russia. He became temporary head of the new state of Poland which was created after the war, but retired in 1921. Five years later he

Marshal Joseph Pilsudski (1867–1935), virtual dictator of Poland from 1930

Lech Walesa in Warsaw, September 1980

returned to power and ruled as a dictator for nine years, although his official position was that of minister for war. Earlier than almost anyone else he prophesied the damage Europe was to suffer from Nazi Germany, but his warnings went unheeded. He died in 1935, and four years later Hitler invaded and conquered Poland. After the war, Poland became a Communist state. In 1980 Polish workers led by Lech Walesa forced the government to recognize the trade union organization Solidarity, which was independent of the Communist Party. This was an important change, but for a time afterwards Walesa and others were imprisoned. In 1989 more changes to Poland's government system were introduced, allowing greater freedom. After elections, a Solidarity leader became prime minister of a new government set on a policy of reform and modernization of the country's industries which had been poorly run by the Communists. In 1990 Lech Walesa was elected president of democratic Poland.

# The Story of Russia

During the Middle Ages a small state called Muscovy had been growing up around what is now Moscow, but its development had been checked by Genghis Khan, Khubilai Khan and Timurlaine. When the Mongol dominance declined in the fifteenth century, Muscovy had a chance to expand. Two rulers added further lands and these included districts in Europe.

The first ruler, Ivan III (1462–1505), whose wife was a relation of Constantine XI, the last Byzantine emperor, started building the Kremlin, that massive citadel of towers, domes, walls and battlements which has for centuries housed the government of Russia, and which is a splendid example of the European and Oriental architecture of the period.

In 1533 Ivan's grandson, Ivan IV (1533–84), became ruler while still a child. As soon as he was old enough he took over the reins of government and called himself the czar (this title is derived from the name of the great Julius Caesar). Ivan IV constructed a modern state out of Muscovy, or Russia, as it later came to be called, and extended its territory to the Ural mountains and to the Caspian Sea. He also made himself head

Ivan IV (1533–84), czar of Russia, known as Ivan the Terrible, lays siege to a Tatar fortress

of the Eastern Orthodox Church, which had moved from Constantinople to Russia in the middle of the fifteenth century.

Ivan determined to bring as much European influence into Russia as he could. He traded with England, Scandinavia and France, as well as with Asia Minor and India. He introduced a printing press, and he modernized the Russian language.

But, on the other side of the coin, Ivan was a very stern, cruel monarch who was not afraid to punish whole communities by exterminating them. Such was his cruelty that he became known as Ivan the Terrible, and towards the end of his reign, Western countries, disgusted by his brutality, declined to trade with him.

None the less he had given Russia the idea of nationhood and had instilled in the country a yearning for culture.

Unfortunately for Russia, Ivan's successors were weak and unprogressive, and a long period of chaos followed. Much of his work was undone, even to the extent of printing being banned, and the Church was not strong enough to pioneer an advance in learning as Churches had done in Western countries.

In 1613 a young Russian noble, Michael Romanoff, got himself elected czar. He ruled for thirty-two years, and in that time he strengthened the government and the country in many ways. He was the first of a long line of czars that lasted until 1917 when Nicholas II, the last Romanoff monarch, was deposed.

Michael's son, Alexei (1645–76), cooperated with the Church and encouraged a gradual return to the civilization introduced by Ivan the Terrible. Alexei was himself a very devout man, who used to sing with the choir in Moscow's cathedral, and who, like Louis IX of France (*See* page 250) spared no effort to help those less fortunate than himself. But this obsession with the Church meant that the

St Basil's cathedral in Moscow, a prototype of subsequent churches, was built by Ivan the Terrible as a memorial to eight saints

Peter the Great was a vital force in modernizing Russia. He encouraged trade with foreign countries as well as every kind of cultural contact with Europe

royal guards who were behaving as if they were the praetorian guards of ancient Rome.

To bring the Russians into the orbit of European civilization, Peter introduced European dress and manners, dancing and entertainments. He eliminated the Oriental habit of keeping women secluded. He squashed privilege and corruption in high places and stipulated a good education should be a worthier reason for promotion in the army and in the civil service than aristocratic birth. He introduced the Western calendar, promoted the teaching of science, mathematics and engineering, and founded schools and universities.

Peter the Great was also ambitious for Russian arms, and in a number of wars he won new territories. In particular he fought to obtain for Russia outlets to the sea in the Baltic, and by the defeat of Charles XII of Sweden at Pultova in 1709, Peter obtained several. In the north he founded St Petersburg on the Baltic, which was to become a great commercial city and naval base. Peter was also a keen naval architect. As a young man he had spent some weeks in the dockyards of Holland and England in disguise as a carpenter, and he used this knowledge to good effect in founding the Russian navy.

When Peter died in 1725, Russia was in a position to expand still further and to take part in the general development of Europe.

One of his successors was Catherine (II) the Great (czarina from 1762 to 1796). This remarkable woman, a German princess who married Czar Peter III and then probably had him murdered in 1762, ruled through a series of very cunning ministers, including Prince Potemkin and Count Orloff. Russia obtained a huge slice of Poland in the

business of government was neglected, and once more Russia was plunged into an era of unstable rule.

In 1682 there came to the throne the greatest Russian ruler of all time, Peter the Great. This strange man had two sides to his nature, like Ivan the Terrible. He was capable of appalling cruelty on an extensive scale, but he was also the most enlightened man in the land.

Peter was only a boy when he succeeded to the throne and for a while he had to submit to the elder members of his family. But in 1689 he took control himself. Having determined to modernize Russia, he tackled the problem in a variety of ways. First he decided to break the power of the nobles, not only by dividing up their lands but also by humiliating them personally. They wore long beards as part of their religious belief; he ordered the nobles to remove them, in many cases assisting in the operation himself. Then he put a tax on beards. He also broke the power of the

First (1772), Second (1793), and Third (1795) Partition treaties (*See* page 398), and in a number of wars with the Ottoman empire, Catherine won new lands.

In the domestic field Catherine reconstructed the civil service, divided the country into governorships, like large local authorities, and gave many towns a large measure of self-government. Her court became a centre of learning and art, especially literature. French was spoken, and she herself corresponded with Voltaire (*See* page 347) and Diderot.

But Catherine did nothing to improve the lot of the serfs who still suffered under feudal conditions. In 1773 a large-scale revolt broke out, led by Emil Pugachev, who claimed to be the czarina's murdered husband, Peter III. Pugachev displayed brilliant military ability and conquered large areas, completely outwitting the royal forces sent against him. Finally, in 1775 he was defeated and executed. Unfortunately, Catherine learned nothing from the revolt; serfs who were found to have been involved were banished to Siberia in large numbers.

After Catherine's death in 1796 Russia joined the various alliances formed against Napoleon, but was defeated at Austerlitz in 1805 and at Friedland in 1807. Peace was made at Tilsit, but in 1812 Napoleon quarrelled with the czar and led his 600,000 strong Grand Army against Russia. He defeated the Russians at Borodino and marched on Moscow which he found empty. When the cold weather set in, the condition of French troops became miserable, and they embarked on a disastrous retreat.

After Waterloo the Russians appeared to retreat within their own frontiers. The czar remained an absolute ruler and the gap between landowners and serfs grew wider and wider. Reform proved difficult because it had to come either from the czar or from revolutionaries. In 1861 Alexander II abolished serfdom and then tried to reform the system of justice, but this was a failure and he was assassinated in 1881.

The abolition of serfdom did not help the peasants, for the lands which they were now allowed to buy for themselves were too costly. A new doctrine arose called nihilism. Everyone wanted to overthrow the existing order of things, but no one had a clear idea of what they wanted in its place.

This nihilism was accompanied by violence and terrorism. Bombs were thrown in crowded places and strikes were organized in factories. Czar Alexander III (1881–94) dealt with these outbreaks severely, and so did his successor Nicholas II (1894–1917). But Nicholas also tried to find ways of improving the conditions of the country. He encouraged trade, had railways built, and set up a programme of road construction. His ministers, however, were either incompetent or corrupt. When the Russian army was easily defeated by the Japanese in 1905 and the Russian fleet routed in the same year, revolution on a wide scale broke out against the general inefficiency of the nation's management. Nicholas called the Duma (the Russian parliament)

Catherine the Great, czarina of Russia, was a ruthless woman of exceptional ability

The doctrines of Karl Marx, the German political philosopher, were the basis of the policies of the Russian revolutionaries

government at home was in danger of collapsing. The reverses at war continued, and in 1917, Nicholas abdicated. The czar, and more so the czarina, had been for some years heavily under the spell of an extraordinary monk, Gregor Rasputin. They listened to his advice on all matters although it was almost always disastrous. Rasputin was assassinated in 1916. A moderate government under Alexander Kerensky was formed.

Kerensky's government was too moderate for the more extreme revolutionaries like V. I. Lenin and Leon Trotsky, who had been encouraged by the Germans. In October 1917 they overthrew it, setting up the first 'Dictatorship of the Proletariat', that is, rule by the poorest class. They made a separate peace with Germany at Brest-Litovsk and withdrew from the war. Their aim was to build up a new Communist state on a truly Socialist pattern. The world watched with wonder, and in some quarters with

into session but dismissed it almost at once because the violent scenes which occurred while it was in session frightened him.

In the First World War Russia joined the Allies but was severely defeated at the battle of Tannenburg. Here and there Russian generals like Brussilov won victories against the Austrians, but

Revolutionaries attack the Winter Palace in St Petersburg during the Revolution in 1917

Lenin (left), with Stalin, who was one of his associates, talking to workers and troops in Moscow

President Roosevelt of the United States and Winston Churchill, prime minister of Great Britain, to decide the future of Germany. The decisions reached favoured the Russians, and when the war ended in the summer of 1945 they extended Communist rule across Eastern Europe. The wartime allies were now divided by what Churchill in a speech made in 1946 called an 'iron curtain' across Europe.

The Union of Soviet Socialist Republics was now one of the two most powerful nations in the world. It rivalled the United States in military might and in achievements in space. It led a group of Communist countries in Europe. Its citizens had better housing, schools and hospitals than ever before. But all was not well. There was no real freedom, farms and factories were not efficiently run, and shops were often short of goods.

By the 1980s there were calls for change. Mikhail Gorbachev, leader from 1988 to 1991, brought in reforms and sought friendship with the West. Communism was no longer the answer and the creaking federation of 15 republics began to break up. In 1991 the 'Soviet Union' ceased to exist. Among the new self-governing republics, Russia became by far the biggest and strongest.

horror, for among the first acts of the new state was the killing of the czar and his family at Ekaterinburg (1918).

Lenin, whose doctrines were based upon the teachings of Karl Marx, the originator of Communism, was the founder of the Union of Soviet Socialist Republics of which Russia was the leading and largest republic. He died in 1924 and was succeeded as leader of the Soviet Union by Joseph Stalin after a period of rule by the presidium of the Communist Party. By 1936, Stalin was absolute master of Russia.

In 1939 Stalin made a non-aggression pact with Hitler who then invaded Poland, in September, and overran most of it in six weeks. This brought Britain and France into war with Germany (*See* page 424). Two years later, Hitler unleashed a massive attack on Russia and in a few weeks overran vast areas in the west, almost reaching Moscow. But the Russians fought with great heroism and at last their armies drove the Germans back into their land, capturing Berlin.

In their advance westward, the Russians freed several European countries from the Nazis. In February 1945 Stalin met

Yuri Gagarin, a Russian astronaut, was the first person to pilot a spacecraft around the earth in 1961

# Nationalism in South-East Europe

After the fall of Constantinople (*See* page 272) and the spread of Ottoman power throughout eastern Europe, traces of nationalism among the various peoples there vanished for centuries. But in the 1800s when Ottoman control of its empire began to break up, nationalist movements made the Balkans an important area of political attention among the great powers.

The leadership of the Eastern Orthodox Church had passed from Byzantium to Russia, and the nearby Balkan countries were Christian, so their political sympathies were with Russia.

### Greece

Greece won its independence after a heroic struggle, which began in 1827, against the might of Turkey. This success thrilled all Europe. Greece was then ruled by a Bavarian prince, Otto, for thirty years. He was deposed and in 1863 a Danish prince was elected King George I. He reigned for fifty years.

Greece became a battle ground during the First World War. Afterwards the monarchy was expelled, but restored in 1935 under George II. In 1940 Mussolini (*See* page 369) invaded Greece and a year later the Germans overran it.

The king was returned to power after the Second World War. In 1967 the young Greek king, Constantine, was driven out and his rule replaced by a military dictatorship. This regime was overthrown and since 1975 Greece has been a democratic republic. It joined the E.U. in 1979.

### Albania

This small country freed itself from Turkey in 1912. Until 1939 Albania had a king, but then Italy invaded and the king was deposed. After the Second World War, the country became a Communist republic. Its people were poor and had few contacts with the outside world. In 1992 Albanians elected a non-Communist government and began to modernize their country.

### Rumania

Rumania (also spelled Romania) was granted some self-government by the Turks in 1862 and full independence in 1877. After the First World War, Rumania obtained Transylvania with its salt mines and oilfields. It had a king, but its chief ministers were powerful, and pro-German. Under General Antonescu they joined Germany in the Second World War, sending troops to fight the Russians. At the end of the war, Russia saw to it that Rumania had a Communist government. Nicolae Ceausescu led Rumania from 1965 to 1989, when he was shot after an uprising which led to the formation of a new non-Communist government.

Map of south-east Europe

## Bulgaria

Bulgaria had been a powerful kingdom in the tenth and eleventh centuries and had then become absorbed by the Byzantine empire. Bulgaria became part of the Ottoman empire in the fifteenth century and remained quiet for four hundred years. In the 1870s the Turks let the Bulgarians have their own separate Church. This prompted the nationalists to agitate for full independence, but in 1876 the Turks crushed this movement with appalling severity. What became known as the Bulgarian atrocities created a European scandal. War between Russia and Turkey followed and Bulgarian independence was established in the northern part of the country. In 1885 under Stefan Stambolov, a great leader, the Bulgarians obtained the remainder of their land from Turkey.

Bulgaria sided with Germany in the First World War and was severely defeated. A dictatorship followed under King Boris (1918-43), and Bulgaria joined the Germans again in the Second World War. The country was overrun by the Russians and a Communist republic was set up in 1946 under Georgi Dimitrov. The Communist ruled harshly. By the 1980s there were growing demands for change, and a non-Communist government was elected in 1991.

## Serbia/Yugoslavia

Serbia had once been a mediaeval kingdom, but its national status disappeared after a crushing defeat by the Turks at Kossovo in 1389. In about 1830 self-government was given to the Serbs and they gained full independence in 1877. From 1903 to 1921 the country was ruled by a tough and popular king, Peter Karageorgevic. He campaigned for independence for the Serbian peoples.

In 1914, a Serbian student, Gavrilo Princip, assassinated Archduke Franz Ferdinand of Austria at Sarajevo, an incident which signalled the start of the First World War. The Austrians blamed the Serbs, declared war and occupied Serbia. After the war, Serbia was joined with Croatia and Slovenia, two smaller states of the old Austro-Hungarian empire. The new country was called Yugoslavia.

In 1941 Yugoslavia was invaded by the Germans. After the Second World War it came under the rule of Marshal Tito, the Communist leader of the anti-German resistance. He led the country until his death in 1981. From 1946 Yugoslavia was governed as a federation of six republics, but there were growing tensions between them. Croatia, Slovenia and Bosnia-Herzegovina declared independence in 1992. Serbia and Montenegro formed a new Yugoslavia. Macedonia also declared independence. Serbia, Croatia and Bosnia-Herzegovina began a savage war to decide the borders and populations of their territories.

The assassination of the Austrian archduke, Franz Ferdinand, at Sarajevo in 1914, was the signal for the outbreak of World War I

# The Mogul Empire in India

At the end of the fifteenth century India was still a collection of feudal states run by powerful and often savage rulers called khans, rajahs or nawabs. Some of them were Hindu, some of them Moslem, and generally the Moslems dominated the Hindus.

As the century was turning, Babur, a Mongol descendant of Timurlaine, who had been born in Persia, rose to power and tried to bring some of the states together into a sort of empire. He trained a small but tough body of troops and with this army invaded Afghanistan, capturing its principal cities, Kabul and Kandahar. Then he moved eastwards towards the centre, captured Delhi and swung southwards. By 1530 he was master of much of India, and ruled the largest Indian empire since Asoka (*See* page 171).

Babur died in 1530 and was succeeded by an ineffectual son who was driven out of some of his father's conquered territories. But in his reign the trade routes from East to West were greatly improved by the construction of about fifteen hundred miles of road. He was followed by Akbar in 1542, who came to be known as Akbar the Great.

Akbar became ruler when he was only a child and it was several years before he could grasp the reins of power. He was a tough, energetic man, capable of great cruelty, but a very able administrator. Above all, he was absolutely determined to make India great and powerful after the centuries of stagnation. His government was efficient, however autocratic. When he broke the power of the feudal lords, no one regretted it except the lords.

Akbar wanted to grant freedom of belief both to the Hindus and to the Moslems, a thankless task, for the two faiths were quite irreconcilable. He encouraged a great revival of learning and art, especially Hindu art and literature, and he organized the spreading of Hindustani as a national language. He was a great builder, and among his works were the city of Agra and the improvements to Delhi. When he died in 1605 he had earned the admiration of countless people.

Akbar's son was Jehangir (1605–27), and he carried on his father's reforming

The Taj Mahal, completed in about 1650, is constructed of white marble, and occupies about 130 square feet, on a marble terrace. The central dome is about 200 ft high

work. He also favoured the Hindus and allowed them to have posts in the government. What is more, he took a liking to Christianity and allowed missionaries to come to India. But he was given to excessive drinking and opium-smoking and he failed to emulate his great father even though his abilities well qualified him to do so.

His son was Shah Jehan (1627–58), a bold and brutal man. He married a beautiful princess and when she died young built her the most magnificent monument known to mankind. This was the Taj Mahal at Agra, and it is perhaps the finest piece of Oriental architecture in the world. His wife's death unhinged Shah Jehan's mind and he had to be deposed from his throne by his son Aurangzeb, who cruelly imprisoned him in the fort at Agra until his death in 1666.

Aurangzeb ruled the Mogul empire from 1658 to 1707. He was a stern, violent and hot-tempered man who

Jelaleddin Mahomet Akbar (1542–1605), the greatest of the Mogul emperors, extended the empire so that it included all India north of the Vindhya mountains. It has been said that his empire was 'the most splendid the world has known'. His anxiety to grant tolerance to Hindus and Moslems alike was typical of his generous nature which also led him to be sympathetic to Christianity

loathed any form of amusement or pleasure. He slept whenever possible on rough ground, refused any stimulating drink, and would not even watch dancing or acrobatics. What is more, he tried to make his followers equally austere. He was at heart a soldier and he spent the best part of his reign with his huge army of a quarter of a million men, always on the move somewhere or other. All the same he failed to conquer a revolt of the Narathas of the Deccan led by Sivaji.

Aurangzeb turned against the Hindus and expelled them from their government offices. He imposed severe taxes on them, and he destroyed many Buddhist temples. The Hindus resisted, generally in a passive manner – such as by lying down outside his palaces and allowing themselves to be trampled to death by elephants. On one occasion many died in this way outside the Taj Mahal.

Aurangzeb's policy was bad for the empire. It held up development, and in conjunction with a series of natural catastrophes – famine and plague – it hastened the end of Mogul greatness. Eventually, even his own army began to desert him and in 1707 he died, lonely, depressed, and indifferent to the fate of the empire which in a very short time was to break up and become easy prey to infiltration by Europeans, among them the French and the British.

After Aurangzeb's death the provincial rulers seized power in their states and ruled like emperors. Some of his Moslem officers also set up kingdoms for themselves. Warfare between the Hindus and the Moslems continued.

Two powerful Moslem states grew up, Bengal and Deccan. Bengal was ruled by a grandson of Aurangzeb. But the continual warfare between the states only made it easier for the British and French to extend their influences as they were called in to help one side or the other. Robert Clive, an East India Company official in Bengal, organized an army and defeated the Nawab of Bangal, Suraj ud-Daulah, in 1757 at the battle of Plassey, and thereby added the large state of Bengal to the growing empire of Britain.

It was the end of Indian independence for nearly two hundred years. Time and again they struggled against the British to get free. In 1948 the British finally left and the country was divided (*See* page 395) between Hindus (India) and Moslems (Pakistan). The first prime minister of India was Jawaharlal Nehru (1889–1964), an extremely able politician who became one of the most respected statesmen in the world.

The large province of Bengal was added to the British empire after Robert Clive had crushed its ruler, the brutal Suraj-ud-Daulah at Plassey, in 1757

# China: From Manchus to Mao

The Ming emperors (*See* page 286) in China cut the country off from the influences of the rest of the world and spent more time worrying about their spiritual life than about the more earthly conditions of their people. Throughout the sixteenth and the first half of the seventeenth century they drifted on in this manner. The Chinese were not afflicted by the terrible religious wars that were ravaging Europe, nor were they bothered by the aggressive activities of the Ottomans. Their people appeared content to endure poverty and inefficient government.

This apparently depressing period, however, was also one of great artistic flowering. Painting became very popular and some of the best Chinese pictures were produced. Porcelain manufacture improved further, and became more exciting still when fresh varieties of colouring were introduced. More books were written and published, though still in the old language, which has been said by some historians to have inhibited the general development of China; pictorial writing is not the easiest written language with which to discuss problems between one civilization and another or to exchange ideas.

The emperor, Wang Li (1573–1620), spent lavishly on royal palaces and buildings, but it was in his time that fresh Mongol invasions disturbed the country's peace. These new invaders, who were envious of Ming culture, were called Manchus and they were distantly related to the Kins. They already controlled parts of China in the north, and dreamed of extending their territories. Wang Li and his successor failed to keep the Manchus at bay, and before 1628 all Manchuria was in enemy hands.

The last of the Ming emperors, Chung-Chang (1627–44), who was a quiet and gentle scholar, was utterly unfitted to resist the warlike Manchus. After ineffective attempts to fight, Chung-Chang committed suicide and the Manchus took over the throne, starting a new dynasty, the last in a very long line.

The Manchu emperor, K'ang Hsi, defeats Mongol tribes on the Chinese border, using cannon

Just like the earlier invaders of China, the Manchus became quickly absorbed and they took over the administration of government and ran it as the Ming dynasty had done. The Manchus even invited the Chinese to co-operate with them.

The first important Manchu emperor was K'ang Hsi (1662–1722). He defeated the Mongols in a long campaign in which he used cannons purchased from western Europe. K'ang Hsi was a cultivated man who tried to teach the Mongols a more settled way of life, showing them the benefits of farming and owning permanent homes. He welcomed Christian missionaries, interested himself in science and literature, and wrote books (he even edited a dictionary). He erected many great buildings, including the Summer Palace at Peking.

But his last years were not happy, for there was a strong political party at home that did not approve of the introduction of Western ideas into the country. When he died in 1722 he was succeeded by his son, Yung Cheng (1722–35), who immediately reversed his policy. Christian missionaries were expelled, science and literature from the West were prohibited, and the Chinese withdrew again into isolation. They were frightened by the tales they had heard of British and French intervention in India.

Yung Cheng was succeeded by Ch'ien Lung, who ruled for more than half a century. He was an enlightened man who improved the administration of the government, but who persecuted the remaining Christians, since he saw them as a potential danger to the loyalty of the people to the state and the royal family. The Chinese people regarded their emperors as gods; it would not do for them to be told that there is only one God, and that He is not on this earth.

Ch'ien embarked on a number of military expeditions. He conquered Nepal and drove the Gurkhas back to Katmandu. He also conquered Tibet but continued to recognize the Dalai Lama, the Tibetan head priest, as the 'Pope' of Buddhism. Then he invaded Burma and compelled its rulers to recognize Chinese sovereignty. By the time of his death in 1796, China was very powerful indeed in the Far East.

The Dalai Lama is the spiritual head of the Tibetans. The present holder of the office fled to India when China annexed Tibet

But after Ch'ien Lung the country began to slide downhill. Its isolationist policy had arrested development in a number of important fields – science, agriculture and industry. It had not progressed in political development and did not yet see the folly of perpetuating semi-feudal conditions for the peasants working the land. Even in trading there seemed no enthusiasm to bargain for the products of the rest of the world.

As the Chinese continued to resist industrialization, so they became an obvious prey to other countries, and in the nineteenth century European nations began to infiltrate Chinese life. For example, in 1839, China had a trade dispute with Britain. This resulted in a British squadron of warships sailing up the Yangtze River and bombarding Nanking, forcing the Chinese to hand over the port of Hong Kong to Britain.

In 1846 a horde of peasants, led by Hsiu Chuan, a semi-religious leader who preached a doctrine of Confucianism and Christianity mixed, rebelled against the Manchu emperor. The rebels were remarkably successful in many districts, and in 1851 they captured Nanking, setting up a state of their own. The Manchus were unable to do anything and invited help from western European powers. This broke Chinese isolationism. France and Britain assisted the Manchus to restore order, and in return obtained fresh trading posts and facilities. Christian missionaries were also admitted again.

At the end of the 19th century some Chinese turned on foreigners living in their land and massacred them. The European powers attacked Peking in retaliation and the riots, known as The Boxer Rebellion, ceased

Western contact threatened the age-old fabric of Chinese society. In 1894 Japan defeated China for possession of Korea, and this was a signal for more Europeans to move into China, setting up trading posts. Emperor Kuang Hsu (1875-1908) tried to introduce some democracy but failed.

In 1900 there occurred the Boxer rebellion. Chinese rose up against foreigners. The Western powers retaliated, sending troops and seizing Peking. Order was restored but the Manchus were doomed. In 1911 came revolution and the last Manchu emperor was expelled. Sun Yat sen, who sought to modernize China, became president of a new republic, but almost immediately he was driven out by his colleagues. Anarchy followed for some time, during which Sun Yat sen was president of a smaller republic in southern China. In 1927 Chiang Kai shek, Sun Yat sen's brother-in-law, seized power and united nearly all China.

In 1931 Japan invaded Manchuria and occupied it, but after the Second World War, when Japan was defeated, Manchuria reverted to China. Chiang Kai shek, who had led Chinese forces against Japan in alliance with Britain and the U.S.A., tried to reassert dominion over all China. A civil war followed between his supporters and those of Mao Tse tung, a Communist revolutionary leader who had fought bravely against the Japanese during the occupation. In 1949 Mao Tse tung's armies captured Nanking, Peking and Shanghai, and a People's Republic was declared, with Mao as its head. Chiang fled to the island of Formosa (Taiwan), where he set up what became the Nationalist Government of China. He died in 1975. The Nationalists still hold Formosa.

Under Mao Tse tung, China was governed as a Communist state. During the 1960s Mao encouraged a frenzied campaign of 're-education', known as the

Mao tse tung, the Chinese Communist leader, as a young man. Mao died in 1976

Cultural revolution, which caused great confusion, damaging government, universities and industry. Mao died in 1976 and China's new leaders sought a less revolutionary path. Most were veteran Communists and opposed to democracy. They sent the army on to the streets of Peking to crush student protests in 1989, but allowed modernization of China's economy and increased trade with non-Communist countries.

# Japan and the Far East since 1500

Japan had become completely shut off from the world during the Middle Ages. In the 1500s a few Dutch and Portuguese traders and missionaries were allowed to enter, but in 1624 the Shogun (the hereditary general in control) expelled all foreigners and once more cut his country off from the outside. Japan then remained isolated until the middle of the nineteenth century. During that time, however, there was a cultural revival in the country, when art and porcelain manufacture reached great heights and compared well with some of the better Chinese periods.

In 1853, Commodore Matthew Perry, in command of a squadron of United States warships, sailed to Japan and obtained permission to fish in Japanese waters. Soon European powers followed and before long Japan had trade agreements with many countries. This opened up the country heralding a new age for the Japanese.

The Shoguns were overthrown. The emperor, who had remained in obscurity

Map of Japan and the Far East

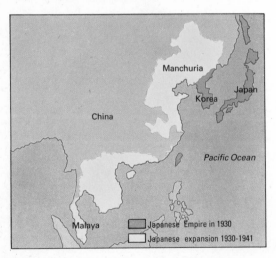

all his reign, as had his ancestors before him, was brought from retirement and installed on the throne with great ceremony in Tokyo, the largest Japanese city. Feudal lords volunteered to give up their baronial rights, and a new government was formed, modelled closely along western European ideas.

At this time Japan converted itself almost wholesale from an Oriental backwater into a modern industrial state. Its army was revolutionized and a new fleet of steel ships was built for its navy. Perhaps this had one of the most important influences on its future conduct.

In 1902 Japan made its first important alliance – with Great Britain – mainly because it feared Russian expansion. The Trans-Siberian railway across Russia from Moscow to Vladivostok was completed and this meant that troops could be transported to the eastern coast for an invasion of the Japanese archipelago.

Japan, which had ambitions of colonizing Manchuria, ran up against the Russians there in 1905 and a full-scale war broke out. It proved to be a most successful affair for the Japanese. At the battle of Tsushima the Russian navy was almost wiped out by a well-trained force. On land the Japanese captured Port Arthur and drove the Russians back into their own land.

During the First World War the Japanese declared war on Germany and cleared her from the Pacific in November 1917. They leapt forward, meanwhile, with their industrialization programme which had started in the 1870s. Soon they had the world's third largest navy.

Unfortunately, in the 1920s Japan was governed by ministers who became increasingly militaristic in their thinking. This was really an inheritance from the past, for the Japanese nobles had a long tradition of military glory.

In 1931 Japan seized Manchuria despite the protests of the world, and in 1937 embarked on an invasion of China itself. It was swiftly overrun in the north and Shanghai was captured. The Japanese used the railways to take their forces into Nanking, which fell in December. To all intents and purposes China had become a Japanese posession.

But this was not really the case, for the Chinese kept up an endless resistance campaign, organized on two fronts, one by Chiang Kai shek and the other by Mao Tse tung (*See* page 415).

Japanese military successes stimulated the government leaders still further and, in 1941, Japan determined to become the head of a grand Far Eastern empire. Japanese forces attacked the American naval base at Pearl Harbor in Hawaii unexpectedly which brought the Americans into the Second World War, and also invaded the mainland of South-East Asia. In a few months practically the whole of the Far East was in Japanese hands — Malaya, Indonesia, the Philippines, Burma and Indo-China, and the very borders of India were in danger.

The Americans managed to defeat the Japanese navy in a number of naval actions in 1942 and 1943, and this stemmed the Japanese advance. By 1945 U.S. bombers were raiding Japanese cities, and British troops were driving Japanese forces out of Burma.

In August the Americans dropped their first atomic bomb on Hiroshima, which wiped out the city and killed many thousands of inhabitants. A few days later a second bomb was released on Nagasaki. At once the Japanese surrendered.

Since the war, Japan has rebuilt its cities and shattered industries. It has a democratic government, in which the emperor is now only a figurehead. It has prospered from trade. Japan's industries are so successful that it is now one of the world's richest nations.

### Indonesia

By the sixteenth century most of Indonesia was Moslem, although there

The Japanese city of Hiroshima was devastated in August 1945 by the atomic bomb, which was dropped from an American airplane

were several areas which were mainly Hindu. The Moslem districts were visited by the Portuguese at the beginning of the sixteenth century for trading purposes. Soon the Spanish, the Dutch, the English and the French followed, all in pursuit of spices which were cheaper to buy direct than from Venice or from traders in the Ottoman empire. Trading stations were set up, and in 1684 the Dutch East India Company was formed, which to all intents and purposes became the principal power in the islands. Within a hundred years the whole area was exclusively Dutch ruled.

In 1942 the Japanese invaded Dutch Indonesia and held it until 1945, when it was returned to the Dutch. They granted full independence to the Indonesians (there had been a strong nationalist movement growing over the previous half century). For a while Indonesia was beset by economic difficulties which were made worse by the excessive military build-up undertaken by its president Sukarno. But since his deposition in 1966, the country had moved ahead steadily and increased its economic strength.

### Malaysia and Singapore

The Malay people came from Indonesia in the fifteenth century and settled in the dense forests of the Malay peninsula. The area also attracted the attention of the Chinese, the Indians and the Moslems. In time much of Malaya was converted to Islam.

The first Europeans in Malaya were the Portuguese, who arrived at Malacca in 1511. There they set up a trading station and held it until the Dutch captured it in 1640.

British influence in Malaya began in earnest in the 1780s when traders settled in Penang. Operations in Malaya by the British were supervised by the East India Company which governed British India.

The important habour of Singapore was annexed for Britain by Sir Stamford Raffles in 1819. Six years later Malacca was taken from the Dutch, and throughout the nineteenth century the whole of Malaya was under the control of the British, although the various sultanates and states were allowed considerable independence. In about 1880 the states were called the Federated Malay States.

Malaya's principal products were tin and rubber, and these raw materials were of great value to western Europe.

After the Second World War, Malaya obtained complete independence from British rule (1957), and in 1963 it became part of the Federation of Malaysia.

South of the Malay peninsula lies the island of Singapore. In 1819 the British founded a trading port there and this, in time, became one of the greatest commercial centres in Asia. The British also built a naval base on the island which was regarded as impregnable.

But in the war with Japan (*See* page 426) the island fell, and with it the naval base. It has been called the greatest defeat in British history. It remained in Japanese hands until the Japanese surrender in 1945.

Singapore became an independent state in 1959 and joined the Federation of Malaysia in 1963. Two years later it ceased to be one of the fourteen states of the Federation, and is now a self-governing country of great commercial importance.

### Burma

Burma was a great Buddhist monarchy in South-East Asia in the eleventh century. The country, however, dissolved into anarchy and remained in a state of civil war for many years, until it came under the influence of the East India Company (English) in 1612.

In the middle of the eighteenth century Burma recovered its own unity under a great ruler, Alompra, but after his death anarchy followed again. Early in the nineteenth century rival claimants for the throne threatened to disturb the peace on the border with Bengal, and the East India Company became alarmed. In 1824 a war was fought in which the British captured the capital, Rangoon. Thirty years later the Irrawaddy River territory was annexed. In 1885, the ruler of what remained of independent Burma, Thibaw, seized property belonging to the Bombay-Burma Company with French connivance. Britain retaliated by occupying Thibaw's kingdom. In 1886 Burma became a province of the British-Indian empire.

In 1937 Burma was separated from India and given a measure of self-government. It was occupied by the Japanese in the Second World War. After the war, when India was partitioned and made independent, Burma also obtained independence in 1948.

### Indochina

The countries of Vietnam, Cambodia and Laos were formerly known as Indochina. Into this region, first settled by Indonesian and Malay peoples, came the Viets, then Thais and Khmers. This was about two thousand years ago, and the Khmers controlled most of the region from the ninth century until the fifteenth. The Viets had their own kingdom, but were often at war with China.

In the nineteenth century the French made Indochina a colony. But French Indochina was overrun by the Japanese in 1940. After the Second World War, Laos and Cambodia became self-governing but were still under French influence.

However in Vietnam, Communists led by Ho Chi Minh fought the French from 1946 and drove them out in 1954. French Indochina then disappeared from the map. Laos and Cambodia became fully independent. Vietnam was split between Communist North and non-Communist South. It was not reunited until 1975, after a second war in which the United States sent powerful forces to aid South Vietnam. In spite of this aid, the North was victorious, and Vietnam became a Communist state. The Vietnamese economy was damaged by so many years of fighting, but the country remains stronger than its neighbours Laos and Cambodia, each of which has suffered from bad government and civil war, causing the people great misery.

### Polynesia

In the Pacific Ocean there are numerous groups of islands that began to attract the attention of Europeans in the eighteenth century when Britain's Captain James Cook made one of his celebrated voyages through the Pacific in 1768-71. The people who live in the islands of Hawaii, New Zealand and Easter Island — which form a triangle — are the Polynesians. Sometimes referred to as the Vikings of the Pacific (for in former days they were great sailors and coast raiders), they came, it is believed, from Asia, about two thousand years ago. Historians think that there may also have been some migrants from Peru in South America.

Although there was no written Polynesian history, the chiefs remembered long sagas handed down to them by their ancestors, and these were repeated in every generation. They lived by farming and fishing; their lives seemed idyllic.

The modern world, of course, could not be kept out, and the islanders' way of life has changed. Europeans and people from Asia settled on the islands. Some are still colonies, others have become self-governing. The most notable of these are Tonga, the Solomons and Tuvalu. Tourism is now a growing industry.

# The Two World Wars

In Chapter Sixty-five, Nationalism in South-East Europe, we saw something of how the Balkan nations desired and fought for independence. Their leaders were not so blind, however, that they did not see that independence could be guaranteed only by the goodwill of the greater powers interested in that area, namely, Russia, Austria-Hungary and Turkey. But this was bound to lead to trouble as nationalism spread. Serbia was the touble spot which caused a world war.

The ancient kingdom of Serbia, which had been crushed by the Turks as a result of the battle of Kossovo in 1389, remained part of the Turkish empire in Europe until the nineteenth century when the Ottomans recognized Serbian independence. By the beginning of the 1900s the Serbians had begun to agitate for the independence of other Serbian peoples still living in areas of the Austro-Hungarian empire, but the Austrians were not inclined to concede such freedom.

On June 28, 1914 the heir to the Austrian throne, the Archduke Franz Ferdinand, was assassinated at Sarajevo by a Serbian student, Gavrilo Princip, a member of a Serbian nationalist group. The Austrian government accused the Serbian government of instigating the murder and within a month declared war.

This provided an excuse for other European powers, which had grievances against each other, to go to war. The Russians mobilized their armies along the German and Austrian frontiers, whereupon the Germans declared war on Russia. This brought in France, which had a treaty of alliance with Russia. To get at France, the Germans then invaded Belgium, despite having guaranteed their

British and German High Seas fleets clashed for the last time in the First World War at Jutland in May 1916. The result was a stalemate

neutrality. Great Britain intervened and declared war on Germany and Austria-Hungary. Turkey joined the Central European powers in November and Bulgaria followed suit in 1915.

The principal allies of Great Britain and France and Russia were Japan (from August 1914), Italy (from May 1915), and the United States of America (from April 1917). The bulk of the fighting took place on land in six main theatres of war. These were the Western Front, a line of trenches running from the Belgian coast through France down to the border with Switzerland; the Eastern Front, a more flexible line from the Baltic Sea to the Black Sea; the Dardanelles, in 1915; the Balkans, including Salonika; the Near East, including Palestine and what is now Iraq; and the Austro-Italian border.

The fighting on the Western Front was static, neither side advancing more than a few miles right up to the end of the war. On the Eastern Front the Germans and Austrians began by winning several victories and they gained much ground. In 1916 the Russian general Brussilov counter-attacked successfully, but in 1917 the Russian monarch was deposed (*See* page 404) and a revolutionary government was set up which made a separate peace with the Germans at Brest-Litovsk.

The Dardanelles campaign was an imaginative scheme devised by Winston Churchill to capture Constantinople by combined naval and military forces, and so come to the aid of Russia by knocking Turkey out of the war. The scheme failed, however, through insufficient co-ordination of naval and military forces and want of daring leadership, and the British evacuated their troops early in 1916. In the Balkans the Serbians were at first successful, but they were later over-thrown by combined Austrian, German and Bulgarian troops. British and other forces in Salonika, however, defeated the Bulgarians in 1918.

In the Near East the British and their allies were triumphant. They drove the

Turks out of Palestine and broke their hold on Mesopotamia. On the Austro-Italian border, not much happened in the first two years of the war, but in 1917 the Italians were severely beaten at Caporetto. The following year the Italians reversed this defeat by crushing the Austrians at Vittorio Veneto. In Africa, the Germans were defeated in their colonies, including Tanganyika and German South-West Africa.

At sea the British and Germans fought a major engagement at Jutland on May 31, 1916. The result was a stalemate, but the German High Seas Fleet did not venture out into the North Sea or Atlantic again during the war. Instead, by means of a determined campaign of submarine warfare against ships coming to Britain with vital supplies, the Germans brought Britain nearly to starvation.

The Second World War in Europe and North Africa

Eventually, however, the campaign was defeated by the introduction of the convoy system, that is, merchant ships in relays guarded by warships, and by the use of a new invention, the depth charge.

The Central Powers collapsed in the autumn of 1918 under the superior strength of the Allies who had been joined by the United States of America. An armistice was arranged on November 11.

The map of Europe was virtually redrawn at the Treaty of Versailles in 1919. The Rhine was to be permanently deprived of troops or arms factories. German territories abroad were to be distributed among the victor nations. Poland was to be recognized as an independent nation. Alsace-Lorraine was to be returned to France. Other adjustments were to be made, mostly leaning towards creating independent new nations. Serbia,

In July 1916 a fierce and prolonged battle between British and German forces began in France on the River Somme. It was the first major engagement in which Kitchener's volunteers took part

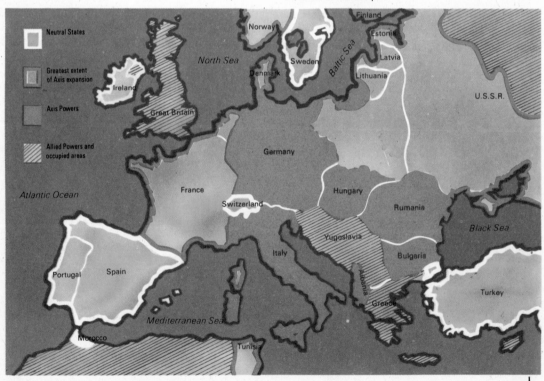

Montenegro and other former Austrian states were made into the republic of Yugoslavia, later to become a kingdom, and a new state of Czechoslovakia was created. The German army was to be cut and limited to 100,000 men, and the navy was not to have ships larger than 10,000 tons. A huge war indemnity had to be paid by the Germans.

The treaty proved to be a failure from the start. Disarmament was cunningly evaded; the German fleet was scuttled; the reparations were eventually cancelled. The Rhine was remilitarized by Hitler (*See* page 358) in 1936 and the German army and navy enlarged and re-equipped

with the most modern weapons. In 1938 Germany annexed Austria without firing a shot, and in 1939 Czechoslovakia was occupied. Here lay the seeds of a fresh European conflagration and it came on September 1, 1939 when Hitler ordered German troops to invade Poland. He had already agreed with Russia to divide the country between them.

When Hitler marched against Poland, Britain and France declared war. Poland was overrun in four weeks, before anyone could come to her aid. Operations then subsided for a while, but in April 1940 the Germans marched against Denmark and Norway and swiftly conquered both.

Not long after the fall of France, in June 1940, the Germans turned on Great Britain. To make it easier to invade, they set out first to destroy the Royal Air Force. This resulted in the Battle of Britain. The heroism and superior skill of the British pilots, however, ensured that Hitler's dreams of invasion came to nothing

The next month Holland and Belgium fell, and in June it was France's turn.

Hitler hoped that Britain would give in and come to terms, but Winston Churchill, appointed prime minister in May 1940, refused to have anything to do with this. By his unforgettable speeches of defiance and encouragement he galvanized the morale of the whole British people, and by his superb organizing powers he prepared them to deal with invasion whenever it might come.

In a prolonged series of aerial engagements which are referred to as the Battle of Britain (1940), the hitherto invincible German air-force was worsted. Hitler

Winston Churchill, prime minister of Great Britain 1940–45, and 1951–55, is widely regarded as one of the greatest men in British history. But for his supreme gifts of leadership, it is probable that Britain would have been defeated in the Second World War

gave up his plans to invade Britain and instead turned elsewhere in Europe. Yugoslavia fell in the spring of 1941 and in June the Germans, without warning, attacked Russia along a 2,000 mile front, overrunning more than a million square miles in a few weeks and all but capturing Moscow and Leningrad. From November 1942, the Russians began to force the Germans back towards their own country.

The Italians, meanwhile, under the fascist dictator, Mussolini, had thrown in their lot with the Germans and had declared war on Britain in 1940. This was a bad mistake. The British – and later on, the Americans who were helping them – gradually drove the Italians right out of their colonies in North Africa, as well as the German forces sent by Hitler to help them. Then the British and Americans invaded Italy itself. Mussolini was deposed and the Italians surrendered. The Germans occupied the northern part of Italy and continued the fight, but were driven out after a fierce and prolonged struggle lasting up to the spring of 1945.

The Russians continued to edge the German armies out and by 1944 were themselves advancing across Poland and the Balkans. In June 1944 the British and Americans invaded Europe in the Normandy landings and in less than a year had reconquered France, Belgium and Holland and pushed the Germans right into their own land. At the same time the Russians entered Berlin in April 1945 and Hitler committed suicide. This was the end of the war in Europe.

On the other side of the world, Japan, ambitious to expand her conquests in Asia and the Pacific – she had already overrun large areas of China – attacked the United States at Pearl Harbor and elsewhere in December 1941. British possessions in Asia were similarly invaded. Germany and Italy declared war on the United States, in support of Japan. Within four months a large part of

Adolf Hitler had a number of associates to whom he gave high office in the state. The two leading men were Hermann Goering and Joseph Goebbels

Field Marshal Erwin Rommel (1891–1944) commanded the famous Afrika Korps of the German army where his early successes against the British army in 1941–2 earned him the admiration of his opponents, as well as his fellow countrymen

Asia was in Japanese hands, including Malaya, Burma, Singapore, Indo-China, Borneo, New Guinea and many islands in the Pacific. They were not freed until the Americans began to defeat the Japanese at sea in a number of engagements in 1942 and 1943. The British then started to expel the Japanese from Burma in 1944 and by the end of the war in Europe, in April 1945, the Americans were nearly ready to invade the Japanese mainland. This was not undertaken, however, because in August the first atomic bomb, equivalent to the destructive power of 20,000,000 tons of high explosive, had been dropped on the Japanese city of Hiroshima, almost obliterating it. Another bomb was dropped a few days later on Nagasaki, and immediately the Japanese surrendered unconditionally. By August 1945, the Second World War was over.

After the war there was an enormous task of reconstruction. Cities and factories lay in ruins. Thousands of people were homeless. One of the good things to emerge from the terrible war was a new desire for international cooperation to prevent further wars. The United Nations Organization was founded in 1945. Its main aim was to settle disputes between nations peacefully. America and Russia were no longer allies, but rivals in what became known as the Cold War. Each of these super-powers had huge stocks of nuclear weapons. The utter pointlessness of a nuclear war which could destroy the human race was clear. Since the end of the Second World War there have been serious local wars, but thankfully a third World War has been avoided.

# The Emergence of Africa

Africa was regarded by many Europeans for several centuries as the 'Dark Continent', chiefly because they knew little about it. Except for some of the north coast, and Egypt, Africa remained closed to Europeans. Few Asians knew much about it either, although Arab and Chinese sailors did explore the east coast.

In fact there were a number of advanced communities in Africa by the 1500s. The Moslems from the north had penetrated into west and west-central Africa and had set up small states. There was a powerful kingdom on the River Niger called Songhoi. By the 1400s, Songhoi had more power and wealth than any other west African kingdom. It was founded by Askia Mohammed, who introduced an advanced administrative system, with tax collection, a police force, and a system of weights and measures for trade. There was even a university at Timbuctoo. When he died in

1530, his work was allowed to decline.

In the east of Africa was the Christian kingdom of Abyssinia. This state lay between Egypt and the Red Sea. Its rulers resisted Moslem attacks and created a civilization in advance of many others of the time.

Further south, Africa was dominated by the Bantu group of tribes. These were, for the most part, fierce warriors. Their lands were difficult to cultivate and so did not attract the first European visitors, the Portuguese, who began to explore in the early 1500s.

The western kingdom of Songhoi revived in the 1550s, under a new king, David. He died in about 1580 and Songhoi was overrun by Moroccans. Of the once-great African kingdoms, only Abyssinia remained independent and cut off from contact with the outside world. Europeans and Arabs now became more interested in

Piet Retief, the leader of the Voortrekkers, tried to come to a peaceful agreement with Dingaan, chieftain of the powerful Zula tribe, about establishing settlements in Natal. However, Dingaan brutally betrayed the Voortrekkers by inviting them to his kraal and then massacring Retief and seventy of his

Africa, seeking gold and slaves. People captured by slavers were taken from their villages in west Africa, and shipped across the Atlantic to work as slaves in the West Indies and America. The Portuguese set up trading bases on the east coast. In the south of Africa, the Dutch established themselves in the seventeenth century.

By the nineteenth century, Africa was at the mercy of European colonizers. There was the 'scramble' for Africa, and Europeans were increasingly involved in the Africans' economic affairs. Through trade, they gained political power and wealth. There was intense rivalry.

The French penetrated the Sahara, colonized Algeria and developed colonies in West Africa. The Germans moved into East Africa, and the Belgians ventured into the Congo. The British fought the Dutch for South Africa. In doing so they ran up against the Zulus, with their well-organized armies. The Zulus had been united under their chief Chaka, who moulded different tribes into a formidable fighting force. The well-trained Zulus

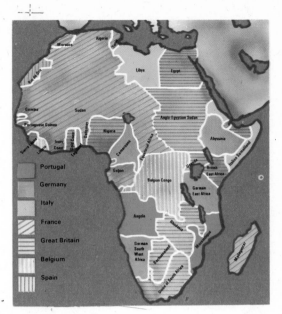

Africa in 1914

dominated the other Bantu tribes and fought the Europeans until their final defeat by the British in the Zulu War of 1878-9.

By the end of the nineteenth century almost all of Africa was ruled by Europeans, who brought their own ideas about religion, education, medicine and govern-

followers. The Zulu attempt to wipe out the rest of the European immigrants failed, and Dingaan himself was decisively defeated at the Battle of Blood River in 1838

ment. African traditional culture was seldom understood and often rejected. A few African kingdoms survived in some form, others vanished. In West Africa the Europeans discovered the wonderful art of the Ashanti and Yoruba peoples. In East Africa there were communities whose culture showed Asian influence, the result of earlier contact with traders from India and Arabia. There were also remains of impressive buildings, such as the stone ruins of Great Zimbabwe.

Europeans settled in some regions, such as Kenya (British) and Mozambique (Portuguese), most living by farming and trade. The oldest white community was that of the Dutch farmers or Boers in South Africa. People from India settled in East and South Africa.

The two World Wars of the twentieth century spread to Africa. In the First World War, Britain defeated Germany for control of East Africa. In the Second World War German and Italian armies overran much of North Africa, but were eventually driven out.

An initiation mask in wood, copper, sea shells and beads from the Congo, symbolizing the relationship between the social classes

The Commonwealth Prime Ministers' Conference in 1964. President Kwame Nkrumah of Ghana (right) is shown with Jomo Kenyatta, later that year President of Kenya

In the 1950s a strong current of African nationalism began to sweep the whole continent. Leaders such as Kwame Nkrumah in the Gold Coast, which later became Ghana, and Jomo Kenyatta in Kenya, argued and fought for independence for their peoples. All over Africa, colonies and protectorates sought independence from European rule. Some won their freedom peacefully, but in others such as Portuguese-ruled Angola and Mozambique there were wars between nationalists and the colonial power before independence was won. White settler-families, long used to governing unchallenged, sometimes resisted moves towards black majority rule. This was the case in Rhodesia which declared itself independent under a whites-only government in 1970 but eventually became lawfully independent under a black majority government, as Zimbabwe, in 1980. South Africa held to its policy of whites-only government and apartheid (separation of the races) until change came there too (*See* page 393).

Civil wars and drought have caused death and famine over large areas in Africa. World organizations help, but still the people suffer

The emerging African nations faced many problems. Most were poor, although Libya in the north and Nigeria in the west had oil. The most powerful country in terms of industries and military might was South Africa, with its vast mineral wealth.

There have been territorial disputes between neighbours and some countries have been divided by tribal rivalries. There were civil wars in the Congo and in Nigeria after independence. Often European-style democracy left in place at independence failed at last, and countries came under one-party governments or military leaders. Uganda fell under the rule of a cruel dictator, Idi Amin, from 1971 to 1979. The Central African Republic was for a time an empire, under the self-styled Emperor Bokassa. The last real emperor in Africa, Haile Selassie of Ethiopia (1891-1975) was overthrown by a revolution in 1974.

In recent years Africa has had to tackle the problem of educating and training many more children and young people. Africa has a very high birth-rate, but many countries lack resources to build enough schools, colleges and hospitals. To help improve trade, transport and cooperation, African nations have formed regional organizations such as the West African Economic Community. The Organization of African Unity tries to settle disputes between African nations peacefully. Africa's problems have been made worse in parts of the continent by drought and famine. A terrible famine hit north-east Africa in the 1980s and many people died, despite the efforts of relief agencies.

President F.W. de Klerk and A.N.C. leader Nelson Mandela of South Africa were awarded the Nobel Peace Prize in 1993

# A Century of American Progress

The victory of the north over the south in the American Civil War saved the Union. But the war left the south in ruins. There were some four million black slaves, now free, who had to be housed, educated and employed.

Lincoln's successor as president was Andrew Johnson (1808-75). He tried to carry out Lincoln's policy of conciliation, but was overruled by Republicans who wanted to punish the southern states. The military government of the south merely increased the bitterness between north and south. Businessmen descended upon the wasted southern farms and plantations and forcibly purchased them.

In 1868 a new president was elected. He was General Ulysses S. Grant (1822-85), the soldier who had commanded the northern armies in the last months of the war and accepted the surrender of Lee. After the Civil War, America opened its doors to more immigrants from Europe. Many Irish came after the terrible famines of 1845-8, so did shiploads of Europeans after the year of revolutions of 1848. The newcomers were determined to build a new life in a new world.

The relentless drive westward began. Pioneers carved new territories out of the great plains and mountains, and new states came into being. There were ruthless wars against the Indians, who were driven from their ancient lands. America was also undergoing an industrial revolution as science and invention bounded forward. Railways and roads were built all over the country, canals were dug, and countless new towns founded. Oil was discovered, bringing new wealth and contributing to the advance of mechanization.

By the end of the nineteenth century, Americans were the most industrialized people in the world. They were also playing a greater part in world affairs. America challenged the supremacy of European powers, such as Britain. In particular, the United States claimed a predominant position over all the American continent, insisting that Europe must not interfere

Immigrants from Europe continued to pour into the United States of America throughout the second half of the nineteenth century. Those in the picture are sailing past the Statue of Liberty in New York harbour

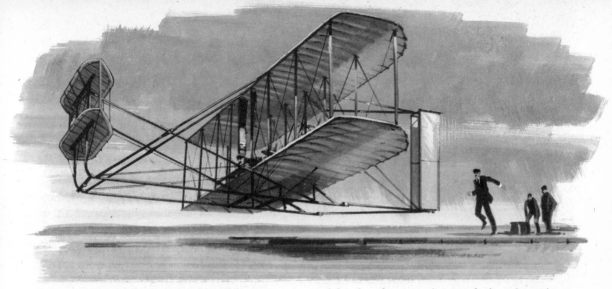

Two American brothers, Orville and Wilbur Wright, were the first men to fly in a heavier-than-air machine. They made four historic flights at Kitty Hawke in the *Flyer* on 17 December 1903, the longest one covering 852 feet in 59 seconds

with the free nations of the Americas, north and south. This policy was known as the Monroe Doctrine, after President James Monroe (1758-1831) who first proclaimed it.

At the same time the United States was becoming a colonial power itself. In 1895 a rebellion broke out in Cuba against the Spanish. An American cruiser, the *Maine*, was blown up in Havana in 1898 and more than 250 sailors were killed. American feeling ran very high, though it was never proved that Spain was guilty of the attack, and in the resulting war the Spanish lost Cuba, Puerto Rico and the Philippine Islands to the United States. Later, the Americans persuaded Panama to break from Colombia so that they might build the Panama Canal.

In the twentieth century, the United States has moved into first place among the nations of the world. One of the presidents who contributed to this rise to power was Theodore (Teddy) Roosevelt (1858-1919), president from 1901 to 1909. He became president when President McKinley was assassinated and awakened the American people to the immense possibilities of their place in the world. He

Theodore Roosevelt (1858–1919) made his name as leader of the 'Rough Riders' in the Cuban War in 1898. As a young man he ranched in North Dakota. He became president in 1901, and again in 1905

The Treaty of Versailles was signed in 1919 by the principal victorious powers in the First World War. This painting shows the three leading statesmen seated at the conference table, in the centre: Woodrow Wilson, president of the United States, George Clemenceau, the French premier, and Lloyd George, prime minister of Great Britain

believed that 'to go far one must speak softly and carry a big stick'.

During the First World War (1914-18) Roosevelt, no longer president, condemned the Germans in speeches and articles. But President Woodrow Wilson (1856-1924) kept the United States out of the war until April 1917. American soldiers and airmen fought in Europe, and in 1918 Wilson announced that, if necessary, eight million soldiers would be shipped to Europe to help win the war. This demoralized the Germans and by the autumn of 1918 they had begun to crack. In November they surrendered.

Wilson had issued Fourteen Points as a basis for peace, emphasizing the need for a League of Nations to preserve world peace. The American president played a leading part in the peace conference at Versailles, France, in 1919. Unfortunately the American Congress refused to ratify the resulting treaty. Republicans opposed to Wilson, a Democrat, disliked his commitment to the League of Nations. They wanted America to stay out of international politics.

In 1929 a financial collapse occurred on the New York Stock Exchange. Share prices plunged, banks failed, businesses went broke, and financiers were ruined overnight. Confidence in money and industry disappeared. There followed years of slump and depression in trade.

American confidence was not restored until the election in 1932 of Franklin D. Roosevelt (1882-1945), a cousin of Theodore Roosevelt. A polio victim, he offered the American people a 'New Deal'. This involved extending the power of the federal (central) government over the states, increasing presidential authority, and funding large public works schemes such as building dams and roads.

Roosevelt succeeded, and was returned to power in 1936 by an overwhelming majority vote. In foreign policy, Roosevelt was not an isolationist. When the Second World War broke out (See page 424) America remained neutral, but when in June 1940 France fell to the Germans, Roosevelt made no secret of where his sympathies lay. He agreed to help Britain with arms and in other ways, for he saw that if Britain fell, the might of Nazi Germany would be

The Pacific Fleet of the United States was savagely attacked by the Japanese by air and by submarine as it rode at anchor in Pearl Harbor, Hawaii, on 7 December 1941

turned upon America. He announced a policy of 'all aid to Britain short of declaring war'. In 1940 he was re-elected president, the first person to be elected three times running.

In December 1941 the Japanese, who had already conquered much of China, unleashed a series of attacks on British and American possessions in the Far East. The American naval base at Pearl Harbor, Hawaii, was attacked without warning on December 7 by Japanese planes launched from aircraft carriers. Among the ships sunk were five battleships.

The Americans were now in the war, against Japan, Germany and their allies. Roosevelt and Winston Churchill, Britain's war leader, worked closely together. Roosevelt was a sick man by 1945 but nevertheless took part in the Yalta conference at which the Allies agreed that the Russians should take responsibility for several parts of eastern Europe, previously occupied by Germany. Roosevelt died in April 1945, having been elected president

for a fourth time at the end of 1944. He was succeeded by his vice-president Harry Truman.

After the war, the Americans found themselves in the centre of world affairs. They initiated the North Atlantic Treaty, a military alliance of the Western allies against Russia. American troops, planes, ships and munitions were sent to Europe to be ready to resist any aggression from the Communist east. America also funded the Marshall Plan. Named after the American chief of the army staff in the Second World War, the plan gave millions of dollars worth of aid to help countries of Europe recover from the war. America also helped rebuild Japanese cities and industries.

America was the first nation to have nuclear bombs. It built up a huge arsenal of weapons, including rockets and missile-firing submarines. Only the Russians tried to match this power, and for some time the two countries were unfriendly. But America's might helped to maintain world

The 'Big Three' war leaders, (left) Churchill, (centre) President Roosevelt, and Marshal Stalin, at the conference at Yalta in 1945

Three of the most important men in the United States in the last thirty years: (from the left) John Fitzgerald Kennedy, elected president in 1960. Martin Luther King, leader of the civil rights movement, is shown here in 1965, in Montgomery, Alabama. He was assassinated in 1968. William J. Clinton took office as president in 1993

peace, although American forces fought a war in Korea (1950-53). President Truman served two terms and was followed by Dwight Eisenhower, who had commanded the Allied forces against Germany in Europe in 1944 and 1945. After Eisenhower, a Republican, came the young Democrat John F. Kennedy in 1960. He was tragically assassinated in 1963, leaving ambitions and hopes unfulfilled. He was mourned throughout the world.

Kennedy's vice-president Lyndon Johnson immediately became president, and was elected in his own right in 1964. In 1965 the first American troops landed in Vietnam, to fight a war which split the nation. The Americans finally withdrew from Vietnam in 1973, and defeat for America's ally, South Vietnam, came two years later.

At home, Johnson brought in civil rights laws to end unfair treatment of black Americans in housing, voting and education. But he declined to seek re-election in 1968. He was followed as president by the Republican Richard Nixon, who had to resign after charges of misconduct, and then Gerald Ford. Democrat Jimmy Carter served from 1976-80, and then former film actor, Ronald Reagan, a Republican, was elected. Reagan

and his successor, George Bush (1989-93), were conservatives in economic affairs, but achieved breakthroughs in relations with the Russians, signing agreements for cuts in weapons and ending the so-called Cold War which had lasted since the late 1940s. During the brief Gulf War of 1991 American forces played the leading part. But Americans were most concerned with home affairs. William J. (Bill) Clinton, a Democrat, defeated Bush in the 1992 election and took office as president in 1993.

The first man on the moon, Neil Armstrong, took this photograph of his lunar module pilot, Buzz Aldrin, in July 1969

# A Changing World

History is a continuing story, without chapters. Yet throughout history there are dates which have a special significance as turning points in the human story. In modern times such dates include 1917, the year of the Russian Revolution, and 1945, the year of the first atomic bomb and the end of the Second World War. That momentous year of 1945 also marked the beginning of the so-called Cold War, the rivalry between the United States and the Soviet Union which seemed to threaten the world with a new war. These two nations, the most powerful on earth, were armed with awesome weapons, capable of destroying each other many times over.

They were rivals because their leaders believed in opposing political and economic systems. The United States was the land of the 'free market', where businesses and individuals were able to run their own affairs without much government interference. The Soviet Union practised Communism. Its government ran factories and farms, and allowed individuals very little freedom, be it in art, politics or religion.

In 1989 came another important date in modern times. This was the year the Berlin Wall fell. *(See photograph above.)* For years it had divided Germany's capital, symbolizing the divide between the free world and the Communists. Now Communism in Europe was faltering and countries which had laboured under its bonds since 1945 moved into an unfamiliar new world of free elections and free market economics. Old leaders gave way to new ones. Lech Walesa, a former shipyard electrician, became president of Poland. Vaclav Havel, a writer who had spent years in prison for opposing the Communists, became president of Czechoslovakia, which soon afterwards split into two republics, one Czech, the other Slovak.

Such were the extent of discontent and the force of change that even the Soviet empire crumbled. The reforms of Mikhail Gorbachev weakened the iron grip of the Communist state. There followed calls for democracy and regional independence. In 1991 there was a brief attempt to turn back the clock. A group of Communist leaders ordered tanks into the streets in a bid to seize power from the reformers and return to old ways. Russian citizens urged the soldiers to return to barracks and the plot collapsed. But in this new world, Gorbachev was left without a Soviet Union to rule. In its place were independent republics, following their own paths. Their leaders, like Russia's Boris Yeltsin, faced the daunting task of rebuilding economies and political systems.

The United States was left unchallenged as the world's only super-power. It and the United Nations were now the peace-keepers in a new world order. But the world was in fact more disordered than for some time.

In Europe a wider union of countries was taking shape, although not all members of the European Community, now titled the European Union, wanted to share one currency and one government. In the Middle East talks between Israelis and Palestinians raised hopes of an end to the long hostility between Israel and most of its Arab neighbours. Ever since Israel was founded in 1948, the Middle East had been kept in crisis by the plight of the Palestinian refugees and the refusal of Arab states to recognize Israel's right to exist.

If there was more hope for democratic government in eastern Europe, and in South America and Africa too, China with its one thousand million people remained sternly Communist. And dictators still waged war. Iraq's Saddam Hussein ordered an invasion of the neighbouring state of Kuwait in 1990. The response was swift, with the United States leading a coalition of forces against him. Kuwait was freed, but Saddam Hussein remained in power to menace those peoples who had most cause to fear him, the Kurds in northern Iraq and the Arabs of the southern marshlands.

Old evils persist in a world seemingly made smaller by miracles of technology. Satellites encircle the earth, beaming television into homes in every continent. Threats to health, such as AIDS and drug abuse, are equally universal. Nations need to cooperate, to fight ignorance and disease, and to share the benefits of trade, scientific discovery and prosperity.

The Cold War may be over, but the world remains divided between rich and poor. Many millions of people still go hungry and live in squalor. The rich industrialized countries consume far more of the earth's resources, such as minerals, water and fuel, than do the poorer nations.

These natural resources are not limitless. The most urgent problem facing mankind is the future health of the earth itself. Forests, lakes, oceans and even the air we breathe are polluted. Many plants and animals face the threat of extinction as their habitats vanish. In 1992 leaders from more than a hundred countries met in Brazil to discuss global efforts to protect and restore the environment. Much more needs to be done to conserve precious resources wisely, for future generations. People have walked on the moon and may one day walk on the planet Mars. But there is no other home for mankind in our family of planets. No other planet can offer us life, as does earth. This is where we live, and will for as long as we can foresee.

Unless we can deal with the effects of pollution like this, in a few years our pleasant earth will be uninhabitable, and man has nowhere else to go

# Index

## W

Waldemar II, king of Denmark 242
Wales 156, 220–2, 300–1
  English conquest of 301
Walesa, Lech 399, 438
Wallace, William, Scottish patriot 293, 305
Wallenstein, Count Albrecht von 353–4, 362, 396
Wallingford, treaty of 291
Walpole, Sir Robert 370
Wang Li, Chinese emperor 412
Wang Mang, Chinese emperor 178
Wang Ngau-Chi, Chinese emperor 236
War of American Independence 383
Warsaw, capture of 397, 399
  1704 Peace Treaty 397
Wars of the Roses 295–6, 299
Warwick, Richard Nevill, Earl of 298
Washington, George, U.S. president 381, 383
Waterloo, battle of 350, 356, 372

Watt, James 372
Wei, kingdom of 233
Wellington, Arthur Wellesley, Duke of 332, 349–50, 372
Wentworth, Thomas, earl of Strafford 338
Wessex, kingdom of 212
Western front, First World War 421
West Indies 377
Westminster Abbey 218
Westphalia 355
Wet, Christiaan de 393
White Mountain, battle of 353
Wilberforce, William 373, 385
William I, 'The Conqueror', king of England 63, 218–9, 247, 253, 291, 300
William II, king of England 291
William III and Mary (joint rulers of England, Scotland and Ireland) 330, 340–1, 361
William IV, king of the United Kingdom 373
William I, German emperor, king of Prussia 356–7

William II, Kaiser Wilhelm, German emperor, king of Prussia 357
William 'the Lion', king of Scotland 304
Wilson, Woodrow, U.S. president 434–5
Witanagemot, Anglo-Saxon council 218
Wittenburg, city of 324–5
Wolfe, General James 389
Wolseley, Field Marshal Viscount (Sir Garnet) 373
Wolsey, Thomas, Cardinal 334–5
Wordsworth, William, English poet 372
Wren, Sir Christopher 340
Wu, kingdom of 233
Wycliffe, John, English religious reformer 294, 324

## XYZ

Xerxes I, king of Persia 89, 118, 122, 124, 128

Yahweh, Hebrew 'God' 87
Yalta, Allied conference at 405, 437–9
Yangtze River 63, 94, 414
Yazdegerd, Sassanid king 207
Ye-le-tchutsai, Chinese statesman 267
Yeltsin, Boris 439
York, English royal house of 295
Yuen-Chang, Chinese emperor 286
Yugoslavia 47, 407, 424, 426
Yung Cheng, Chinese emperor 413
Yung-Lo, Chinese emperor 286–7
Yu the Great, Chinese emperor 61
Zama, battle of 145
Zapotec, Central American culture 241
Zeus, Greek god 103, 129
Ziggurat at Ur 19
Zimbabwe 430
Zoser, Egyptian pharaoh 26–7
Zulus 392–3, 429
  Zulu War 429

# Acknowledgments

Photographs are reproduced by courtesy of the following: Bibliothèque Nationale, Paris 1; The Board of Trinity College, Dublin 225; Trustees of the British Museum 20, 33, 157, 205, 311; Freer Gallery of Art, Washington DC 208; Heraklion Museum, Crete 44 right; Imperial War Museum 435; Louvre, Paris 327; the Marquess of Salisbury KG 336; Musée Bayeux 216 top, 216 bottom, 217 top, 217 bottom; National Gallery, London 281; National Museum, Athens 44 left; National Museum, Copenhagen 160; National Museum of Ireland 222; National Portrait Gallery, London 371; Staatliche Museen, Berlin 29, 84, 85; Staatsbibliothek, Berlin 352; Victoria and Albert Museum 273 top right; The Wellcome Trustees 228.

Sources of photographs: *(the numbers refer to the pages on which the photographs appear)* –

Associated Press 439; Camera Press 373; J.Allan Cash 323; Colorphoto Hans Hinz 15, 44 right; Reginald Davis 322; Giraudon, Paris 273 top left; Hamlyn Group picture library 20, 33, 84–5, 157, 160, 162, 203, 205, 208, 222, 272, 276, 277 top, 311, 336, 435; Hamlyn Group picture library – the Green Studio 225; Hamlyn Group picture library – M. Holford 216 top, 216 bottom, 217 top, 217 bottom, 273 top right, 281; Hirmer Verlag, Munich 29, 32, 44 left, 353; Hulton Deutsch Collection Ltd. 374, 375, 377 top, 399, 408; Jacqueline Hyde, Paris 327; Impact 431 top (Dagnino/ Cosmos); Irish Tourist Board, Dublin 303; Magnum Photos 377 bottom (R. Burri), 437 top left (Wayne Miller), 437 top right (Misha Arwitt), 439 (James Nachtwey); The Mansell Collection 70, 280–281; National Portrait Gallery, London 371; Pictorial Press 278; Popperfoto 397 bottom, 430 top, 431 top and bottom, 437 top centre; Scala, Florence 273 bottom, 277 bottom; Staatsbibliothek, Berlin 352; Sygma 321 top (J. Pavlovsky), 376 (H. Collart Odinetz); Topham 438 (Associated Press); A.C.K. Ware 294; Wellcome Institute of the History of Medicine, London 228; ZFA 401

The publishers wish to thank the following artists for their contributions:

John Berry, D. Bown, Ron Brown, Mario Capaldi, G. Caselli, Peter Charles, M. Codd, Peter Conolly, G. Coppola, Graham Coton, S. Davis, Neville E.F. Dear A.R.C.A., C.L. Doughty, B. Dunlop, B. Elettori, Ronald Embleton, Wilf Hardy, Peter Jackson, A. Jessett, Gordon King, B.R. Linklater, Gary Long, Brian Lubrani, Angus McBride, G.H. Mott, H.J. Neqve, Kenneth J. Petts, Bill Stallion, Eric Tenney, G. Thompson, Carlo Tora, Louis Ward F.S.I.A., I.S. Wells and Walter Wright.